CW00428913

Sanctifying Signs

Sanctifying Signs

Making Christian Tradition in Late Medieval England

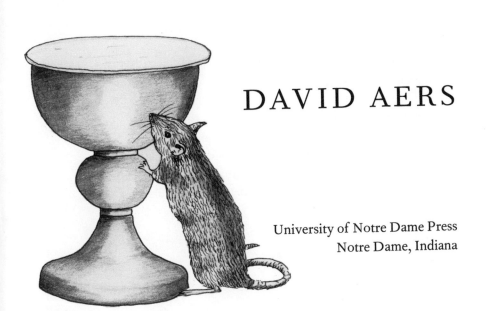

DAVID AERS

University of Notre Dame Press
Notre Dame, Indiana

Copyright © 2004 by University of Notre Dame
Notre Dame, Indiana 46556
www.undpress.nd.edu
All Rights Reserved

Manufactured in the United States of America

Drawings on title page by Christine Derham. Reproduced with permission of the artist.

Library of Congress Cataloging-in-Publication Data
Aers, David.
    Sanctifying signs : making Christian tradition in late medieval
England / David Aers.
        p.   cm.
    Includes bibliographical references (p.   ) and index.
    ISBN 0-268-02021-3—ISBN 0-268-02022-1 (pbk.)
    1. Lord's Supper—History—Middle Ages, 600–1500.   2. Poverty—
Religious aspects—Christianity—History of doctrines—Middle
Ages, 600–1500.   3. England—Church history—Middle Ages, 600–1500.
I. Title.
BV823.A29   2004
264'.36'09420902—dc22

                                                        2003024968

∞ *This book is printed on acid-free paper.*

CONTENTS

PREFACE

*And I found myself far from you "in the region of dissimilarity," and heard
as it were your voice from on high: "I am the food of the fully grown; grow
and you will feed on me. And you will not change me into you like the food
your flesh eats, but you will be changed into me." [Et inveni longe me esse a
te in regione dissimilitudinis, tanquam audirem vocem tuam de excelso:
"cibus sum grandium: cresce et manducabis me. nec tu me in te mutabis sicut
cibum carnis tuae, sed tu mutaberis in me."]*

—*Augustine*, Confessions *VII.10.16*

This book is a study of Christianity in late medieval England. But it is
certainly not a historical or doctrinal survey, and it has no aspirations to
coverage of the topics and texts it addresses. The perspectives and pre-
ferred hermeneutic modes of the book would make such ambitions hard to
imagine, let alone to try enacting. *Sanctifying Signs* emerges out of a fascination with the ways in which certain late medieval Christians and their
Church addressed the immense resources of Christian tradition. They did
so at a time when the common pursuit of salvation generated differences
which came to seem, to some of the participants, uncontainable within the
current ecclesiastical polity. So the fascination, for me, is with complex
processes which are at once theological and institutional, doctrinal, and political. These are the processes of tradition formation, reformation, and
preservation in changing cultural circumstances. And the fascination, for
me, is especially with the contribution of certain texts to these processes.

These are the contexts in which I approach a range of texts, including those judged to be heretical. Perhaps this sounds rather Eliotic:

> These men, and those who opposed them
> And those whom they opposed
> Accept the constitution of silence
> And are folded in a single party
> (*Little Gidding*, III)[1]

But Eliot's vision is eschatological, whereas the concerns of this book are with the heterogeneities and arguments within what has often been thought of as the "single party" not of the heavenly city but of medieval Christianity. Such conversational heterogeneities are not always most fruitfully approached through words like "heresy" and "orthodoxy." The problem with these nouns is that they can encourage us to take our attention away from the particulars of the processes and texts in which they themselves became constituted. The nominalizations can bestow an apparent solidity, an obviousness, on what they refer to, distracting us from the networks of interaction from which these terms are, in a sense, abstractions. They also worked in medieval culture as attempts to direct the tendencies of the relevant conversations. Complex and exploratory texts, like *Piers Plowman*, or Walter Brut's articulation of past and present Christianity, may actually resist medieval and modern application of these terms in their creative engagement with the resources of tradition in their own historical moment. After all, late-fourteenth-century Christians could not know with certainty the theological and ecclesial outcomes of their difficulties, conflicts, fears, and hopes. Their conversations called into question what should count as orthodoxy and heresy. And as is the way with any serious, sustained conversation, all who participate are changed in the process. So are their traditions, whether gradually or, sometimes, abruptly. Orthodoxy, as Rowan Williams observed in his study of relations between "Arians" and "Catholics" in the fourth century, "continues to be made."[2] Such making involves many voices, including some that may be very unwelcome.

This is obviously not to say that the late medieval Church was a sponsor of unstructured diversity and the ideals of liberal pluralism. Where it sought to make clear that certain ways of talking and believing no longer could count as Catholic, whatever their place in traditional discourses, and where it sought to determine just what must be said and believed, I have used the term "orthodox" to describe such positions. But while the term "orthodoxy" may describe an explicitly formulated set of beliefs at a particular historical moment, it may also refer to the complex modes in which the Church maintained such beliefs, together with a wide range of practices (from liturgy to Church courts), modes that varied in response to different pressures in different circumstances. So the first chapter of the book concentrates on the sacramental sign of the altar in the orthodoxy of the late medieval Church. It follows some intriguing problems generated in orthodox attempts to articulate and defend current understanding of the doctrine of transubstantiation. And yet, as the chapter on the sacrament of the altar in *Piers Plowman* shows, a text could draw on traditional resources in a manner that went against the grain of recent and emergent orthodoxy, in ritual practice and theology, without being judged as heretical. Orthodoxy could not ever take control of its own resources and the conversations it incessantly generated, even when apparently seeking to close those conversations.

Sanctifying Signs begins by reflecting on some orthodox accounts of the sacrament of the altar. This introduces the book's exploration of sanctification and signs: sacramental signs (chapters 2–4), indeed, but certainly not only sacramental signs (chapters 5–6), in writings by William Langland, John Wyclif, Walter Brut, and William Thorpe. I hope the reading of Brut and Thorpe may help us think about the variety and inventiveness of theological reflections by those classified as Wycliffites and heretics. The final chapter examines some different models of sanctification and home in the early fifteenth century. Here I address some political dimensions of the theological and domestic differences identified in the chapter.

This book moves into a mode of reflection and analysis that may seem more theological than is customary in work emerging from modern English departments. When it does so, it is seeking to continue a past conversation. I appreciate that this may not be congenial to the ideological predispositions of many colleagues in such departments.[3] For the aspiration demands that we engage with writers like Langland, Brut, or Love in a manner that takes their theological and ecclesiological terms utterly seriously. Such seriousness may involve critical argument with their texts. But it means that we do not treat their theology and ecclesiology as confused (or brilliant) anticipations of some contemporary and thoroughly secularized theoretical paradigm. And it means that where their ethical and political reflections are indissolubly united with theology and ecclesiology, habitually the case with the subjects of this book, our reading will try to grasp the particular force and scope of their terms. I have not proceeded chronologically. This is partly because I sometimes seek to compose theological typologies and in doing so might first discuss a writer who is chronologically later. The idea here is that the lineaments of the later writer can help us see more clearly what the chronologically earlier writer is, or isn't, doing. But my lack of commitment to strict synchronicity and to historical sequence also comes from exploring aspects of what is identifiable as a tradition of discourse and practice in which a writer from the apparently remote chronological past may be taken by a late medieval writer as present, as a participant in the contemporary conversations that concern him or her. That is not because medieval people had no sense of historical and cultural difference; they certainly did. Given their theological, philosophic, and literary experiences, together with their knowledge of past and present conflicts between Christianity and other religions, how could they not have such a sense? But in the tradition which formed them, certain texts and authors from the past were read with a conviction of their relevance to any current conversation or conflict. Obviously enough, this does not mean that Augustine is read at Oxford in 1381 just as he was read at Carthage in 411 or in Palestine around 415 during disputes between Pelagius and Augustine.[4] But it does mean that he will be as present in the conversations involving Wyclif, Langland, Love, or Netter as any contemporary theologian, present in a time not measured by chronometers. And perhaps, sometimes, some of the arguments composed in some of the writings I explore may be more present to me than some of those that are the common currency of the present academic moment. The communication of the dead may not always be "tongued with fire beyond the language of the living" (Eliot, *Little Gidding*, I), but all those studied in this book had a powerful sense that the dead who concerned them were part of a contemporary conversation. These dispositions, intellectual and affective, were probably strengthened by creedal teaching and pervasive cultural practices celebrating the "communion of the saints." So our versions of historical inquiry must always understand how the filiations of conversation were not only synchronic.[5] This kind of engagement goes against many prevalent hermeneutic and ideological assumptions, prevalent in contemporary English departments, about what is possible and desirable in the study of Christian texts from the Middle Ages.

Of course, I too write from the culture of English departments. That culture legitimates a massive assortment of methodologies and topics of inquiry, although some are more favored, more prevalent than others. In this situation we will inevitably have to make some choices about the critical paradigms and materials that are to shape our inquiries. But we make such choices in circumstances we have not chosen and out of histories we have not made. So we should try to understand these choices with as much attention as possible to the traditions that shaped their form and their preoccupations. Just as we inhabit traditions which enable us to carry out certain inquiries, and which preclude others, so Langland, Brut, and those about whom this book is written composed inquiries and made choices (sometimes difficult, sometimes dangerous, sometimes with barely a thought) within the traditions they inhabited.[6] And in their tradition-formed choices, in their inquiries and arguments, they contributed to continuation and change in the formation of these traditions, traditions of discourse which were also forms of life. Paul Ricoeur recently offered some observations that seem to me relevant to this issue, this book, and its subjects: "So in a certain manner, to be a religious subject is to agree to enter or to have already entered into this vast circuit involving a founding word, mediating texts, and traditions of interpretation; I say traditions, because I have always been convinced that there was a multitude of interpretations within the Judeo-Christian domain, and so a certain pluralism, a certain competition between traditions of reception and of interpretation."[7] It is indeed important to see how such "a multitude of interpretations" and "a certain competition" constitute the making of orthodoxy, an issue with which I began this Preface. Of course, the medieval Church showed itself capable of impatience towards these constitutive multiplicities and competing interpretations. Some of its subjects encountered this impatience in the form of violence, violence designed to contain the "pluralism" towards which Ricoeur points. Not only, as I noted earlier, could such attempts not succeed, given the very constitution of the processes out of which orthodoxy was made. But they also entailed setting aside the perspectives on orthodoxy and tradition, thoroughly orthodox perspectives, with which Julian of Norwich concluded her *Shewings:* "This booke is begunne be Gods gift and His grace, but it is not yet performid, as to my syte."[8] This perspective comes from a traditional understanding that the Church and its members should never confuse any particular historical agent or objective with the *eschaton.*

"As sickness is the greatest misery, so the greatest misery of sickness is solitude. . . . Solitude is a torment which is not threatened in hell itself." So wrote John Donne, Dean of St. Paul's, in his *Devotions.* "God himself," he meditates, "would admit a figure of society . . . and all his external actions testify a love of society and communion. . . . [T]here is no phoenix; nothing singular, nothing alone."[9] Every act of learning and teaching, every attempt to articulate a reading or write a history, every essay and book is also "a figure of society," constituted by and contributing to the constitution of traditions and communities in which it is made. So with this book I have tried to acknowledge those to whom I am conscious of being indebted and those with whom I am conscious of being in disputation, living and dead, in text and notes. Here I wish to thank particularly those three conversation partners most directly involved in the present project. Lynn Staley has always been willing to apply her learning to the issues I address, and Stanley Hauerwas has been a deeply informed, endlessly energetic source of theological reflection on what I have been trying to do. All the strands of this book emerged during continual discussions with Sarah Beckwith, conversations over endless cups of tea and also in the classroom in courses we have co-taught. Given that our conversations and arguments began in the early 1980s, it is inevitable that they have become woven into the fabric of my own thinking. No footnotes acknowledging where I draw on Sarah's published works can begin to give a remotely adequate account of my debts to her. I am indeed blessed to have her as my colleague and friend. I continue to be thankful for the generous and brilliant teaching I received from Elizabeth Salter and Derek Pearsall and for Derek's continual encouragement in recent years. I thank James Simpson for a seriously engaged reading of the book's final draft and for a conversation about what I have and haven't done in this project. Thanks too are due to Fiona Somerset for comments on an earlier version of chapter 4 and discussions about Walter Brut. Anne Hudson read drafts of both chapter 3 and chapter 5, and I thank her for characteristically helpful observations. I thank Nicky Zeeman for her careful reading of the first version of chapter 2 and chapter 5. I have also benefited from many discussions of issues that motivate this book with Andrzej Gasiorek. I would also like to express my gratitude for the current support of medieval studies at Duke University and particularly to Dean William Chafe and Dean Karla Holloway. One major consequence of this support has been the presence of medieval graduate students with whom it has been a great pleasure to work. I also thank Rebekah Long, who has been an utterly perfect research assistant for me throughout the making of this book. I thank Barbara Hanrahan of the University of Notre Dame Press for her warm support of this project and Elisabeth Magnus for her immensely helpful editing of the manuscript. Finally I thank Christine Derham, who continues to be my closest friend and my wife. For her, some words from Nancy Griffith's song "These Days in an Open Book":

These days your face
In my memory
Is in a folded hand of grace against these times.[10]

Earlier, shorter, and in one of the cases significantly different versions of chapters 2 and 4 have appeared as follows: "The Sacrament of the Altar in *Piers Plowman* and the Late Medieval Church in England," in *Images, Idolatry and Iconoclasm in Late Medieval England,* ed. Jeremy Dimmick, James Simpson, and Nicolette Zeeman (Oxford: Oxford University Press, 2002), 63–80; "Walter Brut's Theology of the Sacrament of the Altar," in *Lollards and Their Influence in Late Medieval England,* ed. Fiona Somerset, Jill C. Havens, and Derrick G. Pitard (Woodbridge: Boydell, 2003).

chapter 1

THE SACRAMENT OF THE ALTAR IN THE MAKING OF ORTHODOX CHRISTIANITY OR "TRADITIONAL RELIGION"

The consecrated bread and wine become the ultimate aspect in which charity delivers itself body and soul. If we remain incapable of recognizing in it the ultimate advance of love, the fault is not its responsibility—love gives itself, even if "his own did not receive him" (John 1:11); love accomplishes the gift entirely, even if we scorn this gift: the fault returns to us, as the symptom of our impotence to read love, in other words, to love. Hence our tendency to reduce the eucharistic present to everything except to the love that ultimately assumes a body in it. Christ endures taking a sacramental body, venturing into the here and now *that could blaspheme and/or idolize him, because already, he took a physical body, to the point of "not resisting, not recoiling . . . , not withdrawing (his) face from insults . . . , rendering (his) face hard as stone" (Isaiah 50:5–7). The sacramental body completes the oblation of the body, oblation that incarnates the trinitarian oblation— "You wanted neither sacrifice, nor oblation, but you fashioned me a body" (Psalms 40:7 according to the LXX, taken up again in Hebrews 10:5–10). In short, the eucharistic* present is deduced from the commitment of charity.

—*Jean-Luc Marion,* God without Being

The dominant form of Eucharistic ritual, iconography, and theology in the late medieval Church was organized around a particular version of Christ's presence in the sacramental sign. This version was articulated in the doctrine of transubstantiation, a doctrine whose parameters of licit interpretation were narrowed from the later thirteenth century.[1] At the words of consecration, words spoken by a duly ordained priest, the body of Jesus that had lived in Galilee became present under what had become the appearance of bread and wine lacking their proper substance. The body now present was the tortured, torn, bleeding, sacrificial, and life-giving body crucified on Calvary.[2] Such was the presence of Christ elevated in the priest's hands for the faithful to gaze at in adoration, the presence processed through the streets of medieval towns on Corpus Christi Day and around the church on Palm Sunday.[3] In the words of Thomas Aquinas, himself the author of the office for Corpus Christi, the Church proclaimed that in the sacramental sign which sanctified the Christian people the "whole Christ" was present, "not only the flesh, but the whole body of Christ, that is, the bones and nerves and all the rest" [non solum caro, sed totum corpus Christi, id est ossa et nervi et alia hujusmodi].[4]

In his monumental elaboration of orthodoxy against Wyclif and his followers, Thomas Netter again and again insists that the body and blood of Christ are present in the sacrament in their own "nature," according to their "substance," identically one with the body in heaven. This body is now adored by the faithful in its full presence under the bread and wine.[5] Netter calls Wyclif "the doctor of signs" because he is always running to signs, always negating the true substantial presence of Christ's Galilean body. Around this, he says, the whole battle revolves, with Wyclif showing himself to be a heretic by his refusal to accept the Church's version of the way in which the body and blood of Christ are present under the bread and wine. After all, Netter insists, in a rather Wycliffite move, Christ did not say, "This is my body figuratively [figuraliter]."[6] Indeed, we must not use the language of *figura* in talking about Christ's bodily presence in the Eucharist. For this presence is *veritas;* it is neither figuratively nor imaginarily present but substantially.[7] So the true body of Christ is torn and broken in the sacrament, not only in sign, but sensually [sensualiter]. Christ is eaten not only in the intention of the believer's will but also bodily, not only "spiritually" but "carnally."[8] I will return to the version of Christ's real presence articulated by the Carmelite theologian and judge,[9] but for the moment I wish to take note of other strands in the theology of the Eucharist.

The sacrament signified, as Thomas Aquinas wrote, "the unity of the mystical body of Christ which is an absolute prerequisite for salvation, because outside the Church there is no salvation" (*ST* III.73.3, resp). It is "the summit [consummatio] of the spiritual life" and the goal [finis] of all the sacraments: "They sanctify us and prepare us to receive the Eucharist or to consecrate. Baptism is required in order to begin this spiritual life; the Eucharist is necessary in order to bring it to its culmination [ad consummandam ipsam]" (*ST* III.73.3, resp). That this saving life was to be lived in the unity of the faithful, the body of Christ, was a commonplace of medieval Christianity whose genealogy Netter traced back through Augustine to Paul. Moreover, as he makes clear, the consecrated host designates and constitutes Christ's *corpus mysticum*, the Church.[10] It is plain that in this tradition the theology of the sacrament will be inseparable from ecclesiology. Such inseparability will be a recurring theme in this book.

It was also maintained that the presence of Christ's body brought not only spiritual nourishment but also benefits of a thoroughly material kind. The *Fasciculus Morum*, an early-fourteenth-century preacher's handbook, notes that the Eucharist heals bodily sickness and preserves bodily health before providing the standard catalogue of benefits, attributed rather inappropriately to Augustine's theology of the sacrament:

> And Augustine says, in *The City of God*, that on the day one devoutly celebrates or hears Mass, especially if one is free from mortal sin, all necessary provisions are granted, idle words are forgiven, and forgotten oaths are cancelled. On the same day one will not lose one's eyesight and will not suddenly die, and even if one should die, one will be counted as having received the sacraments. And while one is hearing Mass, one does not grow older; and every step one takes in going and returning from Mass is counted by angels.[11]

In chapter 2 I will give Bishop Brinton's version of this list, but as Siegfried Wenzel observes, such lists of the "virtues" or "meeds" of the Mass were "commonplace" and "extremely widespread, in Latin and vernacular texts, both prose and poetry."[12] They could be elaborated or further specified: so the monk John Lydgate writes that presence at Christ's presence in the Mass guarantees to sailors favorable winds for their sailing and to pregnant women a safe childbirth in which they will feel "no myschefe."[13]

Perhaps more important than these benefits for the living were the benefits Christ's full bodily presence in the Mass brought to those in purgatory. Here too the mendicant author of *Fasciculus Morum* expressed standard teaching: "Notice likewise that through its power a Mass lightens and decreases the purgatorial pains of a soul for which it is said in particular, and because of it the other souls in purgatory find a lightening of their pains."

Indeed, "the more Masses one celebrates for the souls in purgatory the more one increases their light."[14] How this Eucharistic belief was central in the relations of late medieval people with the dead and with each other has been explored in a number of fine studies.[15] It is clear that in such contexts any questioning of what had become the dominant understanding of Christ's presence and work in the sacrament would have extremely serious consequences for the whole web of social, political, and economic relations around Masses for the dead, a central practice in the late medieval Church. Furthermore, in a culture where the language, rituals, and convictions of Christianity were constitutive, theological arguments concerning the sacraments would tend to become arguments without boundaries. Sacramental disputes had ecclesiological ramifications and, in a polity where the Church was so pervasive, political implications. We are now fortunate to have some outstanding studies, from illuminatingly different perspectives, which have shown just how the sacrament of the altar had become the most powerful symbol of the formation and contestation of collective and individual identities in the later Middle Ages.[16]

Bearing this in mind, I will now consider treatments of Christ's presence in the sanctifying sign, which is the goal of all the sacraments. My attention is on examples of texts committed to making "traditional religion,"[17] beginning briefly with Bishop Thomas Brinton (who died in 1389).[18] In Sermon 67 Brinton maintains that the real presence of Christ's body is in every part of the broken bread (305).[19] He stresses that this real presence of Christ comprises the same Galilean body that was born of the Virgin, suffered on the cross, rose from the dead, and ascended into heaven (305).[20] The sacramental sign yields a plenitudinous presence, the total Christ, the same body [idem corpus] that was seen and touched in Galilee. In Sermon 37 Brinton considers the reasons why this sacramental presence is hidden under the species of bread and wine. It is hidden lest we should hate what we are offered and what we are actually doing: eating flesh and blood [ne abhorreamus carnis et sanguinis sumpcionem] (162). While the concealment of what is being done is a defense against the derision of infidels and a way of allowing Christians to gain merit for believing what they cannot see (162), it is an act of divine condescension which in no way diminishes the presence of Christ in his full humanity. Between the sign and what the sign discloses there is no gap, only identity, albeit an identity usually hidden from mortals.

Brinton's position is normative in the late medieval Church. The issue of Eucharistic cannibalism was certainly not invented by sixteenth-century reformers and was discussed by Thomas Aquinas in ways similar to those sketched by the later bishop. In the *Summa Theologiae* Aquinas acknowledges that it is apparent to our senses that after the consecration all the accidents of bread and wine remain. This, he maintains, is an arrangement made rationally by divine providence. Humans are not accustomed to eat human flesh and drink human blood: "indeed, the thought revolts them." Because of this fastidiousness about cannibalistic feasts, we are given the flesh and blood of Christ "to be taken under the appearances of things in common use, namely bread and wine" [proponitur nobis caro et sanguis Christi sumenda sub speciebus illorum quae frequentius in usum hominis veniunt, scilicet panis et vini]. Plenitudinous presence, although in "the mode of substance," and although disguised from our carnal eyes, is such that we are indeed eating human flesh and drinking human blood. Divine providence also selects this concealment "[l]est the sacrament should be an object of contempt for unbelievers, if we are to eat our Lord under his human appearances." That is, we are delivered from being known and derided as the cannibals we (really but secretly) are, a view that Brinton also affirmed. Another reason why divine providence makes the flesh and blood we take invisible is to increase the merit of our faith (III.75.5, resp).[21] Bishop Brinton, over a hundred years later, has closely followed the arguments and the order of arguments set down by Aquinas. This is not a claim of direct influence but an illustration of what had become a standard position in the late medieval Church.[22]

I will now move to a very different kind of work, an extremely popular French poem, Guillaume de Deguileville's *Pèlerinage de vie humaine*. This was translated more than once in Lancastrian England.[23] Here Reason and the pilgrim watch the Bishop [Moses] invoking Grace to help him provide a meal of flesh and blood instead of the bread and wine in front of him. With his own eyes the dreaming pilgrim sees the bread changed into "living flesh" [char vive], the wine into "red blood" [sanc vermeil]. Reason too sees the change, even though she claims to have lost her sight in watching the event: "he changed bread into living flesh and changed wine into blood to drink, against nature and custom." Yet Nature too apparently knows exactly what has happened under the accidents of bread and wine. Grace announces that she will change wine into blood, and bread into living flesh, teaching that the sacrament is truly flesh and blood in the "form" of bread and wine. In this version of the sacrament the senses of sight, touch, taste, and smell are "completely deceived" by the appearance of accidents: "it is no longer wine or bread but the flesh that was stretched out on the cross and made it bloody. . . . [Y]ou must not trust your eyes."[24] The presence of the Galilean body of Christ overwhelms the sign and its creaturely elements.

Writing in England during the later fourteenth century, John Mirk similarly closes the gap between sign and the Galilean body of Christ in the sacrament:[25] "Hit is þe same flessch and blod þat Crist toke in mayden Mary, was borne of hyr verray God and man, and aftur soffreþ deþ on þe crosse, and was buryed, and ros from deth to lyue, and now settyth on the faderis right hond in Heuen" (170). Characteristic of the "traditional religion" in formation, Mirk insists that the sacramental sign is the *same* flesh and blood that walked in Galilee and was crucified on Calvary. There is no gap between sign and the realities it signifies. Indeed, every day, in the Mass, Christ "scheddet his blod," a conventional claim that Mirk's contemporary Walter Brut opposed in a fascinating context (see chapter 4 of this book). But Brut articulated a theological approach Mirk was seeking to oppose.[26]

Continuities between Aquinas, Brinton, and writing in English are illustrated in William of Shoreham's long poem on the sacraments (c. 1320).[27] Christ's presence in the Eucharist is said to be even more plenitudinous than if he were among us in his manhood because he is now our *food*, but food that, as Augustine has maintained, "chaungeþ ous in hym" (561–65, 573). The poet is adamant that in the consecrated host "þer nys bote o þyng þere," namely Christ's Galilean body (679–84). So it is not surprising that he should turn to the issue of cannibalism which we saw Aquinas and Brinton addressing:

> For ʒef he schewed hym in flesch,
>   Oþer ine blody þynge,
> Hydous hyʒt were to þe syʒte,
> And to þe tast wlatynge
>   And pyne.
> þanne hys hyt betere in fourme of brede,
>   And eke in forme of wyne.
>
> (694–700)

We need to be deceived about what we know we are doing, but we need to acknowledge what we know even as we proclaim our deception. These paradoxical moves were being made into constituents of "traditional religion"— so much so, in effect, that they became as defining of Catholic Christianity as the Nicene and Athanasian Creeds. Thus Mirk is categoric and conventional when he claims that "ryʒt as eche cristen man and woman þat wol be saued mote need haue perfite charite in þe Trinite, ryʒt so mot he haue ful fayth in þe sacrament of Cristis body þat is made in þe auter" (168). Here "ful fayth" means acceptance of the version of Christ's plenitudinous presence in the consecrated host which we have been following. The sense in emergent orthodoxy that its current doctrine of transubstantiation must always have been an article of faith is nicely illustrated in *The Lay Folk's Mass Book or The Manner of Hearing Mass with Rubrics and Devotions for the People*. There the people are told that while the priest recites the (Nicene) creed (in Latin) after the Gospel, they should "saie þine" in English. But they are to say the Apostles' Creed—and with an unacknowledged difference. Instead of the article affirming faith in the communion of saints (a belief that pervades the Mass), the people's creed has this statement of belief: "And so I trow þat housel es / bothe flesshe & blode" (235–36).[28] This is a remarkable and eloquent interpolation.

Not long after Mirk's *Festial*, Roger Dymmok produced a long Latin book against Wycliffites and presented it to Richard II. The work of this text was to constitute and defend orthodox religion in opposition to Wycliffite "conclusions" proclaimed in 1395.[29] Dymmok reiterates the view that in the sacrament of the altar Christ's body is eaten and chewed but without suffering injury or division (93). The author is certain that Jesus himself intended precisely this interpretation when he instituted the sacrament at the Last Supper. Indeed, it seems that Jesus had in mind the version of Wycliffite theology encountered by Dymmok, for he was, in the Last Supper, carefully rejecting figural misinterpretations of his words ("This is my body" [94]). Like Aquinas, Brinton, and others, Dymmok maintains that while Christ's Galilean body is totally present in the consecrated bread which Christians eat, it is made invisible by God's kindness to our weakness (that is, our reluctance to engage in cannibal feasting). But we must not let this providentially granted invisibility deceive us into accepting the appearances given to our embodied beings. For these appearances conceal what is truly and not feignedly present, namely Christ's body (95).[30] Christ is present, Dymmok reiterates, really and essentially [realiter et essentialiter], not, emphatically not, just figuratively (95). As for the bread, Dymmok maintains the current orthodoxy of his Church: the material bread [panis materialis] does not remain after the priest has uttered the words of consecration (96, 109). When Christ ascended into heaven he did not want his Church to lack his full, bodily presence (100–101).[31] Only the doctrine of transubstantiation could secure this kind of presence, and only this kind of presence would be an adequate sign of Christ's love (102). Undoubtedly, the whole Christ is present in the sacrament, a claim Dymmok formulates according to Aquinas's lead.[32] This sacrament is both the end of all the other sacraments and also the measure of the place of Christians in the ecclesiastic hierarchy: the higher and nobler the Christian, the closer to ministering the Eucharist (108, 110).[33]

Earlier in this chapter I mentioned recent studies which have explored the cultural and political history of the Eucharist in the late medieval Church (see note 16). Roger Dymmok anticipates their reading of this sacrament as a political force in late medieval Europe. He argues that the consequences of the Wycliffite theology of the sacrament (which I will address in chapters 3 and 4) would be catastrophic for Christian faith and its practice. We would forget Christ's passion and the thanks due to God. Fearing the charge of idolatry, people's devotion to the sacrament would cease. They would hold the sacrament in contempt, the Mass would perish, confession would be abandoned, conflicts and hatreds in the community would be perpetuated, and sins would multiply. All this would apparently follow from people believing that they were receiving bread in the Eucharist and not Christ's Galilean body. Christian rituals would disappear and Christianity [sectam Christi] could be destroyed (90–91). Dymmok shows how fully late medieval orthodoxy was *identifying* Christian discipleship with adherence to a particular version of Christ's presence in the sacrament—indeed, to a particular version of transubstantiation. Given this identification, it certainly did follow that a rejection of the latter, even by Christians committed to the Nicene and Athanasian Creeds together with acceptance of Scripture as the revelation of God's word, entailed a rejection of Christianity. It is within some such scheme that Dymmok makes the claim that logically Wycliffites *should* deny traditional teaching on the Trinity, the Incarnation, and the resurrection (111–12). That followers of John Wyclif did no such thing could not, in this ideological scheme, become a topic of careful, self-critical reflection about the complexity of Christian identities and the motives for persecution in the modern Church.

Christian identities were multiple and enmeshed in a web of cultural practices which were themselves inseparable from these historically contingent identities. Indeed, Dymmok's own sustained defense of ecclesiastic wealth and power against Wycliffite zeal for disendowment of the Church, a zeal to reduce the Church to its early poverty, entailed an acknowledgment of the very historical changes endlessly attacked by Wyclif and his followers (40–51). In the light of such acknowledgment and the battle between Wycliffite Christians and the Church for the hearts, minds, and swords of the laity, it is not surprising that the Dominican introduces his defense of what he takes to be "traditional religion" with a dedication to the "most glorious" king of England and France, Richard II (3–10). Rather ironically, but illuminatingly, the dedicatory epistle opens with Dymmok's self-identification as the king's most poor orator and liege rather than as a poor, mendicant disciple of Christ (3). Richard II, a new David, has been raised up in regal magnificence to defend the Church against heretics (5–6). This supplicatory relation of priest to Crown was a core condition of the Church's mobilization of the secular elites against Wycliffite Christians.[34] Here too was irony. Dymmok, along with the ecclesiastic hierarchy whose strategy he shared, was mirroring the politics of Wyclif's project. And this would be fulfilled in the Crown's reformations of the English Church in the sixteenth century.[35]

But Dymmok's defense of his Church's accommodation to historical changes was not serene. For this very defense opened out the possibility that tenets now being made constitutive of the modern Church and orthodoxy might seem as historically contingent and lacking in authority as Wycliffites maintained. One might expect that commentary on the presence of the Holy Spirit in the Church's transformations would be sufficient answer to Wycliffites on this issue. But it apparently did not seem quite persuasive enough to Dymmok in the face of the complex networks of historical relations and claims he himself perceived. Confronted with the specter of a groundless contingency generated by his own defense of the Church, his language becomes marked with panic. He tells the king (and whoever else he hopes will read his book) that any challenge to the version of the sacramental sign of bread and wine currently maintained by the Church will destroy civil society. Invoking Aristotle's *Politics,* he argues that those who undermine the authority of a city's laws cause disintegration of law and order. This leads to divisions and rebellions against all in authority [contra superiorem]: anarchy ensues with the final destruction of the community, whether this is a city or a kingdom (91). Richard II, recently victorious over London and ready to settle old scores with those magnates who had opposed him so robustly in 1387–88, would be a sympathetic listener to such fears and to Dymmok's ideas of order.[36] Dymmok is certain that in their perspective Wycliffite sacramental theology will dissolve the Church's bonds of unity. Fusing discourses of the thoroughly earthly city under the sovereignty of Richard II with theological discourses about the meaning of Christ's words on the food which is his flesh and blood (John 6.56–57), Dymmok maintains that any interrogation of the Church's current understanding of sacramental signs dissolves the union of the faithful in the mystical body of Christ, the Church, and consequently the order of the earthly city (91).[37] Earthly city and city of

God apparently stand or fall together. Most importantly for the concerns of the present chapter, they do so around the doctrine and practices of transubstantiation. Dymmok thus composes a classic example of the inseparability of sacramental theology in late medieval England from the politics of city, kingdom, and ecclesial hierarchy.[38]

Before turning to Nicholas Love, whose *Mirror of the Blessed Life of Jesus Christ* preoccupies the rest of this chapter, I wish to recall an important aspect of the way orthodoxy envisaged Christ's presence in the sign whose sanctifying power was the end of all the sacraments and the consummation of the spiritual life. This aspect is the ubiquitous miracle of the host. Miri Rubin's *Corpus Christi* and her *Gentile Tales* include a veritable anthology of these stories, and they are very familiar to medievalists.[39] While I will be discussing Nicholas Love's use of such stories, their centrality in the version of Christ's real presence that was being constituted as "traditional religion" in the later Middle Ages makes it appropriate to take note of them now. As observed earlier, medieval theologians were clear that Christ's Galilean body was totally present in the consecrated host but mercifully invisible. However, the Church did not believe that Christ had left matters with this invisible plenitude. He had a tendency to show his hidden bodily presence, especially to those who rejected the relevant doctrine. For instance, priests who can't believe that in the Mass Christ once again "schedd his blod" are confronted with a characteristic miracle. One day the officiating bishop making the customary fraction of the host sees blood dripping from this into the chalice. He beckons to the doubting priests. They come and find the bishop's fingers bloody while "blod rane of Cristis body into þe challis." At once they are converted to the current doctrine of transubstantiation, begging the bishop to pray "to hym þat þou hast þer in þi hondys, þat he sende no vengaunce vpon vs for oure mysbeleue!"[40] Another endlessly repeated, characteristic story concerns a woman who bakes the Eucharistic bread. As the maker of the bread she thinks she knows what constitutes bread. So she dismisses teaching that claims Christ's Galilean body to be present in this bread under the appearance of the bread she has baked. Her error is challenged when she sees the consecrated host turn into raw flesh bleeding on the altar. This bloody sight persuades her, and is designed to persuade others, that under the appearance of bread is the bleeding body of Christ: "Lorde, now I beleue þat þou art Crist, Godys Sonne of Heuen, in forme of bred!" In this confession it is the bread she has baked, which the priest has consecrated, that she addresses as "Lorde." Mirk concludes his telling of this story by exhorting "good men and women" to take heed of this "and worschyppeth Godis body with al ȝoure myȝt" (173).

As Roger Dymmok observed, one reads that Christ very frequently appears in the consecrated host as a body or as flesh (100).

How did theologians address these widely proclaimed miracles demonstrating Christ's real but now apparently visible presence in the sanctifying sign? Aquinas insists that the body of Christ cannot be seen by any bodily eye as it exists in the consecrated host. While the body is totally present, it is present not dimensionally but in the mode of substance, hence invisibly, unimaginably, and open only to intellectual apprehension (*ST* III.76.7, resp; see too III.76.1, ad 3).[41] Aquinas thinks these host miracles can take place in two ways. One is through the watcher's perception being moved to see the bloody flesh or child in the host but with no change to the sacrament. Aquinas denies that there is deception in this of the kind found in the illusions produced by magicians. What is the difference? In the miraculous vision the appearance is produced by God "to signify a certain truth, namely that the body of Christ is really present in the sacrament" [ad aliquam veritatem figurandam, ad hoc scilicet quod manifestetur vere corpus Christi esse sub hoc sacramento]. Rather oddly he asserts that this was the manner in which Christ appeared to the disciples on the way to Emmaus. The second way in which Aquinas accounts for these miracles is by ascribing some "objective basis" to the apparition [specie quae videtur realiter exterius existente]. Aquinas struggles to describe what this might be, concluding that "a miraculous change" must take place in the "accidental qualities" so that "flesh or blood appears or even a child." Once more he denies that deception occurs. His reason is that the miraculous apparition "is to show that the body and blood of Christ are really present in this sacrament" (III.76.8, resp). Nevertheless, he stresses that "Christ's natural form is not seen, but a form miraculously produced either in the eyes of the beholders or even in the dimensions themselves of the sacrament" (III.76.8, ad 2). Whether along these or other lines, orthodox theologians affirmed and sought to explicate the widely distributed miracles which disclosed the real presence of Christ's Galilean body in the sacramental sign. There was, of course, an immense difference between the discourse of theologians, immersed in contemporary physics, optics, and metaphysics, and the celebratory discourse of preachers, poets, polemicists, and illustrators. Yet all realms of orthodox discourse, in their different disciplinary modes, shared a commitment to closing the gaps between the sacramental sign of Christ's presence and the bodily presence it signified.

Another important aspect of late medieval sacramental theology is disclosed by such miracles of the host. Many show how the consecrated host could work as the most powerful of relics, quite abstracted from the

Mass enacted in a specific Christian community to which Christ was present.[42] We can take a characteristic example from John Bromyard's popular *Summa Praedicantium*.[43] Bromyard tells of a heretic condemned by one of the Church's inquisitors to be burnt to death. For two days the devil frees the heretic from the fire (by bringing a cloud which extinguishes it). In response to this apparent miracle the people acclaim the heretic as a saint and declare that the inquisitor himself deserves to be burnt. The inquisitor (with Bromyard) interprets this moment of danger for the inquisitor as danger to the Christian faith. His solution involves the sacrament of the altar. On the third day he brings a consecrated host in the pyx. He places this between the devil (with his cloud) and the fire. This defeats the devil, and the heretic is burnt to death. According to the Dominican author the story demonstrates what "a great sacrament" the Eucharist is, quoting Ephesians 5.32 in a context which would have surprised its author (251). We see in this typical narrative just how Christ's Eucharistic presence is extracted from the ritual and worship of a community which itself represents and constitutes the body of Christ. The story, told with no trace of critical reflection by Bromyard, illustrates what seems to me appropriately described as a *reification* of the sacramental sign. It has become a powerful thing extractable and manipulable by those who claim to represent the Church and "traditional religion" against "heretics." Miri Rubin's *Gentile Tales* shows in excruciating detail that such reifications of the host belonged to Christian practices whose consequences could be catastrophic not only for heretics but for whole Jewish communities.[44] It is a reification illustrated in a different mode by the Croxton Play of the Sacrament.[45] God is unequivocally and totally appropriated to the particular, contingent agenda of a particular group of creatures.

Nicholas Love's *Mirror of the Blessed Life of Jesus Christ* was completed by 1410. This work became immensely popular in late medieval England, playing an important role in the making of late medieval orthodoxy.[46] Unlike some modern historians celebrating "traditional religion" in a timeless, unquestioned grammar,[47] Nicholas Love, like Archbishop Arundel, understood that orthodoxy had to be made in a context fraught with theological and ecclesiological conflict. He also decided that his rendering of the thirteenth-century Franciscan *Meditaciones Vite Christi*, itself already a massively influential work, should display this process of making for what it had now become: a theological and ecclesiological battle against Wycliffite Christians.[48] There is no need to go over this ground because it has been excellently covered by Michael Sargent.[49] He shows how carefully Love redirected the Franciscan meditations to specific conflicts in the late-fourteenth- and early-fifteenth-century English Church, a redirection applauded by Archbishop Arundel's personal praise and his decree that it should be "published universally for the edification of the faithful and the confutation of heretics" [vt pote catholicum, publice communicandum fore decreuit & mandauit, ad fidelium edificacionem, & hereticorum siue lollardorum confutacionem] (xlv, 7). As Sargent observes:

> [T]he *Mirror of the Blessed Life of Jesus Christ* was not merely perceived by Archbishop Arundel as a useful book "for the edification of the faithful and the confutation of heretics or Lollards": it was in fact so conceived by its author. For among the greatest of the alterations that Nicholas Love made in adapting his Latin Franciscan original to a contemporary English audience was the addition of a good deal of material commenting directly on Wycliffite positions. These additions group themselves around three primary themes: obedience to the ecclesiastical hierarchy, and the related question of church offerings; auricular confession; and the sacrament of the Eucharist. (xlvi)

While I shall concentrate on the last of these topics, the contexts discussed by Sargent should be kept in mind. We need to remember that long before he reaches the sacrament of the altar Love has acknowledged that the very existence of sacred Scripture has become something of a problem for those who rule the Church. The problem was catalyzed by the insistence of Wyclif and his followers that Scripture should be available to all the faithful in the only language most could understand and, still more threatening, that it should be the judge of all the Church's practices and doctrines.[50] Love's response was to offer his own book as a more salutary alternative for the laity—that is, for "lewde men & women & hem þat bene of symple vndirstondyng" (10). The revelation of the word in Scripture was intended only for the Latinate clergy. Works such as Love writes are allegedly "more pleyne in certeyne parties þan is expressed in þe gospel of þe foure euangelistes," more "edifying to symple creatures þe whiche as childryn hauen need to be fedde with mylke of lyȝte doctrine & not with sadde mete of grete clargye" (10). As with his later acknowledgment that "sume men" who are not Wycliffites do accept "þe fals opinion of lollardes" (92–93), Love does not envisage contemporary Christians as having anything like the "remarkable degree of religious and imaginative homogeneity across the social spectrum" that Eamon Duffy imagines.[51] Indeed, the difference between what he sees and what Duffy sees is both his problem and the motivation for his *Mirror*. His project actually requires the transmission of language and concepts that have much to do with "grete clargye." Yet it calls for a mode that will maintain the sharp divisions he makes so confidently: divisions between "lewde men & women" (by definition those "of symple vndirstondyng," the "symple creatures" like "childryn") and the clergy who can, by definition, grasp Scripture and "grete clargye." This is no simple task.[52]

The treatment of the Last Supper is the place in which we can follow Love's attempt to turn "the gospel" into "mylke of lyȝte doctrine" around the sacrament of the altar (146–58). As befits a meditation, his aim is to "stir oure loue to oure lord Jesu, & kyndele þe gostly fir of oure deuocion" (146). But before he reaches the institution of the sacrament his attention seems turned towards pressure he feels from Wycliffite Christians. Noting how "homely" Jesus is with John in allowing him to "rest vpon his blessed breste," Love adds a passage to his source in which he allegorizes this moment (John 13.23). The allegory, "as clerkes seyn," explicates the scene as John drinking from the well of eternal wisdom, "þe precious drinke of his holi gospel, with þe which aftur he conforted alle holi chirch & ȝafe it as tryacle aȝenynus þe venyme of diuerse heretikes" (149). This kind of polemical exegesis is the stock in trade of Wycliffite preaching.[53] What is it doing here, where readers are expecting "inward meditacion" to stir their love and to "kyndele þe gostly fir" of their devotion? The answer lies in the anti-Wycliffite commitment of the whole work, a commitment prepared to ignore generic expectations and to risk certain convergences with its enemy.[54] Here the risk includes eliciting questions such as the following: If Jesus gave John the "holi gospel" for the comfort of "alle holi chirch," and gave it specially as "tryacle" against the poison of heretics, why does the "holi chirch" now withhold this "precious drinke" from most Christians? Perhaps Love hoped that his "Proheme" would have forestalled such questions and that readers would now accept his work itself as "precious drinke" and "tryacle" more suited to their "symple vndirstondyng" and their need for "mylke of lyȝte doctrine" (10). Be that as it may, Sargent notes that this addition to Love's Franciscan source is "apparently preparing for the anti-Lollard arguments below" (286 n. 149.22–26).

These "anti-Lollard" additions are preceded by a gloss on Christ's words over the bread, *"þis is my body"* (151). Love's gloss is that these are "þe wordes of consecration . . . by vertue of þe which wordes brede was turnede in to his body" (151). Although the gloss directs the meditant to the doctrine of transubstantiation, it does set aside current discussions about the grammar of Christ's words and the nature of a sacramental sign. In doing so, it allows the relations between bread and body to be interpreted in more than one way. But the author is not prepared to leave the meditant to contemplate Christ's words and Love's gloss without further instruction. He adds a passage telling the reader to observe the "devout wonder" with which the disciples saw Jesus "make þat wonderful & excellent sacrament." Readers are being taught to model their approach to the consecrated host on Love's version of the disciples' response to the first "consecration": "at þis tyme þei laft alle hir kyndely reson of manne, & onely restede in trew byleue to alle þat he seide & dide, beleuyng without any doute" (151). So important is this locution to Love that he reiterates it later in the chapter (153).

It is hardly surprising to find a Christian theologian observing that sacramental signs involve gifts surpassing the powers of "kyndely reson of manne." But Love's exegesis of the Gospels he is using has a striking feature. It dissolves the way in which all the Gospels set Jesus's acts in narratives which disclose the disciples' puzzlement and focus on their imminent betrayal of Jesus (Matthew 26.22, 31–45; Mark 14.18–21, 27–41; Luke 22.21–40; John 13.8, 21–38). These are narratives in which Jesus's breaking and giving bread to his disciples is both a sign of the sacrificial breaking of his body and also a sign of the shattering of the community he has created.[55] It thus includes a sign of the vulnerability of the bonds of friendship, of charity, in the face of violent worldly power, power that the disciples had still not adequately differentiated from the kingdom Jesus embodied and to which Jesus called them (Luke 22.20–27). Love has chosen to *abstract* the moment of consecration from the Gospels' dense and profoundly disturbing narrative texture. He transforms the disciples into his own ideal image of contemporary Christians, unreservedly and untroubledly abandoning "alle hir kyndely reson" in their encounter with the consecrated host. In my view, this kind of exegesis and this model of discipleship (so alien to the sacred texts being exegised) was among the sources enabling orthodox coercion, persecution, and killing of Christians whose faith and doubts did not fit such a model. For Love's exegetical abstractionism with his pulverization of narrative obscures what the Gospels make so powerfully clear: the imminent unfaithfulness of even Christ's most devoted and intimate disciples, unfaithfulness that figures forth the readers' condition, one fully grasped by Jesus beyond the awareness of his disciples (John 16.29–32; Luke 22.31–34; Matthew 26.30–35; Mark 14.26–31). As Rowan Williams has commented:

Jesus giving himself over into the hands of the disciples anticipates his own *being given over,* his betrayal. The classical liturgies follow Paul in 1 Corinthians 11 in explicitly locating the action "in the same night that he was betrayed"; and in thus bringing the betrayal within the symbolic scope of the action of taking and breaking bread, the text finally brings into focus the way in which the rite overall embodies the making of a covenant. God's act in Jesus forestalls the betrayal, provides in advance for it: Jesus binds himself to vulnerability before he is bound (literally) by human violence. . . . By his surrender "into" the passion forms of food and drink he makes void and powerless the impending betrayal, and, more, makes the betrayers his guests and debtors, making with them the promise of divine fidelity, the covenant that cannot be negated by their unfaithfulness.[56]

This remarkably attentive reading helps one grasp just how Love's own attention has slipped from the Gospels' narratives as he seeks to cultivate what he considers to be appropriate dispositions in the face of the Church's current teaching on the Eucharist, "þe trew byleue þat holi chirch haþ tauht vs of þis blessed sacrament" (152). Understandably enough, the total presence of Christ's body in the consecrated host preoccupies him, together with the pressure he experiences from Wycliffite Christians: "without any doute he þat we receyuen in þe sacrament of þe autere is he þat self goddus son Jesus þat toke flesh & blode & was born of þe virgine Marie, & þat suffrede on þe crosse for vs, & rose þe þridde day" (152). The Galilean Jesus is fully present, "contynede in þat litel ooste þat þou seest in forme of brede" (152). The exorbitance of this preoccupation leads to substantial addition to his sources (152–56), and Love himself records his motivation: "bycause of þe lewede Lollardes" (154).[57] In such ways Wycliffite Christians were inflecting the meditations of orthodoxy on the central narratives and sanctifying signs of the faith. The importance of this, for the history of orthodoxy, cannot be measured by counting how many Wycliffites there were or were not.

Love does return to the Last Supper. He beholds the apostles seeing Jesus "sittyng with hem bodily, & þerwith haldyng in hese handes þat self body in þat þat semede as to hir bodily siht, nouht elles but brede" (152–53). The Galilean Christ consecrates the bread so that he is holding his own Galilean body in his hands just as the faithful now see priests holding this body "contynede in þat litel ooste" (152). Love's determination to identify the current doctrine of transubstantiation with the founding acts of Christ leads him to reiterate this interpretation of the first Eucharist:[58] "And so þat self body þat þei seyen with hir bodily eye before hem, was soþely vndur þat forme of brede, & þat self blode þat was alle hole in his body was þere in þe chalice in þe forme of wyne. Bot þan was not þat brede as it semede, & as it was before þe wordes of consecracion, nor wyne as it semede in self manere, bot onely þe likeness or þe forme of brede & wyne contynyng verray cristes flesh & blode as it is seide" (153). In discussing a later passage in the same mode I will comment on the linguistic choices Love makes in passages such as this, but for the moment I wish to comment on another feature of this text: namely, that even in its founding moment, before Jesus's arrest and crucifixion, it can allow no gap between the sacramental sign and the signified presence of the crucified *and* risen Christ. Jesus enacts the modern Church's teaching on transubstantiation and signs. So he eats and drinks himself; as Aquinas had argued, Jesus received the whole Christ in the first Eucharist (*ST* III.81.1, resp and ad 2 and ad 3; III.81.3, resp). Sign and signified merge into identity, while the resistances that the Gospels' narratives offer to such metaphysical moves are ignored.[59] So important was this in emergent orthodoxy that we find it being enacted in fifteenth-century East Anglian drama. In the N-Town Play of the Last Supper, Jesus takes "*an oblé*" and instructs his disciples that what "shewyth as bred to ȝoure apparens / Is mad þe very flesche and blod of me."[60] The rubric notes that "oure Lord ȝyvth his body to his dyscypulys," while the observing demon knows that transubstantiation has taken place so that Judas has not only sold Jesus but "etyn hym also" (after 448 and 470). On transubstantiation at the Last Supper, the demon and Jesus are in accord (500–501, 504–5). What about Judas? He follows the disciples to receive Christ's body. Jesus asks him if he knows what he is doing, and Judas replies: "Lord, þi body I wyl not forsake." In response to this declaration Jesus says, "Myn body to þe I wole not denye," but warns his disciple that it will be his damnation (449–56).

Judas also plays a significant role in Love's representation of the Last Supper, although a rather more complex one. Love, as we observed, reiterates that at the consecration "þe trewe apostles . . . laften alle hir bodily reson & witte" (153). That means, all the apostles "saue Judas" (153). In this invention of Judas as the one disciple who refused to leave his "bodily reson & witte," Love sets him up to become the archetypal Wycliffite. Accompanied by a marginal gloss announcing "contra lollardos," Love's text proclaims that just as Judas's alleged refusal to set aside "bodily reson & witte" meant he "receyued þat blessed sacrament to his dampnacion," so "nowe" his successors are those who "seyene þat þe holy sacrament of þe autere is in his kynde

brede or wyne as it was before þe consecracion"(153). One who denies that
the substance of bread and wine ceases to exist is certainly not committed to
denying the real presence of Christ, even his bodily presence, but this fact
does not encourage Love to hesitate for reflection on it, let alone to restrain
his assault. He writes that modern Christians who see no compelling cause to
deny the remanence of the bread's substance are actually "more reprouable as
in þat part þan Judas." The reason Love gives for this judgment is revealing:
"for þei [Wycliffite Christians] seene not Jesus bodily byside þat sacrament as
he dide, and þerfore it is lihtere to hem fort byleue, & more to hir dampnacion
if þei byleue not as god himself & holi chirch haþ tauht" (153). Love's point is
that because Judas could see Jesus holding the bread he had more excuse than
modern Christians for rejecting the identity between sign and signified. Furthermore, we can watch this un-Augustinian identification of sign and referent being invented as a homogenous tradition. Love makes the false assertion
that for "many hundreþ ʒere," back to the time of the martyrs, the Church
has denied any remanence of the substance of the bread and the substance of
the wine in the Eucharist (153).[61] Of course, the rhetorical and practical fusion
of Wycliffites with Judas could only make it easier for orthodox Christians to
light the fires — John Badby was burnt to death as Arundel gave his enthusiastic endorsement to Love's *Mirror*.[62]

But Love's commitment to discredit Wycliffite teaching draws him into
a more complicated register, one which is certainly not "more pleyne" than
the evangelical narratives he found too complex for the laity (10). He decides to set down the "trewe beleue" which Judas and Wycliffites lacked.
The outcome is a classic vernacular statement of late medieval orthodoxy,
and as such it is worth having the whole passage here:

> þe sacrament of þe autere dewly made by vertue of cristes wordes is
> verrey goddus body in forme of brede, & his verrey blode in forme
> of wyne, & þouh þat forme of brede & wyne seme as to alle þe bodily
> wittes of man brede & wyne in his kynde as it was before, neuerles it
> is not so in soþenesse, bot onely goddus flesh & blode in substance, so
> þat þe accidents of brede & wyne wondurfully & myraclesly aʒeynus
> mannus reson, & þe comune ordre of kynde bene þere in þat holi
> sacrament without hir kyndely subiecte, & verrey cristies body þat
> suffrede deþ vpon þe crosse is þere in þat sacrament bodily vnder þe
> forme & liknes of brede, & his verrey blode vndur likeness of wyne
> substancially & holely, without any feynyng or deceit, & not onely
> in figure as þe fals heritike seiþ. (153–54)

The "feith" demanded by "god himself & holi chirch" is thus that the sacramental sign becomes a semblance of its former creaturely being. In this teaching, the presence of Christ means that while bread and wine still "seme" to be bread and wine, "in soþenesse" this is merely seeming. We are actually presented with "liknes" of the creatures with which we began, not with what constituted their being but with their "accidents," now "myraclesly" present to our senses "without hir kyndely subiecte." I will return to the issue of seeming, of deception, but for the moment merely wish to take note of this and set it by. The faith Love explicates maintains that Christ is present in the sacrament in the "verrey" body that walked in Galilee, "þat suffrede deþ vpon þe crosse." This body is fully present "in substance" and yet concealed "vnder þe forme & liknes of brede." In Love's explication we see how orthodox response to Wycliffite questioning becomes acutely anxious about any attempt to understand the relations between Christ's presence and the signs he instituted at the Last Supper through the language of figuration. It seems that "in figure" and "onely in figure" are merged in Love's mind, both being associated with John Wyclif himself, "þe fals heretike." In chapter 3 we will see that what the latter said is rather more complex than the position ascribed to him here, but Love makes very clear a tendency among orthodox apologists to assume that "in soþenesse" is necessarily opposed to "in figure." We encounter a suspicion of signs related to the will to eliminate the gaps between sign and the symbolized, between the present sacramental sign and the plenitude of Christ's presence, including his Galilean humanity. In this tendency Love's text seems as representative of contemporary orthodoxy as the archbishop of Canterbury praised it for being (7).

Immediately after the passage just quoted, Love reflects rather uneasily on the metaphysical language he has used: "þese termes I touch here so specialy bycause of þe lewede lollardes þat medlen hem of hem aʒeynus þe feiþ falsly" (154). He does so because the terms are what Chaucer's friar, himself troubled by a lay person deploying clerical terms and texts, calls "scole-matere" of "greet difficultee."[63] Yet Love does not seem to register the irony in ascribing to "lewed lollardes" the betrayal of his own promise to provide "mylke of lyʒte doctrine" *rather than* "mete of grete clargye" for the lay audience he has represented as "symple creatures," "as childryn" (10). Perhaps blaming his default on the Lollards allows him to avoid examining troubling (for him) implications of the shift in his language during what began as a meditation on the Last Supper. One obvious implication is that the binaries he has set up between audiences and between subject matters are unsustainable misdescriptions of theological and cultural realities.[64] But acknowledging this would force him to reconceive his whole project, perhaps even his understanding of the relations between laity and clergy, English and Latin, in the contemporary Church and its future. A second less obvious implication concerns orthodox discourse on the sacrament in relation to Scripture, around which Love drapes his sacramental teaching. Love's language here, we recall, becomes the language of substance, of accidents, of accidents that appear without their "kyndely subiecte," of bread and wine that seem to be bread and wine but turn out to be "not so in soþenesse," of apparent bread and wine "in" or "vnder" which is the plenitudinous presence of Christ, including his Galilean body. These "termes" are certainly not "more pleyne" (10) than the language of the Gospels they displace and seek to control. But to ascribe the responsibility of such "termes" to "lewede lollardes" is a most eloquent misrepresentation. For while these "termes" are not Augustine's idiom, they certainly are those chosen by *orthodox* theology of the sacrament in the later Middle Ages. Indeed, they are the very kind of "termes" to which Wycliffites *objected* as unscriptural. Were Love to address this problem, his project would be brought under fascinating critical pressure. For what he would have to address would be the relations between the elaborated language of metaphysics and physics in orthodox discourse and the very different language of the key narratives in Scripture. In fact, his commitment to be "more pleyne" than Scripture was actually overturned by his commitment to currently orthodox sacramental theology and its language. So Wycliffites might be justified in asserting that elaborate orthodox accounts of precisely what happens in the mystery of the sacrament were actually resisted by the language and narrative modes of Scripture. But to explore this suggestion would have unraveled Love's project and perhaps his archbishop's admiration.

I wish to return to a difficult issue Love both raises and addresses, one I earlier mentioned and set aside. This concerns seeming, semblance, and deception in the sacramental sign. In his discussion of the Last Supper Love emphasizes that the body and blood of Christ are given "vnder þe lyknes of brede & wyne" (152). Even at the Last Supper, the bread that Jesus apparently was "haldyng in hese handes" only "semede" bread after the consecration and certainly "was not þat brede as it semede," nor was the wine "as it semede in self manere, bot onely þe likenes" (153). Furthermore, in the long passage quoted above (26–27), Love writes that after consecration the bread and wine apparently exist as "before," whereas "it is not so in soþenesse" (153). These reiterations disclose a haunting problem in current orthodoxy's account of the sacrament of the altar. Do not the favored formulations suggest that the sacramental sign of truth involves deception? We have seen how emphatic orthodox writers are that after consecration bread and wine are no longer bread and wine "in soþenesse" but only in seeming. Love himself sees the specter of illusion, of deception in his own conventional language. He seeks to exorcise it by simply asserting that the apparition of bread and wine which are no longer bread and wine occurs "without any feynyng or deceit" (154). But this simple assertion does not begin to address the difficulty he has registered. For if, by his own account, the bread and wine after consecration lack that which makes them bread and wine, being "without hir kyndely subiecte," if the sacramental sign is definitely not what it seems to be, how can it be shown that there is no illusionist "feynyng or deceit" here? Love gives no answer, leaving his readers with his terse assertion. Yet the issue is an extremely serious one, theologically and ethically. The fact that it was actually generated by current orthodoxy was noticed and pursued by John Wyclif, not without some derision.[65] But it was certainly not only a hostile commentator who could see the importance of the questions here, as Thomas Aquinas shows.

Like Nicholas Love, Aquinas opposes the view that after the consecration the substance of bread and wine remains. But unlike Love, he carefully articulates the objections a Christian might make to such a doctrine: "[B]read and wine are employed in this sacrament to bring out its significance of the unity of the Church. As Augustine says, *one loaf is made of many grains and one wine of many bunches of grapes*. But the substance of the bread and wine is required for this significance. Therefore, the substance of the bread and wine remains in this sacrament" (*ST* III.75.2, obj 3). Characteristic of the beauty of the *Summa Theologiae*, this is an excellent statement of the problem in the orthodoxy Aquinas is composing. It reflects an Augustinian understanding of the sacramental sign.[66] But Aquinas's response to this objection is surprisingly thin. He asserts that if the sign's substance remained after consecration this "would destroy the reality of this sacrament which demands that the very body of Christ exists in it" (*ST* III.75.2, resp). This claim shares the assumption we met in Love's *Mirror:* the plenitudinous presence of Christ's body is such that the reality of the creaturely sign cannot be allowed to continue. But what are the theologian's reasons for this assertion? He argues that the doctrine of transubstantiation with nonremanence is the only way of getting the Galilean body into the sign without Christ's body undergoing changes of motion in an interstellar odyssey from its location in heaven to diverse altars on earth. He says that only if the substance of the sign is converted into Christ's body, leaving no remanence of substantial bread and wine, can this unwelcome motion be avoided and the truth of the sacrament maintained (III.75.3, resp).[67] As for Augustinian objections about the nature of a sign, Aquinas merely asserts that accidents without substance are sufficient to convey what the sign signifies. Assertion is not argument, and this one simply ignores the issues of deception raised by orthodox discourse on the sacrament. But Aquinas, not surprisingly, has not finished with this tricky topic.

In a later article he directly addresses the question of "feynyng or deceit," to recall Love's terms. Once again he constructs an excellent objection to the position he wishes to defend: "[I]n this sacrament of truth there should be no deception [In sacramento veritatis non debet esse aliqua deceptio]. Now it is through the accidents that we judge the substance. It seems that our human judgment is deceived if the substance of the bread departs but leaves its accidents behind. It is not right then that this should happen in this sacrament" (*ST* III.75.5, obj 2). At this point Aquinas does not deny that there should be no deception in the sacrament of truth. So he is not denying the difficulties in the position he espouses. Indeed, he offers another equally coherent objection, one especially relevant to the polarizing split between faith and reason on which Nicholas Love, like so many anti-Wycliffite apologists, liked to lean:

> [A]lthough faith is not subject to reason, it is not opposed to it, but rather above it, as was said in the beginning of this work.[68] Now our reason starts from sense-knowledge [ratio nostra habet ortum a sensu]. Our faith then ought not to run counter to what our senses tell us. But to our sense that seems to be bread which our faith affirms to be the substance of Christ's body. It is not then desirable that in this sacrament the accidents of the bread, which are the object of our sense-knowledge, should still remain when the substance of the bread is no longer there. (III.75.5, obj 3)

It is not desirable [non ergo hoc est conveniens huic sacramento] because it entails deception, which is antithetical to "this sacrament of truth." What are Aquinas's replies to these two theologically forceful objections? One answer I have discussed earlier in this chapter: divine condescension leaves the accidents of the substanceless signs so that we are not appalled at the plenitude of Christ's body and revolted by our own cannibalism (III.75.5, resp).[69] This answer hardly addresses the question as to whether we are deceived, although it may give reasons as to why we might well pray to be deceived. Aquinas does, however, address that issue in his answers to the specific objections. "There is no deception," he maintains, because the accidents of bread and wine "are genuinely there" [sunt enim ibi secundum rei veritaten accidentia], and faith preserves our intellect from being deceived by the accidents without their substances, for the specific object of the intellect is substance (III.75.5, ad 2).[70] Furthermore, faith and reason not being contraries, this truth holds good in the present case, since faith is here "concerned with something to which our senses do not reach" (III.75.5, ad 3). These two answers on the question of deception seem, by the standards of this *Summa Theologiae*, unusually slight. Aquinas has already acknowledged that the appearance of bread and wine *is* a semblance to conceal our cannibalism from ourselves and the derision of unbelievers (III.75.5, resp). And the objector is troubled by the elimination of the creaturely signs' substantial reality, an elimination which destroys the very nature of the sacramental sign (life-nourishing bread and wine, fruit of God's creation, work of human hands), introducing a metaphysical split between appearance and reality quite alien to "the sacrament of truth." But if Aquinas himself fails to dissolve the problem of "deception" in orthodox accounts of how Christ's body is present in the host, it is not surprising that Love should rely on arbitrary command to banish the question of "feynyng or deceit."[71]

Perhaps with some relief, Love turns from language appropriate to "scole-matere" and takes up the miracles of the host illustrated earlier in this chapter. Like Dymmok, Love notes that the accounts of such miracles are widely diffused "in many bokes & heren alday prechede & tauht" (154).[72] He is convinced that these stories "confermede" the doctrine of transubstantiation but recognizes the difficulty of persuading Christians who resist the conviction: "Bot here lawheþ þe lollarde & scorneþ holi chirche in allegance [citation] of seche miracles" (154). Why do Wycliffites respond in this way? According to Love they do so because they consider these miracle stories "bot as maggetales [idle tales] & feyned illusions" (154). That is, they interpret them as fabrications made by those seeking to promulgate as creedal doctrine and language teaching for which they can find no warrant in Scripture.[73] Love's treatment of the Last Supper may not have convinced such readers that they were mistaken about this. But Love offers another reason for their opposition to the Church's treasury of miracle stories. Wycliffites lack any personal experience of "þe swetnes" of the

Eucharist (154). Love fails to explain why the experience of "swetnes" in the presence of the Eucharist during Mass entails acceptance of his account of transubstantiation without remanence of substantial bread and wine. He describes someone's blissful joy around the sacrament, through which joy "alle the membres of þe body bene enflaumede of so deletable & ioyful a hete þat him þenkeþ sensibly alle þe body as it were meltyng for ioy as waxe doþ anentes þe hote fire" (154). But however intense the joy, no such experience could necessitate the particular version of Christ's presence to which the late medieval Church demanded assent, a version which precluded, for example, any form of consubstantiation. Love then turns from the appeal to intensity of experience to the miracle tales themselves.

Just as his account of the sacramental sign is a classic vernacular statement of current orthodoxy, so is his exemplification of "miracles." He observes that Christ usually appears "auþer in likenes of a litel childe" or "in a quantite of flesh all blodye" (155). Rather than rehearsing such stories here, Love refers the reader to the treatise on the sacrament "at þe last ende of þis boke as in a conclusion of alle" (156).[74] This was certainly a fitting conclusion to Love's *Mirror*. It centers on the doctrine of transubstantiation and the plenitude of Christ's bodily presence in the sacramental sign (225–41). Once more it is stressed that Christ is present "verrely, & in þat self body þat was so merveilously concyuede by þe holy goste" (225), "verrely & bodily present" (226). Sign and signified characteristically merge into identity.

Love asserts that Christians who resist this account of the sacrament do so only because of their commitment to "hir owne bodily wittes & kyndely reson" (227). We shall see in chapters 3 and 4 that however comforting this simple claim may have been to his orthodox readers, it was false. (Wycliffism, after all, accepted the Nicene Creed, hardly overflowing with propositions read off from "bodily wittes & kyndely reson.") Equally mistakenly (as we shall also see in those chapters), Love says that it is only on vulgarly empiricist and rationalist grounds that Wycliffites object to the Church's current determination that the "substance of bred" no longer exists "in his kynde" after consecration (227–28). Where Love is correct, however, is in his statement that these "heritykes" (227) do not consider themselves bound by the determination of the modern Church in the way Love believes Christians should be. As I observed at the opening of this chapter, theology exploring the constitution of sanctifying signs is finally inseparable from ecclesiology, the constitution of ecclesiastic polity. In this context Love provides a gripping illustration of unconditional and absolutely uncritical faith in the authority of the contemporary Church. He writes that even if the Church's teaching about the sacrament of truth is *false*, Christians should nevertheless *believe and practice* it. Such assent to a false teaching, teaching that is "not soþe," will be rewarded by the God who is truth (see, for example, John 14.6, 15.20, 16.16; 1 John 5.6). Why would the God of truth so reward the pursuit of what is false? To acknowledge "oure gude wille to god & holy chirch" (228).[75] It is interesting to see "gude wille" being shaped to reinforce the closure of any potential gaps between the practices of the contemporary Church and God. Love's approach banishes the possibility that the Church could licitly become the subject of a divinely given prophetic critique and judgment of the kind to which Israel had been so frequently subject in the narratives and prophetic books of the Old Testament. On the contrary, his text seeks to identify the determinations of the contemporary Christian community (the Church) with the will of God. Eschatological frontiers seem to have been dissolved. The Church militant seems to have become the kingdom of God, as "god & holy chirch" (227) become virtually synonymous. The closing up of this gap, of this eschatological frontier, is analogous to the closing up of gaps between sign and signified in the sacramental sign, gaps between the presence and absence of Christ in the sacramental sign, a closing up of gaps we have been following in the late medieval constitution of orthodoxy. For Love and Archbishop Arundel, those who persist in recognizing gaps between the Church militant and the kingdom of God, gaps between the sacramental sign and its referent (the plenitudinous presence of Christ), are undoubtedly heretics. As Love observed earlier in the *Mirror*, these are the people who reject the stories of Eucharist miracles which, so he believes, "confermede" the current doctrine of transubstantiation (154).

Love classifies these precious stories in three groups. The first is given to inspire the faithful (230–32); the second to convert the unfaithful (232–33); the third "to opune prefe" of the sacrament's power (230, 235–37). He offers eight narratives. In the first group Jesus appears "bodily" in the host held between the priest's hands at the elevation; he is the "fairest" of men (230), or "a passing faire litel childe . . . offringe him self in sacrifice" (232). In the second group is a well-known story already discussed in this chapter: a female baker who rejects the doctrine of transubstantiation is forced to see "þe sacrament turnede in to þe likenes of a finger in flesh & blode" until she is converted to "trewe byleue" and until the celebrant prays that the dismembered body part be "turnede in to þe likenes of brede as it was before" (233)—that is, be concealed, be disguised. Also in this group we meet "fresh blode" running out of the consecrated host at the fraction, with the priest holding "flesh" that is "alle ouere wete with þe red blode" (233–34). In the third group Christ shows "opunly by miracles & merueiles" (236) the immensely powerful benefits of the sacrament both in this life and in purgatory: "opun prefe of þe passing profite & vertue of speciale messes done & songen boþe for þe qwikke & þe dede" (237). Love's examples in this third group belong to those benefits of the sacrament illustrated near the opening of this chapter. The first two groups exemplify the closure of the gap between sign and referent, the termination of any play between Christ's presence and absence in their model of the presence of Christ's body. We should also observe that the modes in which the miracles are related (small, exemplary narratives) are designed to exclude the searching questions of orthodox, "scole-matter" questions such as those explored by Thomas Aquinas around the issues of illusionism and deception, noted earlier. Here Love does his best to give us what he promised, matter "edifiyng to symple creatures," to his imagination of lay people who "as childryn hauen need to be fedde with mylke of lyȝte doctrine" and not, perish the thought, with "the gospel of þe foure euaungelistes" (10).

Yet even here Love cannot think of these "symple" lay "childryn" without thinking of Wycliffites. Earlier branded as worse than Judas, Wycliffites are now named as "þe disciples of Anticrist" and charged with having "made mich dissension & division in holy chirch, & putte many men in to errour of þis blessede sacrament" (238).[76] In this situation Love expresses grave doubts about the stable adherence "of þe most party of þe peple" to the Church's teaching on the sacrament (239). The source of all difficulties is Wyclif, that "fals maister of Lollardes & many oþere of hees disciples" (239). Once again Love makes the fascinating kind of displacement and projection we saw in his shoving off responsibility for reproducing orthodox "scole-matere" onto Wycliffites. He accuses Wycliffites of an un-Christian reliance on Aristotle's "kyndely reson" and "naturele science" (238–39). But it was Wycliffites who consistently objected to the way orthodoxy's account of the sacrament drowned the language and logic of Scripture in Aristotelian discourses, a practice amply illustrated by Love's own rendering of the Last Supper.

However, Love's commitment is not to a just representation of Wycliffite theological reflection. As observed earlier, he is striving to close up any gap between the contemporary Church and God, seeking to secure an identification. In this project the sacramental sign which signifies the mystical body of Christ and makes present the Galilean body of Christ plays a central role. Here too the gap between the signs given to the Church at the Last

Supper and the bodily presence of Christ, "that is, the bones and nerves and all the rest" (*ST* III.76.1, ad 2), has to be closed up into an identification. Those who question these identifications are "þe Angele of Sathans & not of god, as bene alle þe fals Lollardes," people who are the antithesis of "we þat þorh grace standen in trewe byleue as holi chirch haþ tauht vs in þis souereyn holiest sacrament" (239). In this version of the Church and its sacramental sign, eschatological frontiers have been dissolved and eschatological difference apparently overcome in the plenitudinous presence of Christ. It is easy to see how such a theological rhetoric around sign, Church, and Christ facilitated the committed persecution and burning to death of Wycliffite Christians, "disciples of Anticrist," by "we þat þorh grace standen in trewe byleue as holi chirch haþ tauht vs." The sacramental sign which signified the body of Christ and was the end of all the sacraments, the consummation of the spiritual life, the spiritual food which transformed its receivers into Christ (*ST* III.73.3), became a test as to whether a Christian deserved capital punishment, death by burning.[77] Such consequences, it seems to me, flowed from the will to close up the gaps and seek for the identifications I have traced in this chapter. Such were the consequences of abandoning the dialectic between presence and absence, between historically contingent pilgrimage and eschatological teleology.[78] In the revealing contrast between Love's rendering of the Last Supper and the narratives it seeks to control, we see how the modern writer resists the Gospels' reticences, their theological reserve, just as he resists taking seriously their accounts of the disciples' puzzlement, false confidence, and betrayal. What he, with the archbishop who so enthusiastically endorsed the *Mirror,* seems to have had no ear for is the way here, as in the resurrection stories, the Gospels disclose what Rowan Williams describes as "laborious recognition, as often as not, the gradual convergence of experience and pre-existing language in a way that inexorably changes the register of the language."[79] Love seems to have no time for such processes of "laborious recognition." This impatience goes with the tendency to set aside eschatological frontiers in the assurance of orthodoxy's own favored formulations, to set aside the Gospels' emphasis on the gap between the capabilities of the disciples' community and the Christ they seek to follow. Love's orthodoxy of sacrament and Church opposes the perceptions of Arundel's distant successor, the current archbishop of Canterbury: "The risen Jesus is not, for Mark, available for work in the negotiating of the Church's business, and the empty tomb (combined, of course, with Mark's radical skepticism about the wisdom or insight of the Twelve) serves to keep empty the seat of ultimate authority in the Church. In the terms of my governing metaphor, the empty tomb is precisely an empty throne or *cathedra*."[80] The author of *Piers Plowman* created a work in which perception such as this is a shaping force, in which "recognition" would be both "laborious" and immensely patient. As for those Nicholas Love perceives as "þe disciples of Anticrist," we will turn to them in chapters 3 and 4.

chapter 2

THE SACRAMENT OF THE ALTAR

IN *PIERS PLOWMAN*

Signs are given to men [hominibus]. Now it is characteristic of men that they achieve awareness of things which they do not know through things which they do know. Hence the term "sacrament" is properly applied to that which is a sign of some sacred reality pertaining to men; or—to define the special sense in which the term "sacrament" is being used in our present discussion of the sacraments—it is applied to that which is a sign of a sacred reality inasmuch as it has the property of sanctifying men.

—*Thomas Aquinas*, Summa Theologiae *III.60.2, resp*

    This chapter explores Langland's understanding of sacramental signs, particularly of the sacrament of the altar. Scholars of *Piers Plowman* seem to have found such an inquiry rather irrelevant, and the reason is probably the one given in the chapter "Langland's Theology" in *A Companion to Piers Plowman*. There Robert Adams writes that Langland's theology of the sacraments is "ethical and social rather than sacramental and mystical."[1] It is indicative that we have a massive and often informative work on *Piers Plowman* and the sacrament of penance, a substantial work on *Piers Plowman* and marriage, work on *Piers Plowman* and the liturgy, but nothing comparable, as far as I am aware, on the sacrament of the altar and *Piers Plowman*.[2] This is not surprising. The poem returns again and again to the sacrament of penance, depicting its troubles as symptomatic of those problems in the contemporary Church which most preoccupied its author. The sacrament of marriage is not as disturbing and pervasive a topic in the poem, but it is directly addressed and put to important figurative uses. The sequences in which Langland turns to the order and texts of the liturgy may be less obvious than those in which penance and marriage are addressed, but they are identifiable by those familiar with the liturgy and its version of Scripture, readily identifiable within the kind of literary history medievalists were trained to practice. Yet it seems that *Piers Plowman* does not give the kind of attention to the sacrament of the altar which could generate such studies, either by addressing it at length and directly or in those dazzling figural modes which are an endless lure to meditation and commentary. In the light of such apparent reticence it may well seem that one should not go further than Adams's cautious statement with which the paragraph began: the poet's theology is "ethical rather than sacramental," even if the sacrament on which one wishes to focus is the sacrament of the altar.

But such a conclusion is inseparable from assumptions about what is properly "sacramental" and how this relates to the "ethical." Assumptions of this kind are often so habitual, so primitive in a reader's formation, that they remain unexamined constituents of perception and interpretation. Here I think assumptions as to what is properly sacramental have been shaped by an understanding that is the product of divisions and determinations that had not been made quite irrevocable when Langland wrote *Piers Plowman*, although they were well on the way to being so.[3] Once the Church had tied its very identity to a particular account of *how* Christ was present in the Eucharist and of precisely *what* happened to the substances of bread and wine, then the absence of such an account (with its circumambient iconography and miracle stories) left the reader to choose between two interpretations. *Either* the writer was a heretic, deliberately eschewing the Church's insistence that Christ's Galilean body was present in a form of transubstantiation which left no substantial bread or wine but only their accidents, *or* the writer's interests were not properly sacramental. Langland was not a heretic (whatever later "heretics" did with his poem).[4] So the absence of the kind of sacramental writing we find in Brinton, Mirk, Dymmok, or Love has led literary historians to the conclusion exemplified in Adams's learned essay "Langland's Theology."

However, the relevant factors are much denser and more complicated than has been appreciated. They are partly and most obviously historical. If we are to understand just what the poet was doing with the sacrament of the altar, we will need to explore the conversations in which his work takes part, its "webs of interlocution."[5] This is so because he necessarily approached the sacrament with words which assumed determinate traditions of practice and argument at a particular moment in English culture. In addressing these we must be careful not to read *Piers Plowman* with the prejudice that it must fit an "orthodoxy" shaped by the Church's war to eliminate Wycliffite inflections of Christianity.[6] The relevant factors here are also theological. If we are to discern the body of Christ in *Piers Plowman* we will have to follow a complex dialectic of absence and presence, a dialectic which is inseparable from Langland's representation of the mystical body of Christ, the Church. The latter received the sacrament from Christ, but the presence of this Church is, as we shall see, also shot through with absence, and worse. We will need to develop an inquiry which is sensitive to different kinds of absence in relation to the sacrament of the altar and Christ's real presence.[7] If we do so, as I am seeking to do in this chapter, we will discover that the poet was making extremely complex and thoroughly coherent decisions in his approaches to the sanctifying sign on which I focus (see the quotation from Aquinas in the epigraph). I aim to show how these decisions are part of a profound contribution to late medieval reflections on the sacrament which, according to Aquinas and others, is the goal and consummation of all the sacraments, the sign and cause of the unity of the Church.[8]

The orthodox form of Eucharistic theology and iconography in Langland's Church was organized around the doctrine of transubstantiation with the version of Christ's presence this sponsored. The Galilean body of Jesus, the torn, twisted, bleeding body crucified on Calvary, was now present under the appearance of bread and wine after the priest's words of consecration (see chapter 1). This was the presence of Christ elevated in the priest's hands for the faithful to gaze at in adoration. Amongst the laity in late medieval England, communion was habitually rare: normally (and mandatorily) once a year. But gazing devoutly at the body of Christ under the appearance of the bread was at the center of the Mass and carried with it a range of rewards which were widely taught. For example, taking Bishop Brinton's list, from a sermon of 1376: the necessities of the day's food; forgiveness of light speech and oaths; eyesight not diminishing; freedom from aging during Mass; steps to and from Mass being counted by angels.[9] Lydgate's list adds favorable winds for sailing and safe childbirth, but the basic list of privileges for devout gazing at the present body of Christ was standard.[10]

From the late 1370s Wyclif developed a critique of this orthodoxy and its commitment to the doctrine of transubstantiation. This critique sought fidelity to Christ's institution of the sacrament as described in the Gospels and Paul's first letter to the Corinthians. As we shall see in the next chapter, the line taken by Wyclif included a reverent belief in the real presence of Christ, a sacramental, spiritual presence in which the communicating faithful participated but which included neither the presence of the Galilean and risen body of Jesus nor the annihilation of bread and wine.[11] Attention was shifted from the metaphysics of consecration and from the spectatorial focus of the Mass, with the rewards of attendance, to the faithful's reception of Christ, a shift that transformed the role of priests.[12] In orthodox views, this role was primarily defined through the consecration of the elements leading to the presence of the Galilean body of Christ (*ST* III.67.2, resp). This fact, together with the centrality of transubstantiation as the focal symbol of late medieval Christian culture, shaped the hierarchy's response to Wycliffite Christianity.[13] In chapter 1 we followed this response, one I wish to recall here. We saw how it was represented in Roger Dymmok's long anti-Wycliffite book dedicated to Richard II in 1395.[14] He maintained that because Wycliffite teaching on the sacrament of the altar rejected transubstantiation its consequences were catastrophic for Christianity [sectam Christi] and catastrophic for the existing political order.[15] Against this apocalyptic and revolutionary menace he opposed the defense of transubstantiation, the presence of Christ's Galilean body in the consecrated elements. He reiterated the then-traditional explanation that this is given under the appearance of bread and wine because of our infirmity: if we saw the actual flesh and blood we could not bear it. Still, we know that the bread is truly converted into this body, a conversion demonstrated in numerous and familiar miracles.[16] As Aquinas emphasized, orthodoxy maintained the absolute necessity of professing the presence of the whole Christ [totus Christus] in the Eucharist, "not only the flesh, but the whole body of Christ, that is, the bones and nerves and all the rest" [non solum caro, sed totum corpus Christi, id est ossa et nervi et alia hujusmodi] (*ST* III.76.1, resp and ad 2).

Defending this doctrine was bound up with defense of current practices of the Mass and the rewards mentioned above. As John Bossy observes, much of the Mass "was enacted in secret behind a screen; much of the words of its solemn and central passage, the canon, was inaudible to the public [*sic*] and not thought proper to be divulged to them."[17] Not only was the canon "inaudible," it was in a language few understood and was uttered by a priest whose back was mostly turned to the faithful. In Sarah Beckwith's words, "[B]y the late Middle Ages the mass was becoming more and more of a spectacle and less and less of a communion. The emphasis was increasingly on watching Christ's body rather than being incorporated in it."[18] On this event and on just what happens in the priestly consecration of

the elements, the physics and metaphysics of the presence of Christ's crucified body, orthodoxy chose to focus its self-identification against Wycliffite
Christians.[19] The "web of interlocutions" in which Langland wrote the C
version of *Piers Plowman* included these voices, these positions, and these
conflicts.[20] We must not begin our reading of the poem with the assumption
that to set aside the dominant, orthodox representations of the sacrament of
the altar is to set aside sacramental theology, the sacrament of the altar, and
all the resources of tradition—even if that is what the polemics of emergent
orthodoxy was now claiming.

    The poem's opening vision includes bleak representations of the Church
and its hierarchy. Conscience finds it fostering idolatry, false sacrifices and
misbelief while allowing exchange for material profits to permeate all its
practices. The result is pervasive simony and Masses that lack devotion
(Pr.95–127; see too Pr.47–84). Against this the dreamer receives a vision of
Holy Church descending from heaven to give him the guidance that the
contemporary Church seems unable to provide (I.3–II.54). Her speeches include beautiful and evocative disclosures of the saving power of divine love
and forgiveness in Christ's life combined with an insistence that this calls
people to active practices modeled on such love (I.81–83, 137–202). Without
such loving practices, she stresses, Masses will bring no rewards (I.177–80).
Her teaching sets aside conventional accounts of the rewards for attending
Mass noted earlier. She seems to see her task as revealing the love of God
while resisting reification of the Mass and its benefits, resisting the assimilation of sacramental signs to "the mase" (I.6) which we are shown so vividly
in these early passus (Pr.47–127; II.1–24; III.38–49, 311–12). After Wille has
directed his heavenly teacher's attention to what understandably obsesses
him, Mede and the powers she represents, she vanishes, never to reappear in
the poem.[21] So Holy Church becomes, as it seems to our sight, absent. For the
rest of the poem we are left with the visible Church introduced in the Prologue, the Church that to orthodox Catholics is the mystical body of Christ.
Perhaps the interplay of absence and presence here will be an important clue
to Langland's sacramental theology, a theology which, we will see, cannot
be separated from ecclesiology.
    Under pressure from the sharp questions of Conscience and Reason,
Wille (named at I.5) repents and goes to the church (V.92–108).[22] His penitential activity here is intense but seems isolated. Although he has not confessed to a priest he does not seem to be seeking one. Nor does he seem to

have come to Mass. There are potentially questions here, but in church Wille receives a vision of collective repentance. He sees a community seeking to follow the reformation initiated by Theology, Conscience, and Reason (II.119–V.200). In this context it would be reasonable to expect the sacrament of penance to lead into the Mass and the Eucharist, recalling standard teaching summarized in the epigraph to this chapter. Sacraments are signs that cause grace and incorporate creatures into Christ (*ST* III.62.1, resp), while the Eucharist is the sacrament of the Church's unity (*ST* III.73.1, contra, III.73.4, resp), the completion [consummatio] of all the spiritual life, and the sacrament to which all the others are ordered (*ST* III.73.3, resp). Yet during confession, the brief allusions to the Mass in which the sacrament is celebrated are rather ominous.

Wrath recounts his activity in church pews during Mass (VI.143–50).[23] We are certainly shown signs of unity: people sit together in the church, and the holy bread, blessed by the priest for distribution after the Mass, is a substitute for reception of the consecrated host which would have been adored earlier. But these signs of unity become catalysts of competition for social precedence and status, signs and causes of disunity in the Christian community. This is congruent with Bossy's acknowledgment that liturgical symbols whose end was "to express the wholeness" of local communities often became centers of conflict. So, for example, passing round the *pax* board readily activated disputes over hierarchy in the community: "*Pax* became a symbol of discord, not of amity."[24] Langland's approach continually refuses to ignore such difficulties for the sacrament of unity and its theology in his Church. But such a refusal does not register lack of attention to the sacrament. On the contrary, it reflects a determination not to abstract the Eucharist from complex social processes in which it is embedded. Some readers might take such determination itself as resistance to the divine resources given in the sacrament, or as a displacement of the "sacramental" by the "ethical." But this kind of evaluation is premised on a range of splittings strenuously opposed in *Piers Plowman*: namely, splitting off the spiritual from social and material practices, sacramental theology from ethics, and individual spirituality from the community's forms of life. Langland's approach to the sacraments assumes that individual spiritual life will flourish only in a community that fosters it, that salvation entails incorporation into the body of Christ, the community that is the Church.[25] So the practices of the community cannot be treated as irrelevant to the Mass and the sacrament. We will see how *Piers Plowman* unfolds numerous ways in which divine gifts, including sacramental signs, may become drugs and poisons, to use the language of its final passus.[26] His poem, as we will see, turns its readers towards eschatological dimensions lacking in much of the Eucharistic discourse from which it emerges, a dimension in which the presence *and* absence of Christ are joined.

Once the confession has been completed in the seventh passus, Repentance utters an exquisitely beautiful prayer for grace to amend and for divine forgiveness. In a densely allusive mode, he evokes salvation history disclosed in Christ's work (VII.119–50). In this lyric we encounter a complex allusion to the Eucharist.[27] Repentance recounts that after the crucifixion Christ fed with his blood "oure forfadres in helle" (VII.132–35). Within the Eucharistic discourses of late medieval England this could have striking implications. For it suggests that Christ's body and blood can be received, really received, *without* the Galilean body crucified on Calvary, a body that was, at this moment, still on the cross or entombed. Those who receive the saving food are distinguished, like Abraham (XVIII.181–289), by their faith in Christ's future coming (see *ST* III.49.5). Their reception is real *and* figurative *and* without the whole Galilean body, "bones and nerves and all the rest" (*ST* III.76.1, ad 2). This was just the conjunction now being anathematized by the authorities in Langland's Church. Had the poet been obsessed with the consecration of the elements and the plenitudinous presence of the Galilean body of Christ under the accidents of bread and wine, he might well have followed scholastic speculation on the nature of the consecrated host during the *triduum*.[28] But Langland's sacramental theology resists abstraction of the sacrament from the narratives of Scripture and from the contexts of reception. So he imagines Christ feeding the faithful in hell with his blood and sets aside questions that emerged here within orthodox theology of transubstantiation.

Being told that "oure forfadres in helle" were fed with Christ's blood still leaves us to ask how the repentant people complete their penitence. J. A.W. Bennett noted that Repentance's prayer draws on the liturgy of Holy Week and points towards the Easter communion.[29] Yet despite Repentance's memory of Christ feeding the people that dwelt in the region of the shadow of death, the people seem to have forgotten the sacrament of the altar. Crying out to Christ and his mother, none of them knows "the way" after repentance: blundering about "as bestes," they seem quite lost (VII.155–61). Furthermore, they lack any spiritual guide, let alone a priest to officiate at Mass. This strange outcome invites at least two interpretations. First, the people have not been adequately instructed in the theology and practice of the sacraments, in the relations between penance and the Eucharist, in their incorporation, through the sacraments, into the body of Christ. The fact that they are penitent but unguided suggests a laity abandoned by their priests, an image already given us in the prologue and one to be greatly expanded later (Pr.55–65, 81–94; XVI–XVII). Second, even though "the way" has been revealed (as Holy Church in Passus I and Repentance in Passus VII proclaimed), Christ who is that way still remains hidden, elusive, absent—revealed but absent even in the Church he will not abandon (Matthew 28.20). Perhaps the implication here is that the versions of "real" presence in conventional accounts of the sacrament are an impediment to the understanding of sacramental signs and an impediment to the kind of seeking that turns out to be "the way" in *Piers Plowman*.[30] This perspective is congruent with the strange scene that follows the image of lost and apparently abandoned Christians. They encounter what had become a neo-Wycliffite figuration of the cult of signs and pilgrimages in the contemporary Church.[31] The figure is a Christian dressed "as a paynyem in pilgrimes wyse," loaded with "Aunpolles"[32] and "Signes" of holy places (VII.160–69). His signs are marks of an achieved journey, of a presence sought, found and possessed as he returns home. His journey has included the place of Christ's nativity and "the sepulcre" where Jesus was buried (VII.171–72). But he has never heard of Truth, nor has he any clues about the way sought by the penitents (VII.177–81). He thus images the pursuit of signs in which the signs, including signs of Christ's life and work, have become reified into objects of the quest. Such signs do indeed lead to "the sepulcher," and there they silence the challenge put by the angels at the empty tomb to Christ's astonished and terrified disciples: "Why seek you the living with the dead?" (Luke 24.5).[33]

The two interpretations of the scene just offered cohere. Langland is imagining ways in which conventional signs and practices in his Church could obstruct the completion of penance in the sacrament of the altar and the sanctification it promises. Significantly, the servant of Truth who emerges in this impasse is not a priest but a layman, "a plouhman" (VII.182–IX.296).[34] Taking up some of the themes of Repentance's prayer, he outlines a journey which fuses the commandments revealed to Israel on an earlier journey with the sacrament of penance. His promise is that participants, led by grace, will discover saving Truth and Charity, making an inner Church which provides food for the souls of all (VII.205–60). Piers's map doubtless belongs to a long tradition of Christian spirituality which encourages its practitioners to find God more intimately present to themselves than their innermost being.[35] Yet the familiarity of this tradition may encourage us to overlook an aspect of Langland's strategy here, highlighted by a small change in the C version. In the B version the journey culminates in a vision of Truth within the individual heart, in a chain of charity, "as thou a child were / To suffren hym" (B V.605–8). In C VII the culmination is still the vision of Truth within the heart, but instead of the chain of charity and obedience we read of Charity making a Church in the heart, one which will allegedly provide shelter and food for the souls of all (VII.254–60). By imagining the virtuous soul as a Church nurturing others with shelter and food, Piers evokes comparisons with the visible, institutional Church to which all Christians belong, the Church heavily satirized and strikingly absent at crucial moments so far in the poem. Piers's journey inwards has developed signs of the way which leads those obediently following them away from attachment to any signs. The journey educates the will against seeking to accumulate signs in the manner of the Christian pilgrim just encountered.[36] But, in the light of the whole poem, we can identify a problem here. Despite mentioning the sacrament of penance (VII.247), the journey actually sidelines the visible Church. Piers claims that the inner Church can shelter and feed everyone. But the very language he uses evokes what is conspicuously absent from his map: the sacrament of the altar ministered in the Catholic Church. Piers himself seems quite unaware of this crucial resonance.

What is the poet doing here? In Piers, at this stage of the work, he gives us a devout Christian, a loyal parishioner, and a meticulous tithe payer (VIII.100–104). His guidance to the lost people is neither an attempt to displace the teaching authority of the Church (cf. IX.281–93) nor an attempt to increase his own status. Yet whatever its wisdom and timeliness, it belongs to a long exploratory process it does not transcend.[37] In the perspectives given us by this process we can appreciate how his insights accompany the lack just identified, the lack of the visible Church and its Eucharistic food. His confident claim that the inner Church he describes will "fynde alle manere folk fode to here soules" (VII.255–60) should evoke memories that qualify his formulation. For his language recalls Repentance's recent words about Christ feeding with his "fresshe blood oure forfadres in helle: / *Populus qui ambulat in tenebris vidit lucem magnam & c.*" (VII. 133–33a). At this point, his first appearance, Piers's understanding of "charite," "churche," and spiritual food does not participate in the later Christocentric vision in which a converted Piers will be a crucial if mysterious figure. There he will be given power, by Grace, to make the bread of heaven, Christ's body, in and for the thoroughly visible Church (XXI. 385–89; discussed below). Here, in Passus VII, his image of an inner Church and its universally nurturing food seems to be the consequence of the Church's ministry in this part of the poem (and not only in this part). This absence encourages the devout Piers to *spiritualize* the Church into an inner domain apparently autonomous of the actual ecclesiastic polity and the earthly society in which it journeys. Such a move, however, forgets that our spiritual life is like our bodily life in that our flourishing depends on our belonging to a community in which we necessarily live as naturally social creatures, the very community in which we receive sacramental food (*ST* III.65.1, resp; III.73.2–4; III.79.4, resp). The next passus, the plowing of the half-acre under the shadow of the Statute of Laborers (VIII), involves a return of what Piers had repressed, a return with a vengeance.[38]

But not till much later in the poem will we be given the resources for understanding Piers's error and its sources. When we meet the layman in Passus VII he is pursuing the path of discipleship and is a guide whose discernment far exceeds that of the lost pilgrims and the readers they represent. Yet the disciple has to offer guidance from a particular moment within the complex process which will become *Piers Plowman,* a moment shaped by the contingencies and limitations of the contexts in which that guidance is required. Here the guide, as I observed, cannot transcend the long process in which he is formed and to whose identity he contributes. In this understanding of the plowman's teaching the poet figures forth his own understanding of how authority is made, revised, and received in any living tradition. While Piers is a devoted servant and knower of "treuth" (VII.177–99), an authority on "þe way" (VII.178, 205–91), he is immersed in the contingencies of his historical and ecclesial moment. His map is inevitably shaped by these, its ecclesiology bearing witness to a lack already painfully clear in the poem. Authority, Langland would have his readers learn, is always in the making, always subject to processes it cannot grasp but always tempted to reify itself, always tempted to posit a false transcendence for itself. The poem would not have us collude with such temptations, and in the present case it will show, time and again, that Christians cannot sideline the visible Church, whatever its current state. Liberum Arbitrium, "cristes creature," well known "in cristes court," explains how the Church herself *is* "Charite," the virtue that alone can lead the will (and hence Wille) to the divinely ordained end (XVI.167–72; XVII.122–29). His remorseless attention to the Church and its reformation (XVI–XVII) is a sustained corrective to the tendencies I have identified in the map Piers offered in Passus VII. Such a corrective is as Augustinian as it is Thomistic, for the introspective journey to God in Augustine's writings is a journey that "is possible only through the agency of the church."[39] With figural wit and theological profundity, Langland shows us a converted, transformed Piers as a crucial agent making and sustaining the *visible* Church *in the world* (XXI).

But we do not have to wait for Liberum Arbitrium or the transformed Piers to grasp that Langland's haunting satire around the consumption of food often gains force from its allusion to the sacramental food which has been set aside both in the guide's map and in the representations of the Church around it.[40] This is exemplified in Study's account of contemporary meals among the wealthy and theologically curious (XI.26–48):

> Thus they dreuele at the deyes the deite to knowe
> And gnawen god with gorge when here gottes fullen.
> (XI.38–39)

Gnawing God with full stomach, they simultaneously "carpen of god ofte / And haen hym muche in here mouth" (XI.50–51). The poet refers to the poverty in the social contexts of their consumption and theologizing (XI.40–42, 45–75). In doing so he evokes the beatitudes and curses of Christ's sermon on the plain (Luke 6.17–26), later a central topic for Patient Poverty (XV.277–XVI.157). But the juxtaposition of wealthy people gnawing God while their neighbors are destroyed by hunger also invokes Paul's account of sacramental meals in Corinth (1 Corinthians 11.20–30). Characteristically, Langland is concerned with reception and discernment, not with the familiar issues around consecration. His concern is with receiving the sign, with what Paul calls discerning the body of the Lord, a mystical, sanctifying body composed of all Christ's members (1 Corinthians 10.17, 12.12–13; Romans 12.4–5). Like the sacramental sign of the altar, Langland's figure signifies "the unity of the mystical body which is an absolute requisite for salvation" (*ST* III.73.3, resp). Gnawing God and talking of God, Langland shows (XI.40–41, 52–53), is perfectly compatible with the refusal to discern the body signified by this sign. That is what Paul calls eating "unworthily" [indigne], an eating that brings one under "judgment" [iudicium] (1 Corinthians 11.27, 29).

Wille soon hears of another meal fraught with eschatological meaning and danger. This happens when he has been abandoned by the particularly mercenary domain of the Church he had hoped would help him in his current despair, aging, poverty, and spiritual need (XII.1–40). Scripture preaches Jesus's parable of the wedding feast (Matthew 22.1–14; XII.41–49). Wille is transfixed by its final comment, "[M]any are called, but few are chosen," a comment he isolates from the narrative to which it belongs.[41] In terror he disputes whether he is chosen. Thinking of Holy Church, he recalls his baptism into Christ's body and his calling (XII.50–55, with I.72–75; see *ST* III.68.1, resp and ad 1, III.69.2, resp and ad 1–2). He remembers Christ's invitation to all who thirst (Isaiah 55.1; John 4.20, 13–14, 7.37–38), that they should "souke for synne saue at his breste / And drynke bote for bale, brouke hit hoso myhte" (XII.54–57). This is a conventional image replete with Eucharistic significance.[42] It seems that Wille is moving from baptism to the sacrament of the altar, the sacrament to which all the others are ordered. But this does not happen. Instead, he stays with the promises of baptism, clinging to its inalienable character (XII.58–71; see *ST* III.63–65; III.66.1, ad 1; III.69.10, resp). Why does he not respond to the directions of his own image? I think the contexts give us an answer. As noted above, Wille has been abandoned by the friars on whom he claims to have relied—abandoned in great spiritual need. He can recall aspects of teaching he has learnt about his baptism, and this gives him hope, though certainly not joy (see XII.60–71). He cannot elaborate the resonances of his own Eucharistic image because he is stuck, and he is stuck because, like the earlier lost penitents, he lacks the community of faith that might enable him to move on to the consummation of the sacraments, as his abandonment by the friars and apparent isolation signifies. Langland does not have to be a "Donatist" to explore the consequences for Christians if the Church were to fail in its ministry of the sacraments, to be absent in the way Wille experiences. And by the poet's account, such experience is not only Wille's. Aquinas's comments on the relations between the sacrament of baptism and the sacrament of the altar are relevant to the situation Langland has composed: "Baptism is the beginning of the spiritual life and opens the door into the sacramental world; the Eucharist is the summit of the spiritual life [consummatio spiritualis vitae] and all the sacraments are ordered to it.... They sanctify us and prepare us to receive the Eucharist or to consecrate it. Baptism is required in order to begin this spiritual life; the Eucharist is necessary to bring it to its culmination" (*ST* III.73.3, resp). For Wille, as Holy Church had told him (I.72–75), the door has long been open. But how to enter, how to go on? How to find the sacrament of the altar, and how to receive it not "unworthily" (1 Corinthians 11.23–29)? For Langland, the sacrament of penance is certainly a major part of the answer, and it preoccupies him throughout the poem.[43] But that too finds its end in the Eucharist. And the Eucharist is the sacrament of the Church's unity (*ST* III.73.2, contra), the sacrament which signifies the unity of "the mystical body of Christ which is an absolute prerequisite for salvation" (*ST* III.73.3, resp). It *signifies and causes* this unity, the communion [communio] through which believers are joined to Christ (*ST* III.73.3, resp). To the Church is entrusted "the *goal and consummation of all the sacraments,*" and, as Aquinas summarizes the teaching of his and Langland's tradition, "what it contains within itself is Christ" (*ST* III.63.6, resp). As Christ is the still seemingly absent center and end of *Piers Plowman,* so the relations between Christ, the contemporary Church, and the sacrament of the altar which the Church ministers remain elusive at this stage, hidden from Wille and the reader. We may remember Wille's cry to the heavenly Holy Church many passus earlier: "kenne me kyndly on crist to bileue" (I.78). By now we should at least be realizing that although God's saving power "is not restricted to visible sacraments" (*ST* III.68.2, resp), as Langland will soon remind us through his version of Trajan (XII.75–88),[44] yet the sacraments given to the Church are the ordained way for Christians. But where is the Church whose sacramental sign enacted at the altar brings "communion" with Christ? One of the constituting forces of *Piers Plowman,* Langland returns to the question again and again. He consistently resists any separation between sacramental theology, the current ecclesiastic polity, and eschatology.

The issues just raised are put with great concision and urgency to Liberum Arbitrium by Wille: "What is holy churche, chere frende?" (XVII.125). Langland's answer weaves through the discourse of Liberum Arbitrium (XVI–XVIII) and the poem's final passus (XXI–XXII), shaping what he has to say about the sacrament of the altar and Christ's presence, the goal and consummation of the sacraments. But before these passages, Langland offers a brief contribution to his representation of Christ's presence in signs that sanctify (see the epigraph to this chapter).

As we have observed, Langland and the tradition to which he belongs maintained that Christ is to be sought in his mystical body, the Church, and in the sacrament of the altar.[45] But we have already seen that *how* he will be discerned and *whether* he will be discerned are, at least for Langland, painfully difficult questions. In Passus XII there is a powerful vision of Christian fraternity derived from the crucified and risen body of Christ (XII.109–19).[46] Christ is present in the body he constitutes, but this presence seems absence. He is disguised in "pore parail and pilgrimes clothes" on the road to Emmaus, and his own disciples "knewe hym nat that he crist were" until he blesses and breaks the bread between them (XII.120–133). But as soon as he is known in the act of blessing and breaking bread at the evening meal, "he vanished out of their sight" (Luke 24.29–31). This is Langland's model for the presence of Christ in his mystical body and in the sacramental sign enacted in the breaking of bread. Neither here nor elsewhere is he interested in elaborating the currently orthodox understanding of the real presence in the sign as, in Aquinas's words, "not only the flesh, but the whole body of Christ, that is, the bones and nerves and all the rest" [non solum caro, sed totum corpus Christi, id est ossa et nervi et alia hujusmodi] (*ST* III.76.1, ad 2). This orthodoxy was expressed in Nicholas Love's words on Christ's consecration of the bread on the night in which he was betrayed: "brede was turnede in to his body" so that the very body the disciples saw with their bodily eyes "was sothely vnder that forme of brede." Furthermore, the bread "was not that brede as it semede, & as it was before the wordes of consecracion, nor wyne as it semede in self manere, bot onely the likenes or the forme of brede & wyne contynyng verrey cristes flesh & blode."[47] Langland's decision for theological reticence here is a significant part of his poem's generation of its own model of sacramental sign and real presence. While this reticence is certainly very different from the language and practices of orthodoxy around him, it should not be mistaken as a lack of interest in the "sacramental." Such a mistake would simply and unexaminedly reproduce the assumptions and iconography of the contemporary orthodoxy Langland so delicately refuses simply to reproduce. Far from lack of interest in the "sacramental," his refusal here belongs to a careful engagement with sacramental theology and the forms of Christ's real, sacramental presence "until he come" (1 Corinthians 11.26).

Before moving to Liberum Arbitrium I wish to discuss a moment that was deleted from the final version of *Piers Plowman* but is relevant to the present inquiry, relevant as written and relevant as deleted. In B XII (C XIV), Ymagenatyf addresses a number of issues which have troubled the dreamer and the poem. Among these is the role of "clergie" (book learning) in Christian life. In defending its place Ymagenatyf claims that "clergie" is rooted in Christ's love (B XII.71). Ymagenatyf seeks to exemplify this position from the sacrament of the altar. He asserts that "goddes body myȝte noȝt ben of breed withouten clergie" (XII.85). Just as "clergie" is a comfort to the penitent and a curse to the unrepentant, so the Eucharist is "boote to the riȝtfulle" but "deeth and dampnacion to hem that deyeth yuele" (B XII.83–87). This threat comes from Paul's letter to the Corinthians considered earlier (1 Corinthians 11.27–29). Ymagenatyf does show the poet's own habitual concerns with reception of "goddes body" rather than with the metaphysical and physical constitution of the presence of Christ's body and the elements, the act of gazing in adoration at the elevated host, and the list of benefits for attending Mass. But this passage is deleted in Langland's revision. My tentative explanation of the reasons for this decision is twofold. First, the sacrament of the altar is the completion of all the sacraments, yet here it is used to defend book learning. The use is opportunistic, theologically superficial, and certainly not pursued with any serious attention.[48] Given this, the nature of the subject, and the current conflicts projected onto it, the poet decided to set the passage aside as raising too many problems unfruitfully and unnecessarily. Second, the passage abstracts Paul's warning to the Corinthians from its contexts, ones appropriately suggested in an earlier passage discussed above (C XI.33–51). The effect of this abstraction is to claim that the Eucharist is given only for "the riȝtfulle" (B XII.86). Those who do not receive "worthily" will be damned (B XII.90–91). Extracting Paul's threat like this leaves the issue of "worthy" and "unworthy" reception utterly vague and yet utterly threatening. Furthermore, Ymagenatyf seems to have forgotten Jesus's emphasis that he came to the outcast and sinful, the unworthy, not the righteous (for example, Matthew 9.13). Even more strikingly, he seems to ignore the preceding narrative in which he recounted Jesus's refusal to condemn the woman taken in adultery (B XII.70–84; John 8.3–11; cf. C XIV.35–42). Perhaps he becomes so preoccupied with appropriating the story for the defense of learning that he fails to grasp its wider ramifications, ones brought out with characteristic force by Augustine.[49] Ymagenatyf's brisk and generalized judgmentalism here certainly contrasts with Christ's own later orations (B XVIII.366–409, XVII.202–350; C XX.403–51, XIX.164–329). The consequence of Ymagenatyf's line is to make the sacrament of the altar seem a divisive threat rather than a gift of healing and reconciliation. That would hardly help Christians accept Conscience's invitation to receive communion far more frequently than late medieval norms and regulations (B XIX.383–90; C XXI.381–90, discussed below). Even though Ymagenatyf is merely one fallible voice in a complex process moving towards the showings of Christ and the Holy Spirit, the poet decided that in this passage he had created problems that were not, in the context of a defense of "clergie," productive. So it was deleted.

I move now to Liberum Arbitrium (XVI–XVIII). He is a figure from "cristes court," well known there "and of his kynne a party." Indeed, to him the gates of heaven are open (XVI.158–72). His long discourse engages with a wide range of issues but pays most sustained attention to the contemporary Church and its relations to the theological virtue of charity. He maintains that all current evils in the polity are rooted in the contemporary Church's failings

(XVI.231–85), responding with what had become a distinctively Wycliffite call for disendowment of the Church by the lay powers (XVII.208–40).[50] How does the sacrament of the altar fare in such a Church? When Liberum Arbitrium mentions the feast of Corpus Christi, we might expect reflections on the question (XVII.119–21). These expectations are heightened by the fact that the clerks are reciting the hymn "Pange Lingua Gloriosi/Corporis Mysterium," which, as Derek Pearsall observes, affirms the "transubstantiation of the communion wafer and wine into Christ's flesh and blood in the sacrament of the eucharist."[51] However, the poet declines to fulfill these expectations. We hear no conventional affirmations of Christ's presence as "the whole body of Christ, that is, the bones and nerves and all the rest" (*ST* III.76.1, ad 2). We hear nothing like Nicholas Love's words: "in that litel ooste" is "verrey cristies body that suffrede deth vpon the crosse" there "bodily & not onely in figure as the false heretike [Wyclif] seith" (152, 153–54). We hear nothing about the familiar benefits of attending Mass. Instead the focus is on *sola fides sufficit*, the power of faith to save "lewede peple" in the face of priests who fail them, and fail them at Mass (XVII.117–24, XVI.242–98). As tradition taught, the sacrament of the altar (*corpus Christi*) is approached through faith alone, but here faith is not directed to the habitual late medieval focus on consecration, transubstantiation, and the crucified, immolated Galilean body. We are certainly being deprived here of the form of Eucharistic presence celebrated in the miracles recounted by Bromyard, Brinton, Dymmok, Mirk, Love, and others.[52] But our deprivation belongs to a long process in which Christ's presence and the sacrament of the altar are *not yet*, a *not yet* which is at the heart of the poet's sacramental theology.

Liberum Arbitrium leads Wille's search for charity (XVI.286–374, XVIII.1–2) into the extraordinarily brilliant allegorical writing around the tree of "trewe loue" and the ensuing disclosures of salvation history in the Trinity and Christ's work (XVIII.1–XIX.336).[53] During this narrative Langland has Abraham (traveling in Wille's England during the appropriate liturgical time) recall God's promise confirmed in the command to worship him with wine and with bread on an altar, in worship of the Trinity. With the wine and the bread he is to "make sacrefice so: somwhat hit bitokneth" (XVIII.254–63). As all commentators have noted, this invokes Abraham's meeting with Melchisedech in Genesis 14.18–20 (Hebrews 7), traditionally taken "as a preparation of the eucharist."[54] Abraham's words, "somwhat hit bitokneth," underline this allegory. The bread and wine are signs of God's presence and promises of a future gift. Interpretation and promise demand faith ("I leue that ilke lord"), since the promised kingdom is conspicuously absent (XVIII.264–64a). In this prefiguration of the Eucharist later in the poem (which we shall eventually reach), Langland conveys the dynamic form of the sacramental sign of the altar in his theology. The sign is embedded in a profound vision of salvation history centered on the Incarnation: it signifies both divine presence *and* divine absence calling the participants to a faith that acknowledges the eschatological frontier (*"Hic in enigmate, tunc facie ad faciem,"* we recall; XVI.296a). The sacramental sign, like its prefiguration here, draws its participants into a prophetic understanding that Christ "shal delyuere vs som day" (XVIII.281–85). It is inescapably eschatological. The Christian visionary who has just been shown Christ's life and is about to encounter Christ himself responds from and to the poet's present:

> "Allas!" y saide, "that synne so longe shal lette
> The myhte of goddes mercy that myhte vs alle amende."
> Y wepte for his wordes . . .
>
> (XVIII.286–88)[55]

For Langland, then, the sign of bread and wine in Genesis figures forth the relations of *sacramentum* and *res* in the sacrament of the altar. It figures forth his own distinctly Augustinian understanding of presence *and* absence in this sign. It brings worshippers the divine presence even as it simultaneously acknowledges the absence of the kingdom it represents.[56]

Traveling with Abraham (also the theological virtue Faith) and Moses (also the theological virtue Hope), Wille encounters the incarnation of Charity, Christ manifested as the good Samaritan (XIX.48–336).[57] Faced with the deadly consequences of sin figured forth in the bound, naked "semyuief" man in the wilderness, Faith and Hope are helpless. Only the Samaritan Christ can give attention to the wounded creature, only he can offer healing remedies (XIX.48–79). The gap between the promises to Faith and things seen is massive. Christ explains that only his works can save and that this work is applied in baptism and the Eucharist (XIX.80–95). His comments on the Eucharist display a linguistic and imagistic restraint that is far from commonplace in late medieval accounts. Baptism, he insists, is not enough to make anyone "stronge," not enough to sustain a flourishing spiritual life (XIX.89–91). Christ teaches that such healing strength is not attainable "Til he haue eten al the barn and his bloed drunken" (XIX.90).[58] That is all he finds it necessary to say about the Eucharist before offering a long discussion of the Trinity and the way that unkindness alone will quench the divine forgiveness (XIX.108–334). The length of the exposition shows that it is not the poet's lack of time or wish to avoid complex theological issues which explains Christ's concision on the Eucharist. It is, rather, a choice made by the poet, ascribed to Christ, a choice against the habitual conceptual and imagistic prolixity, the "prolongation" of language in orthodox treatments of the Eucharist and its transubstantiation.[59] It is also a choice against the equally habitual emphasis on the consecration of the elements and the benefits for attending Mass as a devout spectator.

A consequence of these choices is the absence from *Piers Plowman* of the processions in which the consecrated host was carried by clerics, with the lay community's official version of hierarchical order being represented "around the supernatural power of the eucharist."[60] Not even when he mentions the feasts of Corpus Christi or Palm Sunday does Langland acknowledge these processions (XVII.117–21; XX.6–34a). We are not shown, in Margery Kempe's words, "how the preystys dedyn her observawnce, how thei knelyd to the sacrament and the pepil also" (ch. 78, 176). Nor are we shown the sacrament being used to work the kind of miracle Margery Kempe records in her parish church. A "hydows fyer" seemed likely to burn down St. Margaret's church and much of Lynn. Margery's confessor asks her "yyf it wer best to beryn the sacrament to the fyer er not." She replies "Yys, ser, yys, for owr Lord Jhesu Crist telde me it schal be ryth wel." So her confessor, the parish priest, "toke the precyows sacrament and went beforn the fyer as devowtly as he cowde and sithyn browt it in ageyn to the cherche, and the sparkys of the fyer fleyn abowte the cherch." Combined with Margery Kempe's own prayer, the result is a snowstorm which puts out the fire (ch. 67, 157–58).[61] Once again, we should note that the absence of such practices and assumptions in *Piers Plowman* is not an absence of attention to the sacrament of the altar. On the contrary, it is a studied response to current devotional, ritual, and theological norms from the perspectives of a significantly different sacramental theology.

Langland's emphasis is on the actual reception of what *both* the orthodox *and* many early Wycliffites agreed to be the body and blood of Christ.[62] All Christians are to eat and drink the sacrament (a possible, fleeting hint of utraquism?) with loyal faith if they are to be finally healed, according to Langland's vision of Christ (XIX.89–95). They are also to know that Christ's presence in this sacrament does *not* dissolve eschatological frontiers. The Samaritan Christ endows the Church with word and sacraments for the care of the "semyuief." Then he rides off, promising that he will return (XIX.71–79).[63] This dramatic moment is replete with theological and ecclesiological meaning. Christ will give his body and blood to the Church. He gives a sacramental sign that must be eaten and drunk in a manner that always registers his absence, the absence that only his eschatological return can supersede. Neither the sacramental sign that is the Eucharist nor the one that is the Church can be owned or controlled or known with finality by those immersed in history and the darkness of sin, known with finality by those for whom the sacrament is given as they are found, "semyuief." This eschatological perspective warns against all temptations to fetishize the sacrament of the altar or the Church to which it is given. It works against the will to fix it into a sign whose precise modes can be so determined (for example, no material bread remains, only its accidents) that its expert knowers (the current ecclesiastical hierarchy) can use it as a test for distinguishing Christians who belong to Christ's body from Christians who are "heretics" deserving capital punishment. When Christ is harrowing hell he proclaims that even as divine lord of life he still thirsts with the thirst he felt on the cross (John 19.28), a thirst for human salvation which will last until he finally has "out of helle alle mennes soules" (XX.403–14). Christ's thirst throughout history comments on the mystery of the sacrament (XIX.87–88). Christians are given essential food and drink here, but this is inseparable from Christ's own thirst, a thirst that belongs to *all* celebrations of the Eucharist. Humans eat and drink because Christ thirsts for them. So they are also incorporated in this thirst until its eschatological fulfillment.[64]

After the vision of Christ harrowing hell, Wille wakes on Easter Sunday. He calls his wife and daughter to arise and "reuerense godes resureccion" (XX.467–75).[65] He goes to church to hear Mass and to receive communion, "to be hoseled" (XXI.1–3). But when "men ȝede to offrynge"—that is, before the canon of the Mass—he falls asleep into his seventh vision (XXI.4–7). Expectations shaped by late medieval devotional texts would lead us to anticipate a Eucharistic vision confirming the way transubstantiation brought the presence of Christ's Galilean body—showing, as Nicholas Love writes, that "goddus flesh and blode in substance . . . verry cristies body that suffrede deth vpon the crosse is there in that sacrament" (153). The opening of the vision seems to fulfill such expectations as Wille sees a figure "peynted al blody" carrying a cross. But this seems to be "Peres the plouhman," yet "riht lyke in alle lymes to oure lord iesu" (XXI.5–8). Christ's presence is more mediated, more elusive than writers such as Bromyard or Mirk or Love led us to expect. His presence is mediated not only through the shifting, elusive figure of Piers but also through Conscience, the interpreter summoned by the puzzled Wille:

> "Is this iesus the ioustare," quod y, "that iewes dede to dethe?
> Or hit is Peres the Plouhman? Who paynted hym so rede?"
>
> (see XXI.9–11)

Like Jesus's disciples encountering the risen Christ on the road to Emmaus (XII.123–33), Wille encounters a fluid, ambiguous figure. As he had to rely on Faith to interpret the figure "semblable to the samaritaen and somdeel to Pers the plouhman" (XX.6–25), so now he must rely on Conscience to interpret for him. (It is striking, given the poem's representations of the contemporary Church, that neither Faith nor Conscience is personified as a priest.) Conscience's interpretation entails another extensive narration of Christ's life and work, culminating in his establishment of the early Church and looking towards the time when he "wol come at the laste" (XXI.12–198). This movement from the offertory of the Mass to the *eschaton* demonstrates Langland's understanding of Christ's presence and absence to those seeking him in his Church and the sacrament of the altar.

The application of Christ's redemptive work requires the building of the Church, "that hous vnite" built under the guidance of the Holy Spirit (XXI.200–334). In this vision of the early Church's making and of social relations informed by grace in such a Church, Langland unfolds his final response to spiritualizing tendencies such as those he explored in Piers's early teaching (VII, discussed above). Now transformed, Piers is endowed with the keys of the kingdom (Matthew 16.19), keys that are nevertheless contingent on restitution, *Redde quod debes.*[66] In a compressed image of the Church's historical life, Langland first envisages a successful defense in which "vnite holi churche" stood in "holinesse" (XXI.335–80). Celebrating this, Conscience calls all Christians to the sacrament of the altar:

> "Here is bred yblessed and godes body þervnder.
> Grace thorw godes word gaf Peres power,
> Myhte to make hit and men to eten hit aftur
> In helpe of here hele ones in a monthe
> Or as ofte as they hadden nede, tho that hadden payed
> To Peres pardon the plouhman *Redde quod debes.*"
>
> (XXI.385–90)

Not one of the more discussed passages of the poem, it is extremely resonant in the contexts explored in this chapter. Conscience encourages *monthly and more than monthly* reception of the sacrament. This calls people to communion far in excess of even the practices of the especially devout laity. As Eamon Duffy observes, "[F]requent communion was the prerogative of the few. Lady Margaret Beaufort received only monthly, and even so was considered something of a prodigy." Indeed, communion with anything remotely like the frequency Conscience suggests would come under suspicion.[67] We should, once more, also note that the people are asked to dine, to eat the "bred yblessed and godes body thervnder." There is no question here of an invitation to gaze at the consecrated host elevated between the priest's hands as he turns from the altar he has been facing.[68] Langland affirms that Christ's body is present in the sacrament, through the Holy Spirit, God's word, and the divinely empowered Piers. But once more he refuses to prolong discussion around the presence, around the consecration, around the metaphysics and physics of substance and accidents. With this goes his refusal to reproduce the popular iconography and miracles around orthodox accounts of Christ's presence in the sacrament. Instead of such conventional language and iconography, Langland reiterates one of the poem's consistent penitential demands, "*Redde quod debes.*" Conscience is quite unequivocal: to receive communion in Christ's body and blood one must have rendered one's dues to others in the community. This obligation is itself a condition for receiving the pardon which flows from the work of Christ (XVII–XXI), a pardon now mediated by Piers and an essential preparation for communion (XXI.383–90). This passage is carefully linked to an earlier moment in the passus. There, just before his ascension, Christ gave Piers "pardoun" and power:

> Myhte men to assoyle of alle manere synnes,
> To alle manere men mercy and forȝeuenesse
> In couenant þat þey come and knoleche to pay
> To Peres pardoun þe plouhman *Redde quod debes.*
> (XXI.184–87; see 183–90)

As Samaritan, Christ had already corrected earlier confusions about the nature and grounds of pardon (IX; cf. XIX.48–95, 164–334). Now he shows that while the gospel has the last word (XX.113–475), it contains a "couenaunt" to which the virtue of justice belongs. Justice has become a form of the gospel: it manifests the bonds of love and reconciliation in Christ's Church, making the acknowledgment of one's broken obligations an act of healing love. In this perspective, the will for communion in Christ's body (Corpus Christi, Corpus Mysticum) is unimaginable without the will to fulfill the law of and in the gospel: "*Redde quod debes*" (XXI.184–87, 386–90). Since the sacrament of the altar is the sacrament of unity, that unity cannot remain a dead letter but must be an embodied, living spirit, "þat hous vnite, holy chirche an englisch" (XXI.328).[69]

So Langland now envisages contemporary Christians responding to Conscience's invitation to endless communion, having tried to fulfill their part in the new "couenant" established by the risen Christ (XXI.383–90, 183–87; cf. the threatening earlier account of God's invitation, XII.45–50). Their first reaction is incredulity that the demand for restitution is a constituent part of the sign of unity and the bond of charity:

> "How?" quod alle þe commune; "thow conseylest vs to ȝelde
> Al þat we owen eny wyhte or we go to hosele?"
>
> (XXI.391–92)

Conscience maintains the teaching he has received from Christ. In trying to fill out what not eating and drinking unworthily might entail (1 Corinthians 11.28–29), he invokes the Lord's Prayer, "forgive us our debts, as we also forgive our debtors" (Matthew 6.12; XXI.393–95). This elicits outright and outraged rejection (XXI.396–402). The scene, with what follows, suggests that Christians now want the Eucharist only if it has absolutely no entailments for their social practices: they want Christ's gifts of the new covenant to have no consequences for their forms of life. In rejecting the sacrament as Conscience presented it, they reject that which signifies "the unity of the mystical body of Christ which is an absolute requisite for salvation" [res sacramenti est unitas corporis mystici, sine qua non potest esse salus] (*ST* III.73.3, resp), the sacrament which signifies and effects incorporation in Christ's body through living faith (*ST* III.80.4, resp). From within the Church they turn against "þat hous vnite, holy chirche" founded by Christ and the Holy Spirit (XXI.328).

The consequences of the decision and the processes to which it belongs unfold in the final passus (XXII). The forces of Antichrist seem to overwhelm the Church: only a few "foles" resist (XXII.52–79). The poem's critique of the contemporary Church, focused by Liberum Arbitrium (XVI–XVII), falls on deaf ears. Instead of reformation, we are shown how "inparfit prestes and prelates of holy churche" undermine Conscience (XXII.228–29) and subvert the sacrament of penance. This path to the Eucharist is transformed into a drug which destroys the will to repent and establishes an enchanted amnesia in the people (XXII.309–79). No one in this state recalls the sacrament of "bred yblessed and goddess body þervnder" (XXI.383–85), no one remembers the teaching of Christ the Samaritan (XIX.83–95), no one meditates on the work of Christ recapitulated so powerfully in *Piers Plowman* (XVII.1–XXI.199). The poem has shown how the sacramental meal is a constitutive act in the memory and practice which makes a Christian community where Wille's early questions about faith and salvation can be addressed (I.76–80). In its closing passages it shows how the rejection of this sacrament, given with Christ's conditions, is a symptom and cause of the community's unmaking.

But no more than Augustine does Langland encourage application of apocalyptic materials to conjure up imaginings of an imminent end, still less of an imminent new and sublime stage of Church history, a neo-Joachite reformer's utopia.[70] On the contrary, in the time of desolation figured in the final passus, Wille is ordered by Kynde to remain within the Church (XXII.204–13), now herself "semyuief" (XIX.49–95, XXII.348–79). While he remains, Conscience, rejected by Christians, sets out on another pilgrimage in search of Piers the Plowman, he who has been entrusted by Christ with the pardon and its completion in the sacrament of the altar, with the mediation of the new covenant. Once again, Langland's vision forces us to remember the limits and horizons of our understanding and imagination in face of the eschatological frontiers beyond which the rejected sacrament is the given path. *Piers Plowman* composes a profound and coherent theology of the sacrament of the altar, a theology at the heart of its ethics and ecclesiology.

chapter 3

JOHN WYCLIF

De Eucharistia (Tractatus Maior)

[H]oc sacramentum ex fide evangelii est naturaliter verus panis, et sacramen-
taliter ac veraciter corpus Christi. [According to evangelical faith, this sacra-
ment is naturally true bread and sacramentally and truly the body of Christ.]

—*John Wyclif*, Trialogus, *IV.6*

Signa enim ecclesie que Christus instituit [cultores signorum] denegant esse
signa. [The worshippers of signs deny that the signs of the Church which Christ
established are signs.]

—*John Wyclif*, Tractatus de Apostasia, *ch. 12*

Recent work on Wyclif, early Wycliffism, and the Church's responses
to Wycliffism has established the centrality of the sacrament of the altar in
this field of conflict while providing accounts of Wyclif's beliefs about this
sacrament.[1] Anne Hudson summarizes the position shared by Wyclif and
his early followers as "a denial of the contemporary views of transubstantiation and a belief that after the words of consecration in the mass the substance of bread and wine remained on the altar along with the accidents, or,
in less sophisticated language, that material bread still existed there."[2] Anthony Kenny, Maurice Keen, Anne Hudson, and Ian Levy all rightly emphasize that Wyclif affirms not only the remanence of substantial bread and

wine but the real presence of Christ in the sacrament of the altar.[3] In Kenny's words, Wyclif believed that the bread "does truly become the body of Christ," while Keen comments, "Christ's presence was sacramental and spiritual; none the less real, but real in the same sense as when he said 'I am with you always,' not in the sense as when he hung upon the cross bodily."[4] So he denied currently orthodox claims about the presence of Christ's Galilean body under the accidents of bread and wine. But he affirmed the real presence of Christ in the sacrament. For those with the power to determine what should constitute orthodoxy, the denial of the former, the presence of Christ's Galilean body, entailed the denial of the latter, Christ's real presence in the sacrament. *Either* Christ was present in his whole earthly body ("bones and nerves and all the rest," *ST* III 76.1, ad 2) *or* he could not be present. Nothing besides these alternatives was thinkable, or at least licitly thinkable. The espousal of this binary placed whoever maintained Wyclif's understanding of Christ's form of presence outside the Church. As we saw in chapter 1, it was asserted that such Christians would destroy Christianity and unravel the very fabric of human community. A nightmare of hatred and anarchy would be unleashed by such sacramental theology. In this anarchy the authority of the city's laws and statutes would be destroyed; from this would follow social divisions and insurrections against superiors. So wrote the Dominican Roger Dymmok, in a work dedicated to Richard II in 1395.[5] Paul Strohm, Peter McNiven, and Margaret Aston have given detailed accounts of the political formation in which such rhetoric was produced, together with fine analysis of its violent teleology.[6] Their work, together with the account of orthodox practices and doctrine in the first chapter of this book, provides the main contexts for the present chapter. It follows what Wyclif himself claimed he had often said "to the people" concerning the sacrament of the altar.[7] I am not concerned with the details of Wyclif's objections to current doctrines of transubstantiation when these tread the terrains of physics (for example, theories of motion and optics), logic, and metaphysics.[8] Despite his eminence in these spheres of academic work, he himself apologized for his engagements there as digression into a scholastic mode consequent on his struggle to deliver the Church from its current practical and theoretical errors (324–25).[9] My attention here, like my interests, is specifically on his theology of the sacramental sign, on what it is and what it is enabling. I have chosen *De Eucharistia (Tractatus Maior)* (1380) because it is replete with sustained arguments on the topics that preoccupied Wyclif and many of his contemporaries. The same could be said of *Tractatus de Apostasia*, but *De Eucharistia* seems a slightly more completed work, perfectly representative of his final views on the Eucharist, and perfectly sufficient for the limited tasks of this chapter.[10] Whatever William Woodford's claims about Wyclif's shifts on the Eucharist, my own reading of *De Eucharistia* alongside *Tractatus de Apostasia* (late 1380) and the later *Trialogus* (1382–83) has not found significant differences of position in the areas I address here.[11]

I set out from Wyclif's starting point, one he says he has often taught to the people: the constitution of the sacramental sign in the sacrament of the altar (11). This sign certainly brings us the body and blood of Christ. But is the body present "really" [realiter]? (11). Yes, as really as is the soul of a human being to his or her body, present throughout the body. Yet when a lion eats the body it does not eat the soul. With such a model, Wyclif maintains, we should think about the sacramental presence of Christ (11–12). This will not satisfy those who want a different kind of presence, those who assume that unless they can potentially see the body of Christ and eat this body with their teeth they do not receive the body of Christ (12–13).[12] In Wyclif's view, such Christians fail to distinguish corporal vision from spiritual. We see Christ in the sacrament, certainly; but we see with faith, through a glass, enigmatically (1 Corinthians 13.12) (13). Similarly, in receiving the body of Christ we don't touch and eat Christ's body carnally, we don't tear apart the body of Christ with our teeth, but we receive him whole (13). Wyclif goes on to argue that such reception is spiritual, concerned with feeding the soul from a fruitful faith through which our spirit is fed in God (16–17). Contemporary Christians, however, are being led into cannibalistic and horrible misunderstanding of Christ's invitation in John 6.48–52 and 54–59. It is not surprising that in the face of such misunderstanding many disciples turned their backs on Jesus, observing that "[t]his saying is hard, and who can hear it?" (John 6.67, 61).[13] Christ himself, however, was clear that "[i]t is the spirit that quickeneth: the flesh profiteth nothing. The words that I have spoken to you, are spirit and life" (John 6.64). Wyclif glosses this life-giving "spirit" as the spiritual sense of Christ's words: "*spiritus est,* hoc est spiritualis sensus, *qui vivificat*" (17). The faithful must therefore believe that the soul is fed by spiritual food, that Christ's flesh and blood bring love, the food of the soul (17). Not surprisingly, Wyclif turns to Augustine's commentary on John 6:

This it is therefore to eat that meat and drink that drink, to dwell in Christ and to have Christ dwelling in him. And so he that dwells not in Christ, and in whom Christ does not dwell, without doubt does not eat Christ's flesh spiritually even though carnally and visibly he presses the sacraments of the body and blood of Christ. On the contrary, he eats and drinks the sacrament of so great a thing [tante rei sacramentum] to his own judgement [1 Corinthians 11.29]. (17)[14]

In this Augustinian perspective neither the ubiquitous scholastic mouse nor the damned eat the body of Christ when they chew the consecrated host (18, 19; see too 11, 130, 308).[15] Furthermore, the binary propagated by current orthodoxy is superseded. So Christ is *not* present in his Galilean body, but he *is* really, decisively, salvifically present.

With help from Augustine's commentary on John 6 and from Augustine's understanding of sacramental signs, Wyclif argues that contemporary orthodoxy has collapsed the dialectic of absence and presence intrinsic to the sacramental sign.[16] The consequence is a false presence in which *nudum sacramentum* and *res sacramenti* are identified. So the collapse of the dialectic informing the constitution of the sacramental sign sets us on the paths of identification whose end is idolatry. For Wyclif the horrible irony here is that the faith in transubstantiation demanded by the contemporary Church becomes the worst form of faithlessness, one in which the fetishized creaturely sign is *identified* with Christ and worshipped as God; the sacrament's crucial negative moment, its eschatological reminder, has been presumptuously set aside.[17] In the light of this analysis Wyclif places the popular host miracles so conspicuously eschewed by his contemporary, William Langland (19–20).[18] He does not pursue any of Aquinas's explications, ones we followed in chapter 1. They are human inventions, he claims, driven by the idolatrous worship of signs. Plausibly enough, he argues that even if they *were* miracles they would not entail the current doctrine of transubstantiation (20). Misrecognition of signs, the collapse of the relations of difference that constitute sacramental signs, has catastrophic consequences and so is sponsored by Antichrist in his subversion of Christ's Church (20). No wonder that the analysis of signs and their performance is pervasive in *De Eucharistia* and presented with such urgency.

Wyclif maintains that the language of Christian tradition is permeated with figurative relations. Yet the modern Church seeks to exclude the sacramental sign of the altar from such relations, insisting instead that the relevant locutions unequivocally make claims of identification free from figurative or tropical modes.[19] His approach is organized around the distinction between *predicacionem ydempticam* and *predicacionem tropicam*. An example of the former would be the statement "Christ is man." An example of the latter would be Paul's statement "Petra autem erat Christus" [and the rock was Christ] (1 Corinthians 10.4).[20] Wyclif quotes the whole of this passage from Paul's first letter to the Corinthians, recalling how "our fathers," led by God in the wilderness, all ate the same spiritual food and drank the same spiritual drink: "they drank of the spiritual rock that followed them, and the rock was Christ" (35) (1 Corinthians 10.1–4).[21] Wyclif describes the relations here as ones in which that rock in the wilderness figured Christ mystically, part of traditional Christocentric allegorical exegesis of the Old Testament narrative: "hoc est, illa petra Christum mystice figuravit" (36). From this conventional reading Wyclif moves to the following chapter in Paul's letter, one of the New Testament texts describing Christ's institution of the Eucharist (1 Corinthians 11.23–26). He quotes Christ's words, "This chalice is the new testament in my blood" (1 Corinthians 11.25), and comments that the wine figured forth the New Testament as the calf's blood had been the sign of the Old Testament's covenant (Exodus 24.5–8). Setting Paul's criticism of the Corinthians' sacramental meal in these contexts (1 Corinthians 11.20–29), Wyclif observes that these Christians each brought their own bread and wine, one getting drunk and another going hungry (36–37). There can be no doubt that in Paul's narrative the apostle is talking about material bread and wine, both its abuse and its proper sacramental, collective use [ubi patet quod loquitur quadrupliciter de pane et vino materiali]. On this material foundation, Christ proclaims the words instituting the sacrament (1 Corinthians 11.24–25). Just as the chalice figures forth the New Testament in the locution "This chalice is the new testament," so the Corinthians' bread and wine figure forth the body and blood of Christ (37). Paul teaches these Christians to perform a rite *in figura*, a rite which remembers, makes present, and faithfully proclaims the future "until he comes" (11.26). Paul emphasizes that this rite is to be performed worthily if the receiver (receiver, not spectator) is not to be "guilty of the body and of the blood of the Lord" (1 Corinthians 11.27) (37–38). Furthermore, Wyclif notes that this sacramental sign of bread and wine is enacted in the homes of Christians, not only in Paul's account, but in the Acts of the Apostles: "And continuing daily with one accord in the temple, and breaking bread from house to house, they took their meat with gladness and simplicity of heart" (Acts 2.46). Having recalled these domestic scenes, he comments that here too the venerable sacrament is simply called bread. He

concludes that those who now burden the Church with speculative and practical perplexities around the sacramental sign sin grievously (38).[22]

In this context I return to Wyclif's understanding of Christ's presence
in the sacrament, to the dialectical relations of absence and presence
through which this sign is constituted. This topic permeates *De Eucharistia*,
and I shall consider a characteristic discussion of it from chapter 4 of that
work. As customary, Wyclif gathers together the accounts of Christ's institution of the sacrament in the evangelists and Paul (Matthew 24, Mark 14,
Luke 22, and 1 Corinthians 11). Once more he argues that Christ speaks
figuratively [figurative vel tropice] over the bread and the cup of wine (83).
But a sacramental sign involves a distinctive form of figuration. This may
perhaps be obscured by Wyclif's own habitual choice of terms (*figurative,
tropice*) and examples (such as Matthew 11.14, "he [John the Baptist] is
Elias," or Matthew 13.37–40, "the field, is the world. . . . [T]he cockle [ziza-
nia] are the children of the wicked one" [83]). Certainly his opponents
never seem to have grasped his continual attempts to show the distinctiveness
of sacramental figuration, its transcendence of the orthodox binary noted
earlier in this chapter. Perhaps his own vocabulary may not have helped
them do so.[23] Nevertheless, Wyclif stresses that there *is* a difference between
the mode of figuration we call tropological or moral and the mode we call
allegoric or sacramental [Differencia tamen est in modis loquendi, cum
unus sit tropologicus vel moralis et alius allegoricus vel sacramentalis] (84).
What is this difference?

The mode of speaking that Wyclif calls "allegorical or sacramental"
has a power lacking in all other figural discourses, including those found in
Scripture.[24] The divine gift of the sacramental sign includes the unique
power of making present the body and blood of Christ under the bread and
wine [habet enim efficaciam faciendi corpus Christi et sanguinem esse de
facto sub sacramentalibus speciebus, a quo defecerunt alie figure tam nove
legis quam veteris] (84).[25] Such is the "difference" in question. Matthew,
Mark, Luke, and Paul all recollect Christ's words of the institution because
of the extraordinary power of the sign (86). More than any other sacrament
it makes present the humanity of Christ and unites members of the Church
with Christ. Also more than any other sacrament, it benefits the person
duly celebrating it (87). So here we have at the same time allegorical or
sacramental utterance [allegoricus vel sacramentalis] *and* the presence of
that which is allegorically or sacramentally signified. As he goes on to show,
in this sacrament we are given both truth and figuration [simul veritas et
figura], a sacrament which figures forth Christ and the union between him

and his Church, one which makes and figures forth the sacramental presence of Christ beyond the power of any other figures [sacramentum enim figurat Christum et unionem cum ipso atque ecclesia; et vere facit atque figurat presenciam Christi sacramentalem ultra figuras alias] (97–98). But affirmations of sacramental force and Christ's real presence do not invite us to dissolve the dynamics of the sign; we are not to *identify* the bread with Christ's body (100). On the contrary, in the sacramental sign the bread becomes an "efficacious figure" [figura efficax] of Christ (100). This happens because the word of God works through the words of consecration; the great "artifex" is working through abject instruments in which Latin holds no privileged place (89, 90, 91–93). In sum then, this sacrament brings us Christ's body so that Christ dwells in the recipient's soul (101, 111).

In the process of this divine gift we must not fetishize the sacralized object through which the miracle is enacted by the divine word. This warning pervades *De Eucharistia,* and we have already met the term he uses to evaluate the consequences of ignoring it: idolatry. In Wyclif's vocabulary, "idolatry" points to our misrecognition of the sacramental sign's constitution and our forgetting that its teleology is *our* conversion, not the conversion of the elements, even less the annihilation of their substance. His vision and his warning is congruent with these comments from Rowan Williams's chapter "The Nature of a Sacrament" in *On Christian Theology:* "Signs are signs of what they are not: they are transformations of the world by reordering it, not destroying it, so that the tension of 'otherness' remains, itself part of the fluid and dynamic nature of sign-making. The object relocated and worked at in the process of making sense does not disappear in the process: it is still itself in the new context."[26] This careful formulation incorporates the dialectic of Christ's absence and presence in the sacramental sign, a dialectic Wyclif was convinced had been lost in the Church's daily practice of the Eucharist. There he found an exorbitant and one-sided cult of the presence of Christ's Galilean body under the consecrated elements, in words of Aquinas I have frequently recalled, "not only the flesh, but the whole body of Christ, that is, the bones and nerves and all the rest" (*ST* III.76.1, ad 2).[27] So exorbitant was this conventional understanding that the Church currently insisted on the substance of bread and the substance of wine ceasing to exist altogether, converted totally into the body and blood of Christ.[28] Wyclif was maintaining that the transformations of the world in currently orthodox doctrine were transformations not by relocating and reordering but indeed by destroying substantial elements of the world.[29] To Wyclif the very idea that Christ's blessing of the creatures (bread and wine) led to their substantial nonexistence, their destruction as the creatures they were, was a blasphemy against the creator's gracious and joyful goodness (117–18).[30] He was convinced that such blasphemous speculations, becoming enshrined as articles of faith, were dependent on current misunderstandings of the sacramental sign's constitution. These his work sought to remedy. Among such misunderstandings was the way the doctrine of transubstantiation opened out a chasm between appearances and reality. This was a problem I identified in Nicholas Love's *Mirror* in chapter 1 of this book, where I also considered Aquinas's engagement with it. Wyclif does not accept any attempts to resolve this problem because he thinks that current teaching inevitably turns God into a maker of illusions, a deceiver, one who calls humans to love and venerate the truth while setting up a web of deceptive appearances. Wyclif's reflections here raise fascinating issues about the potential for self-subverting skepticism within orthodox accounts of transubstantiation, and these reflections have been lucidly discussed by Anthony Kenny.[31]

One of the languages in which Wyclif sought to explain his own sacramental theology was the language which sought to distinguish "figurative or tropical" locution from "allegoric or sacramental," as we observed earlier in this chapter. Here the theologian probably draws on the traditional understanding of the difference between the Christocentric theory of allegory as emerging from God's revelation in sacred history disclosed in Scripture and the allegory that was common to both classical and medieval writing, an allegory that need have nothing to do with Christianity.[32] This genealogy seems to be part of his decision to treat *allegoricus* and *sacramentalis* as synonymous, distinguishing these terms from *figurative* and *tropice* (83–84). The point made in theological tradition was that humans, especially poets, invented figures for delight; through delight we could be persuaded to accept instruction, but in principle such instruction could be as lucidly expressed without tropes. But sacred Scripture, source of sacred doctrine, delivers to our apprehension divine and spiritual realities organized in events and figurative language by God, historical and linguistic orders without which we could not receive the gift of revelation, we being the kind of creatures who can reach the world of spiritual intelligence only through the senses.[33] God, the ultimate author of sacred Scripture, adapts events and things to become signs of the realities God discloses to human beings for their salvation. The key to all such allegorical signification was the Incarnation, life, death, and resurrection of Christ. In this mode of signification the spiritual or allegorical sense was not to destroy the historical or literal sense (this was the theory, whatever the practice of exegesis); it was to be founded on what was a historical and literal sense given by God.[34] Such theory, it seems to me, guided Wyclif's understanding of the allegorical modes given in the divinely instituted sacramental signs of the bread and wine—allegorical modes, we recall, that he insisted were distinctive, indeed unique.[35]

It also encouraged his resistance to a binary logic which had become entrenched in orthodox discourse concerning the Eucharist. I introduced this topic in the first paragraph of this chapter but have not developed it since then, so it is appropriate to recall the logic in question: *either* Christ's Galilean body is present in the sacrament *or* Christ's body is not present. *Either* the presence of Christ's body is of the real, literal, carnal kind apparently illustrated by Eucharistic miracles (see chapter 1), miracles of which Wyclif was highly critical (19–25); *or* there is no real presence, merely tropes for an absent Christ. But Wyclif was convinced that this binary involved a serious misunderstanding of the sacramental sign, a misunderstanding currently being fixed to provide a litmus text for detecting "heresy."[36] He believed that the presence *and* absence of Christ in the sanctifying sign could be adequately represented only by decisively setting aside this binary and substituting a different kind of model with a different kind of logic. This, as we have seen, affirmed that the body of Christ is *both* present "allegorically or sacramentally" *and* present transformationally, "really but sacramentally" in the consecrated sign. This sign can sanctify us with unique power (for example, 121–23, 153, 303–4), uniting us with Christ (111–12, 164). But the Galilean body is absent, at the right hand of God. Those governing the contemporary Church refused to accept such an understanding of Christ's real, allegorical presence in the sacrament as one that is at least compatible with Christian faith.[37] So the sacrament which contains Christ, in a mystery of faith, and is the bond of charity, sign of unity, and saving spiritual food (see for example, *ST* III.79.1–2, 5, and III.80.4) became subject to the binary logic I have described. This reduction allowed ecclesiastic judges to present their fellow Christians with a brutally clear alternative: Does the Galilean body of Christ totally displace the bread or does it not? No complex answer is allowed. If it is "no," then the judge rules that the respondent is outside the Catholic Church.[38]

Wyclif's systematic resistance to the abstraction of the Eucharist from its processes of constitution was, in his view, a resistance to the reification of the sacramental sign. For him the Eucharist belonged to processes narrated in the relevant stories of the New Testament and their enactment in present communities where the sacrament was received with the eschatological memory it proclaimed. To resist the sacrament's abstraction from these processes was to resist a range of contemporary ritual practices and assumptions identified by J. I. Catto.[39] The body of Christ loses its role as a specular relic independent of the consecration and reception of the bread and wine in a particular community. It ceases to be an object of adoring gaze, whether elevated above the priest's head or processed through town streets in the Corpus Christi festival as the most holy of relics. Wyclif, indeed, is quite explicit in maintaining that the sacrament of the altar should not be elevated by the priest (308), let alone carried around the streets of the town. Against such practices and their assumptions, his concentration is on the sanctifying reception of Christ spiritually (for example, 13, 17), and his model of communion is the breaking of bread in the homes of early Christians (Acts 2.46) (38, 119). It is in this act of reception that the communicating Christian is incorporated in Christ's body (308, 18). Anyone propagating these views on reification and the sacramental sign in the late medieval Church was bound to arouse intense hostility from those committed to current ritual and the ecclesiology to which this belonged.

But Wyclif of course also challenged the theological authority of those ordained to speak for the Church. Characteristically he maintained that neither Church nor heavenly angel is to be believed in any matter concerning faith unless what they claim is clearly founded on reason or the faith of Scripture (273; see too 116). The implications of this for current doctrines concerning transubstantiation are clear. In so far as this elaborate edifice is based on neither reason nor Scripture, it is not to be believed, whatever "Church" is claimed as its authority (273; see too 278–82).[40] But don't we need someone to pronounce authoritatively [autentice] the sense of Scripture and to declare other catholic truths which Scripture does not articulate expressly? Wyclif acknowledges the desirability of apostolic "pastors and doctors" (Ephesians 4.11) whom one could believe *as* pastors and doctors. But he laments that we now lack such luminaries and must limit the nature of our theological claims to fit our resources. Instead of building massive speculations in metaphysics and physics around the sacrament, we must remain at the most explicit level of faith given in Scripture rather than risk fabricating novel meanings. The rest we should leave to the Holy Spirit (281). Following this rule we will call the consecrated host "bread," and we will reject all nonscriptural language around this sign, including all talk about unknown accidents and holy quantity [quantitas sacra] (281). We will also revise our understanding of "heresy" (155–56, 312). This was customarily defined as the obstinate maintenance of what the Church determines to be false, the Church being the source of all authority, even Augustine's.[41] But Wyclif maintains that those the Church currently charges with heresy are actually following Christ. The latter was charged with heresy and blasphemy, while the martyrs were similarly charged and then tortured by tyrants for faithlessness to current gods. In the modern Church, Wyclif observes, a faithful Christian is charged with heresy (by ecclesiastic judges) because he or she defends the truth of Scripture [quia defendit veritatem scripture] against the claims of the current Church (312).[42] In this perspective Wyclif constantly classifies his orthodox opponents as heretics, for he defines heretics as those who subordinate reason and Scripture to the determinations of the modern Church.

In concluding this chapter it is worth noting why J. I. Catto seems mistaken to claim that Wyclif's challenge to his Church had the consequences of generating an "asocial mysticism."[43] Indeed, one can hardly imagine a more political engagement than Wyclif's sustained attempt to reform the theory and practice of the Eucharist in his culture. His reforming arguments have important implications for many contemporary practices and beliefs, as Catto himself has shown so clearly. Perhaps Catto's claims were generated by his unwary use of John Bossy's influential work. For there we find a familiar, misleading story in which we move from a virtually subjectless medieval culture, with its externalizing Christianity, to one in which interiority emerges at the expense of earlier orthodoxy and its social "integration."[44] Be that as it may, Wyclif's theology of the sacrament is inseparable from his ecclesiology and its politics. His strategies for ending what he takes to be an unscriptural fetishization of the consecrated host are replete with consequences for current forms of life in Church and polity. Nor is this, as it were, accident without its substance. The premises and sources of Wyclif's sacramental theology draw a reader to move authority away from the hierarchy of the visible Church and its priests. His transformation of penitential theology and practice rejects the mandatory role of the priest. One confesses to God, and no priestly mediation is required. If one needs human help and counsel, that can come from any devout Christian. So a priest is no longer necessary in the preparation a Christian makes to receive the Eucharist— hitherto, as we saw in chapter 1, the consummation and end of the sacraments. But Wyclif's understanding of the latter severely diminishes the status of the priesthood, a status the medieval Church grounded in the priest's uniquely given power to confect the body of Christ.[45] In fact, this activity was the principal task defining the priestly office. As Aquinas says, priests are consecrated so that they can confect the body of Christ (*ST* III.67.2, resp). Wyclif saw himself as restoring sacerdotal power to its proper (that is, scriptural), ministerial limits. The priest blesses, consecrates, and confects the sacrament, the efficacious sign of Christ's body. But he does not confect the body of Christ. Nor is praise due to him for this act but for his holy life (15–16). The difference between priest and laity is much narrowed, a movement intensified by Wyclif's demand for universal access to a vernacularized Scripture.[46] Nobody, he declares, would deny that God could [ad potenciam Dei absolutam] allow laity to confect the Eucharist. Indeed, he claims that Augustine and other saints agree with him that all elect laity are priests anyway (98). Nevertheless, he states that the Church has acted rationally [racionabiliter] in ordaining that only its priests should confect the Eucharist (99). But even this apparent acceptance of orthodox practices is immediately qualified. Consecration is rationally restricted to priests not because they have received the indelible mark or character of ordination but because of the priest's pious form of life [propter religiositatem et dignitatem in moribus]. Furthermore, he confesses his doubts about the scriptural foundations of the arrangements he accepts as rational enough (99). As I have noted earlier, his favored model is the early Church's practice in Acts 2.46. There the faithful break bread in their own homes, action Wyclif takes to involve consecrating the Eucharist (119). At the opening of this chapter I recalled Roger Dymmok's vision of the political anarchy that would flow from Wyclif's sacramental theology. This vision undoubtedly blocks out the striking Caesarean dimensions of Wyclif's political theology. And one can see why Dymmok should have decided to occlude these dimensions when addressing a king who had apparently developed some Caesarean aspirations or fantasies of his own. Richard II was unlikely to be anxious about a Caesarean theologian whose program would centralize and strengthen royal power. But Dymmok was absolutely correct to argue that Wyclif's theology had a range of major political consequences which would radically change both the English Church and English society. The Dominican grasped exactly what Catto overlooked: there can be no separation of inner and outer for a Wycliffite Christian.[47]

Wyclif himself constantly argued that theological errors concerning the Eucharist had disastrous consequences for forms of life in the community, for the bonds of peace and charity. He insisted that his reformed sacramental theology would initiate a significant reformation in social relationships. Among the sources of this conviction was the belief that the current reification of the sacramental sign, and the rites in which this was embodied, had drastically impeded attention to Scripture. Consequently the particularity of Christ's form of life and teaching (nonviolence and abnegation of worldly dominion and wealth, for instance) had been occluded while the true end of the sacrament was forgotten: namely, union with Christ lived in the practice of the Christian virtues.[48] Because a proper grasp of the sacrament reminds Christians of the forms of discipleship to which they are called by Christ in Scripture and the Eucharist, it is logical enough that *De Eucharistia* should discuss the role of Parliament and temporal lords in expropriating the worldly wealth of the Church (319–22). Here Wyclif explicitly returns to concerns on which he focused in *De Simonia* (early 1380), the immersion of the clerical order in networks of buying and selling divine gifts. These practices destroy the kingdom but will be stopped only if their foundations are uprooted. That means disendowment of the Church.[49] With equanimity he follows this by envisaging a disendowed ministry as a priestless one devoted to following Christ in poverty: having renounced personal possessions, it would hold all in common (322: cf. Acts 4.32–34).[50]

Such were the kind of consequences Wyclif unfolded from his reformation of current Eucharistic theory and practice. It is hardly surprising that persecution was very much on his mind even before it was inscribed on the bodies of his later followers.[51] We saw how *De Eucharistia* recalled that as Christ was charged with heresy so were his disciples—because they refused to worship the gods of the earthly city. Just so, in the modern Church, faithful Christians are charged with heresy for defending Scripture, Christ's word, against ecclesiastic and secular powers (312). And it was on Scripture that Wyclif claimed to found his understanding of sacramental signs and of the Eucharist in particular. Since he believed that contemporary misunderstanding of sacramental signs was a consequence of failure to practice forms of life congruent with Christ's scriptural word there could be nothing "asocial" about Wyclif's devotion and sacramental theology. Indeed, the very mode of his writing is pervasively engaged in conversation and polemic, itself a thoroughly and self-consciously social practice.

chapter 4

EARLY WYCLIFFITE THEOLOGY OF THE SACRAMENT OF THE ALTAR

Walter Brut and William Thorpe

"Amen, amen I say unto you: He that believeth in me, hath everlasting life. I am the bread of life."

—*John 6.47–48*

I

Walter Brut is an early Wycliffite whose extraordinarily rich testimony has received surprisingly little attention.[1] This latinate layman and Herefordshire farmer (278, 284) had been accused of heresy in the 1380s by both the archbishop of Canterbury and Bishop John Gilbert of Hereford, cited to answer articles allegedly against the Catholic faith which he had been maintaining in public (279). The testimony we have is written in Latin at the command of Bishop John Trefnant, the successor of John Gilbert, who accused Brut of erring in many matters of the faith (285). Anne Hudson has described the "seriousness" with which Trefnant addressed Brut's views and the ways in which "interest in the trial spread far beyond the bounds of Hereford or its diocese."[2] Her study of his learning and latinity, his identity as "laycus litteratus," shows the academic sources of Lollardy and corrects K. B. McFarlane's condescending and inaccurate account of Brut's work and its significance.[3] But while Hudson gives us important contexts in which to study Brut, she acknowledges that "[t]he views of Brut are not my primary concern."[4] It is one central aspect of these views that concerns the first half of the present chapter: namely, Brut's reflections on the sacrament of the altar. The more carefully we study Walter Brut, the more we will be encouraged to unpack the ways in which the linguistic, theological, and political homogeneity of Wycliffites has been seriously exaggerated by enemies and friends, past and present. Perhaps this chapter on Brut and Thorpe will encourage further study of individual Wycliffites and of their treatment of particular topics. The documents around Brut are rather unusual in giving us an extensive statement of a Wycliffite's self-description *alongside* the ecclesiastic judges' construals of that statement and their responses to what they so construed. Exploring the clash in representation here would illuminate the well-known problems presented to Wycliffite studies by the fact that so many Wycliffites are known only through their judges' construals. Brut's trial enables readers to see how the authorities went about the business of composing a version of this Wycliffite—what they included, what they excluded—and it invites us to think about the role of different genres in producing different versions of teaching. Such invitations will not be pursued in this chapter, but they are in its margins and call for further attention.

Brut's testimony as a whole is a remarkably wide-ranging and often extremely shrewd work of theological inquiry by a very searching Christian. Brut attempts to subject the Church's practices and doctrines, together with his own reflections on these, to the authority of sacred Scripture, especially the New Testament, and to the authority of probable reasoning grounded in Scripture (285–86).[5] He confesses that he will believe the "bare words" [nudis verbis] of no teacher unless they are grounded in the truth of experience or Scripture [in veritate experiencie aut scripture]. He thinks that this position is supported by Scripture's own account of the discovery of erroneous teaching even among the apostles chosen by Christ: Paul publicly rebuked Peter because Peter was undermining evangelical understanding of justification by faith in Christ rather than by the works of the law (286, citing Galatians 2 [see especially 2.11–21]). It is hardly surprising that if Peter could err so seriously the "holy doctors" of the later Church should have generated errors, as they themselves have acknowledged. As for modern masters of theology, Brut observes that they often maintain conflicting positions, with the result that the very same proposition may be approved as true and condemned as heresy or error. So contemporary teachers are capable of erring (286). Furthermore, Brut recalls that Scripture does not encourage Christians to give unreserved and uncritical submission to those officially approved as wise and authoritative. He acknowledges to his "reverend father," the bishop of Hereford, his own ignorance and sinfulness, his unworthiness to untie or carry the shoes of the Church's doctors. But he reminds the bishop that God, in his great mercy, sometimes discloses to the simple and to sinners [ydiotis et peccatoribus] what he has hidden from the holy and wise (290; see Matthew 11.25 and 1 Corinthians 1.17–31). As he shows with abundant quotation, Scripture often proclaims that God hides its mysteries from the wise, the prudent, and the just but, when he so wishes, reveals them to sinners and to simple lay people [peccatoribus et laycis ydiotis] so that God alone will receive the honor in all things (1 Corinthians 1.27–31) (291).

Brut's appeal to Scripture and to reasoning disciplined especially by the New Testament never advocates anything remotely like the vulgar materialism or the abstract rationalism with which contemporary orthodoxy habitually charged Wycliffites. Such charges are illustrated in Nicholas Love's *Mirror of the Blessed Life of Christ.*[6] Love, we recall, asserts that Wycliffites are worse than Judas because of the trust they place in "bodily felyng, as in siht, tast & touching" (153). They refuse to set aside "manus reson" in the face of divine activity (153–54), "presumptuously leuyng vpon hir owne bodily wittes & kyndely reson" (227). How wide of the mark this characteristic generalization is will emerge below. Nor is Brut's exegesis shaped by the kind of scriptural fundamentalism with which Wyclif and his followers are so often associated.[7] His exegetical approach is thoroughly Christocentric. This is clearly illustrated in his fascinating reflections on charity (301–4, 308–16). These follow his exploration of the relations between the prophetic criticism of Rome's violence in the apocalypse, the figure of Antichrist, and the commitment of the modern Roman Church to violent practices, to the use of the carnal sword (291–301). Brut's approach is to focus on Christ's teachings about love, nonviolence, and self-sacrifice in the Gospels. He also considers a network of related texts in the New Testament. In the light of these teachings on charity and grace he places and subordinates the Old Testament law, together with its rather different views on the roles of violence and war in the pursuit of sanctification. Discipleship of Christ entails following Christ's teaching and practice of nonviolence (308–16, drawing especially on Matthew 5–7). Christ's fulfillment of the old law is a fulfillment which decisively supersedes its uses of coercion and violence in this life. He taught love of enemies (Matthew 5.43–48, Luke 6.27–35) (308–9), and he practiced the nonviolence he taught, following its path to the cross. Brut objects that the Roman pope has set aside Christ's new law, now approving war and the killing of people, both non-Christians [infideles] and Christians (309). He wryly notes the strategies by which the Church seeks to sideline Christ's clear but hard teaching (309–11). Old Testament wars are no model for Christ's disciples, and they are best read allegorically by Christians, taken as figurations of spiritual battles in the new dispensation (311–12). Christ taught his disciples that they should endure persecution rather than fight back with the carnal weapons of their persecutors (Matthew 5.10) (312). Tracking the teaching and practice of Christ and the early Church, Brut unravels standard post-Constantinian theories of the "just war." He argues that these are the product of a marked diminishment in the intense charity which had informed the early Church. As the practices of Christocentric charity waned, so Christians invented glosses forcing the precepts of Christ to fit and justify their current actions, however violent. In this way the Church came to fight wars against "infidels" seeking conversions to the faith by violence, a practice that is utterly faithless [ut per bella covertantur ad fidem est satis infidele factum], since no one believes in Christ through violence and unwillingly (313). Brut recalls Christ's sharp rebuke to James and John when they wished to destroy the Samaritans who had rejected Jesus (Luke 9.52–56): "You know not of what spirit the son of man is: he did not come to destroy souls but to save" (313; Brut's text varies slightly from the vulgate here).[8] A Christocentric practice of charity makes the wars of Christians illicit: illicit for *all* Christians. Whoever approves the killing of Christians or "infidels" justifies that which is contrary to Christ's law. In doing so, one shows oneself to be Antichrist's follower, seducing people to believe what Christ had expressly forbidden is actually both licit and meritorious (316). And this, of course, is the current position of Brut's Church.

This description of Brut's meditation on charity and Christian discipleship illustrates his form of exegesis and the way it shapes his theology, his ecclesiology, and his politics. Committedly Christocentric, he resists the orthodox splitting of sacerdotal Christianity from lay Christianity, of Christ's counsels from Christ's precepts. Continuing against the grain of his culture's Christianity, Brut extends his reflections on Christ, charity, and violence to wonder how the Church has come to encourage disciples of Christ to kill thieves and heretics and how Christians can impose the death penalty (on thieves and heretics) in the light of Christ's teachings on charity, judgment, and mercy (316–19, 321–24). He certainly allows for the activities of reasoning and imaginative speculation in reading Scripture, but he tries to prevent these from becoming totally autonomous of what he, like his orthodox opponents, understands to be the revealed word of God.

Within this model of Christian inquiry Brut approaches the sacrament of penance with its three parts of contrition, auricular confession, and satisfaction through the penance determined by the priest followed by sacerdotal absolution (324–36). He offers a patient exploration of the relations between the Church's doctrine, exegesis of Scripture, and practice, but I shall discuss only his analysis of the judicial power ascribed to the priest in the sacrament of penance (328–30). Brut is puzzled by the disparity between his Church's current teaching and Scripture's narratives of Christ's practice (328–29). In studying Christ's way of forgiving sins, Brut finds Christ absolving sins not as a judge but as a savior [non invenio ipsum hoc fecisse in forma iudicis sed in forma salvatoris]. This accords with his divine calling, described in John 3.17: "God sent not his Son into the world to judge the world, but that the world may be saved by him" (329). Brut also quotes Christ's words to the woman taken in adultery: "Woman, where are they that accused thee? Hath no man condemned thee? Who said: No man, Lord. And Jesus said: Neither will I condemn thee. Go and now sin no more" (John 8.10–11) (329). From these and other texts Brut concludes that in his first coming Christ did not come as a judge to punish sinners. The latter office was deferred eschatologically (Matthew 25.31–32) (329). If Christ himself did not come as judge, why, asks Brut, do priests maintain that they hold the place of Christ to judge sinners according to the quantity of their sins [ut iudicent peccatores secundum quantitatem delictorum] (329)? Brut argues that while forgiveness of sins is ultimately God's gracious act, all disciples of Christ are his ministers and as such have power to forgive sins "ministerially," for they have received the Holy Spirit (in baptism and as the gift of Christ promised in John 20.22–23) (330). The Roman Church acknowledges that all Christians can baptize efficaciously, so all Christians have access to the keys of the kingdom. But these keys, in Brut's theology, are faith in Christ and hope in Christ, the faith which is the spiritual water flowing from Christ and washing the soul from sin. Such keys have nothing to do with judgment and punishment (330). Brut observes that nowhere does Christ give the Church any kind of model for a priest to impose retributory punishment ("satisfaction") on a confessed sinner; Christ's habitual locution is "Go, and now sin no more" (John 8.11) (332; see too 329). While Brut thinks confession to good Christians is useful (following James 5.16) (332), he finds its importance to be exaggerated in the modern Church (332), and he can see absolutely no scriptural warrant for the current constitution of the priest as a judge administering corporal punishments to satisfy God (333).[9] Indeed, Christ alone could make this satisfaction, and he has done so (Isaiah 53.4–8) once and for all. Human beings, Brut recalls, were incapable of making any adequate and transformatory satisfaction (333). This critique of the sacrament of penance is elaborated to include the Church's claims to have power to issue indulgences, a practice Brut finds alien to Scripture, simoniacal, and empty (335–36).

From the sacrament of penance Brut moves to the sacrament of the altar. He notes something the Church was increasingly invested in denying: that over the centuries diverse authorities have produced diverse accounts of this mystery (336).[10] In this complex situation his own commitment, he says, is to what Christ taught explicitly or implicitly. For Christ is ("I believe and I know") the true bread of God who descended from heaven and gives life to the world (336). He sets out from the words of Christ in John's Gospel, citing John 6.32–35, words that represent Christ as the life-giving bread from heaven. The mode of exposition here seems so unpolemical that a reader not immersed in late medieval discourses of the Eucharist and their conflicts might well overlook the force of Brut's decision. To grasp this, one needs to recollect cultural and ecclesial contexts addressed in chapter 1. For the vast majority of late medieval Christians, the sacrament which brought them Christ's body was a spectacle performed by a priest who whispered behind increasingly elaborate screens in a language very few would have understood even if they had been able to hear the words. For most of the service the priest had his back turned to the people, who were not called on to make any responses. Indeed, as vernacular texts such as the *Lay Folk's Mass Book* show, the laity were encouraged to make prayers and readings which might often bear little relation to what was being enacted at the east end of their church. The Mass thus embodied and fostered the clearest division between clergy and laity. The consecration bell would tell the people that the elements had been transubstantiated, and as the priest turned to face them they could adore the actual body of Christ, elevated between the priest's hands.[11] As the Franciscan historian Paul Lachance observes, "One went to Mass, however, not so much to receive the body of Christ as to see it."[12] The late medieval Mass was for the vast majority of Christians a spectacle where pious attendance at the display of Christ's body guaranteed a range of benefits endlessly reiterated. Let us recollect, for example, Bishop Brinton of Rochester, a contemporary and opponent of Wyclif who taught that these benefits included the necessary material food for the day, forgiveness of light speech and oaths, one's eyesight not diminishing, freedom from sudden death that day, freedom from aging during Mass, and the privilege of having one's steps to and from Mass counted by angels.[13] Even members of the Franciscan Third Order would receive communion only three times a year, and Eamon Duffy has rightly observed that to communicate monthly was viewed as " something of a prodigy."[14] This is the context that so frustrated the Wycliffite priest William Thorpe in Shrewsbury, soon after Brut composed his testimony. In a well-known scene Thorpe recounts how he was "in þe pulpitte, bisiinge me to teche þe heestes of God," when a "sacringe belle" was rung from an altar in the church. Immediately "myche peple turned awei fersli and wiþ greet noyse runnen frowardis me" to behold the body of Christ being elevated for adoration.[15] This is the context assumed and implicitly challenged in the way Brut decides to approach the sacrament of the altar through John 6.

Christ the bread of life is to be *eaten,* and those who do eat will live eternally ("ex quo pane qui manducat vivet in eternum, ut patet in eodem capitulo [John 6])" (336). Abstaining from direct polemic, Brut's text simply does not contain the slightest suggestion that devoutly watching the bread of life could be an appropriate response to the sacrament, or that presence at the display of the consecrated host would bring the benefits described in Brinton's standard list. Brut's strategy foregrounds reception of the bread of life, communion, before he engages with the consecration of the elements, the issue that obsessed late medieval defenses of current orthodoxy.[16]

He considers what is entailed by eating Christ, the bread of life. This consideration turns to faith in Christ's redemption of humanity, which, by grace, justifies those who have been immersed in sinful lives, unable to fulfill the teachings of the divinely given law (336–37; he quotes from Galatians 2.16, 3.11–12, and 21–24 and from Romans 5.20–21). In this move Brut is following connections made in the chapter of John's Gospel from which he began: "Jesus said to them: I am the bread of life. He that cometh to me shall not hunger: and he that believeth in me shall never thirst" (John 6.35). Jesus warns that seeing is *not* the same as believing (John 6.36). Responding to this, Brut emphasizes the role of faith in communion with the flesh and blood of Christ. Whoever eats the flesh of Christ and drinks his blood dwells in Christ and Christ in that person (he cites John 6.57), but as it is faith alone that justifies the Christian, so it is faith alone that enables this reception (337).[17] By unfolding the connection of reception and faith through reading John 6, Brut introduces his understanding of what is entailed by eating Christ's flesh and by Christ's real presence in sacramental communion. He does so *before* he engages with current arguments over what exactly happens to the elements at their consecration, arguments which are a mixture of physics, metaphysics, and theology.[18]

He decides to open out another important dimension of the Eucharist before addressing these issues, one that seems to get obscured in the apologetic writings of those responsible for formulating orthodoxy against Wycliffite Christians. The dimension I have in mind here is the eschatological. As Aquinas wrote of the sacrament, it looks to the past (Christ's passion and sacrifice), the present (the unity of the Church), and the future: "It prefigures that enjoyment of God which will be ours in heaven. That is why it is called '*viaticum*,' because it keeps us on the way to heaven . . . [and] called 'eucharist,' that is, 'desirable gift or grace [bona gratia],' because *the free gift of God is eternal life* [Romans 6.23]" (*ST* III.73.4, resp). Brut maintains that in believing the Church's teaching on the Incarnation we eat the bread of heaven and the body of Christ and that in believing that he freely shed his blood for our redemption we drink his blood. Unless we eat Christ's flesh and drink his blood, we do not have life in us because the flesh of Christ is truly food and his blood truly is drink (337). As he contemplates the future figured in the sacrament, Brut develops a striking sacramental eschatology. In heaven the most sublime aspect of the faithful, the "intellect," will be eternally fed with the divinity of Jesus Christ, the bread of heaven, God containing all delight, while the faithful's exterior and interior powers will be fed with the flesh—that is, the humanity of Jesus Christ. Brut envisages Christ's humanity as the gorgeously attired queen standing at God's right hand [regina astans a dextra Dei in vestitu deaurato circumdata varietate]: this is the queen of heaven united with the word of God and exalted above the choirs of all angels. Through this queen all our cognitive corporal powers will be fully fed just as our spiritual intelligence will be fully fed with the contemplation of Christ's divinity (337). This eschatological vision is essential to Brut's understanding of the sacrament of the altar. Brut quotes the accounts of Christ instituting the sacrament in Matthew (26.26–28) and Luke (22.19–20), observing that Christ gave us the sacrament in memory of the twofold feast, now and in eternity (337). The Eucharist is a present feast which commemorates the Last Supper and the future banquet of eternal beatitude. Only now, only in the carefully articulated context I have described, does Brut take up the issues around consecration and, in particular, the currently orthodox version of transubstantiation.[19]

To appreciate what Brut is doing, and the way he is doing what he does, one needs to recall that the late medieval Church had made the reception of the bread and wine, the body and blood, a *supplementary* adjunct to the Eucharist, whose essence was now defined as the act of consecration. While this is certainly implicit in the liturgical practices outlined above, the position had been explicated and defended. For example, in the *Summa Theologiae* Aquinas had argued that the Eucharist "is fully established when the matter is consecrated." In this it is quite unlike the other sacraments, since these demand the faithful's participatory use of them. He emphasized that "the use by the faithful of this sacrament is not required for validity, but is something that takes place afterwards" [usus autem fidelium non est de necessitate sacramenti, sed est aliquid consequens ad sacramentum]. And again, "in this sacrament use is not an essential part" [usus materiae consecratae qui non est de necessitate hujus sacramenti].[20] Not only was this theology embodied in contemporary liturgical practices, it also informed the processions of the consecrated host on Palm Sunday and Corpus Christi, the latter a procession around the town in a form which not only sanctified urban spaces but also sacralized current distributions of political power.[21] It is evident in Eucharistic miracles such as the one Margery Kempe reports in Lynn: "an hydows fyer and grevows" destroyed the Guild Hall and seemed about to burn down St. Margaret's, the parish church.[22] Her confessor asked her whether "it wer best to beryn the sacrament to the fyr er not," and Margery replied that this should be done. So the priest "toke the precyows sacrament and went beforn the fyer," returning to the church around which sparks were flying. This, combined with Margery's own prayers, brought a "myracle": God sent snow to quench the fire and preserve the church. As we observed in the previous chapter, the essential role of the priest in orthodox teaching was that he consecrated the Eucharist, and such practices are congruent with these accounts.[23] But Brut's approach to the sacrament sets such theory and practice aside. His emphasis on reception in faith, on communion with Christ, negates the habitual foregrounding of consecration as the *essence* of the sacrament with its corollary that the "use" of the sacrament by the faithful is a supplementary and quite separable aspect. He builds on this decision to revise the role of communion when he later argues that current doctrine misleads the people into eating the body of Christ only at Easter and on the verge of death, something for which he notes that he can find no precedents in the New Testament and early Church (339).

When he does address the issue of consecration directly, Brut affirms that Christ's words "hoc est corpus meum" and "hic est sanguis meus novi testamenti" were spoken over the bread and the cup of wine (337–38). How do these words relate to the current version of transubstantiation affirmed in the English Church and the controversies around it? Brut emphasizes that the bread is indeed Christ's body *in whatever mode* Christ determined [credo illud fuisse corpus eius illo modo quo illud voluit esse corpus eius quoniam cum sit omnipotens cuncta que voluit fecit] (338). He acknowledges that if the omnipotent Christ wanted to convert the bread into his body so that after the conversion no bread remained, as current orthodoxy insisted, then he certainly could do so. Brut does not hold a realist metaphysics in which such transubstantiation would demand that God enact a self-contradiction, like making a game of cricket be at the same time a game of basketball, or making a square be a triangular circle (338).[24] Nor does he hold to a dogmatic empiricism or materialism. His ground for rejecting the doctrine of transubstantiation as a necessary component of Catholic Christianity is that he cannot find any such insistence in the Gospels (338). There he simply sees no denial that the bread remains substantial bread after consecration. And if the revealed word of God does not insist on this teaching, then Brut thinks the modern Church has no authority to do so. He confesses that as God was able to assume human nature while remaining God, so Christ could have made the bread become his own body while the bread remained substantial bread (338).[25] Yet here too Brut finds nothing in the New Testament expressly maintaining that this possibility was actually willed by Christ. Like John Wyclif (see chapter 3 of this book), he maintains that Scripture expresses nothing about an identity [ydemptitatem] between sacramental sign and the things signified (338). Once more Brut uses the language and narratives of the New Testament as a disciplinary check on the theologians' imagination and intellect, an approach far removed from any form of fundamentalism or vulgar materialism.

What, then, does Scripture suggest? Brut observes that in saying "I am the true [verus] bread" (see John 6.34–35, 41, 48, 51–52), Christ continued to be the same person he had been before he uttered these words; he was speaking of himself figuratively [secundum similitudinem] (338). Similarly, Brut thinks, Christ could have intended his disciples to understand that the bread he gave them at the Last Supper while he said, "This is my body" (Matthew 26.26), actually remained the same bread it had been before he uttered these words but now also became sacramentally or memorially his body [sacramentaliter aut memoriter corpus eius] (338). We remember that such memory, for Brut, includes the Eucharist's eschatological dimensions, a memory that joins past, present, and ecstatic future. This is the interpretation of Christ's words that Brut finds most congruent with the command "Do this for a commemoration of me" (Luke 22.19). Meditating on the narratives of the Last Supper in the Gospels, Brut sees sacramental sign and signified event, symbol and symbolized, in an intimate union which never becomes an identity in which distinctions between sign and things signified are dissolved. Christ broke bread and gave it to his disciples to eat with their bodily mouths; so he gave them himself, the self-sacrificing, forgiving savior, as spiritual food to be received through faith (338–39). In this event Brut thinks that the physical bread was eaten carnally while the true bread of the soul was eaten in spirit through faith [et ipse verus panis anime ab eorum spiritu per fidem] (339). The bread which the disciples chewed passed into their stomachs and thence into the "privy," as Jesus himself noted in Matthew 15.17 (339). But the true bread of the soul, Christ himself, was eaten spiritually, entering the disciples' minds through faith and remaining in their innermost beings through love [per fidem ingressus est eorum mentem, et mansit in eorum interioribus per dileccionem] (339). This is Brut's model for contemporary communion and its theology; such is Christ's real presence in the sacrament he gives his disciples, past and present. Brut reiterates that the broken bread is really [realiter] food for the disciples' bodies, bread that is ordinary, untransformed bread. But through Christ's agency this bread has become sacramentally [sacramentaliter] the body of Christ (339). This, he maintains, is Paul's assumption in 1 Corinthians 10.16: "[T]he bread which we break, is it not partaking [participatio] of the body of the Lord?" Paul calls "the material bread" [materialem panem] which is broken the body of Christ in which the faithful share. So bread remains bread but is simultaneously the body of Christ sacramentally [non ergo mutat panis suam essenciam sed est panis realiter et corpus Christi sacramentaliter] (339).

Brut then aligns Christ's language at the Last Supper with earlier identifications of Christ in the gospel: "I am the vine; you the branches: he that abideth in me and I in him, the same beareth much fruit" (John 15.5); "Destroy this temple, and in three days I will raise it up. The Jews then said: Six and forty years was this temple a building; and wilt thou raise it up in three days? But he spoke of the temple of his body" (John 2.19–21). Throughout John's Gospel Christ's disciples and interrogators are continually misreading such figural language, and Brut is suggesting that his Church's teaching on the sacrament reproduces errors exposed and corrected in the Gospels. If this is how a sacramental sign works in the language of the Gospels, if this is the mode of figuration within which Christ chose to disclose his identity, if this is the language in which Christ ordered priests to consecrate the sacrament of the altar in his memory, and if he wishes to be sacramentally present rather than present in his Galilean body, then priests who ask him to convert the bread into the Galilean body err grievously. They substitute their own version of Christ's presence in the Church for the gift he has actually given. This gift is to be eaten *spiritually and really* [spiritualiter et realiter] by those who believe (340).

But whatever the mode of presence Christ himself has chosen, Brut is sure that contemporary Christians are seriously misled when they believe that in the Mass they are looking at the Galilean body of Christ elevated between the priest's hands. So pervasive is this view, he says, that it has generated the conventional oath, "through him whom I saw today in the hands of the priest" (339; see too 341). Brut's account of conventional attitudes matches that of the Catholic historian Eamon Duffy.[26] Not surprisingly, for the Church was committed to propagating the belief that the Galilean body of Christ was present in the priest's hands, "not only the flesh, but the whole body of Christ, that is, the bones and nerves and all the rest," as Aquinas maintained (*ST* III.76.1, ad 2). In propagating this belief, the Church generated a collection of Eucharist miracle stories to illustrate it, ones widely recited in Brut's England and considered in the first chapter of this book. These stories are replete with examples to demonstrate that any questioning of current teaching on the mode of Christ's presence is unbelief, heresy, or Judaism.[27] But for Brut, Christ's sacramental presence, real as it is, includes forms of absence, forms of lack, of waiting for a plenitude which is eschatological.[28] As Paul reminds the Corinthian Christians, the sacrament includes a memorialization of Christ's promise "until he come" (1 Corinthians 11.26). That is, the form of Christ's presence amongst those receiving the sacrament is simultaneously an acknowledgment that this feast also involves a lack, a prefiguration of a future plenitude. These forms of absence include the absence of Christ's Galilean body, resurrected and ascended as it is. With such recognition of absence in the present gifts of Christ goes a refusal of the extraordinary confidence with which orthodox formulations of transubstantiation were being deployed as markers determining whether a Christian was orthodox or heretical, a member of Christ's body or a rotten branch fit for burning.[29] As we have noted, very soon after Brut's trial, Dymmok argued that any interrogation of the doctrine of transubstantiation was a threat to the very existence of Christianity and of the polity with which he characteristically confused Christianity.[30]

Brut's reflections on the sacrament of the altar include a consideration of its orthodox representations as the sacrifice of Christ, immolated on the altar by the priest and presented to God for the sins of the world.[31] His approach is to juxtapose the New Testament with the practices and theology of the modern Church, concentrating on Hebrews 8–10 (342–43). What fascinates Brut is the canonical text's insistent contrast between "often" [saepe] and "once" [semel], between the high priest who had to sacrifice often for the people's sins, with the blood of oxen and goats, and Jesus who sacrificed once only, and with his own life, not another's. The epistle to the Hebrews emphasizes that the priest's daily sacrifices could never remove sins, whereas Christ's sacrifice, once offered, achieved forgiveness and sanctification of those reconciled to God. Now Christ intercedes for his people in the presence of God (343). Musing on priestly sacrifice, Brut observes that Christ says little to distinguish priests from others and apparently did not use the term "priest" to describe his followers, preferring to call them "disciples" and "apostles" (343). Where the New Testament does refer to priests (as in 1 Timothy 3 and 5 and Titus 1), it seems, according to Brut, that the distinction between priests and others lies in knowledge and good works, not in any consecrational or sacrificial functions (343–44). This contrasts with the Roman Church, where priests are ordained to sacrifice, pray, and bless, and where only priests are able to offer Christ's body day by day, at the altar, for the sins of the people. With this contemporary understanding of priesthood goes a very sharp and very hierarchical distinction between clergy and most Christians (344), one that was, as observed earlier, embodied in the Mass.

Brut expresses amazement at the relations between his Church and the views of the early Church (presented in Hebrews 9–10) on sacrifice. He wonders why contemporary priests claim to offer sacrifice for our sins every day (contrasting Hebrews 10.10–14). He observes that he can find no warrant in the New Testament for this understanding of the sacrament as a continually reenacted sacrifice of Christ. Instead he finds that the body of Christ is a sacrament and memorial of his unique sacrifice of himself for our sins. It is not fitting, he argues, that Christians should claim that Christ is now, once again, sacrificed on their altars, a claim which has priests crucifying Christ. In insisting that no Christian should believe this [quod non est a cristianis credendum], Brut goes against conventional iconography and the widespread miracle stories of the bleeding Christ who appeared in the consecrated host to confirm the Church's current doctrine on the sacrifice of Christ in the Mass.[32] So central was this sacrificial economy and its enactments to the late medieval Church that Brut's judges had no hesitation in classifying as heresy Brut's denial that Christ is once again sacrificed for the sins of the world in the sacrament of the altar (items 28–29, pp. 364 and 382).

Having made clear how he sees no support in the New Testament for his Church's teaching on Christ's immolation in the Eucharist, Brut retraces scriptural narratives of the Last Supper and the practices of the early Church in the breaking of bread (especially Acts 2.42, 46). Here too he reads nothing about disciples *sacrificing* the body of Christ. The disciples are remembering Christ's love and self-sacrifice for the remission of sins, remembering in such a way that they lovingly offer *themselves* to God, prepared to sustain death for their faith and the welfare of the Christian community (344). This indicates how Brut envisages sacramental memory as an active power in the present, individual and collective. The memory of Christ's sacrifice shapes and enables the believers' commitment to the faith and community, a faith that knows nothing of priestly immolation of Christ. Such discipleship, Brut remarks, fulfilled Christ's commands that his followers should love one another as he had loved them (John 15.12) (344).

With this Brut could have concluded his remarks on sacrifice. But he adds a brief speculation on the path by which the practice and doctrine of the early Church could have been transformed into the present situation. He suggests that the pressures of persecution gradually led to the transformation in question. At some stage of persecution priests began to flee from death in a variety of ways. This was a flight from the loving self-sacrifice practiced by early disciples. During this failure of charity, Christians reconstituted the sacrament of the altar. From an eschatological memorial of Christ's unique sacrifice, calling disciples to absolute self-sacrifice, they turned the sacrament into the supposedly actual sacrifice of Christ. The modern Church's sacrificial economy is thus represented as an ideological legitimization of what were the consequences of lack of faith and charity (344–45).[33]

Brut's analysis of sacrifice and the ecclesiastic history he imagines dovetails with Wyclif's insistence that were Christ to visit the contemporary Church as an unknown Christian to preach and practice as he had done, with the same tenacity, he would be persecuted and burned as a heretic.[34] Just as Caiaphas thought it "expedient" that Jesus should be sacrificed "for the people and that the whole nation perish not" (John 11.50), so the modern Church sacrifices Christ both on its altar and in its members. These sacrifices are bound together as the Church becomes a persecuting and a sacrificing community perpetuating the very violence its founder's self-sacrifice and forgiveness were designed to end forever.[35] This conclusion supports Brut's analysis of the way the sacrament of penance had become a forum of judgment and punishment quite alien to the models Christ gave his disciples.

His brief but resonant reflections on sacrifice and persecution are closely related to his earlier demonstration that Christ was committed to the path of nonviolence, essential to the kingdom of God he proclaimed, a path whose hallmark was the love and forgiveness of enemies (he quotes Matthew 5.21–22, 38–48; see 308–21). There he had turned his irony on the modern Church which approved and even organized contemporary wars, inventing fables and justifications to set aside Christ's own unequivocal commands to those who would be his disciples (309–10, 313–17).[36] The abandonment of these commands is bound up with the cultivation of a sacrificial economy legitimizing war. So the sacrament, its theology and liturgical forms, is inextricably bound up with ecclesiology, politics, and conflicts between very different models of authority. This was well appreciated by both orthodox apologists and Wycliffites, and the links between these domains and practices remain as decisive in the contemporary world as in the fourteenth century.[37]

Brut's attempts to reform sacramental practices include the question as to whether women can confect and administer the body of Christ (341, 345–47).[38] Given the way in which the sacrament of the altar, *Corpus Christi*, had become a central symbol in late medieval culture, one intrinsic to the formation of identities, any radical challenge to its current forms would have implications for a diversity of practices.[39] Brut acknowledges that his theology of the sacrament and his related understanding of priesthood have consequences that go against the deeply rooted misogyny of his culture and Church.[40] His affirmative answers to the questions about women's power and authority in the ministry of the sacrament flow from a number of his positions: his rejection of transubstantiation; his rejection of the view that priests immolate Christ on the altar; his high valuation of preaching (which he says women have certainly done, converting many when priests did not dare speak the word);[41] his analysis of the fact that the Church allows women to administer the sacrament of baptism (in emergencies), the sacrament that is the gateway to all the other sacraments and, according to the Church's teaching, the only one necessary to salvation (345–46). Brut characteristically emphasizes the tendency of the Roman Church to exaggerate its own authority in relation to the revealed word of God and to God's sovereignty. Given that lay people can licitly enact the sacrament of marriage without a priest (346), given that God's power can work through women in baptism, and given that God's power works through even the most sinful priest consecrating the bread (as the Church taught), Brut feels unable to say that

Christ cannot or will not consecrate through holy women. To maintain such a position one would have to say that Christ could not consecrate unless he did so in conformity to the current ordinances of the Roman pope. Restrictions of this kind on Christ's powers seem unthinkable to Brut. So he sees no grounds for denying that Christ could be willing to consecrate in response to the prayers of holy women speaking the sacramental words (346–47). Discipleship of Christ, once more, is shown to have potentials unacknowledged by the Church. Its hierarchy is too hasty in its willingness to sacrifice others for its own conformity with the world. Brut's discussion of women's authority to administer the sacrament follows the logic of his theology and ecclesiology. In doing so it crosses immense cultural barriers.

Yet Brut is not particularly concerned with women's discipleship and current restrictions on its practice. Time and again he limits the force of his arguments about women's ability to perform priestly offices, asserting that women should do so only when those ordained "in the church" are absent (345–47). He does this although the only warrant for such a restriction in his own testimony seems to be that the Roman Church restricts the administration of the sacrament of baptism by lay people to emergencies, when no priest is available. Why this should have a binding force for Brut is not clear, for he continually undermines the authority of determinations made by the Roman Church which seem to have no compelling sources in the New Testament. So why back off here? Because, it seems to me, he wished to draw back from the version of the priesthood of all believers which was to be articulated by later Wycliffites such as Hawisia Mone, one that finally dissolved boundaries between male and female and between priest and lay person in Christian discipleship: "Every man and every woman beyng in good lyf oute of synne is as good prest and hath as muche poar of God in al thynges as ony prest ordred be he pope or bisshop."[42] Brut's refusal to pursue this line suggests that his position on priesthood is very close to Wyclif's.[43] But it must be acknowledged that while the confession we have tells us a great deal about what Brut took to be the betrayal of Christ's gospel by the modern Roman Church, it does not construct a coherent ecclesiology. One might think that this absence was purely contingent on the genre and the work's relative brevity. In my view, however, the absence represents unresolved and corrosive problems in Wyclif's own theology, an absence that Wycliffism may not have had the resources to address coherently. But that is another story.[44] It is, however, a closely related one, and I will return to it when concluding the following reflections on Thorpe's *Testimony*.

II

While the remarkable lay theologian Walter Brut was formulating his views for the bishop of Hereford, William Thorpe seems to have been a traveling priest teaching a Wycliffite inflection of Christian traditions.[45] His *Testimony* is an account of his interrogation by Archbishop Arundel, patron of Love's *Mirror,* conversation partner with Margery Kempe, and a committed persecutor of Wycliffites, one who oversaw the introduction of death by burning to England.[46] There are complicated problems about the "historicity" of Thorpe's text and its genre which have been lucidly set down by Anne Hudson in her edition of the *Testimony* (xlv–lix). But what remains indubitable is that the *Testimony* is an early-fifteenth-century Wycliffite text probably written when it claims to have been composed (1407; see 29 and Hudson's observations, lii and 106). Here I intend to consider the most fully discussed question in the work, the sacrament of the altar (42–56).

But before addressing this question we should note the context in which it has been set. The *Testimony* begins by describing the modern Church as a persecuting Church whose "tirauntrie" resists "þe fredom of Cristis gospel, for which fredom Crist bicam man and schedde oute his hert blood" (24, 25; see 24–29). The "freedom of Cristis gospel" is, for Thorpe, closely related to the liberty from slavery that Christ died to achieve: "siþ Crist Iesu diede vpon þe cros willfully to make man fre, men in þe chirche now ben to bolde and to bisie to make men þralle" (84). In his prologue Thorpe also evokes a community which, though scattered and vulnerable to persecution, consists of "men and wymmen" seeking to cultivate the knowledge and practice of Christian discipleship based on their encounter with "Cristis gospel." This community might hope to learn from the persecution Thorpe now witnesses, a community he writes to strengthen and whose expansion he hopes to facilitate (25–28). Those who oppose and persecute this community are described as "antecristis lymes," currently led by "prelatis of þis londe and her mynystris, wiþ þe comente of prestis" (24). Like Brut, Thorpe sees a Church committed to practices of violent coercion and killing as a tyranny antithetical to "Cristis gospel."

Although Thorpe does not offer anything like Brut's far-ranging, profound reflections on violence and sacrifice in the Church, he does argue that the modern Church has substituted a persecutory understanding of "sacrifice" for one modeled on Christ's life and therefore pleasing to God (27–28). It is logical enough that he first mentions the sacrament of the altar after this, within his affirmation of the creed and a life of Christ (30–32). Eucharist theology is inseparable from ecclesiology, whether this inseparability is made a topic of critical reflection or not:

> And aftir þis, whanne Crist wolde make an eende here of his temporal lyf, I bileue þat in þe dai next before þat he wolde suffre wilfulli passioun on þe morn, in foorme of breed and of wyne he ordeynede his fleisch and his blood þat is his owne moost precious bodi, and ʒaf it to hise apostlis forto eten, comaundinge hem and bi hem alle her aftir-comers þat þei schulden, in þis foorme þat he schewid to hem, vsen hemsilf and techen and comowne forþ to oþir men and wymmen þis moost worschipful and holiest sacrament, into myndefulnesse of his moost holiest lyuynge and moost trewe techyng, and of his wilful and pacient suffrynge of þe moost peyneful passioun.
>
> And I bileue þat þis Crist oure sauyour, aftir þat he had þus ordained þis moost holi and worþi sacrament of his owne most precious bodi, he went forþ wilful aʒens his enemyes; and he suffride hem moost pacientli for to leyen her hondis moost violentli vpon him. (31)

I have quoted at length here because this is a particularly resonant and illuminating passage. Thorpe's reverence of the sacrament is unequivocal. He also affirms the presence of Christ's "precious" body "in foorme of breed and of wyne." These are among the favored terms of current orthodoxy, as we may recall from the discussion of Nicholas Love's *Mirror* in chapter 1: "þe sacrament of þe autere dewly made by vertue of cristes wordes is verrey blode in forme of wyne" (*Mirror*, 153). Certainly these are terms we find Arundel himself using (53) in a sequence discussed later.[47] But in the light of the materials studied so far in this book two aspects of this passage come into a sharper focus than they might in other contexts.

First, one sees how Thorpe sets the orthodox terms in a narrative which stays close to the relevant New Testament narratives (1 Corinthians 11.23–26; Mark 14.22–25; Matthew 26.26–29; Luke 22.17–19). The narrative (unlike Nicholas Love's treatment of the Last Supper) does not pause to abstract the consecration and the consecrated elements for analysis, whether in the discourse of metaphysics or physics. To narrate or not to narrate is a decision fraught with theological and ecclesiological consequences, especially in this historical moment. Thorpe's decision is a decision against the orthodox prolongation of Eucharistic analysis that we have seen in Love and other examples of late medieval orthodoxy. We shall return to this issue below.

A second aspect of this passage that should now come into clear focus is its ecclesiological implications. Following scriptural narratives in the way he does, Thorpe has shown the institution of the Eucharist to be the decisive confirmation of Christ's choice of nonviolence. Christ chooses self-sacrifice and the embrace of terrible suffering rather than self-defense and "just" war (cf. Matthew 26.53: "Thinkest thou that I cannot ask my father, and he will give me presently more than twelve legions of angels?"). Thorpe emphasizes that Christ gave this "holiest sacrament" to create "myndefulnesse of his moost holiest lyuynge and moost trewe techyng, and of his wilful and pacient suffrynge." The narrative discloses a form of life to which all "men and wymmen" are called in the sacrament, one in which Christ "went forþ wilful aȝens his enemyes." This phrase involves an extraordinary dislocation of what it habitually conveys. For here the "wilful" going "aȝens his enemyes" is an enactment not of heroic violence but of nonviolent love of enemies (see Matthew 5.38–44 and Luke 6.27–29, together with the discussion of Brut's theology of nonviolence above). Having given himself into the hands of his disciples who will soon betray him, he gives himself to those who come against him "violentli," as "his enemyes." The narrative and the language in which Thorpe tells this story make an extremely powerful comment on the issue from which the *Testimony* set out: a persecuting Church that claims that its persecutory practice is enacted in obedience to Christ. So the potentially critical relations between the sacrament of the altar and the Church in which it is performed emerge with great clarity and force at the beginning of the *Testimony*.

From here Thorpe turns directly to his understanding of the Church which those who recite the creed (as Wycliffites unreservedly did) are committed to believing.[48] This move brings out the most decisive difference between Thorpe and his archbishop, one that shapes their disputation. Thorpe articulates his understanding of the relevant article of the creed:

> I bileue holi chirche: þat is, I bileue þat þere haþ ben, and þat þer ȝit now is, and alwei to þe worldes eende schal be, a peple whiche schulen bisie hem for to knowe and to kepe þe heestis of God, dredinge ouer al þing to offende God, and louynge and sechynge moost to plesen him. And I bileue þat alle þei þat had, and ȝit haue, and alle þei þat ben to haue þese foreside vertues, stabli stondynge in þe bileue of God, hopinge stidefastli in his merciful doyngis, perseuerynge into her eende in perfit charite, wilfulli, pacientli and

gladly suffringe persecuciouns bi ensaumple of Crist chefli and of his apostlis, alle þese haue her names writen in þe book of liif. (32)

The Church which Christians believe is thus composed of those who have been given persevering grace, eternally predestined. Thorpe emphasizes that "þis peple, lyuynge now here in þis liif, is þe holi chirch of God" (32). This, and this alone is the creed's Church to which Thorpe wills his assent: "I submitte me to þis holi chirche of Crist, to be euer buxom and obedient to þe ordinaunce and þe gouernaunce of it and of euery membre þerof" (33). How does one recognize the faithful gathering which constitutes this Church of Christ to which one owes obedience? Already Thorpe has made very clear that the persecuting Church led in England by his interrogator, Archbishop Arundel, cannot be recognized as such. The only grounds for recognition Thorpe allows is through the form of life practiced by those who claim to belong to the Church, a form manifesting the virtues he has outlined. He states that he will submit "oonli" to those he himself knows to be practicing "þe forseide virtues" (33). Not surprisingly, Archbishop Arundel returns to Thorpe's ecclesiology, telling him to spell out its implications (51). Thorpe obliges. The Church on earth is the "pilgrymes of Crist wandrynge towardis heuene" in a life "sadli groundid vpon þe corner- stoon Crist, heerynge his word and louynge it, bisiinge hem feiþfulli and contynuelli in alle her wittis to do þeraftir" (51–52). Such an understanding of the creedal Church plainly had decisive consequences for the understand- ing of the actually existing Roman Church and the obedience one owed it.[49] Before he unfolds the *Testimony*'s main treatment of the sacrament of the altar, Thorpe dramatizes how this understanding works.

Archbishop Arundel tells him to "forsake alle þe opynynouns whiche þe sect of Lollers holdiþ," to work against "alle suche distroublers of holi chirche," and to stop preaching until Arundel is convinced of his conver- sion (34–35). Addressed by the leader of the Church in England, called to obedience in the Church against its "distroublers," Thorpe moves inwards in a manner that determines and reflects the practice he has been pursuing: "And I heerynge þese wordis þouȝte in myn herte þat þis was an vnleeful askynge, and I demed mysilf cursid of God if I consentid herto" (35). Thorpe appropriates the judicial power of the Roman Church and makes judgments and determinations accordingly. He sees himself as Susannah trapped by the elders who wish to rape her (Daniel 13.1–23) (35). Forbid- den the retreat of silence, he is commanded to answer the archbishop (35). His response articulates his loyalty to those the Church leadership defined as "distroublers of holi chirche" (34), insisting that were he to obey this Church he would be "traitour to God" and subverter of his own evangelical mission in the communities his *Testimony* addresses (35–36). The next stage in this dramatic disputation is predictable enough, after 1401: Arundel warns Thorpe that either he will submit to the Church the archbishop represents or "þou schalt be schauen and sue þi felow into Smeþefelde!" (36; see too 81). This, of course, brings us back to the place from which Thorpe set out: the transformation of what claims to be the body of Christ into a persecuting, burning Church. Once more Thorpe depicts a turn inward ("in myn herte") during which he reflects on the killing of William Sawtry and the archbishop's role in this.[50] The outcome of his interior activity is another remarkable appropriation of the Church's traditional jurisdiction: "I was moued in alle my wittis for to holde þe Archebishop neiþer prelat ne preest of God" (36). The defrocker is defrocked, the degrader is degraded, the deposer deposed[51]—but only in Thorpe's "inner man," not yet in Saltwood Castle, where the Church's earthly presence and power are tangible. Here Thorpe is ordered, once more, to declare whether he will obey or disobey the prelate he has just deposed in his "herte," his "inner man." Thorpe's reply is a fascinating story of his path to the sacrament of orders and a Christianity inflected by Wyclif's teaching and Wycliffite groups (37–42). Arundel's response to this genealogical narrative is untroubled. Thorpe's "maistir and auctour" was indeed "a greet clerk" whom many considered a holy man, "ȝit his doctryne is not apreued of holi chirche but many sentencis of his lore ben dampned" (42). For Arundel there is no division between the Church of the creed and the Church in which he is archbishop, the Church in which Thorpe received the sacrament of orders making him a priest. By this stage Thorpe must have hoped that his text would have discredited the orthodox identification between the Church of the creed and the Church of the persecuting archbishop.

In this context, into this carefully organized sequence of arguments and narratives, Thorpe introduces the sacrament of the altar (42–56). He does so by having Arundel now read from a letter written by the Crown's officers in Shrewsbury recounting "þe errours and þe eresies" he has been proclaiming in the town from the third Sunday after Easter in 1407 (42–43).[52] The archbishop observes that Thorpe "so troubled þe worchipful comounte of Schrouesbirie" that they now seek the enactment of the death penalty on him, "openli þere among hem" (43). These citizens of Shrewsbury rightly approach Arundel as one who joins ecclesiastic and lay power: "me þat am Archebischop of Cauntirbirie, primate of al Yngelonde and chaunceler"

(43). The first charge in the letter from Shrewsbury concerns the sacrament of the altar (43). The question about the Eucharist takes up 421 lines in Hudson's edition (43–56), but it is only after almost 300 lines that the *Testimony* focuses on the doctrinal charge that Thorpe preached, in St. Chad's church, "þat þe sacrament of þe auter aftir þe consecracioun was material breed" (43, 52–56). Digressive as Thorpe's mode may seem, the intervening lines are thoroughly relevant to this sacramental sign, since they concern the constitution of "holi chirche" (44, 51–52), the bonds of peace in a Christian community (44–45), the office of priesthood, and the sources of authority in the Church (45–52). We should recall the traditional teaching that in this sacrament Christians are "joined with Christ and incorporated in his members," his mystical body (*ST* III.80.4, resp; III.73.3, ad 2). As it is the sacrament of unity, so it is the sacrament of faith and love: in the words of Augustine quoted by Thomas Aquinas, "O sacrament of piety, O sign of unity, O bond of charity" (*ST* III.79.1, resp; see too III.79.7, ad 2). It is in this perspective that one should set both Thorpe's account of his arguments with Arundel and his account of his relations with the Church in that "worschipful comounte of Schrouesbirie" (43).

I noted above that the letter from Shrewsbury calls for Thorpe to receive the death penalty in the community he has allegedly "troubled." Thereby, so the "worschipful men" write, divisions for which he is held responsible will be healed and those "peruerted" by his teaching will be "reconseilid aȝen to þe vnyte of holi chirche," while those who resisted him will be "moore stablischid" in the "trewe feiþ of holi chirche" (43). Thorpe seems to be envisaged in the role of scapegoat, a figure of the history of sacrifice sketched out by Walter Brut and eloquently and substantially described by René Girard.[53] "O sacrament of piety, O sign of unity, O bond of charity" (*ST* III.79.1, resp). How then does Thorpe relate the events in Shrewsbury to his understanding of the sacrament and Christian community?

He does not deny the charge "þat I haue troubled þe comounte of Schrouesbirie" (44–45). But he does not see himself as breaking the bonds of peace, unity, and charity in the Church, the body of Christ. He argues that those persecutors who take themselves to belong to the mystical body are in this matter utterly deluded. Thorpe believes he can discern this from their works. In his view such people are actually "troublid" by those trying to "lyue iustly after þe heestis of God"; out of their own self-division they persecute Wycliffite Christians like Thorpe as divisive troublemakers (44–45). The model that Thorpe cites to justify his actions is a very different version of Jesus from the one composed by Nicholas Love, one warranted by Arundel himself:[54] "And where, ser, ȝe seie þat I haue troublid þe comounte of Schrouesbirie, and manye oþer men and wymmen, wiþ my techynge, þis doynge if it þus be is not to be wondrid of wiise men, siþen alle þe comountee of þe citee of Ierusalem was troublid wiþ þe techynge of Cristis owne persone, þat was veri God and man and þe moost prudente prechour þat euere was or schal be" (44–45). So the "comounte of Schrouesbirie" and the "comountee of þe citee of Ierusalem" have produced a unity and a peace which is opposed to the divine presence. This unity and peace, fusing ecclesiastic and lay powers, defends itself with violence against the divine presence whose teaching and form of life has "troublid" them. Thorpe recalls that the reactions of the community of Jerusalem had been prefigured in Nazareth where the citizens sought to kill Jesus after his prophetic and eschatological challenge (45; Luke 4.16–30), an episode Nicholas Love transforms and domesticates in his *Mirror* to ward off just such readings and applications as Thorpe's.[55] In these contexts any sacrament of unity will create a false unity which God will trouble through his prophets: "Also acoordingli herto þe Lord witnessiþ bi Moysees þat he schal putte deuysioun bitwixe his peple and þe peple þat contrarieþ and pursueþ his peple" (45). So the visible Church in England makes an "Egyptian" unity opposed to God's will (Exodus 8.23) and Christian liberty (25). Thorpe then discusses the priestly office. As observed earlier, traditional understanding of the office saw its principal function as the consecration of the host.[56] Thorpe maintains, however, at length, that the end of priesthood is proclaiming the word of God (45–50). Indeed, he describes the priesthood as "þe office of prechinge" (50).[57] The difference between this Wycliffite view and late medieval tradition is nicely exemplified in the incident in St. Chad's referred to earlier in this chapter. The people who ran from Thorpe's sermon to the altar from where they heard the "sacringe belle," sign of the presence of Christ's body, had an understanding of the relations between preaching and Eucharist that was different from his, but they also had a very different understanding of the sacrament itself. Their actions embodied a habitual readiness to abstract the consecration of the elements from the Mass (which these people had not attended) and from reception, an abstraction discussed in chapter 1. Just as Brut had done, though in different ways, Thorpe opposes these conventions.

Arundel tries to keep Thorpe within their terms by asking him for his views on the issue he denied preaching about in Shrewsbury, the nature of the consecrated elements, whether "þe sacrament of þe auter was material breed after þe consecracioun" (52; see too 43). When he seeks to reject this language as alien to "holi writt," much as Brut did, Arundel asks him what he does believe (53). Thorpe's response, one we have noticed before, is a shift to narrative, once again the narratives of the Last Supper in liturgy and New Testament (53). Reiterating these, he concludes that belief in what the sacrament is should be left with these narratives and their terms, "Takiþ þis and etiþ of þis alle; þis is my bodi." These terms affirm, according to Thorpe, "þat þe worschipful sacrament of þe auter is verri Cristis fleisch and his blood in forme of breed and wyne" (53). Although Thorpe does not ac-. knowledge this fact, his own language here adds a brief gloss on the sacred narratives and does so in the thoroughly conventional terms used by Nicholas Love (*Mirror*, 153). The archbishop acknowledges this and agrees with Thorpe's formulation: "It is soþ þat þis sacrament is Cristis bodi in fourme of breed"(53). However, he immediately adds another gloss to deny that Christ's body is present in the "substaunce of breed" and asks for Thorpe's view on this (53). In doing so he illustrates the orthodox fixation on the consecrated elements in abstraction from the full process of the Mass, including its reception. Thorpe tries to answer the question on his own terrain by glossing the term "fourme," on which he and Arundel have agreed, with Paul's use of the word in Philippians 2.5–6. There Christ is said to be in form of God [in forma Dei], meaning, Thorpe says, "þe subtaunce or þe kynde of God" (53). Arundel blocks this path: "Woldist þou make me to declare þese tixtis to þi purpos? Siþ þe chirche haþ now determyned þat þere dwelliþ no substaunce of breed aftir þe consecracioun of þe sacrament of þe auter, bileuest þou not to þis ordinaunce of holi chirche?" (54). This orthodox insistence that the substances of bread and wine do not remain after the consecration brings the plenitudinous presence of Christ's Galilean body to the altar was illustrated in chapter 1. Here the exchange makes especially clear the way it encourages the abandonment of the sacred narratives which Thorpe sought to recall in the face of Arundel's remorseless returns to the familiar obsession with the precise fate of the elements at consecration. For the relevant narratives are marked by a theological reticence around the institution of the Lord's Supper [Dominicam coenam] (1 Corinthians 11.20), a reticence which may be an incitement to metaphysical prolongation but is also a severe stumbling block to such elaboration.

Blocked in his attempt to reflect on the implications of language he shares with the archbishop, Thorpe moves to the reception of the sacrament. He invokes Paul's first letter to the Corinthians (10.16–17) and the canon of the Mass ("þat þing þat we haue taken wiþ oure mouþ, take we wiþ clene and pure mynde"). To this he adds a statement ascribed to Augustine in canon law: "þat þing þat is seen is breed, but þat þing þat mannes feiþ axiþ or desireþ to be enformed of is verri Cristis bodi" (54). This thoroughly Augustinian emphasis is designed to lead sacramental discourse away from fixation on the abstracted elements and towards meditation on "communion of the blood of Christ" [communicatio sanguinis Christi], on "partaking of the body of the Lord" [participatio corporis Domini], on the faithful and transforming reception of the sacrament in a specifiable community: "For we, being many, are one bread, one body, all that partake of one bread" [Quoniam unus panis, unum corpus multi sumus, omnes qui de uno pane participamus] (1 Corinthians 10.16–17).[58] Thorpe wishes to think about the sacramental sign as earthly substance which nourishes and spiritual substance, which, received in faith, gives divine life to human beings (54–55; see similarly *ST* III.79.1, resp). But the archbishop sets aside Thorpe's resistance to prolonging discourse about the consecrated elements in abstraction from reception, ritual, and community. He asserts that the devil blinds Thorpe from understanding "þe ordenaunce of holi chirche" and from obeying it (55). Once more he orders the priest to answer his prelate's question: "Bileuest þou aftir þe sacringe of þis forseid sacrament þere dwelliþ substaunce of breed or nay?" (55) So Thorpe must accept the abstraction of consecration and the elements from the narratives, liturgy, and rituals to which they belong. Here he becomes rather derisively mocking. He remarks that the issue is whether "þis moost worþi sacrament of Cristis owne bodi is an accident wiþouten soget," showing the familiarity with academic idiom one would expect from a man who had moved in the Oxford circles he had earlier outlined (55; see 39–41).[59] Then he claims that he is unable to grasp such "scole-mater" even as he contemptuously gives the Latin terms for the issue, commending them dismissively to "þo clerkis which deliten hem so in curious and so sotil sofestrie" in the "*pro* and *contra*" of university disputations (55). Thorpe is emphasizing the incommensurability between the modes of "holi writt" and the modes of contemporary "scole-mater" in approaching the sacrament of the altar. He is also, crucially, resisting the orthodox prolongation of discourse around the consecration. But such reluctance is simply unacceptable to the leader of the contemporary English Church: "I purpose not to oblische þe to þe sotil argumentis of clerkis, siþ þou art vnable herto, but I purpose to make þee to obeie þe to þe determynacioun of holi chirche" (55). But the Church's determination in this domain had become inseparable from the language and arguments of its "clerkis," just as his own performance was disclosing. Indeed, in chapter 1 we saw how Nicholas Love himself ran into serious difficulties when conveying the Church's determinations on transubstantiation to the laity and how he sought to blame the difficulties generated by orthodox Eucharistic discourse onto Wycliffites — that is, onto those who did not wish to propagate such discourse.

Thorpe's final response to this pressure on his Eucharistic beliefs is another turn to narrative. He now inserts "þe determynacioun of holi chirche" in a history of the Church. This participates in the contemporary battle over what is actually "traditional," over what is to count as "traditional."[60] Thorpe offers a characteristic Wycliffite history of the modern Church's definition of "þe moost worschipful sacrament of Cristis bodi an accident wiþouten soget" (55–56). In this history the modern Church is represented as imposing a drastic break with the tradition constituted in the early Church and faithfully followed for "a þousand ʒeer after þe incarnacioun of Crist." It is this tradition Thorpe claims to follow in his understanding of the Eucharist, an understanding accepted "of al holi chirche as sufficient of saluacioun" during those thousand years. The rupture with this tradition, Thorpe maintains, was the work of Thomas Aquinas, led by the recently emancipated fiend mobilizing his forces around the novel claim that the sacrament of Christ's body is "an accident wiþouten soget," a terminology alien to "Goddis lawe" and therefore resisted by Thorpe (55–56).[61] It should be noticed that Thorpe is far from consistent in his terminological demands, for he has no hesitation in using language about the Trinity developed in the Church's traditions but absent from Scripture (30; cf. 53, lines 951–53). But it is appropriate, indeed inevitable, that the question on the Eucharist concludes with ecclesiology, authority, and tradition.

We observe that nothing in Thorpe's disputation with Arundel qualifies his affirmation that Christ's body and blood are present in this sacramental sign. "I beleue and teche oþer to beleue, þat þe worschipful sacrament of þe auter is verri Cristis fleisch and his blood in forme of breed and wyne" (53). We saw that this statement was accepted by Arundel. His objections focused on what the statement did not say, namely its reticence over the metaphysical and physical state of the bread and wine after consecration.[62] But Thorpe's *Testimony* shows that reticence in this domain is perfectly compatible with faith in the real presence of Christ's body and blood in the Church's sacrament of the altar. What Thorpe affirms is clear enough, as is his reverence for the sacrament which he acknowledges "verri Cristis fleisch and his blood" (53). What he does not wish to say is also clear. Yet it seems to me that despite this clarity there are problems in Thorpe's theology which have escaped his attention. With these I shall conclude the chapter.

If the modern Church is as errant as Thorpe maintains, if it has made a demonic break with the norms of the early Church founded by Christ, as Thorpe claims, if it is devoid of authority and hopelessly misled by "frere Tomas Alquyne" in its performance and doctrine of the Eucharist, why is Thorpe so confident that its enactment of this sacrament remains "þe worschipful sacrament" in which Christ makes himself present? His answer to this unasked question would have to take some form of the Church's conventional arguments against Donatistic attacks: the aberrant, sinful minister who consecrates the sacrament is only the vehicle of a divine grace unaffected by the instrument's culpability (see *ST* III.64.1–5, 64.8–9). But two consequences follow from this necessary response, neither of which is compatible with Thorpe's treatment of the Roman Church in his *Testimony*. First, the visible Church is then acknowledged to be the Church founded by Christ and currently graced with the divine presence in the sacramental sign he instituted. Here, Thorpe, recognizes, the faithful receive "verri Cristis fleisch and his blood in forme of breed and wyne" (53). No fallible ministers or doctrinal elaborations apparently unwarranted by scriptural narratives and language can resist the grace that God pours into his Church. Second, if this is so, Thorpe has no good reason to theorize "þe worschipful sacrament" independently of the forms of contemporary authority evolved in such a divinely founded and graced Church, one in which he himself was baptized, educated, and received the sacrament of orders ("myn office of presthode" [86]) and in which, by his own testimony, he receives "verri Cristis fleisch and his blood." After all, his very identity as a Christian, his very ability to participate in Christian discourse and practice, derives from this Church, one in which he is a subject, a member. It was here, in this Church, that Scripture was received, understood, and handed on as sacred text.[63]

We should now remember Thorpe's account of the creedal Church discussed earlier in this chapter. Thorpe describes the creedal Church, we recall, as composed of those who have been given the grace of final perseverance— that is, the predestinate (32–33). This was Wyclif's view.[64] To this community alone does Thorpe give belief and obedience, and he does so unreservedly (33). Consequently he rejects the archbishop's standard claims that this priest owes belief and obedience to the Roman Church. We followed his confident appropriation of the authority to depose the archbishop (34–36). Presumably he thinks that his obedient membership of the creedal Church gives him authority to grasp that the archbishop is now "neiþir prelat ne preest of God" (36). But there is something hollow about Thorpe's promise to believe and obey the creedal Church, a claim he reiterates towards the end of the *Testimony:* "Ser, as I haue seide to ȝou dyuerse tymes todaie, I wole wilfuli and lowely obeye and submitte me to be obedient and buxsum euer aftir my kunnyng and my power to God and to his lawe, and to euery member of holy chirche as ferforþ as I can perseyue þat þese membris acorden wiþ her heed Crist, and wolen teche, reule me or chastise me bi autorite specially of Goddis lawe" (92). The vacuity of this confession is that it actually entails no belief or obedience to any embodied Church. Thorpe's own perceptions will determine who is and who is not the Church, who are members of Christ and who are not. He himself will determine who is related to Christ and God's law in a way that compels his belief and obedience. That is, he maintains authority over the community to which he imagines himself conceding authority to "reule" or "chastise" him. In effect he banishes that embodied, earthly mediation of divine grace, that actually existing Church, appropriating for himself the kind of immediacy in relation to "Goddis lawe" against which Augustine argued so carefully in the preface to *De Doctrina Christiana*. There Augustine reminded readers of their dependence on human mediations in the gifts of Christ and knowledge about these gifts. Against his own dissolution of the Church's mediations Thorpe could have placed Augustine's reminder:

> Let us not tempt the one in whom we have placed our trust or we may be deceived by the adversary's cunning and perversity and become unwilling even to go to church to hear and learn the gospel or to read the biblical text or listen to it being read and preached, preferring to work until 'we are caught up into the third heaven, whether in the body or out of the body' (in the words of the apostle [2 Corinthians 12.2–4]), and there hear 'words that cannot be expressed, which human being may not utter' or see the Lord Jesus Christ in person and hear the gospel from him rather than from men.[65]

Augustine goes on to reflect that even Paul, enlightened by a divine voice, "was sent to a human being to receive the sacrament of baptism and be joined to the church" (Acts 9.3–8).[66] For Augustine the necessity for human institutions of learning, for human mediations in the actually existing Church, is a divinely given one through which love can "make souls overflow and as it were intermingle with each other." All truth does indeed come "from the one who says, 'I am the truth'" (John 14.6), but we receive that truth mediately, through the actually existing Church.[67]

Thorpe's claim that he would believe and obey those whom his own authoritative perception determines to be credible and authoritative may seem to be a concession to Augustine's emphasis on our divinely given commitment to human mediations and hermeneutic limits. But this is not the case. First, as noted above, he himself retains full authority to determine who and what is to count as authoritative. Second, the Christians to whom he claims he would defer are those predestined to beatitude, those with the gift of persevering grace (32). But as Wycliffites and orthodox medieval Catholics all agreed, nobody can know who has the gift of persevering grace, who belongs to the predestined community of the saved. Not even the predestined subject can know. Thorpe's confidence that his own isolated perception of someone's works sufficiently declares their predestined state (32–33) is one of the less coherent moves he learnt from Wyclif. It is one thing for Jesus to say, "[T]hough you will not believe me, believe the works" (John 10.38), quite another to determine someone's final life from current acts. It fails to acknowledge the temporality of human lives and works, the obscure, unpredictable temporalities of grace. The betrayer who denies Christ is also the rock on which Christ chooses to build his Church, the one to whom he gives the keys of the kingdom is also and simultaneously an obstacle in his path, thinking not as God but as human and called "Satan" at that time (Matthew 26.69–75 and 16.13–23).

In bestowing on his own contingent perceptions the authority to determine the final relation of Christian subjects to "her heed Crist," Thorpe also fails to take into account Christian commonplaces about the inescapable sinfulness of the *viator*. In the B version of *Piers Plowman* Will expresses this bluntly: "For soþest word þat euer God seide was þo he seide *Nemo bonus*."[68] It pervades the later work of Augustine: "[N]o one, no matter how just he may be, lives in this corruptible body without some kind of sin."[69] Such sinfulness obviously involves the perceiver as much as the perceived, and the only cogent position for those belonging to such a tradition (as Thorpe did) is the one Langland's Anima figures forth in teaching Will about charity.[70] The virtue of charity, which joins humans to God (*ST* II–II.23, II–II.24.2), cannot be perceived by human scrutiny of "werkes and wordes" alone, since its source is the "wille." It can be known "þoruȝ wil oone." From humans this is hidden, but not from God: "*Et vidit deus cogitaciones eorum* [And God saw their thoughts]."[71] Thorpe apparently did not see the relevance of such commonplaces from his own tradition to his thinking about discernment and the Church.

The cluster of unaddressed problems in the *Testimony* cast Thorpe's ecclesiology into some confusion and seem to undermine his sacramental teaching. One is left with his unequivocal acceptance of the Church's teaching about the real presence of the body of Christ in the sacrament and the efficacy of this sacrament in a Church, which, far from being the creedal Church, is a Church for "renegatis"—that is, for apostates (90). But if Christ gives his presence in this sacrament of the Church, the participants in this event seem, in Aquinas's Pauline words, "joined with Christ and incorporated in his members," incorporated in his mystical body through his actions in this particular Church (*ST* III.80.4, resp). This is the end of the sacrament (one recalls Thorpe's invocation of 1 Corinthians 10.16–17). From this communion (proclaimed by Thorpe) it follows, once again, that despite its sinful violence this Church remains a divine gift. It remains a sanctifying sign mediating Christ's presence and calling people to *become* a community embodying the "bond of charity" and, consequently, to *discover* forms of reconciliation that go against the grain of its members' dispositions and against the grain of cultural norms in medieval or any other historical society (*ST* III.79.1, resp).[72] Where does Thorpe speak from if not from within this Church and its various traditions? These traditions include the very resources for the criticisms of the lust for dominion and the zealous participation in human violence made so lucidly by Brut and, albeit in a less concentrated manner, effectively enough in the *Testimony*. Perhaps the shaping problem in Thorpe's ecclesiology is the one touched on above when I discussed Thorpe's confidence that he could judge who was joined to Christ eternally by his perception of their current works. There I showed how strikingly this confidence clashes with the representation of Peter in narratives Thorpe accepts as foundational and normative. The scarcity of serious reflection on contradictory processes in human lives and communities meant that Thorpe probably could not think of the Church as a community both immersed in sin and yet also the divine gift in which Thorpe received the sacraments.

Yet the texts Thorpe accepted as unquestionably authoritative showed that the early Church was founded in the disciples' collective and individual betrayal of Jesus. Having abandoned and betrayed Jesus, this community was given the risen Christ, who showed that even betrayal and apparently unequivocal denial ("I know not the man," Matthew 26.72) did not defeat divine forgiveness, fidelity, and the divine powers of reconciliation in that community. As I observed in chapter 1, Rowan Williams has argued that this process was prefigured in the Last Supper and performed in the classical liturgies which "follow Paul in 1 Corinthians 11 in explicitly locating the action 'in the same night that he was betrayed.'"[73] The Church and the sacrament of the altar are bound up with betrayal and the redemption of betrayal in a process fraught with painful contradictions. Williams emphasizes that those who betray Jesus are his "guests and debtors," promised "divine fidelity that cannot be negated by their unfaithfulness." The narratives of the sacrament's institution, to which Thorpe paid close attention, condense "the longer and more diffuse historical sequence of passion and resurrection—the betrayal followed by divine vindication and the return of Jesus as host at the table (as in Luke 24 and John 21)."[74] Thorpe and Arundel share these narratives, Wycliffite Christians and orthodox Christians both declare commitment to the Scriptures as foundational to Christian theology and ethics (ST I.1.2, I.1.8–10).[75] Here they might have encountered a model for thinking of the sacrament as the sign of a community whose redemptive potential is given in betrayal and the recognition of such betrayal. Once more in Williams's words:

> God's promise to be faithful, even in advance of betrayal, points towards a community whose bonds are capable of surviving betrayal, and which thus can have no place for reprisal, for violent response to betrayal and breakage, or for pre-emptive action to secure against betrayal. There is no promise that people will not be unfaithful and untrustful towards each other, but there is an assurance that the new humanity does not depend on constant goodwill and successful effort to survive: its roots are deeper. If it is, properly, defenseless, that is because it does not need defending and *cannot* be defended by means that deny its basic assurances (again a theme familiar in Augustine, as in the final book of the *City of God* [XXII.6]).[76]

Williams refers here to Augustine's pervasive contrast between Rome's lust for dominion enmeshed in the practices of violence and the city of Christ, which "never fought against her wicked persecutors for her temporal preservation, even though while still on pilgrimage in this world she had on her side whole armies of mighty peoples; instead, she refrained from fighting back, to ensure her eternal salvation." Her people chose martyrdom rather than violent self-defense.[77] Augustine stresses that "the safety of the City of God is such that it can be possessed, or rather acquired only with faith and through faith; and when faith is once lost no one can attain to that safety."[78] Brut and Thorpe certainly shared this view. The sacrament of the altar is understood in this Augustinian context as the self-sacrifice of those who constitute the body of Christ (Romans 12.3–21) in "acts of compassion" [misericordiae].[79] Perhaps this perception informed Brut's own history of sacrifice in the Roman Church's theology of the Eucharist. Be that as it may, one recognizes that Thorpe's archbishop apparently lacked any vision of a "properly, defenseless" Church sacramentally signified in the sacrament of the altar. Here it seems that Thorpe's criticism of a persecuting Church, together with the narratives of the Last Supper, could have opened out towards Williams's reading of the sacrament and its implied ecclesiology. But it did not. Perhaps one reason it did not was that Thorpe's thinking about the Church had become, understandably, captivated by that which it sought to oppose, by the Church, power, and persecution which had shaped his identity as priest, theologian, and now heretical member of the "sect of Lollers" (34), one of those whom the archbishop believed God has called him back to England "to distrie" (91).[80]

chapter 5

THE SIGN OF POVERTY

Piers Plowman *(The C Version)*

> *a bereth þe signe of pouerte*
> *And in þat secte oure saueour saued al mankyde.*
>
> —*Patience, in* Piers Plowman *C XVI.98–99*

> *Et si distribuero in cibos pauperum omnes facultates meas, et si tradidero cor-*
> *pus meum ita ut ardeam, charitatem autem non habuero, nihil mihi prodest.*
> *[And if I should distribute all my goods to feed the poor, and if I should de-*
> *liver my body to be burned, and have not charity, it profiteth me nothing.]*
>
> —*1 Corinthians 13.3*

This chapter explores "þe signe of pouerte" in the final version of *Piers Plowman*. My approach follows the procedures of reading practiced in chapter 2 as I traced the poet's treatment of the sacramental sign of the altar. It thus remains immanent to the poem's own order as I seek to describe the dialectical process in which the sign of poverty is constituted and, so I shall argue, superseded—superseded but never forgotten, a constitutive part of the process which generates it. In this mode I hope to show how the powerful orations of Rechelesnesse and Patience, with their Franciscan inflections, are placed and why they are placed as they are. Overall the chapter engages with Langland's theology of poverty and its relations to a thoroughly troubled inheritance.[1] In doing so its analysis is also directed, as in chapter 2, at the ways in which signs work, and cease to work, in *Piers Plowman*.

The poem opens with a vision of a polity immersed in market relations and the modern Church subsumed to these energies. Even orders vowed to poverty turn preaching, exegesis, and the sacraments to "profit of þe wombe."[2] But this image of a Church which has lost all power of critical resistance to what "þe world ascuth" (Pr.20) is immediately followed by a vision of "Holy churche," the creedal Church which Christians are committed to believe (I.72–75): "Credo . . . unam sanctam catholicam et apostolicam Ecclesiam."[3] She comments on the poem's prologue as a vision of how "bisy" people are "aboute þe mase" and how unreal to them is any "othere heuene then here" (I.3–9). Rightly enough, Wille (so named at I.5) seeks salvific instruction from her (I.76–80). She responds generously. Her teaching is immensely rich and deploys a wide range of modes. In a number of areas it will take the whole poem, a lifetime's searching for Wille, to unfold the implications of her utterances. This unfolding will necessarily disclose the negations her affirmations assume. And Wille's inquiries will take us down paths which Holy Church does not take. But it will emerge that only thus can we understand the implications her teachings hold in the poet's culture, only thus come to understand "þe mase" from which we begin. Wille himself does not initially recognize the Church that made him a "fre man" and whom he has promised to obey, believe, and love throughout his life (I.72–75). In response to her calling, Wille's memory stirs, and he, for the moment, acknowledges her: "Thenne y knelede on my knees and criede here of grace" (I.76).

Holy Church perceives God's creation (invisible to those absorbed by "þe mase") as divine generosity, divine "cortesye" to humans (I.14–20). The latter are embodied, communitarian spirits. For them, she maintains, faithful worship means living in accord with the virtues that enable a good use of the gifts of creation, however abundant [thow muche] these are. The "formor of alle" intends humans to be at ease [attese] in the material world. This ease, however, depends on cultivating dispositions to live "in mesure." These dispositions are known as the cardinal virtues, and already they are bound up with the means of salvation left to the Church by the risen Christ (Pr.128–33; cf. XXI.274–308).[4] Wille asks Holy Church to say more about "þe moneye of þis molde," the "tresour" desired by most people in the Prologue (I.42–43). Her answer directs him to Christ's statement about relations between God and Caesar, adding that "welthe" should be used with "resoun" and "kynde witte" (I.44–53). Holy Church's approach to the gifts of creation, to human productivity and exchange, is as free from glorification of riches as it is from glorification of poverty. Despite the vision of the Prologue and despite her engagement with evangelical doctrine ("'Go to þe gospel,' quod she," I.44) she does not even give a nod to the fierce and extensive debates on the status of poverty and mendicancy that had riven the Church in the hundred years before *Piers Plowman* and would continue to do so in different forms for many years.[5] Does her focus change in response to Wille's passionate prayer to learn how he may save his soul (I.76–80)? It does not, despite her meditation on Christ's Incarnation.

In this her response to Wille is significantly different from the response given in a comparable episode where Patience instructs Actyf (*Activa Vita*), an important episode discussed later in this chapter. Holy Church fuses the perspectives she has been cultivating with a Christocentric discourse which brilliantly develops a dense range of scriptural texts. Wille has asked her to teach him how he can save his soul, and she shows that reflection on Christ's Incarnation returns us to concern with just practice in a determinate community (I.81–204).[6] According to Holy Church, truthful practice, in word and deed, flowing from a good will to all, participates in the divine life (I.81–87).[7] Just as Holy Spirit will insist near the poem's conclusion, so Holy Church states at its opening that such practice, participating in the perfections of divine life given to humans, will include dominion and just coercion (I.90–102; see XXI.245–47).

All positions in the battles over poverty and its status in Christian living claimed that they were warranted by Christian Scripture and were following Christ. From a particular model of Christ devotional writers and polemicists read off a version of obedient discipleship and its most perfect form. If writers claimed that Christian perfection consisted in absolute poverty, having nothing in person or in common and consequently pursuing a life of mendicancy, they envisioned a Christ who renounced both personal and common dominion, who taught that absolute voluntary poverty was the highest form of virtue, the cause of infinite goods, the root of all spiritual goods, the pearl of the gospel, the twelve pearls of the apocalypse. The Christ of such Christians, like themselves, pursued the life of mendicancy.[8] When such people addressed the fact that according to Scripture Christ and his disciples kept a purse and had the resources to buy provisions (John 13.29, 12.6), they maintained that this was merely a condescension to the weak, to those unable to pursue the path of voluntary poverty; they also made much of the fact that he who carried the purse was Judas, thief and betrayer.[9] Langland's Holy Church includes an exquisite lyric on the Incarnation during her instruction of Wille, but it is a very different mode from that of apologetics and polemics in the poverty conflicts. Her attention is on the divine will to heal humans in soul *and* body:

> Loue is þe plonte of pees, most precious of vertues,
> For heuene holde hit ne myghte, so heuy hit semede,
> Til hit hadde of erthe yʒoten hitsilue.
> And when hit hadde of þe folde flesch and blode taken
> Was neuer lef vppon lynde lyhtere theraftur
> And portatif and persaunt as þe poynt of a nelde
> That myʒte non Armure hit lette ne none heye walles.
>
> (I.148–54)

This dazzling image of divine generosity conveys an extraordinary sense of divine embodiment not as constricting but as charged with boundless energy and joy.[10] The speaker resists conventional late medieval tendencies to focus with massive elaboration on the passion and crucifixion of Christ. Holy Church's focus is on the Incarnation as a plenitudinous release of divine power piercing through imprisoning physical and spiritual walls, foreshadowing the emancipation of hell and the extensive representations of Christ in *Piers Plowman* (XVIII–XXI).[11] From this figuration of healing power in the Incarnation Holy Church turns to Christ's forgiveness of those who killed him and takes this as an example of the unity of power and mercy demanded from human beings who are "riche." She apparently knows of no demands for voluntary poverty in Christian discipleship, however devoted. She teaches that those with possessions must give to "þe pore, / Of such good as god sent goodliche parte" (I.161–80). The first passus ends with her affirmation that virtues uninformed by charity will be "cheyned in helle," that those who are "vnkynde" reject the saving actions of the Trinity (I.181–204). We will meet this cluster of ideas and language once more when encountering Christ as the Good Samaritan, but by then we will have gone down ways to which Holy Church has not directed us, ways in which poverty is construed as a sanctifying sign given by the life of Christ: Franciscan ways.

Like Holy Church, Reason and Conscience show no knowledge of such a sanctifying sign during their struggle to initiate a reform of the polity which would loosen Mede's hold on institutions and individuals (II–IV). Reason does mention St. Francis (IV.117). But he seems to assimilate the latter's order to the enclosed life of monks, a life built on common dominion and possession (IV.116–17). In the light of the poem's conclusion, studied at the end of this chapter, Reason's remark might be a significant hint. But here it constitutes no more than a passing reference without any sustaining context in Passus IV. One might be tempted to say that Reason's is a casual reference which he does not examine. Yet the issues around Franciscan conceptions of poverty, mendicancy, and mobility are of such vexing concern to the maker of *Piers Plowman* that it is difficult to leave one's explication with this. Nevertheless, in the contexts within which Reason mentions St. Francis, this reserve seems necessary.

In the next passus (V), the reformers meet the figure of the poet in an episode which has elicited considerable and wide-ranging commentary.[12] The poet Wille is "yclothed as a lollare" (V.2). This recalls his first entry clothed "as y a shep were; / In abite as an heremite, vnholy of werkes" (Pr.2–3). But he now also claims to be a maker of texts directed against "lollares of Londone and lewede Ermytes," writing as "resoun" has taught him. The apparent self-division ('lollare' against 'lollare') is probably what one should expect of a Christian subject (Romans 7.18–25), but it is of course the particular form that is puzzling. For Langland chooses a term that was already tricky and shifting, as a substantial scholarly literature has shown.[13] He also chooses to defer his own explication of this term until Passus IX, addressed later in this chapter. Passus V begins with the poet as a 'lollare' who has reasoned against 'lollares' and now, in good health, wills "no dede to do but drynke and slepe." In this situation he meets Conscience and Reason (V.1–9). Roaming through his memory, the latter challenges him. Reason is, as Derek Pearsall notes, "the personification of the waking dreamer's own rational self-analysis" as well as being "the authoritative figure of Passus IV."[14]

Reason introduces a word that proves to be extremely important in *Piers Plowman* and plays a major role in its conclusion: the verb *fynden,* the noun *fyndynge,* a word meaning "material provision, material livelihood." He asks the apparent "lollare" to declare the "craft" he contributes to the community in reciprocity for those "þat byleue the fynden" (V.12–21).[15] Although Reason offers the opportunity to define "craft" broadly enough to include singing in a church (V.12), Wille answers as though he has only been asked why he does not do manual labor (V.22–25). Given this provocation, Reason asks whether Wille has landed or noble means "[t]hat fyndeth the thy fode." He observes that this self-declared "lollare" seems to be "an ydel man," "a spilletyme" (time is not only the time of the worker which employers seek to buy and control but God's gracious gift to his creatures;

B. IX.99–102; C X.181–87). Or perhaps Wille is a married mendicant who
chooses to beg his livelihood, preferring, as he himself has confessed, "no
dede to do but drynke and slepe" (V.26–32, 7–9). If so, Reason determines
that Wille would indeed be living the life he is dressed to represent: "lollarne
lyf þat lytel is preysed," a life that goes against what will become one of the
central understandings of divine demands for justice and love in *Piers Plowman*, the demands that Christians render to others their due (V.31–32a).[16]
But rather than judge according to Wille's appearance and self-declaration,
Reason asks whether he has some affliction that would necessitate his mendicancy (V.33–34). Wille's answer takes up the term that Reason introduced
as he tells a story of how his father and friends "foende" him to a clerical
education (V.35–39).[17] The consequence of this education, Wille says, is that
he likes a life "in this longe clothes," deploying clerical skills if he has to
labor (V.40–43a). He stays with the issue and term of *fyndynge* as he describes a mobile, clerical livelihood, using the tools ("lomes") of his craft for
the souls of those who help him, "tho þat fynden me my fode" (V.44–51).
Yet Wille himself classifies this way of gaining a *fyndynge* not as "mercede"
(III.290–340a) but as mendicancy, although a nonaccumulating mendicancy:
"y begge / Withoute bagge or botel but my wombe one" (V.51–52). In defining himself as married (V.2, XX.467–72, XXII.193–98) and clerical, Wille
stresses that he acts alone, that he does not belong to one of the Church's
mendicant orders, that he is detached from the obedience, collective rule,
and practice that constitute these orders, a fact Conscience soon confirms.
But as he elaborates his self-defense he seems to claim that he is in the state
of "a parfit man." He claims that his poverty and mendicancy manifest a
supreme faith that God will provide his *fyndynge:* "*Fiat voluntas dei* fynt vs
alle thynges" (V.82–88). His way of life, he is affirming, answers the evangelical call to perfection found in Matthew 6.25–34 and Luke 12.22–34; he
thus anticipates Patience's Franciscan teaching on poverty and perfection in
Passus XV–XVI.[18] Conscience, however, is profoundly unimpressed by this
anticipation of teaching which we will consider below. He takes up Wille's
assumption that the life of voluntary poverty and mendicancy is the life of
"a parfit man": "it semeth no sad parfitnesse in Citees to begge, / But he be
obediencer to prior or to mynistre" (V.90–91). Here Langland introduces
hints of arguments which will be explored, dramatically, later in *Piers Plowman*. But now the figure of the poet assents wholeheartedly to Conscience's
objections to his choices and acknowledges the justice of Reason's suspi-
cions that his appearance "as a lollare" may betoken "lollare lyf" in which
one becomes "a spilletyme":

> "That is soth," y saide, "and so y beknowe
> That y haue ytynt tyme and tyme myspened"
>
> (V.92–93)

So Reason and Conscience have elicited a confession which leads not into despair but "hope." Wille's new hope is that through this encounter with Reason and Conscience he may be moved, "thorw wordes of grace," towards the treasure so prominent in Holy Church's discourse, the treasure hidden in a field symbolizing the kingdom of heaven (V.94–98a):[19]

> So hope y to haue of hym þat is almyghty
> A gobet of his grace and bigynne a tyme
> That alle tymes of my tyme to profit shal turne.
>
> (V.99–101)

These moving words express a still obscure hope that a crumb of God's grace can begin a time in which even the sad waste of time past can be redeemed. Such would be an "acceptable time [tempus acceptabile] . . . the day of salvation" (2 Corinthians 6.2).[20] At the moment, however, this is very shadowy: How can there be a new time which can redeem time past as well as the future? Here we are pointed towards the heart of the poem's slowly unfolding meditations on salvation history, ones in which the will for individual autonomy, the will to be "synguler" (VI.36), can be only a disastrous impediment. In accord with this hope, Wille responds to the advice of Reason and Conscience "to bigynne" the beginning for which he yearns by going to the church (V.102–4). This also obscurely foreshadows a distant moment in Wille's journey, truly "at the laste ende" (V.97, XXII.204–16). I will leave this much discussed episode with one further observation. It is, as Lawrence Clopper says, one of the "incidents" in *Piers Plowman* which has "ties to the Franciscan issues of the poem."[21] The "ties" are in the evocation of questions about the form of life appropriate to one who aspires to become "a parfit man" and questions about the relations of mendicancy, "lollarne lyf," and sanctification. Most crucially, in the long run, they are also questions about the kind of *fyndynge* most congruent with the search for the treasure hidden in the "fair feld ful of folk": "Simile est regnum celorum thesauro abscondito in agro" [The kingdom of heaven is like unto a treasure hidden in a field] (Matthew 13.44) (Pr.19; V.98a; I.42–53, 81–82). But the mode in which this episode is written, its extraordinary density and brevity, together with its refusal to make any direct reference to Franciscanism or friars, shapes its meaning and should shape our interpretation. Wille's self-divisions are emphasized, as we noted. Initially a confident defender of his singular vocation, he is an equally confident assailant of what he takes to be forces undermining feudal hierarchies in the Church and its social world (V.35–83). But through his self-divisions we are shown his strong yearning for a "gobet" of God's grace to make that beginning in which the sad waste of time will become redeemed. Yet the episode refuses to specify what form of life would sustain Wille's repentant longing for grace and his return "to þe kyrke" (V.105). As we are not given, carefully not given, the resources to answer these questions, we are denied the resources to read the signs of poverty. We are thus obliged to suspend judgment about the nature of the episode's "ties" to "Franciscan issues," about the relations between sanctification, poverty, and a *fyndynge*. But even as the episode obliges us to wait, it has given us strong provocations to search further into these issues.[22]

From the episode of Wille's confession the poem moves to a collective confession of vices followed by the apparently churchless, priestless people losing "the way" (V–VII). In this loss the people meet Piers the Plowman, who leads them to plow the half-acre. The ensuing passus (VIII) is devoted to conflicts in contemporary agrarian England and resistance to "lawes" sponsored by "þe kyng and alle þe Kynges Iustices."[23] How should Christian polities organize their *fyndynge?* The task was, after all, God-given: "Go to oure bygynnynge tho god the world made," as Hunger observes, quoting Genesis 3.19 (VIII.239–41a). Holy Church too had made very clear that the task was a central one (I.12–67, 81–100, 171–200). But in Passus VIII the poet does not give sustained attention to issues of Christian perfection and the sanctity of poverty glimpsed in Passus V. Piers has "pitee vppon alle pore peple" but distinguishes those he considers counterfeit poor from the "blynde or brokelegged or bolted with yren"; it is the latter with whom he will share his provisions (VIII.204, 136–45). He and his workers will also "fynde" for ascetic anchorites, hermits, and friars together with the "pore folke syke" (VIII.146–48).[24] But "freres þat flateren" are excluded (VIII.147). This language will have a major role in the poem's conclusion, as we shall see, but at the moment its complex potential is not unpacked. We are not told anything about the conditions of such a *fyndynge* or its bearings on the peculiarly Franciscan identification of Christian perfection with the state of poverty, or its implications for Franciscan claims to live the most perfect form of poverty, or the consequences it might have for fraternal mendicancy. These issues will all be teased out in due course, but here Piers is preoccupied with work in the production of the community's *fyndynge*. He asks Hunger about those who seem unproductive: "Of beggares and biddares what beste be to done?" (VIII.209).[25] The dialogue with Hunger shows that his mind is on nonreligious mendicants, ones who are making no special claims to Christian perfection (VIII.210–95, 324–28). Among the terms of abuse used in Hunger's comments on "Bolde beggares and bygge" is the word "lollares" (VIII.223–88). This is the term applied to the figure of the poet and to those he opposed in Passus V, but Langland again defers elaboration until the sign of poverty becomes a topic for reflection, in the next passus.

Passus IX involves the "pardoun *A pena & A culpa*" for Piers and "his ayres for euere to ben assoiled" (IX.1–4). This has generated a substantial critical literature on both the B version and its revisions in the C version. I wish to restrict my attention as much as possible to the central issue of this chapter but I will preface my remarks with a *caveat* I have been making since I first wrote on the pardon, one that has not impressed my colleagues.[26] The *caveat* concerns a simple problem the poet sets his readers in all the poem's versions. Let us recall it. When Piers actually unfolds the pardon, it turns out to contain just two lines "and not a letter more" (IX.281–85). These two lines are written "in witnesse of treuthe," taken from one of the Church's creeds, *Quicunque vult*, the Athanasian Creed (IX.286–88).[27] But if the pardon so unequivocally contains only two lines, who is responsible for the preceding 276 lines which gloss the creedal proclamation? What status do they have as a gloss by an indeterminate glossator or glossators? In my view, the massive gloss, for all its passion and distinctions, contains some striking omissions. It fails to note the Trinitarian and Christological contexts of the two lines from the creed "in witnesse of treuthe" (IX.286) and so, inevitably, fails to present a minimally adequate version of the processes of pardon as envisaged within Catholic traditions. These processes, Trinitarian and Christocentric, will be disclosed with great theological subtlety and dramatic power across Passus XVIII–XXI. The fact that the gloss fails to disclose a specifically Christian account of pardon does *not* mean that it lacks serious reflections on many of the issues with which it is concerned, issues that preoccupied the poet and his poem. But still, to whom should we attribute the gloss? In the C version Langland makes clear that it speaks with almost as many voices as T. S. Eliot's *Waste Land*. For example, at lines 159–61, a comment on "lollares" is explicitly ascribed to Piers ("quod Peres"). Derek Pearsall punctuates his edition to stop Piers commenting at line 161. This decision is followed by George Russell and George Kane.[28] This is perfectly plausible. But so are editorial decisions not to punctuate so as to end Piers's commentary at line 161.[29] We are actually left to guess where Piers's glossarial voice ends. Other examples: Who is claiming to read glosses "in þe margine" concerning the estate of merchants and its exclusion from the full pardon "*a pena & a culpa*" (IX.22–26)? Who claims to have access to "a letter" qualifying this marginal gloss, allegedly sent by Truth, "vnder his secrete seal" (IX.27–40) and "purchased" by the plowman Piers (IX.42)? What kind of warrant does this indeterminate voice have for claiming a special revelation to writings outside the Scriptures and in extremely obscure relationship to the Church? Certainly Christ the Samaritan makes no reference to any such special deal and "secrete" glosses in his long oration (XIX.83–335). Whose is the prophetic warning voice that seems to irrupt into the gloss at IX.51: "Beth ywar, ȝe wis men and witty of þe lawe"? It is a voice we meet in many different parts of *Piers Plowman*, a voice that usually seems an authorial self-presentation, as at the end of Piers's failed attempt to organize collective *fyndynge* in the face of substantial opposition: "Ac y warne ȝow werkmen . . ." (VIII.342). But what is this prophetic voice doing within the pardon and its commentary, and with what authority? If Piers is not still commenting after IX.161, whose is the "Y" in the passages around IX.239 and 247, passages at the heart of the discourse on "lollares," including the etymology of the term in "þe engelisch of oure eldres" (IX.215)? The fact that there is no way of providing any definitely correct answers to the questions I have been asking should at least be acknowledged in commentary on this sustained glossorial writing. What at first seems to be offered as an authoritative account of a revelation from Truth to Piers providing pardon from punishment and guilt for him and his "ayres for euere" turns out to be a multivoiced mixture of often extraordinarily eloquent cultural and ethical reflections whose authority the poet chooses to place in unresolvable question. Having recognized this, I shall temporarily bracket the formal problems while I consider the treatment of poverty and mendicancy in the gloss to the pardon.

The traditional demand that a *fyndynge* and legal help should be given to those understood as poor and dependent is affirmed (IX.34–36, 46–54). Furthermore the poet adds to the B version a passage of extraordinary force telling readers that if we are properly attentive we will find that the most needy people are our neighbors. Most unusually in medieval writing about worthy recipients of alms, Langland concentrates here on able-bodied, hardworking women and men, landless laborers whose wages and unpaid domestic work leave them and their children on the dangerous margins of subsistence (XI.70–95).[30] As Derek Pearsall observes, the poet "describes in precise and minute detail the lives of those who are employed in the most menial part-time and piece-work jobs—scraping flax, peeling rushes, carding and combing, patching and washing clothes—and who, though employed, can barely scrape together a living."[31] Because I find this passage an important landmark in the C version, as we will see, I will quote from it at some length. These "pore folk in cotes" are

> Charged with childrene and chief lordes rente.
> þat they with spynnyng may spare spenen hit on hous huyre,
> Bothe in mylke and in mele to make with papelotes
> To aglotye with here gurles that greden aftur fode.
> And hemsulue also soffre muche hungur
> And wo in wynter tyme and wakynge on nyhtes
> To rise to þe reule to rokke þe cradel,
> Bothe to carde and to kembe, to cloute and to wasche,
> To rybbe and to rele, rusches to pylie,
> That reuthe is to rede or in ryme shewe
> The wo of this wommen þat wonyeth in cotes
> And of monye oþer men þat moche wo soffren,
> Bothe afyngred and afurste, to turne þe fayre outward
> And ben abasched for to begge and wollen nat be aknowe
> What hem nedeth at here neyhebores at noon and at eue.
> This y woet witturly, as þe world techeth,
> What other byhoueth þat hath many childrene
> And hath no catel but his craft to clothe hem and to fede
> And fele to fonge þerto and fewe panes taketh.
>
> (IX.73–91)

Geoffrey Shepherd observes that this "is probably the earliest passage in English which conveys the felt and inner bitterness of poverty."[32] It certainly does convey the crushing urgency and immediacy of material demands, the literally endless demands of children, the overwhelming reiterations of a host of daily and nightly labors unmediated by the forms of help material resources could provide. But we should note that pervaded with compassion as this wonderful passage is, it does not contain *any* allusion to those strands in Christian tradition which have emphasized the sanctity of poverty, at least of poverty patiently endured. In fact, this powerful passage does not attempt to suggest any sense that the crushing actualities of poverty

should be understood as a sanctifying, sacramental sign. The force and re-
lentless particularization of this poetry is itself extraordinarily disciplined
and an unusual act in its culture of discourse. It calls readers to especial and
sustained remembrance as they continue down paths of the poem in which
they will meet Franciscan ideas and voices.

The gloss to the pardon includes some equally passionate writing about
a very different form of poverty, one already met in the Prologue, in the encounter between Wille, Reason, and Conscience and in the plowing of the
half-acre. It is enacted under these classifications: unholy; beggar with bags;
faytour; waster; lollar; losele; Lorelle; friars that flatter.[33] Passus IX gathers
together these terms in a sustained attack on "beggares with bagges þe whiche
brewhouses ben here churches," able-bodied "lollares" pursuing "lollares
lyf" against divine law and the teaching of "holi churche" (IX.98–104).
Those attacked include mendicant hermits drawn to the dwellings of ale-
wives and devoted to avoiding the hard work for which they were prepared by plebeian status and training. These people are categorized as "lollares, lachedraweres, lewede Ermytes" (IX.189–214). At this point, in the
margin of the pardon, Langland produces his etymology for the word
"lollares" in "þe engelisch of oure eldres." He writes that traditional usage
of the term designated someone who was "ymaymed in som membre"—
that is, someone lamed; such lolling out of joint is said to be an apt symbol for those who "Lollen aȝen þe byleue and lawe of holy churche"
(IX.215–19).[34] But the "byleue and lawe of holy churche" here turns out
not to be the "byleue" and "lawe" currently challenged by Wycliffite lollards. Instead it is the law of feudal order and ideology, one allegedly
underpinned by "holy churche" (IX.220–55).[35] There is good reason for
Geoffrey Shepherd's view that

> throughout the poem we first catch that uncompromising aversion to
> public beggary which in the post-medieval centuries has remained
> the normal response of northern Europeans. Beggars are shocking,
> beggary is somehow obscene. A bond of shame unites public giver
> and public recipient. Beggars are parasites upon and enemies and be-
> trayers of society, the dangerous drones who according to the pros-
> perous Franklin in *Mum and the Sothsegger* should be nipped out of
> the busy commonwealth of bees and destroyed utterly.[36]

No indication here that poverty is a state exceptionally conducive to sanctification, a sacramental sign.

But for the gloss on the pardon in its C version Langland added the frequently discussed account of "lunatyk lollares" (IX.105–40).[37] These are "men and women bothe" who although appearing to be in good health actually "wanteth wyt": "madden as þe mone sit," indifferent to all weathers they "aren meuynge aftur þe mone," people who are "witteles." Compelled by the movements of the moon they are veritably "lunatyk" and, in their mobile dependency, "lepares aboute"; they are "lollares" (IX.105–11, 137). Because they lack "wyt," their dispositions driven by the moon, they *unequivocally* lack the resources to a *fyndynge*.[38] Their undemanding (IX.121) and *involuntarily* needy presence should, we are told, encourage those with access to a *fyndynge* to share this with the "lunatyk lollares" (IX.124–26, 134–40). The "riche" are exhorted not to give anything to "lollares" with their wits, even if they should die for hunger. But they are told to welcome these witless "lunatyk loreles" (IX.98–101, 134–37).

These utterly indigent women and men belong to the poem's categorization of the deserving poor, traditionally elaborated from Luke 14.21 and Matthew 25.34–40.[39] As such they belong to that group of people medieval Catholics viewed as one of God's main contributions to the salvation of the rich. On this Geoffrey Shepherd observed, "[T]he rich need the poor as much as the poor need the rich."[40] The poverty of the poor is given to elicit charity from others, to catalyze sanctification in those who possess the dangerous goods of the world (Luke 6.24, 18.25). The relation between poor and rich supposedly enacts, to the illumination of both groups, an analogy of the gracious abundance of the Creator's plenitude in a world still scarred by lack and grievous need. But the poor who participate in the analogy, the deserving poor, must be utterly unthreatening, undemanding, and monumentally patient. To remain deserving, they must not take action against policies or persons responsible for exacerbating their sufferings. They would not, for example, join the rebels of 1381 to resist unprecedented burdens and forms of taxation or to resist the burdens of serfdom.

The "lunatyk lollares" plainly belong to those classified as deserving and unthreatening poor, but they are unusually complex figures. We are told that in their "witteles" and "moneyeles" mobility, walking through "mony wyde contreyes," they resemble Jesus's apostles (IX.109–12, 118–20a). As such they are "munstrals of heuene / And godes boys, bourdyors" and God's "mesagers" (IX.126–38). Understandably enough, this analogical language has persuaded some readers to identify "lunatyk lollares" with a far more exalted version of poverty than the one endured by our own neighbors "þat most neden" (IX.71–97) and those evoked in Luke 14.13–14 as the due recipients of alms. This more exalted account of poverty is Franciscan and its presence here and elsewhere in the B and C versions of *Piers Plowman* has been widely recognized.[41] The most unqualified convergence of "lunatyk lollares" with Franciscan ideology has been made by Lawrence Clopper. He argues that these people "are not madmen. . . . They are not lunatics" because they "follow or manifest the apostolic life and the Franciscan ideal." Although they are admittedly not "designated as regular members of the order," Clopper maintains that "they are (perhaps nostalgic) images" of Francis and "may also include those friars who follow the *Rule* in strictness." They reflect the "Franciscan perspective" of the poet's own "Franciscan agenda."[42] But if they were to "follow the *Rule* in strictness" these "lunatyk lollares" could not be "witteles." They could not be compelled by the movement of "þe mone," "lunatyk," lacking "wyt." Yet the poet says that this is exactly what they are. So one cannot assimilate these figures to a "Franciscan agenda" without some major reinventing of the text. Such rewriting is essential for another aspect of a straightforwardly Franciscan reading. Since St. Francis follows the path of voluntary poverty, Langland's "lunatyk lollares" must be "the humble voluntary poor," those "who chose voluntarily to live a life of poverty."[43] To make such voluntary choices one plainly needs options (the choice not to live the life of poverty) and intellectual faculties capable of meditating on the available choices and determining to follow one path rather than others. Such agency could not be driven by the moon, could not be lacking in "wyt," could not be "witteles." But there is no indication in Langland's description of "lunatyk lollares" that they are "voluntary poor." As we have seen, they lack the means to a *fyndynge* and are not shown making a "voluntary" act of any kind, let alone having possessions they choose to abandon in pursuit of the perfection that proved too difficult for the virtuous, rich young man of Matthew 19.16–22.

Another difficulty with an unqualified Franciscan reading of these figures is an absence that the poet names: "þey preche nat" (IX.112). They are "as" the apostles in certain ways (IX.110–38): mobile, destitute, apparently nonviolent minstrels of God whose presence summons those with possessions to charitable and salvific action (Mathew 25.31–46). But despite these affinities they do not preach. Clopper notes this: "they do not have the office to preach." So if they include friars, they are "mendicants not licensed to preach."[44] This is doubtless true, but Langland gives not one hint that these women and men have any knowledge of offices and licenses: they are "lunatyk lollares," "lepares aboute" who do not display customary respect for status and hierarchy but are apparently not at all punished for this (IX.122–23a). We are simply told that they do not preach, although often "hem happeth / To profecye of þe peple" (IX.113–14). Nor are we given any reason to confuse "lunatyk lollares" with any form of Wycliffite lollard, to confuse these nonpreaching, "witteles" women and men with those for whom the activities of preaching, scriptural reading, and ecclesiastical reformation were constitutive of their mission. The fact that they do not preach also separates them as decisively from the apostles of the early Church as it does from St. Francis and Franciscan tradition. In a text used in the justification of fraternal orders, Jesus called his apostles and "sent them to preach the kingdom of God, and to heal the sick" (Luke 9.2). And as Clopper himself has noticed, Bonaventure says in the *Legenda Major* that when Innocent III approved the rule, he gave friars a mission to preach repentance [dedit de poenitentia praedicandi mandatum] and conferred clerical tonsure on all the laymen [laicis] among the companions so that they could preach the word of God freely [ut verbum Dei libere praedicarent].[45] Just as the elimination of preaching from the apostolic ministry would have transformed the identity and mission of apostleship, so the elimination of preaching from medieval Franciscans would have transformed the identity and mission of Franciscanism.

These nonpreaching "lunatyk lollares" are thus extremely peculiar messengers of God in Christian traditions. Their lack of "wyt" and their moon-drivenness does not match the language of "foolishness" which Paul used to describe his *preaching* of Christ's gospel to the Corinthians, language sometimes aligned with Langland's "lunatyk lollares." Paul makes clear that the gospel of Christ's cross is "foolishness" only to those who reject it, "to them indeed that perish," whereas "to them that are saved, that is, to us, it is the power of God." He emphasizes that "it pleased God, by the foolishness of our preaching, to save them that believe." Evangelists "preach Christ crucified: unto the Jews indeed a stumbling block, and unto the Gentiles foolishness: But unto them that are called, both Jews and Greeks, Christ the power of God and the wisdom of God." As for lack of loftiness of speech or wisdom in Paul's proclamation of Christ, "[M]y speech and my preaching was not in the persuasive words of human wisdom, but in shewing of the Spirit and power; That your faith might not stand on the wisdom of men but on the power of God" (see 1 Corinthians 1.17–31; 2.1–16; 3.1–2, 18–23; 4.6–13). Langland's "lunatyk lollares" are God's minstrels and messengers, but unlike Paul they do not proclaim Christ's gospel, do not proclaim his Incarnation, life, death, harrowing of hell, resurrection, and ascension; nor do they talk about Christ founding the Church with its sacramental gifts. Not only are they unlike Paul in this, they are unlike the Christocentric poet of *Piers Plowman* (XVIII–XXI; see also chapter 2 of this book).

The invocation of Peter and Paul in the passage describing the activities of "lunatyk lollares" suggests other important differences even as it invites us to search for affinities. After the passage on the "foolishness" of the gospel of Christ compared to "the wisdom of this world" that we have just considered, Paul reminds his readers that the apostles, "fools for Christ's sake," actually "labour, working with our own hands" (1 Corinthians 4.10–12; see too 1 Corinthians 9.6–27). We are also shown Paul laboring at his trade, tent making, in Acts 18.3 (see too Acts 20.34). Furthermore, in texts endlessly regurgitated in antifraternal polemic (with a long life ahead of them in the Reformation), he not only stresses that he labors for a livelihood but demands that all Christians do the same (1 Thessalonians 2.9, 4–11; 2 Thessalonians 3.7–8).[46] In *Piers Plowman* itself, Langland has one of the most authoritative speakers ("Cristes creature . . . in cristes court yknowe wel," XVI.165–71) bring Paul and Peter together in a manner that bears on the present discussion:

> Paul aftur his prechyng paniars he made
> And wan with his handes al þat hym nedede.
> Peter fischede for his fode And his fere Androwe;
>
> (XVII.17–19)

Not only does Liberum Arbitrium recollect that Paul worked for his livelihood and that Peter and Andrew did the same, but he inserts the latters' work into the nexus of monetary exchange: "Som they solde and som they sode and so they lyuede bothe" (XVII.20). These apostolic forms of life are strikingly remote from the quasi-apostolic ministry of the "lunatyk lollares" of Passus IX.

The latter undoubtedly carry the sign of poverty and summon those with possessions to almsgiving. But the passage hints at potential difficulties in reading the sign. These able-bodied "lunatyk lollares" are "in hele as hit semeth" (IX.105). It might thus seem that they are not to be classified among the deserving poor (Luke 14.13; cf. VIII.136–47). But appearances are deceptive because these women and men "wanteth wyt," are "witteles" and compelled by the moon's cycles (IX.106–8). They are thus also not "in hele" and, as I observed above, cannot provide their own *fyndynge*. They are "beggares" (IX.105). But they do not beg: "beggeth they of no man" (IX.121). The sign of poverty even when borne by "messagers" of God (IX.136) poses tricky hermeneutic work for those who encounter it in the poet's culture. Nor are we allowed simply to set aside these hermeneutic problems, even though some strands in Christian tradition, including some represented in *Piers Plowman*, found acts of discriminating almsgiving contrary to evangelical teaching.[47] Passus IX instructs readers to distinguish between those leading "lollarne lyf," counterfeiting neediness to avoid work, and "lunatyk lollares." The rich must interpret and act on their interpretation. As we noticed, they must withhold alms from the former, not caring if they die in consequence, and they must welcome the latter (IX.98–101, 134–52).[48] So interpretation will have practical consequences. If the sign of poverty is to be a sanctifying sign, we are already discovering that it generates extremely sharp hermeneutic and theological difficulties. When inventing "lunatyk lollares," the poet undoubtedly invoked elements of Franciscan discourse. But simultaneously he negated these. The "lunatyk lollares" do not preach Christ's gospel, and they are not voluntarily poor. Passus IX leaves open a host of hermeneutic, ethical, and theological questions around the sign of poverty and its relations to Franciscan sources. But it has forcefully brought these into the poem's dialectical explorations, and *Piers Plowman* will pursue them tenaciously.

Poverty, however, has not yet been represented as a state of perfection in which the theological virtue of charity most flourishes. Rather it has been treated as the potential cause of charity in others. The allusions to Franciscan discourse could have introduced a different model, but, as I have shown, these were effectively negated. Indeed, the C version strengthens the B version's negation of these elements. Langland, famously enough, deleted the scene in which Piers tears the pardon and promises to stop his sowing "& swynke no3t so harde" (B VII.119–23). In the B version he cites Jesus's commands that disciples should not be solicitous for their lives or for what they eat or wear. Following Jesus's words, he promises to take as his model God's provision of a *fyndynge* for birds that neither sow nor reap (B VII.119–35; see Matthew 6.25–34 alongside Luke 12.22–31; cf. B VII.115–43 with C IX.289–93). In the B version this scene represents a rupture with major tendencies in B VI and B VII, tendencies which could generate a work ethic congruent with the material self-interests and legislative innovations of the tiny minority of people who constituted the governing classes. A plowman who renounced his customary work would be rejecting "þe statut" (B VI.320), turning himself into one of the very people castigated

by contemporary labor legislation and petitions as underminers of the com-
monwealth. In this rejection of the political disciplines encapsulated in "þe
statut," Piers introduces a vision of evangelical poverty propagated by
St. Francis and his followers.[49] In the C version, however, Piers neither
tears the pardon nor invokes Jesus's teaching from Matthew 6.25–34 and
Luke 12.22–31. All we are now told is that a priest and Piers "of þe pardon
iangelede" (IX.294).[50] Readers who knew and recalled the B version would
experience this rewriting as the negation of a powerful moment which had
opened out a Franciscan vision under the authority of a converted Piers.
Readers who had not read the B version would still have been able to experience the invocation and negation of Franciscanizing ideology and iconography in an extensive gloss of elusive status, as I have argued above. All
readers have been shown that controversial and vexing issues around the sign
of poverty are very much on the poet's mind.

When the next passus sets up a dialogue between Wille and two Franciscan friars, readers have reason to expect some elaboration of the issues raised
in Passus IX. They might be especially expectant as Wille invites the mendicants to discuss virtue [Dowel], drawing on their own calling (X.1–17). But
the friars' responses do not contain a word about poverty or mendicancy
(X.1–60). Given the centrality of these to the order's history and understanding of Christian virtues, this is a striking silence. But what kind of silence? The absence of Franciscan teaching on poverty in this context seems
another negation of the kind we followed in the previous passus. A reader
might wonder how much longer an articulation of Franciscan ideology will
be deferred, but for the moment the critical question concerns the teaching
Wille does receive from the Franciscans and whether there is anything the
poem identifies as specifically Franciscan about it.[51] I think the poet has chosen these religious mendicants to exemplify an attitude towards the consequences of sin which the poem has already exposed as utterly frivolous.
The mendicants assume that falling into sin, seven times a day, leaves one
with an unequivocally "fre wil and fre wit" always able to repent and rise
up from sin (X.41–43, 51–53; cf. 21, 49–50). But the intractability and effects
of sin figured forth in the poem so far give the lie to this comfortable pic-
ture. One should remember the extreme difficulties facing even those who
have apparently managed to repent under the guidance of Reason, Conscience, Repentance, and Hope (V–VII). Crying to Christ and his mother
for grace to go to Truth, they soon find themselves thoroughly lost:

Ac þer was wye non so wys þat þe way thider couthe
But blostrede forth as bestes ouer baches and hulles

(VII.155–60)

This model accords with the brilliant account of the gradual enchainments of the sinning will in Augustine's *Confessions*.[52] But the friars confidently ignore this understanding of the consequences of sin, ones which include our tendencies to ineradicable selfishness, our self-deceptions, our addictive compulsions. These all make unqualified talk about "fre wil and fre wit" worse than bland. The Franciscans only know sin without the consequences of sin, sin that somehow does not fall from charity (X.42–43).[53] They apparently know nothing of the realities of our situation disclosed so vividly both earlier in *Piers Plowman* and in the gripping images which herald the dramatic entry of Christ the Samaritan:

Bothe abraham and *spes* and he mette at ones
In a wide wildernesse where theues hadde ybounde
A man, as me tho thouhte, to moche care they brouhte
For he ne myhte stepe ne stande ne stere foet ne handes
Ne helpe hymsulue sothly for semyuief he semede
And as naked as an nedle and noen helpe abouten.

(XIX.53–58)[54]

In contrast to this haunting model, the Franciscan masters are confident that "fre wil and fre wit foleweth man euere / To repenten and arise and rowe out of synne" (X.51–52). The introduction of these Franciscan teachers with a version of sin's consequences so different from the one Christ encounters leaves us with at least two questions. What kind of confessors and spiritual guides will such masters make? Does their complacent misrepresentation of sin's consequences, within the souls of sinning subjects and within their communities, have any bearing on Franciscan teaching about perfection and poverty? Such questions are not addressed in Passus X, but they are carefully taken up in later explorations of poverty.

Meanwhile Wille continues his search for a fuller and more concrete grasp of Christian virtues. The five instructors he encounters after the Franciscans (Thought, Wit, Study, Clergy, Scripture) are not concerned with composing "þe signe of pouerte," but it is still worth noticing how poverty is treated in this sequence. Wit (the figuration of that which "lunatyk lollares" lack) has no pride in clothing but "no pouerte noythere" (X.117). His account of virtue offers a Christian anthropology in which "inwit" is a divine gift, treasure from God enabling a human "to fynden hymselue" and to help those who cannot provide a *fyndynge* for themselves. In such a community of virtue, where friendship and the Church act as they should, Wit sees no reason for mendicancy (X.174–91). It is not a form of life he envisages as a way of praising the Creator's gifts to humanity. Christ himself is not presented as absolutely poor, absolutely devoid of possessions and rights: "The catel that Crist hadde, thre clothes hit were; / Thereof was he robbed and ruyfled" (X.194–95). Wit himself does not elaborate this image and its terms, but within the century-old contexts of disputes about Christ's form of poverty the statement conjures up a distinctively non-Franciscan model.[55] Although Wit shows no concern with such disputes, he does introduce a term that becomes prominent when the C version of *Piers Plowman* gives full attention to the sign of poverty and its Franciscan affiliations. The term is *rechelesnesse*. This will become the name of one of the two speakers who are most enthusiastic about Franciscan ideology. But for Wit "rechelesnesse" is an unambiguous mark of sinful inattention to God's commands (X.213–19).[56] Of course, Wit's voice is just one stage on an unfolding path, but it is by no means a trivial or insignificant one, despite Study's objections to his readiness to teach Wille, whom she initially, and too hastily, associates with those unteachable swine who trample holy pearls under their feet before turning with violence on their teachers (XI.5–10; Matthew 7.6).

Study complains that those to whom God has given "most goed" fail to support the "nedy pore," leaving "þe carfole" crying and quaking at their gates, "afyngred and a furst," dying for lack of provisions (XI.23–51, 61–77). Hers is a traditional statement of rich people's obligations to give alms, "as puyr charite wolde" (XI.63). Such giving is to be discrete (to the "nedy pore") and an acknowledgment that the wealthy are chosen mediators of God's gifts (XI.26–28). She knows nothing of poverty as a special sign of Christian perfection, nothing of any urgent pressures on the wealthy to identify with the poor in any remotely literal manner, and nothing of any dangers to those who receive God's material gifts and help the "nedy pore." As for friars, her perception of them is twofold. They are linked with "faytours"— that is, those whom the poem consistently depicts as counterfeiters of the need to beg, those who could achieve a *fyndynge* but prefer mendicant life.[57] And they are held especially responsible for undermining Christian faith among the "folk," both "riche and pore" (XI.50–58).

Although the Franciscan friars of Passus X had nothing to say about poverty, we observed that they displayed a Pelagianizing disposition towards the consequences of sin in the quest to do well. Whether the poet might discern Pelagianizing tendencies within Franciscan ideas about poverty and the state of perfection was a question raised but not addressed. In the B version of *Piers Plowman,* Scripture briefly turns to the issue of poverty. She asserts that those who follow poverty patiently gain heaven "by trewe riȝte" whereas the rich arrive there "but of ruþe and grace" (B X.344–48). This overlooks the need to specify what makes patience distinctively Christian.[58] The oversight here seems to prepare the ground for the bizarre Pelagianism of the assertion that those who are patiently poor are saved by "riȝte."[59] This again raises the possibility that discourses on the power and perfection of poverty lived patiently might encourage Pelagianizing attitudes towards the consequences of sin. But Langland's decision to delete such an inadequate theological utterance from Scripture's conversation means that the C version simply sets that question aside for the moment.

This brings us to the poem's most sustained composition of the sign of poverty and its most sustained deployment of Franciscan ideology on the state of poverty (XI–XVI).[60] Wille meets Rechelesnesse when he yields up moral questions in "wo and wrathe," in a despair through which he is "rauysched" by Fortune into "þe lond of longyng" (XI.164–68, 193–98). Rechelesnesse wears "ragged clothes" and encourages Wille, as Wit's use of this term anticipated, in his abandonment of his quest for Christian virtues and salvation: "Folowe forth þat fortune wole" (see XI.193–95). He also presents the despairing dreamer with a brash and extraordinarily superficial theology of predestination which manages to sideline Christ, the Incarnation, and the sacraments of the Church (XI.202–27). This is the context established by the poet for Rechelesnesse's oration on poverty.

Lawrence Clopper argues that Rechelesnesse, "while personally a failure in attaining the ideal, defines and defends Franciscan 'rechelesnesse,' the absence of solicitude that marks the calling of the Franciscan order." His "'raggede cloþes' [XI.193] are intended to identify Rechelesnesse as a Franciscan friar," serving as "a sharp reminder of the poverty of the order's beginnings" and "recalling the Franciscans to the calling, the poverty, to which they had been called." However lapsed Rechelesnesse's practice may be, according to Clopper it cannot undermine the speaker's cogent "statement of the Franciscan ideal," one to which the poet himself unequivocally adheres.[61] To examine the force of Clopper's claims we need to read Rechelesnesse's oration on poverty (XII–XIII). Having done so, we will then need to see how the positions maintained in the oration fare in the dialectical processes which still have a long way to go in *Piers Plowman* and which still await the poem's most authoritative figure: Christ, the still hidden one who draws Wille on (I.78).

Rechelesnesse certainly does present a model of poverty as a sanctified state especially favored by the divine presence (XII.97–106, 117–26). Indeed, he announces that Christ is "neuere in secte of riche" (XII.132–33). This confident *neuere* will be decisively undermined later in *Piers Plowman*, as we shall see (XVI.337–69). But for the moment the assertion seems thoroughly evangelical (see Luke 6.24, 20). Rechelesnesse develops the evangelical register by quoting from Jesus's teaching on absolute renunciation in Matthew 19.16–29 and Luke 14.26, 33 (XII.152–67a). These words were especially congenial to Franciscan claims that the form of poverty constituted the state of perfection practiced by Christ and his apostles: "*Si vis perfectus esse vade & vende, & c.*" [If thou wilt be perfect, go sell what thou hast, etc.] (XII.167a; Matthew 19.21).[62] Rechelesnesse's aim is to defend the characteristically Franciscan claim that the supreme Christian virtue is patient poverty: "pacient pouerte prince of alle vertues" (XII.177). He pursues this argument without discussing the relations between this allegedly supreme virtue and the theological virtue of charity. Charity is certainly patient, as Paul wrote (1 Corinthians 13.4). But many kinds of patience have nothing to do with charity and can be enacted in causes inimical to charity. That is why Christian theology specifies distinctions between Christian and other versions of patience.[63] But instead of any such specification, Rechelesnesse equates his Franciscan version of patience with ones found in non-Christian cultures (XII.174–77; see similarly XII.140–44). It is not surprising that in his devotedly Christocentric vision the poet decided to ascribe such a "rechelesse" construal of the sanctifying sign of poverty to Rechelesnesse.[64]

The exploration of this sign through the figure named Rechelesnesse continues into Passus XIII. He offers an extended simile to illustrate the advantage of "þe pore pacient" over "þe ryche" (XIII.29–99). The aim is to reassert that "pore and pacient, parfitest lyf is of alle" (XIII.99). But here the Franciscan composition is done in a manner that has already been called into question. For Passus IX has already produced the most realized, focused writing about the crushing daily and nightly pressures of endless work endured by so many poor people living on the margins of subsistence (IX.70–97, discussed above). Despite this, Rechelesnesse, like Patience after him, represents poverty as a life of "merye" emancipation from the burdens under which the rich labor. The poor are like a messenger who is "ay merye and his mouth ful of songes" (XIII.59, see 33–98a). The bland images of poverty propagated by Rechelesnesse clash both with the passage on "pore folk in cotes" in Passus IX and with Study's representation of the poor dependent on alms in Passus XI.[65] By clashing these earlier representations with Rechelesnesse's, Langland suggests the potentials of Franciscan ideals of poverty to become sentimental abstractions which dissolve the material *and* spiritual realities of lives lived on the margins of subsistence outside the institutional supports experienced by religious mendicants. It is helpful to compare Rechelesnesse's approach here with Aquinas's approach to the defense of voluntary poverty in the *Summa contra Gentiles*. He writes that riches are "necessary for the good of virtue; since by them we support our body and give assistance to other people." So riches are good as a means to an end according to which they and their use are to be measured. "Hence, it happens to be a good thing for some people to possess riches, for they use them for the sake of virtue, but for others it is a bad thing to have them, for these people are taken away from virtue by them, either through too much solicitude or affection for them, or also because of mental pride resulting from them." Simultaneously, poverty is a good "according as it frees man from the vices in which some are involved through riches." Insofar as it removes "the solicitude which arises from riches" it is useful, at least to those "disposed to busy themselves with better things"— that is, "to divine and spiritual matters." Aquinas notes, however, that poverty "is harmful to others," often enough to those who become poor voluntarily. All externals, abundance or lack, "are good to the extent that they contribute to virtue, but not in themselves."[66] I will return to Aquinas later in this chapter, but these remarks from the *Summa contra Gentiles* point towards the kinds of distinctions *Piers Plowman* is beginning to compose, even if Rechelesnesse is not interested in them.

Before Rechelesnesse leaves the poem he initiates an argument that could subvert his own identity. Having asserted that the most perfect state of life is in poverty patiently endured, he demands that "a parfit prest to pouerte sholde drawe" (XVI.99–100). Congruently with his Franciscanism, he says that perfect priests should not hold money: "han no spendynge suluer" (XIII.101). If they hope in God, work and trust God, they will not lack "lyflode." This is the Franciscanizing position that Piers announced in the conclusion to the pardon scene in the B version, the conclusion whose deletion from C IX I discussed earlier. But Rechelesnesse then merges this position with one that seems dependent on a very different model. Priests, he says, should be ordained only if the bishop guarantees them "wages." Rechelesnesse illustrates this situation (one based in canon law) with an analogy to the making of knights. Nobody should be knighted without adequate material and social resources being given to him. Just so, priests, however perfect, should rely, not on receiving "lyflode" in absolute poverty, but on material resources guaranteed by the Church. Without these, priests are likely to take "siluer for masses" (XIII.100–116). This is an argument for a guaranteed *fyndynge* to protect poor priests (however perfect their state) from the overwhelming difficulties of living in absolute poverty without any material security whatsoever. The argument does not support the one from which Rechelesnesse set out. It has potentials to undermine the Franciscan ideology he represents. We do not yet know whether the poem will actualize these potentials or whether it will negate them. Not yet. We are probably also not yet able to determine how damaging Recheles-nesse's "rage" against Clergie and Scripture (XIII.129–30) is to the Franciscan ideas he "defines and defends."[67]

Ymagenatyf emerges after Rechelesnesse and addresses some of the difficulties his oration has generated (XIII.218–XIV.217). Although issues concerning poverty and Franciscan ideology are largely deferred for later treatment, Ymagenatyf does brush up against these when discussing the Nativity. In accord with his concentration on "clergie" (against whom Rechelesnesse's rationalizing "rage" had been directed, XIII.129), he focuses on the shepherds and wise men, both of whom (*pastores* and *magi*) figure priests and "clerkis." Having derisively betted that no "frere" would be found among the *pastores* and *magi* worshipping Jesus, he seems to reject those traditions which emphasized the severe poverty of the circumstances in which Christ was born (see Luke 2.7): "in no cote ne Caytyfs hous crist was ybore / Bote in a burgeises hous, the beste of þe toune" (XIV.90–91; see XIV.84–102).[68] Such a bourgeoisified image of the Nativity, together with the dismissal of friars, seems incompatible with Franciscan versions of Christ's birth and poverty. It goes against Rechelesnesse's vision, but the passage is brief, and Ymagenatyf does not have the last word on any of the topics he addresses, as we observed in chapter 2.

In the next two passus the sign of poverty becomes prominent (XV–XVI). Through the figure of Patience, a virtue, Langland provides his most sympathetic representation of Franciscan ideas about poverty, as many readers have observed.[69] Our task is to analyze the particularities of this representation so that we can follow the way the ideology it encapsulates fares during the rest of the poem.

Passus XV opens with a return to the scene in which the mobile, mendicant Wille was challenged by Reason and Conscience, a challenge which led to penitent prayer and tears in "þe kyrke" (V.1–108, XV.1–136). Now

Wille's penitential moment is incorporated within a contrasting, impenitent meal eaten by a mendicant "maister" who is a doctor of divinity and canon law (XV.38, 84).[70] Reason, Conscience, and Clergie have Scripture bring the bread of repentance and the drink of perseverance prepared by Contrition for Patience and Wille, both mendicants whose status as such, in this context and its allegory, poses no problems to Reason or Conscience (XV.39–62). The fraternal mendicant, however, rejects the spiritual food and drink, choosing unallegorical sustenance. This displays a sharp split between a public ideology of penitential poverty and a practice of worldly consumption which incenses Wille (XV.64–93).[71] The scene invites us to compare the practice of poverty with the ideology of poverty among those whose profession is to bear the sign of poverty in the modern Church, to compare fraternal practice with the personification Patience. But what ecclesiastical affiliations will be ascribed to the latter?

Patience is certainly a mendicant in poverty. Furthermore, he is willing to cry out for alms and actually to handle money, unlike St. Francis.[72] He is also said to be "Ilyke peres the ploghman, as he a palmere were" (XV.32–35). It is hard to see exactly in what sense he is like Piers because, as we saw, the C version of the poem deleted Piers's renunciation of material production and deleted the Franciscan rhetoric in which the B version composed it (IX.293–94; cf. B VIII.119–44). Where Piers briefly becomes a speaking presence later in Passus XV (137–49), he celebrates patient love, what Derek Pearsall describes as "the ruthlessness of perfect love: 'Love your enemies' (Matthew 5.44, Luke 6.27), the revolutionary core of the sermon on the Mount."[73] Certainly Patience is far more like Piers in this respect than Rechelesnesse, whose disposition is described as "rage" towards "clergie," not love. But Piers does not say anything about mendicant poverty or about voluntary poverty being the most perfect Christian state of life. The mendicant Patience, however, does.

The discourse on poverty in Passus XV is wittily set up by bringing together *Activa Vita*, or Actyf, and Patience (XV.181–231). The former is associated with Piers the Plowman, the agricultural producer and overseer of labor whom we followed in Passus VIII. He identifies himself as "Peres prentys þe plouhman," and he works "alle peple to conforte." He states that he labors for Piers, "his man, þat ydelnesse hate" (XV.193–94, 212–13). So in *Piers Plowman, Activa Vita*, Actyf, is the way a community achieves the *fyndynge* which sustains its embodied existence (XV.197–201, 214–16). He represents the human cooperation and labor which enables mendicants like Patience to demand "mete for a pore man or moneye" (XV.35).

Patience, however, challenges Actyf with what he presents as a *rival* account, picking up the language of *fyndynge:*

> Hit am y þat fynde alle folke and from hunger saue
> Thorw the helpe of hym þat me hyder sente
>
> (XV.235–36)[74]

Seeking to silence Actyf ("Pees!" XV.232), Patience presents the "lyflode" (XV.237) he offers as a displacement of Actyf's claims that his labor is for the community's essential *fyndynge.* We have already been told that the food Patience carries in his bag is sobriety, simple speech, and true faith, comforting food in "hungry contreys" where "vnkyndenesse and coueytise" dominate (XV.185–88). Allegorical food. He now offers another example from his bag ("his poke," XV.246). This is a piece of the "paternoster": *"fiat voluntas tua* þat sholde fynde vs alle" (XV.247–49). Patience assures Actyf and Langland's readers that this will deliver one from all potential afflictions, whether hunger or cold or imprisonment or lordly oppression (XV.246–53). This is confidently proclaimed. But although Patience is a powerful and sympathetic figure, representing the authority of patient poverty in the poet's Christianity, he was actually introduced to us begging for far more carnal sustenance, "mete" or "moneye" (XV.35). That is, Langland carefully introduces him in his dependency on the productive, material labor of Piers's apprentice, Actyf. The poet then shows Patience soon forgetting this fact as he claims to be quite independent of such labor. Patience attempts to defend this alleged independence from Actyf's *fyndynge* by appealing to God's miraculous provision of food to his chosen people (XV.263–69).

But this displacement of Actyf's *fyndynge* is inadequate. My reasons for this judgment are predominantly theological and in no way question the reality of divine miracles. I also think the theological reasons put forward below are congruent with theological processes unfolding in *Piers Plowman.* In his zeal Patience has slipped into a polarization of his relationship to Actyf, a dichotomization which occludes what the poet himself has showed us: namely, that Patience in his poverty and dependence begged for material food and money, the very products of Actyf's labor in a world where we have seen both Mede flourishing and the crushing lives of those laboring "pore folk in cotes" (IX.73–91). In his dichotomy Patience assumes that Actyf's work and the attention it demands to material and social relations entail the "solicitude" forbidden by Christ (Matthew 6.25–26).[75] But we have no good reason to assume that *all* concern, *all* attention to a *fyndynge* for oneself and others is forbidden by God as "solicitude" incompatible with faithful Christian discipleship. As Aquinas observed in the *Summa contra Gentiles:*

> Indeed, every act requires solicitude. So, if a man ought to have no concern for corporeal things, then it follows that he ought not to be engaged in corporeal action, but this is neither possible nor reasonable. In fact, God has ordained activity for each thing in accord with the proper perfection of its nature. Now, man was made with a spiritual and bodily nature. So, he must by divine disposition both perform bodily actions and keep his mind on spiritual things. However, this way of human perfection is not such that one may perform no bodily actions, because, since bodily actions are directed to things needed for the provision of life, if a man fail to perform them he neglects his life which every man is obliged to preserve. Now, to look to God for help in these matters in which a man can help himself by his own action, and to omit one's own action, is the attitude of a fool and a tempter of God. Indeed, this is an aspect of divine goodness, to provide things not by doing them directly, but by moving others to perform their own actions, as we showed above [III.77]. So, one should not look to God in the hope that, without performing any action by which one might help oneself, God will come to one's aid, for this is opposed to the divine order and to divine goodness.[76]

Aquinas, as usual, takes our embodied and social nature seriously. Our embodiedness within a community is part of the divine disposition, part of the proper perfection of our life which combines "a spiritual and bodily nature." In this perspective Patience's invocation of divine miracles to displace and dismiss Actyf's productive labor could seem the utterance of a "tempter of God." It undoubtedly involves a serious abuse of divine miracles. How this is so is brought out with great clarity by the Dominican theologian Hervaeus Natalis in his reflections on solicitude and voluntary poverty written for John XXII. Objecting to Franciscan uses of Matthew 6.34 ("be not therefore solicitous for tomorrow" [Nolite ergo solliciti esse in crastinum]), he argues that providing for the future does not diminish personal perfection—that is, love of God and love of neighbor. In fact, God created us as the kind of creatures who need temporals and need to give these attention. Total lack of solicitude is, as Aquinas maintained, incompatible with the life God has given us to live on earth.

Even contemplative life would be impossible without a *fyndynge,* he argues. One is actually obliged to make provision for necessities in the circumstances in which God has placed one. As for the appeal to divine miracles of provision, such as Elijah experienced (3 Kings 17), to which Patience appeals, Hervaeus observes that while no one denies God's power to feed people miraculously, the miracles done for a few do not make a common rule. Many holy people, he recalls, have never received such help.[77] There can be no coherent objection to this line of argument.

And Patience does add two lines that come from a rather different paradigm from the one he has deployed against Actyf, a paradigm eloquently drawn on by Holy Church in Passus I. Changing tack, he proclaims that if Christians lived "as mesure wolde," Christian communities would experience no "defaute" (XV.270–71a). But what Patience does not appreciate, unlike Aquinas or Hervaeus Natalis, is that for this thoroughly desirable state to exist, Actyf has to give great attention and time, "solicitude," to the production and distribution of the requisite material *fyndynge* about which Patience has been so briskly dismissive. Were Patience to acknowledge this, his turn to allegorical, spiritual food would have to become far more complex than it has been, and his appeal to divine miracles far more theologically careful. But his lack of such nuanced reflections is intrinsic to his enthusiastic espousal of the Franciscan ideology and vocabulary of poverty, an enthusiasm the poem is exploring.

Immediately after this passage Langland gives Patience two questions from Actyf. In the first, he asks, "What is properly parfit pacience?" (XV.272). This is dealt with briefly, in four lines. Patience defines the fulfillment of the virtues he represents in terms of a unifying humility which is led "to our lordes place" by love, "þat is charite, chaumpion chief of all vertues" (XV.274–75). Here Patience acknowledges that his completion depends on the supreme Christian virtue, charity. But he does not conclude his first answer with this. He goes on to gloss charity, "chief of all vertues": "þat is pore pacient alle perelles to soffre" (XV.276). Charity undoubtedly "is patient" and "beareth all things" [omnia sufferet] (1 Corinthians 13.4, 7). But not all "pore pacient" is necessarily identical with the theological virtue of charity, a gift of divine grace.[78] The poem has a great deal more work to do in its exploration of the relations between charity and poverty. In the second question, Actyf asks: "Where [whether] pouerte and pacience plese more god almyhty / Then rihtful rychesse and resonablelyche to spene?" (XV.277–78). This elicits a much longer answer whose exploration of poverty and wealth leads into the most explicitly Franciscan declaration in *Piers Plowman* (XVI.98–113).

Patience sets out with great confidence:

> "ʒe? *quis est ille?*" quod pacience; "quik, *laudabimus eum!*
> Thogh men rede of rychesse rihte to þe worldes ende
> Y wiste neuere renke þat ryche was þat whan he rekene sholde
> When he drow to þe deth that he ne dradd hym sarrore
> Then eny pore pacient; and þat preue y be resoun."
>
> (XV.279–83)

The quotation with which this passage begins comes from Ecclesiasticus [Liber Iesu Filii Sirach] and deserves to be set in its context:

> Blessed is the rich man that is found without blemish: and that hath not gone after gold, nor put his trust in money nor in treasures. Who is he, and we will praise him [Quis est hic? Et laudabimus eum]? For he hath done wonderful things in his life. Who hath been tried thereby, and made perfect, he shall have glory everlasting. He that could have transgressed, and hath not transgressed: and could do evil things, and hath not done them: Therefore are his goods established in the Lord, and all the church of the saints shall declare his alms. (Ecclesiasticus 31.8–11)[79]

As Derek Pearsall notes, Patience's extraction of a sentence from this passage is to suggest "ironically that rich men such as Active mentions will be hard to find."[80] Such irony may be a little too impetuous, in theological terms, perhaps a little too impatient. For the passus has already quoted a statement by Christ that should make us pause: "*Nemo bonus*" [None is good] (XV.135a; Mark 10.18). *Nemo bonus:* rich or poor. If Patience ignores this warning he is likely to reproduce the Pelagian tendencies in Rechelesnesse's oration and in the teaching of the Franciscan friars in Passus X. If he does so, when moving into his most determinately Franciscan utterances, then it would seem that the poet is again asking whether Franciscan accounts of the supreme sanctifying perfection of poverty may encourage such theological and psychological Pelagianism.

Patience continues in a manner that encourages this line of questioning. He seeks to prove his argument about the status of rich and poor at the

Last Judgment "be resoun" (XV.285). He argues that "þe pore" (he does not specify the poor graced with the theological virtues) "dar plede and preue by puyr resoun / To haue allouaunce of his lord" and that "by þe lawe he hit claymeth" eternal joy (XV.285–86).[81] The speaker's enthusiasm for the state of poverty lures him into a strange forgetfulness about a fallen condition that never was r estricted to the wealthy. *Nemo bonus.* Or, in Paul's words, "[A]ll have sinned" (Romans 3.23); "I am carnal, sold under sin. . . . I do not that good which I will; but the evil which I hate, that I do" (Romans 7.14–15). Patience's conviction that the poor "dar plede and preue by puyr resoun" an entitlement to salvation is not warranted within orthodox Christian traditions.[82] Patience's enthusiasm for the virtue he represents in mendicant poverty may be leading him into theological difficulties, but the passus ends with an implicit and moving correction to the passage I have just been considering. Instead of claiming rights of salvation, he reflects on the distribution of visible blessings and material "defaute" among God's creatures. This leads him to say that in such a universe beggars may "aske" for a bliss to redeem the "languor and defaute" they have suffered (XV.287–97). Prayer replaces the proclamation of rights. Furthermore, there is no hint here that Patience's allegorical *fyndynge* is a superior, spiritual *alternative* to Actyf's material and social *fyndynge*. He acknowledges miserable "defaute" that is not transcended, let alone dissolved, by the food in Patience's "poke" (XV.185–88, 246–53). The poetry recreates the mode in which Langland had earlier represented lives of those that "most neden," landless "pore folk in cotes" (IX.70–97):

> Ac beggares aboute myssomur bredles they soupe
> And ʒut is winter for hem worse for weetshoed þey gange,
> Afurste and afyngered and foule rebuked
> And arated of riche men þat reuthe is to here.
>
> (XVI.13–18)

What these people lack is access to Actyf's *fyndynge,* and that is now included in Patience's compassionate prayer. As Aquinas habitually observed, we are made "with a spiritual and bodily nature."[83] The implication in Patience's comments here is that the rich should be distributors of Actyf's *fyndynge* to those living the kinds of life Patience describes. What Patience has not addressed is how the material *fyndynge* he wishes the rich to share with those in "defaute" can be produced in a way that is compatible with his Franciscan understanding of the commands to eschew solicitude for one's life (Matthew 6.25). He is overwhelmed by his evangelical sense of the immense dangers of wealth: "Allas þat rychesse shal reue and robbe mannes soule / Fro þe loue of oure Lord at his laste ende" (XVI.1–2). In the power of the response there is no suggestion of any such way. Patience's vision seems to put Actyf in a double bind.

Perhaps he glimpses a way beyond this in the proposal that Christians should be "in commune ryche, noon coueytous for hymsulue" (XVI.42). The abandonment of personal dominion while retaining common dominion and possessions seems to extend monastic and Dominican ideas of the best possible arrangement of Christian living to the whole community. But this would involve a rejection of the Franciscan version of the most perfect life as abandonment of both individual and common dominion. It also leaves the questions raised before: How can a Christian community attend to just modes of production and distribution without contravening Patience's Franciscan understanding of "solicitude"? And how is this suggestion of Christian communism compatible with his earlier celebrations of a purely allegorical *fyndynge* supported with divine miracles? Patience does not pause to address these issues. Instead he moves on to defend the familiar position that material poverty makes everyone safe from the "seuene synnes" (XVI.43–97).

Part of the problem with this position on the benefits of involuntary poverty, as I pointed out when discussing Rechelesnesse's oration, is the poem in which it is set. We recall that Langland chose to represent the seven deadly sins in practices which were largely free from "rychesse," largely free from dominion, land, and wealth. Indeed, they were often presented as conspicuously poor (V–VIII; IX.98–104, 189–214). *Piers Plowman* itself has thus shown that the lack of wealth and power does not necessarily encourage virtuous living. Nor is this theologically surprising given the understanding of our condition as fallen creatures in Christian tradition: "*Nemo bonus.*" So when Patience asserts that the poor are less prone to anger, one is not left to wonder whether the poet has considered the provocations to wrath generated by the acute lack of material resources and social power that constitute poverty. The poem itself has shown that Wrath dwells among "alle manere men" and has provided the image of Wrath smiting "with stoon and with staf"—that is, with the weaponry of those who are distinctly lacking in wealth and status (VI.105–7). We find similar problems with Patience's claims about Gluttony (XVI.71–78). Patience argues that because the poor cannot afford "ryche metes" they are less prone to this deadly sin. But he himself acknowledges that ale is desired and drunk by the poor in a manner that is "glotonye" and "grete synne." How could he not acknowledge this, given the memorable scene at "Betene hous the brewstere" and its aftermath? (VI.350–435; see too VIII.122–26, 324–40). The same can be said about covetousness. Patience claims that because "pouerte is bote a pety thing" it tends to escape the clutches of this vice (XVI.79–84). But the poet's representation of Couetyse has not supported this line (VI.196–285a; see too 308–14). He displays this deadly sin among those who could certainly not be classified as "þe ryche" and are often depicted as living in poverty. For example: Couetyse confesses to having been a servant of "symme at þe style," apprenticed in a service that entailed deception for his master's profit (VI.206–14). He offers other similar figurations: thieving from merchants' bags (VI.235–36); secretly stealing from a neighbor's purse or house, or encroaching on the margins of his land (VI.264–71). These are hardly figurations of the rich and powerful. In them we are carefully being shown that covetousness is a disposition of "will" (VI.272–75). And we see Wille, a poor beggar, being overwhelmed by "coueytisie-of-yes" (XI.164–75, XII.3–4). Pride and Envy (the latter omitted by Patience) also go across classes and explicitly include the poor (VI.14–102). The final sin considered by Patience is Sloth (XVI.94–99). He recognizes that poverty may be accompanied by this sin. Nevertheless, he claims that wretchedness [Meschief] is always [ay] an instrument that compels the poor person [maketh hym] to acknowledge God as his greatest help "and no gome elles." Patience also asserts that the wretchedness of slothful poverty compels the subject to acknowledge that he is always God's servant "and of his secte bothe."[84] This is a fascinating assertion. We are told that poverty in itself and necessarily generates the remedies to a deadly sin. It allegedly compels the slothful to recognize what Rechelesnesse had proclaimed: "god, as þe gospel saith, goth ay as þe pore" (XII.101).[85] But to recognize "god" in Jesus, the poor Christ, let alone to follow him as his servant, is an act of faith, and faith is a theological virtue, a gift of God's grace.[86] Here Patience, like Rechelesnesse, fails to acknowledge the utter paralysis of the will in the deadly sin known as sloth, so close to despair (see VII.55–80), itself related to Rechelesnesse (XI.196–98).[87] Patience fails to see that someone in a state of sloth *cannot* exercise the virtues of faith and discipleship. Sin resides in the habits of the will, and the will is thus enchained.[88] It is, as *Piers Plowman* will dramatize, against the Pelagian or "semi-Pelagian" wishes of many voices within and without the poem, *semyuief* (XIX.57; Luke 10.30). Neither poverty nor wealth can free such a will. This kind of failure to grasp the consequences of sin for the freedom of the will and the practice of the Christian virtues is traditionally designated

Pelagianism. As in Rechelesnesse's case, the motivation for such insouciance is the zeal to persuade us of the immense ethical and spiritual benefits of involuntary, material poverty.

At this point Patience may perhaps indicate an awareness of the serious difficulties informing his position. For he prefaces his next proposal with a statement disclaiming the relevance of his previous argument to the one he is about to offer. It makes no difference to the latter, he says, whether the slothful poor are or are not servants of Christ who think that God is their help: "And where he be or be nat, a bereth þe signe of pouerte" (XVI.98). He follows this preface by declaring that the poor "bereþ þe signe of pouerte / And in þat secte oure saueour saued al mankynde" (XVI.98–99). This echoes Rechelesnesse's emphasis that, "god, as þe gospel saiþ, goth ay as þe pore" and that Christ has often been known in the "likenesse" of the poor (XII.101, 122). But even Richard Fitzralph acknowledged that Jesus lived a life of poverty, and the issue was always the contexts in which this observation was set and the consequences drawn from it.[89] Patience's conclusion is that because Christ was poor he constituted "þe signe of pouerte" which makes the will of the poor person irrelevant to the efficacy of the sign. His implicit model seems to be the classic teaching on sacramental signs. They are divinely instituted, and their sanctifying powers are not diminished by the inadequacies of the ministering priest. So the poor person's sloth is said to be irrelevant to the force of the sign. But no theology of the sacramental signs maintained the total irrelevance of the adult recipients' dispositions. Could any theologian forget Paul's threatening words about the sacrament of the altar: "whosoever shall eat this bread, or drink the chalice of the Lord unworthily, shall be guilty of the body and of the blood of the Lord. . . . [H]e that eateth and drinketh unworthily, eateth and drinketh judgment to himself, not discerning the body of the Lord" (1 Corinthians 11.27, 29)? Patience, however, seems so certain about the sanctifying power of the sign of poverty in itself that he is prepared to set aside the subject's dispositions. In accord with this line, he returns to the language of rights:

> Forthy alle pore þat pacient is of puyr rihte may claymen
> Aftur here endynge here heuenryche blisse.
>
> (XVI.100–101)

Since I have illustrated the dire theological difficulties with this kind of claim, there is no need to rehearse the analysis. Even Patience's addition of the qualifier "pacient" to poverty does not mitigate the problems of asserting a claim on eternal life by "pure rihte." Such a claim is simply incompatible with orthodox Christian traditions and their complex discourses of human "merit." We are once more left with the Pelagianizing assumptions encountered earlier in Patience's speech and in Rechelesnesse's.

The poem now moves from involuntary poverty to voluntary poverty and its most explicitly Franciscan passage:

> Moche hardyore may he aske þat here myhte haue his wille
> In lond and in lordschipe and lykynge of body
> And for goddes loue leueth al and lyueth as a beggare.
>
> (XVI.102–4)

Unlike "lunatyk lollares" or other involuntary poor, these people could have sustained life among the wealthy but chose to renounce "al" to become mendicants, "for goddes loue." Because Patience believes that the involuntary but patient poor may claim eternal joy "by puyr resoun," "by puyre lawe" and by "puyr rihte" (XV.283–86, XVI.99–100), it is not surprising that he believes the voluntary poor living as mendicants can make such claims even more securely. He speaks with the kind of assurance we find in the fourteenth-century Franciscan manual *Fasciculus Morum*. There we read that the "standard" of God the eternal king "is the sign of poverty, to which he had given special preference" [vexillum signum est paupertatis quam ipse specialiter preelegit].[90] Patience himself reiterates the unique status of "þe signe of pouerte." Since patient poverty is "syb to crist sulue and semblable bothe," the voluntary poor enact a Francis-like marriage to poverty (XVI.111–13).[91] This is the heart of the poem's reconstruction of a Franciscan understanding of "þe signe of pouerte" as a sanctifying sign, especially efficacious for those voluntarily espousing it in a mendicant life. And it is forcefully done. But serious questions in Patience's oration, to which I have drawn attention, remain unaddressed. This Franciscan marriage to poverty, "syb to crist hymsulue," is not, by a long way, the poem's last word on the sign of poverty.

Langland continues the exploration by allowing Actyf to respond. Patience, after all, was answering his questions about the theological evaluation of poverty and licit wealth reasonably spent (XV.277–78). Far from being impressed with Patience's Franciscan answers, Actyf is thoroughly irritated. He now asks "al angryliche and Arguinge as hit were" just what "pouerte" is (XVI.114–15). The poet wants to give still more space to the Franciscan voice articulating "þe signe of pouerte." Actyf's resistance invites the teacher to expatiate. It provides an opportunity to get a little more specific about the issue Aquinas and Hervaeus Natalis so cogently saw as central to disputes over evangelical poverty, namely, the issue of "solicitude," of anxiety in the production, acquisition, and consumption of a *fyndynge*.[92]

But Patience is unable to take this opportunity. Instead, he defines poverty in an encyclopedic and aphoristic mode which largely recapitulates his earlier emphasis on the immense advantages of material poverty, including involuntary material poverty (XVI.116–57; see XVI.48–97). His praise of poverty and its role as a powerful device against sin merely raises many of the questions we considered in his earlier statement of this view. Perhaps it is worth recalling, once more, that the pressure to put such questions to Patience's speech comes from *Piers Plowman* itself. For example, Patience tells Actyf that poverty is in itself a removing of cares [*Remocio curarum*] and a subverter of pride (XVI.116–22; see XVI.48–65). However, if we remember the poet's powerful images of the crushing and endlessly demanding poverty shaping the lives of families living on the margins of subsistence as landless laborers (IX.70–97), this assertion will seem, at best, smugly ignorant. We have been shown such poor people striving to meet the demands of "chief lordes rente" and told about the crying of their children who "greden aftur fode" that the family lacks despite working endlessly. This is not a "*remocio curarum*," material or spiritual. Nor is it "*sanitatis mater*," mother "of mannes helthe" (XVI.137–38a). In fact, *not* to be crushed by such poverty in the midst of unending patient labor would require the theological virtues which are the gifts of divine grace and emphatically not the necessary consequence of any such social state. The poem itself works strongly against tendencies to reify the sign of poverty in the oration of this Franciscanizing speaker. And its critical exploration of the relevant issues still has a long way to go.

In the middle of Passus XVI Patience is succeeded by Liberum Arbitrium, Actyf's "ledare." This leader is introduced as "*liberum arbitrium*," one who knows Conscience and Clergie well. He is "cristes creature" and well known "in cristes court" (see XVI.159–72).[93] From this moment Patience never reappears. Nor is he ever recalled and referred to as an authority. These facts set us the task of grasping just what kind of succession is involved here and just how Patience's teaching in poverty and perfection relates to those who follow him.

The transition from Patience to Liberum Arbitrium is made with the latter agreeing that land and lordship are debilitating for anyone "at his partynge hennes" (XVI.160–61). But the model of virtue and salvation that he develops is significantly different from Patience's (XVI.158–XVIII.180). At the center of his discourse Liberum Arbitrium binds together the contemporary Church, "persones and prestes and prechours of holy churche," and the theological virtue of charity (XVI.231–85; see too XVII.41–321). Virtue is inextricably bound up with the Church, the divinely given root through which people are to become sanctified (XVI.242–55). *"Si sacerdocium integrum fuerit tota floret ecclesia; Si Autem coruptum fuerit omnium fides marcida est"* [If the priesthood is sound, the whole church flourishes; if however it is corrupt the faith of all is rotten] (XVI.273).[94] Instead of contexts set by the questions "What is properly parfit pacience" and "Where pouerte and pacience plese more god almyhty / Than rihtful rychesse and resonablelyche to spene" (XV.272, 277–78), the search is now explicitly for charity. Wille tells Liberum Arbitrium that he has yet to find charity except "figuratyfly" (XVI.286–97). His searching question is, "Where may hit be yfounde?" (XVI.287). Liberum Arbitrium begins an answer "as holy churche witnesseth," outlining the qualities and disposition of charity (XVI.298–315). Langland then gives Wille the question to which his poem constantly returns, the question of *fyndynge:* "Ho fynt hym his fode?" (XVI.316). As Wille had remembered that his father and his friends "foende" him to school (V.36), so now he asks whether Charity's *fyndynge* comes from "frendes" or rents or other forms of "richesse to releue hym at his nede?" (XVI.316–17). Wille thus links Charity with issues of *fyndynge* and material *nede.* In this, he serves his maker's preoccupations.

At first it seems that Liberum Arbitrium is simply going to repeat the strategies of Rechelesnesse and Patience over the issue of *fyndynge.* This involves allegorizing the *fyndynge* into spiritual food so as to displace the need for Actyf's labor and invoking saints whose bodily needs were met by divine miracles. Liberum Arbitrium tells Wille that Charity has a friend "þat fynd hym" every day. Like Patience he quotes Scripture: *"aperis-tu-manum"* [Thou openest thy hand: and fillest with blessing every living creature] and *"Fiat-voluntas-tua"* [Thy will be done] (Psalm 144.16; Matthew 6.10) (XVI.320–21; see XV.246–49). He may also be alluding to Rechelesnesse when he says that Charity never "reccheth" of rents or wealth (XVI.318–21). But unlike his predecessors he actually has no intention of substituting allegorical for material *fyndynge.* He tells Wille that Charity actually pays for the food and clothes of poor people and prisoners. Liberum Arbitrium thus *combines* unequivocally material comfort with a spiritual comfort which centers on preaching about Christ's suffering and visiting "fetured folk and oþer folke pore" (XVI.324–30). Patience had been shown begging for ma-

terial food and money, as I highlighted (XV.34–35), while failing to acknowledge this, let alone to examine its significance, in his speeches to Actyf.
Liberum Arbitrium, however, recognizes that Charity is involved in a market where food becomes a commodity acquired by monetary exchange. If
Charity is to pay for food he must have social resources that the poor do
not have while still maintaining his identity as Charity. Perhaps remembering the Franciscan assumptions of Rechelesnesse and Patience, Wille asks
whether the "clerkes" of an endowed "holy churche" can know Charity
(XVI.339).

Liberum Arbitrium does not deny that "clerkes" can know Charity but
says that the one who knows Charity "most parfitliche" is Actyf's master,
Piers the Plowman (XVI.339–40a). In the previous passus Piers briefly appeared to proclaim the love of enemies and the material endowment of this
love "with thy catel" and with "kynde speche" (XV.137–46). Here the supreme form of Christian love plainly has material resources which Piers
does not present as an impediment to perfect love, let alone as a danger to salvation. Liberum Arbitrium tells Wille that one cannot discern Charity by
clothing or by words. It is, after all, a theological virtue perfecting the subject's will. But although God alone sees people's thoughts, we learn that we
may discern Charity "thorw werkes." Liberum Arbitrium quotes John 10.38:
"*Operibus credite*" [believe the works] (XVI.340a–42a). His approach begins
to unravel a pervasive assumption in the speeches of Rechelesnesse and
Patience: namely, that external poverty is a decisive sign in the quest for
sanctification. It delegitimizes Patience's assertions about the relations between involuntary poverty and the deadly sins. The unraveling continues.

Liberum Arbitrium insists that Charity is found anywhere: "in russet,"
"in gray," and in the hallmarks of the extremely rich and powerful, "in grys
and in gult harneys." He is also found among monarchs and ecclesiastics
(XVI.345–49). We see that Charity can indeed "paye" for the food of the
poor and provide material *fyndynge* for them. And "them" includes the
vociferous mendicant Patience (XV.34–35). The answer to Wille's question, "Ho fynt hym his fode?" (XVI.316), has now been given: Actyf does.
This was not Patience's understanding. Liberum Arbitrium finds Charity
almost anywhere and everywhere. He has seen Charity as priests, as ecclesiastics, as those wealthy enough to ride horses, as those "in raggede clothes,"
as the extremely rich and as those in the king's court giving true counsel
(XVI.350–61). The poor are of course included in this vision, but there is no
knowledge of poverty as a special sanctifying sign. Indeed, the speaker explicitly *precludes* mendicants from identification with Charity: "Ac biddyng

als a beggare byhelde y hym neuere" (XVI.352). Most striking about this
utterance is Liberum Arbitrium's refusal to make customary distinctions
between different kinds of mendicancy (beggars with bags, beggars without bags, witless "lunatyk" nonbegging beggars, counterfeit beggars, religious beggars).[95] He simply "neuere" sees Charity as a mendicant. Surely
he has, like us, seen Patience clamoring for food and money (XV.34–35)?
If he has, and how could he not, he is questioning Patience's gloss of his
own mendicant poverty as, necessarily, charity (XV.275–76). It seems that
the sign of poverty, so lovingly composed by Rechelesnesse, Patience, and
their author, is now being superseded. Even a brief concession to Franciscanism contributes to this supersession as Liberum Arbitrium remembers
that Charity has been found in the clothing of a religious mendicant but
only "ones," and then long ago, "in franceys tyme" (XVI.355–56). Now he
walks "in riche robes rathest" (XVI.353).

In this context Liberum Arbitrium corrects the use Patience has made of
a text in his arguments with Actyf: Ecclesiasticus 31.8–11 (XVI.358–59a,
XV.279). The Old Testament text (quoted earlier in this chapter) praises the
virtuous rich man and promises that his material goods will be "established
in the Lord." Patience, however, took one verse from its context to suggest
the immense unlikeliness of any rich people pleasing God anything like as
much as the patient poor (XV.279–83, discussed above). Liberum Arbitrium
has just developed an account of Charity which rejects the simple dichotomy
and the ideological model which generates it. Having done so he reaffirms
that Charity commends rich people who live "lelelyche" in love and faith. In
this he quotes from Ecclesiasticus 31, taking the verse preceding Patience's:
"*Beatus est diues sine macula*" (XVI. 359a): "Blessed is the rich man that is
found without blemish: and that hath not gone after gold, nor put his trust in
money nor in treasures" (Ecclesiasticus 31.8). As Aquinas says of this text,
this kind of rich man "has done a difficult thing. . . . [T]hough placed among
riches, he did not love riches" (*ST* II–II.186.3, ad 4).

At the end of Passus XVI, Liberum Arbitrium states once more that
Charity does not beg. Charity, he maintains, considers all begging a vice
(XVI.372–74). His supersession of the Franciscanizing sign of poverty and
the elaborate casuistry of mendicancy it encouraged does, however, offer a
qualification Wille takes up in the next passus. One kind of begging *is* practiced by Charity: begging directly to God. This is in obedience to Christ's
instruction: "*Panem nostrum cotidianum & c.*" [Give us this day our daily
bread] (XVI.374a, Matthew 6.11; see XVII.1–2).

Wille opens Passus XVII by commenting that at "som tyme" every human must beg, "be he ryche or pore" (XVII.1–2). If Wille means that the survival and development of any human involves complete dependency on others, he is unquestionably correct. But if he hopes that because human beings beg from God, as Christ taught (XVI.373–74a), Liberum Arbitrium will withdraw his condemnation of modern mendicancy, his own form of life (V.44–52, XV.3–4), then he is to be disappointed. Having "neuere" seen Charity living as a beggar (XVI.352), Liberum Arbitrium now confirms this claim and returns to Patience's invocation of divine miracles to replace Actyf's form of *fyndynge* (XV.246–71a). In accord with the nuanced approach of Hervaeus Natalis, Liberum Arbitrium carefully restricts the scope of Patience's claims. God has indeed miraculously fed certain people. The ones Liberum Arbitrium mentions are solitaries enclosed in cells or living in isolation from human communities.[96] They are not mendicants and they illustrate what he means by begging only from God (XVII.4–16, 21–31). Explicating the implications of his argument, he turns to apostles who pursued Actyf's mode of *fyndynge*. Paul, after he preached, worked for his livelihood: "wan with his handes al þat hym nedede." Peter and Andrew not only fished but also, according to Liberum Arbitrium, "solde" fish for their livelihood (XVII.17–20).[97] Twice in this passage Liberum Arbitrium insists that these holy people lived "[w]ithoute borwynge or beggynge" (XVII.8, 27). But by observing that Paul, Peter, and Andrew worked and produced commodities while God fed certain holy hermits by divine miracles, Liberum Arbitrium does not mean that the modern Church has no place for *nonmendicant* holy hermits. He proclaims that the latter should have a *fyndynge* provided for them: "trewe man alle tymes sholde / Fynde honest men and holy men" (XVII.33–34).

Liberum Arbitrium has thus done a number of things in this passage. He has decisively reiterated his view that Charity "neuere" chooses mendicancy as a way of life in the modern Church (XVI.352). He has carefully corrected and restricted Patience's broad appeal to divine miracles. He has corrected Patience's displacement of Actyf's form of *fyndynge:* nonmendicant hermits serving God are to be fed from Actyf's *fyndynge* and are not to rely on Patience's allegories or divine miracles.[98] Indeed, he tells the rich that charity begins at home, with their "kyn." This precedes giving to the religious or priests or pardoners. After one's "kyn" the obligation is to those in "moest nede." Such is charity in obedience to Christ (XVII.56–64). The Church can and should (but doesn't [XVI.242–80; XVII.69–85, 206–40]) act on similar principles. It can do so because it has a material *fyndynge* from which it should minister to those "in defaute" (XVII.68). This material *fyndynge* Liberum Arbitrium designates, traditionally enough, as "goddes goodes" and "Cristes tresor" committed to "pore peple" (XVII.67–70). Like Holy Church in Passus I, this teacher envisages the Trinity as a Creator calling, not for starkly ascetic lives but, even in a fallen world, for "plente and pees" (XVII.91–96). Such a gracious and abundant God is praised in just and generous division of resources.

Liberum Arbitrium insists that Holy Church, the creedal Church, *is* Charity, as he himself has been explicating this virtue (XVII.125–29).[99] But he laments the failure of the contemporary Church's mission to "Sarraysens" and Jews (XVII.122–24, 132–300). His sadness and frustration at this takes a Wycliffite turn. Because the Church's failures include alleged abuses in its material endowments, Liberum Arbitrium sees the latter as a poison destroying clerical powers and perfection (XVII.220–32). His solution is to call in the lay elite as physician. Its remedial "medecyne" is coercive disendowment of the "heuedes of holy churche and tho that ben vnder hem." This coercive political action, according to Liberum Arbitrium, is charity: "Hit were charite to deschargen hem for holy churche sake" (XVII.227–31). Charity thus includes not only wealthy ecclesiastics and the powerful elites symbolized by gilt armor (XVI.346, 353–54) but also the coercive action of the laity to disendow the modern Church, "for holy churche sake." Who speaks for "holy churche" against its embodiment (or disfiguration) in the modern Roman Church, and by what authority? Liberum Arbitrium fails to address such vexing questions but draws on a distinctively Wycliffite understanding of charity, as W. W. Skeat and many others have noted.[100] Once they have taken "londes and ledes, lordschipes and rentes" from the Church, the lay powers are exhorted to provide a *fyndynge* for the clergy through "dymes [tithes]" (XVII.216–28). One implication of such an arrangement is that no path will be reopened to the mendicant life discredited by Liberum Arbitrium as inimical to Charity. It is precluded by the *fyndynge* he envisages in a move that foreshadows the poem's final reflections on the reformation of the friars (XXII.380–84).

But this fact does not mean that on every issue Liberum Arbitrium reaches the poem's final determination. He is powerful and authoritative, well known in Christ's court and "cristes creature," as we observed (XVI.165–70). But his arguments and passionate ecclesiological proposals belong to a process which he is making but which he does not contain: adapting the language with which Chaucer ends *Troilus and Criseyde*, he is circumscribed by that which he cannot circumscribe or grasp. The poem's Christocentric explorations of charity and Church certainly do not end with Liberum Arbitrium's Wycliffite image of ecclesiastic reform in Passus XVII. He himself moves to rather different meditations in the next passus, where he introduces the tree of Charity. His very authority as a Christian teacher is displayed in the way he leads Wille and us to figures of indubitably greater authority: the Samaritan Christ, Christ in the poet's *vitae Christi*, Christ in the harrowing of Hell, Christ resurrected, the Holy Spirit and Piers as the divinely appointed mediator of the work of Christ in his Church (XVIII–XXI). Through these figures the poem enriches its understanding of Charity and Church, of what it means to proclaim that "Charite" actually "is holy churche" (XVII.125). Any reading that identifies Charity and reform of the Church with Liberum Arbitrium's Wycliffite moment is in error. Just as the poem composed the Franciscan perspectives of Rechelesnesse and Patience within a process where their positions were essential moments but ones whose full unfolding was still to come, so the poem composes a Wycliffite moment in an authoritative figure's attempt to envisage a practical response to his conviction that the modern Church has allowed itself to be assimilated by the lures of possessions and dominion generalized as "the world." This Wycliffite moment is a forceful response to the situation as perceived by Liberum Arbitrium, an understandable response to his frustration with what he sees as a lack of reforming energies within the ecclesiastical hierarchy. It encourages his readers to think seriously about the potentials of a Wycliffite reformation to address, charitably, the sources of Liberum Arbitrium's frustration, namely, the Church's current failures of evangelism in the poet's country and far beyond its shores and traditions.

Yet this Wycliffite moment stimulates a range of questions which Liberum Arbitrium fails to address: How exactly would the wealthy laity's expropriation of the Church's collective material wealth enhance the evangelism Liberum Arbitrium demands? Would the will of this lay elite be informed by charity as it took "here londe"? Langland's treatment of the virtues and the will in *Piers Plowman* makes it plain that if the expropriators' will were not already informed by the theological virtue of charity, then Liberum Arbitrium would be wrong to assume that "[h]it were charite to dischargen" the common wealth of the Church into the hands of the lay ruling classes. It would, obviously enough, be the deadly sin of covetousness, probably accompanied by the deadly sins of pride, wrath, and envy. Do the poem's own representations of the lay elites do very much to give Liberum Arbitrium good reason to think that their appropriation of the Church's material goods would be an act of charity? They do not (see, for example, XI.21–51, XXI.459–76). Nor do the poem's representations of the broader Christian community suggest that the elites' cupidity and lust for dominion would be significantly tempered by other social groups. Liberum Arbitrium himself claims that "the peple . . . contraryen now cristes lawe and cristendoem dispisen" (XVII.250–51). So we are shown how profound theological, ecclesiological, and political questions are evaded in Liberum Arbitrium's Wycliffite assertion that charity and coercive lay disendowment of the Church are one (XVII.231).

Furthermore, a Wycliffite reformation would utterly subvert traditional understanding and practice of the sacraments and priesthood, just as it would transform traditional understanding of how, and through whom, "holy churche" speaks and is interpreted. Yet Liberum Arbitrium does not attack the traditional ascription of spiritual and sacramental powers to the priesthood. On the contrary, he consistently maintains that all that is good in a community comes from the priesthood (XVI.242–47, 252–53). The other side of this exalted evaluation of the priestly office is that if the priesthood [sacerdocium] is sinful, then the whole people is turned to sin (XVI.273). These views assume a traditional sense of the priesthood and its power in Christian communities. Immediately after the passage on disendowment he reiterates that were the priesthood more perfect, led by the pope, then pope and priests would bring all lands to Christ's peace and love (XVII.233–40). This approach to the priesthood is congruent with the poem's pervasive concern with the *sacrament* of penance, a concern which has nothing in common with Wycliffite desacerdotalization and desacramentalization of penance.[101] The final two passus of the poem will not encourage anyone to pursue Liberum Arbitrium's momentary turn to Wycliffite ideology, its ramshackle ecclesiology, or its regal politics.[102]

The poem moves from Liberum Arbitrium's longing for a thriving Catholic evangelism (XVII.238–321) to its dazzling treatment of salvation history and the means of grace which flow from Christ's Incarnation, death, and resurrection. This treatment involves as profound an achievement of specifically Christian allegory as the tradition has produced.[103] The transition to the tree of Charity is made by Wille's hope that Liberum Arbitrium will tell him and teach him "to charite" (XVIII.1–2).[104] He is not to be disappointed, nor is the reader.

But the complex disclosures of charity and salvation history in Passus XVIII set aside the sign of poverty. Given Patience's Franciscan claims about the sign and its role in Christian perfection, this is very striking. Does it signify the supersession of the sign of poverty as the poem concentrates intensely on charity and Christ? Two moments in Passus XVIII seem particularly relevant to this question. The first is in the elaborate depiction of the fruits on the tree of Charity (XVIII.53–102).[105] The first fruits are of one kind (charity) but include three degrees ("weddede men and wedewes and riht worthy maydones") classified into two "lyues": "lyf of contemplacion" and "*Actiua* lyf."[106] The former is illustrated by "monkes and monyals, men of holy churche." Here all traces of Wycliffite ideology have been erased. This life also includes widowed people who forsake their own wills and live chastely. Those pursuing *contemplatiua vita* are the fruit of charity situated at the top of the tree and soonest ripened by the sun—that is, "þe hete of þe holi goest" (XVIII.58–82a). In this model of charity and perfection there is no mention of poverty, no identification of its special status. Yet we are being given one of the poem's major images of Christian perfection. Furthermore, the representation of the tree's fruit explicitly revises one of Rechelesnesse's most striking pieces of exegesis. In proclaiming the special sanctity of the poor, the "beste" and most perfect state, he took the story of Martha and Mary (XII.117–77; see Luke 10.38–42). We remember that Martha "was busy about much serving" while Mary, sitting "at the Lord's feet, heard his word." When Martha complained that her sister left her alone to serve, Jesus replied that Martha was "troubled about many things," whereas only "one thing is necessary. Mary hath chosen the best part." This well-known story was traditionally read as an allegory of relations between the lives of contemplation (and/or consecrated virginity) and the active life.[107] But Rechelesnesse imposed a different allegory, tailored to promote the role of poverty. He glossed "the best part" not as contemplation or holy virginity but as "pouerte": "pouerte god potte byfore and preued for þe betere: / *Maria optimam partem elegit que non auferetur ab ea*" [Mary hath chosen the best part which shall not be taken away from her] (XII.141–41a; see 129–41a). In the tree of Charity episode we find no support for this exegesis and its ideology. The shift here is eloquent. The relations between poverty and charity are not quite as Rechelesnesse and Patience imagined.

The second moment of particular relevance to the issue of poverty is the representation of Christ's life. This emerges from the vision of the tree of Charity, dramatically and with great theological coherence. Through Christ's Incarnation the poet discloses the source, survival, and fulfillment of charity in all its forms (XVII.117–76).[108] Other lives of Christ are composed in the following passus (XIX–XXI). Langland shows a remarkable intensity of purpose in excluding some of the most pervasive conventions in late medieval Christian culture from his representation of Christ. As I showed in *Powers of the Holy*, he sets aside the dominant figurations of Christ's humanity, with their concentration on infancy and passion narratives, the latter replete with details of the torn, tortured, naked, bleeding body of Christ.[109] This decision is congruent with the supersession of specifically Franciscan ideology of poverty and distinctively Franciscan iconography of Christ's life. Langland's representations of Christ focus on the power of Jesus, spiritual and bodily. Even in his infancy he is "Byg and abydyng, and bold in his barnhoed / To haue yfouthte with þe fende Ar fol tyme come" (XVIII.133–36). His incarnate ministry displays his divine power. He is an omnipotent physician. Instead of authorizing Franciscan forms of *identification* with lepers, so graphically illustrated by Angela of Foligno, he *cures* them.[110] Instead of embracing and exalting ascetic rigors of poverty, he feeds people (XVIII.137–44, 152–54). His ministry includes prophetic assertion and dominion (XVIII.155–60). As Conscience later explains to Wille, Jesus's ministry is that of a conqueror (XXI.96–139). Even the passion and crucifixion are briefly narrated in modes that eschew conventional forms imbricated with Franciscan iconography and ideology (XX.26–112a, XXI.140–53).[111] The crucifixion is figured as a joust culminating in the triumphal liberation of souls imprisoned in hell. Langland's displays of divine compassion are inseparable from divine power and energy (XX.74–112a, 269–475). Without polemic or fuss, the iconographic and theological foundations of a Franciscan sign of poverty have been effectively removed.

Are they reconstituted? I will now address this question, beginning with the representation of the three theological virtues as Abraham, Moses, and Christ himself as the good Samaritan (XVIII.181–XIX.336). Abraham arrives on "a myddelenton sonenday," stepping forth from its epistle, Galatians 4.22–31. This text celebrates the transition from the law of the flesh to the promise of liberty in Christ. As Derek Pearsall notes, this is "one of the many N[ew] T[estament] texts in which the life of Abraham is taken as the model of the life of faith under the old dispensation."[112] But it is worth recalling that the figure Langland chooses to symbolize the theological virtue of Faith is a figure called by God to perfection (Genesis 13.14–17; 17.8, 22). Rechelesnesse himself acknowledged this (XIII.5). Not surprisingly, Abraham became a figure much invoked in medieval disputes over the status of poverty. For example, in *De Perfectione Vitae Spiritualis* Thomas

Aquinas reflects on Abraham's call ("esto perfectus" [be perfect]) after considering the famous invitation of Christ to the young man with great possessions ("si vis perfectus esse . . ." [If thou wilt be perfect, go sell what thou hast and give to the poor and thou shalt have treasure in heaven. And come follow me], Matthew 19.21).[113] For the Dominican theologian there is no conflict between God's call to Abraham, whose wealth multiplies in his calling, and Jesus's call to the young man, invited to sell all he has, for the poor, and to follow Christ. This is because Christian perfection does not consist in renunciation itself but in a *way* of perfection [quasi quandam perfectionis viam], a way which consists in following Christ. So someone possessing riches may certainly be on the way to perfection, obediently following Christ and informed by the theological virtues, just as Liberum Arbitrium maintained in *Piers Plowman*. We see how Abraham, the possessor of immense riches, was perfect. He was not ensnared by wealth but joined to God in love. He was, that is, faith perfectly informed by charity. Christ's point in Matthew 19.23–26, according to Aquinas, was not that wealth cannot enter the kingdom but that it does so with great difficulty.[114] In the *Summa Theologiae* he argues that voluntary poverty should be regarded as an emancipatory stage on the way to the perfection which is charity, while involuntary poverty is likely to be a state of torment. Once more he insists that Christian perfection does not essentially consist in poverty but rather consists in following Christ. Poverty must be, not fetishized, but regarded as "an instrument or exercise for attaining perfection" [sicut instrumentum vel exercitium perveniendi ad perfectionem]. As for wealth held in common, "solicitude" for this actually pertains to the love of charity [sollicitudo quae adhibetur circa res communes, pertinet ad amorem caritatis]. To hold money or any other goods in common for the sustenance of the religious community or any poor people, to hold a *fyndynge*, is unquestionably compatible "with the perfection Christ taught by his example" [est conforme perfectioni, quam Christus docuit suo exemplo]. He notes too that after Christ's resurrection his disciples, the source of all models of religious life, kept the price of lands that were sold [pretia praeditorum conservabant], distributing to each according to his need (Acts 4.34–35).[115]

Whether or not Langland had in mind such resonances when he selected Abraham to exemplify faith, he has Abraham articulate an account of Christian belief in the Trinity and a statement of "holy churche" as the mother of "childrene of charite" (XVIII.184–256, 206). Faith never utters a syllable about the place of poverty in the fulfillment of such charity. Not that the *involuntary* poor are absent here. Abraham holds the beggar who lay at the rich man's gate, "a lazar" (XVIII.269–74; Luke 16.19–31). But the passage here has nothing to do with the sign of poverty and its putatively salvific qualities. On the contrary, Lazarus lies in Abraham's lap with "patriarkes and profetes," still bound by "þe deueles power" until Christ liberates him and them, rich and poor. Such is the liturgical time in which Wille encounters Faith/Abraham, time present, time past, and time future contained in time past yet redeemable through Christ's agency in time. The dreamer lives in a time after the harrowing of hell yet to be envisioned (XX), a time that is nevertheless, like Abraham's, a time of waiting and absence. He responds to what he is shown, in his present, with appropriate intensity:

> "Allas!" y saide, "þat synne so longe shal lette
> The myhte of goddes mercy that myhte vs alle amende."
> Y wepte for his wordes . . .
>
> (XVIII.286–88)

Wille's tears are tears shed in the acknowledgment of apparently boundless material and spiritual suffering. They are Christocentric tears of penitential yearning which know nothing of any alleged perfection in the state of poverty, voluntary or involuntary. And these tears, with the words they seal, are the signs of faith informed by charity, signs of Wille's fully attentive, receptive engagement with Abraham.

In Passus XIX the poet introduces Moses and the good Samaritan who is Christ. They figure forth the other two theological virtues, hope and charity. Hope, or Moses, seeks Christ, who will fulfill the law of love in salvation. But in the dialogue between him, Faith, and Wille, we hear nothing about poverty (XIX.1–46). Still, if the sign of poverty were to be revised and reconstituted, it might be done by the incarnate Christ figured as the good Samaritan, even though its absence from the other sustained representations of Christ's life in *Piers Plowman* (XVII–XXI) hardly encourages us to expect it here.

The Samaritan Christ enters a scene composed to correct any Pelagian delusions that may have survived from earlier orations.[116] Riding swiftly to joust in Jerusalem, sitting on a mule, Christ/Charity encounters Abraham/Faith, Moses/Hope, and Wille in a wild wilderness where thieves have attacked a man and left him in a disastrous state, bound up and only half alive:

> Bothe abraham and *spes* and he mette at ones
> In a wide wildernesse where theues hadde ybounde
> A man, as me tho thouhte, to moche care they brouhte
> For he ne myhte stepe no stande ne stere foet ne handes
> Ne helpe hymsulue sothly for semyuief he semede
> And as naked as an nedle and noen helpe abouten.
>
> (XIX.53–58)[117]

The figure who represents fallen humanity cannot move foot or hands, cannot "helpe hymsulue" at all. Half alive, half dead, the person is utterly incapable of *any* act of virtue. Such is the reality of "free" will in a fallen, enchained state. The scene makes all talk about fallen human beings voluntarily embracing a state of perfection in poverty seem rather hollow. The fallen person is unable to cooperate with the rescuing Christ even in the slightest way.[118] The poet shows Christ recognizing that the man is "in perel to deye." He soothes his wounds, picks him up, and organizes his treatment while he continues to Jerusalem. He assures Wille that in this catastrophic situation not even hope and faith, let alone any human medicine, can help. Only sacraments flowing from Christ's work can do so (XIX.48–95). And these necessary sacraments are entrusted to the Church (XIX.73–78, 86–95).[119]

From here the Samaritan's powerful oration composes models of the Trinity and the consequences of belief in the Trinity for the lives of Christians. Gradually it emerges that loving *kindness* is the form of charity which saves *and* perfects humans through grace flowing from relations within the Trinity (XIX.96–334). In this long and moving oration Christ has nothing to say about poverty as a sanctifying sign and nothing remotely resembling the Franciscan versions of Christian perfection outlined by Patience.

He does consider the rich whose salvation had so troubled Patience (XIX.209–75; cf. XV.279–XVI.9). But here too the one decisive issue is *kindness*. Only "vnkyndenesse" to one's fellow creatures quenches the loving forgiveness and grace of the Holy Spirit, regardless of social and economic status. Christ thus affirms the approach to charity articulated by Liberum Arbitrium. Instead of deploying the favored Franciscan texts (such as Matthew 19.21: "If thou wilt be perfect go sell what thou hast and give to the poor"), Christ the Samaritan takes his own parable of Dives and Lazarus, recently alluded to in *Piers Plowman* (XVIII.271–74). He focuses on Luke 16.21, a summary of Lazarus's situation: "Desiring to be filled with the crumbs that fell from the rich man's table, and no one did give him."

That is, Christ focuses on the rich man's refusal to give even the crumbs from his table. It is for his "vnkyndenesse" that Dives is damned (XIX.225–30). So emphatic is Christ about this that he reiterates the judgment twice within ten lines (XIX.225–35). He also makes it very clear that the rich man's place in hell had nothing to do with illicit winnings. Dives accumulated wealth without wrong, without subtle tricks (XIX.233–40). Langland's Christ says absolutely nothing to suggest that wealth in itself is the overwhelming danger that Patience asserted, nothing to suggest St. Francis's convictions about the inevitable contamination of contact with money. On the contrary, he even uses Luke 16.19 (as Hunger did) to advocate that if one has accumulated wealth unjustly, the way to right this in God's judgment is to make friends of the mammon of iniquity by generous giving (XIX.241–52). So Christ affirms the traditional line that riches become a damning trap only if they are used with cruel selfishness, exemplified in the rich man's refusal of meat and money "to men þat hit nedede," "to the nedfol pore." This is failure of charity in its starkest forms: denial of those on the margins of subsistence, turning one's face away from the neighbor in need, and, later, actual murder (XIX.231–43, 255–61). Only such "vnkyndenesse" irrevocably quenches "the grace of the holy goest, godes owene kynde" (XIX.255–56). And without this grace one is worse than *semyuief*.

Here it is worth noting that Langland's Christ treats the story of Dives and Lazarus in a thoroughly Augustinian way. In a sermon preached on the day of the Scillitan saints, Augustine takes up this parable. He reflects on its treatment of wealth and poverty, rich and poor people, addressing the construal of those who have nothing, including mendicants:

> It's certainly not riches that were blamed in the rich man's case, nor poverty praised in the poor man's; but impiety was condemned in the one, piety praised in the other. Sometimes, you see, people hear these things in the gospel, and those who have nothing are delighted, the beggar is overjoyed at these words. "I," he says, "shall be in Abraham's bosom, not the rich man." Let us answer the poor man: "It's not enough, your being covered with sores; add something to yourself for merit."

What the poor can add for merit, Augustine declares, is kindness to those in even greater need (symbolized by the dogs licking Lazarus) and by faith. As for the condemnation of the rich man, Augustine identifies its source: "He ignored the poor man lying at his gate, who for his part was longing for the scraps that fell from his table; no covering, no shelter, no humanity was shown him. That's what was punished in the rich man, callousness, unkindness, conceit, pride, infidelity." He insists that "it was impiety and infidelity that was condemned in him, not riches and affluence in the present." Addressing resistance to his approach, Augustine asks his listeners to think about the place into which Lazarus was lifted up: Abraham's bosom. "Look at the poor man in Abraham's bosom," something *Piers Plowman* had led us to do at the end of Passus XVIII. Augustine then dwells on an issue discussed above, Abraham's immense wealth: "read in the book of Genesis about the riches of Abraham, gold, silver, flocks, household." He then asks: "Why are you objecting to the rich man. The rich man [Abraham] welcomed the poor man." So the rich must "possess wealth like Abraham, and let them possess it with faith. Let them have it, possess it, and not be possessed by it." But what does that mean? Augustine's answer is as powerful as it is disconcerting. He notes that in his culture, as for many in Langland's culture, people "save their riches for their children." He also maintains, in a statement that some aspects of my final chapter will cast in a strange light, that all "love their children more than their riches, love those for whom they are saving up more than what they are saving up." And yet, this is his point, Abraham set his love of God above the earthly life of the "only begotten son" for whom he had been "saving up" and whom he loved (Genesis 22.1–18). So he would undoubtedly have been willing to give all he had to the poor and follow Christ, had he been so called (Matthew 19.16–22). Perfection ("If thou wilt be perfect," Matthew 19.21) is a quality of the will's love of God, whether one possesses wealth or not. Augustine concludes that those possessing wealth with "works of kindness and piety" should "wait for the last day without anxiety," counsel that both Liberum Arbitrium and Langland's Christ affirm.[120]

It is extremely important that the figure who embodies charity, the model of perfection and the complete, redeemed identification of humanity with God, never mentions the special status and desirability of poverty. He never suggests that the excruciating poverty suffered by Lazarus, and the immense host like him, constitutes the sanctifying sign of poverty, even when endured patiently. Langland's Christ chooses to show that Christian perfection consists *not* in poverty but in following Christ, as Aquinas had argued in a subtle distinction directed against Franciscan ideology.[121] In *Piers Plowman* that means following the version of Christ whose particular features and teaching we have been tracing. Christian perfection is constituted by the form of love exemplified and embodied in the poet's dramatization of

Christ's parable of the good Samaritan. In Luke's Gospel the Samaritan, "moved with compassion" [misericordia motus est], enacts the perfection of love to which the divine precepts call their followers: "Go, and do thou in like manner." But the narrative of Samaritan and *semyuief* together with Christ's elaborate commentary in *Piers Plowman* makes it clear that no one can even begin to hear this precept, let alone fulfill it perfectly, without having been placed in the Church, where Christ has left the essential sacraments (XIX.65–77, 83–95). The perspectives established in Passus XIX do not include the Franciscanizing sign of poverty. The arresting representation of our state as *semyuief* also calls into question Patience's version of the will, both in voluntary poverty, freely willing the alleged state of perfection, and in involuntary poverty, freely willing patient endurance of this state. Christ's actions for *semyuief* and his long speeches suggest that Patience's vision lacked adequate attention to the Church and its sacraments, the necessary means of grace left by Christ for the healing of *semyuief*. No one should identify the vision of *Piers Plowman* with the vision of Patience, a constitutive moment in the dialectical process to which it belongs.

It is to the founding of the Church in *Piers Plowman* that I now turn. Here the enigma of the massively glossed "pardoun" of Passus IX is resolved. We have now been given the resources to understand how Christ himself, as "conqueror," gave "Peres power and pardoun" to forgive all people provided that they confess their debts and perform loving restitution, "*Redde quod debes*" (XXI.12–198). The last two passus (like V–VII) show how the demand for such justice is inextricably bound up with the sacrament of penance and its practice in Christian communities. Given this conviction, it is logical that Langland should explore the divine resources poured into the Church after Christ's ascension. The present condition of the Church, so critically depicted by Liberum Arbitrium, is returned to in the light shed by these gifts (XXI.199–XXII.386). My thread through this characteristically inventive, densely concentrated sequence will be to follow the place of poverty in the founding gifts of the Holy Spirit to the Church and in the poem's final representation of the modern Church. That will bring this chapter to its close.

In founding the Church at Pentecost, the Holy Spirit provides "tresor" which is both material and spiritual, both literal and allegorical, both individual and collective (XXI.199–260). He elaborates the treatment of "tresores" by the creedal Church in Passus I (I.41–53, 79–101, 137–202). As

Derek Pearsall observes, we are shown that the Christian community "the world of the Visio," is actually "Christ's Church."[122] In showing this, *Piers Plowman* continues to work against the amnesia and failures of self-knowledge about which Holy Church had complained so long ago as she descended "fro þe castel" to converse with Wille (I.3–9, 72–75). The poem now tries to make its diversely gifted readers recognize their gifts and themselves as Christ's Church, answerable to the source from which they have been poured forth. *Redde quod debes* (XXI.182–94, 259).

Among the remarkable facts about the poem's contemporary application of Paul's epistle to the Corinthians (1 Corinthians 12; XXI.228a) is its apparent comfort with commodity exchange and markets. The Holy Spirit teaches some to earn their livelihood by "sullyng and buggynge" (XXI.234–39). Even intellectual and verbal gifts to "prechours and prestes and prentices of lawe" are envisaged as labor power exchanged for livelihood (XXI.229–33). Here it seems that the Holy Spirit corrects one of the glosses on the two-line pardon of Passus IX. There men of law had been confidently told that "hit is symonye to sulle þat sent is of grace" (IX.55; see IX.44–57). This conventional aphorism is now shown to need careful complication, especially if it is to be free from any risks of the communism ascribed to envy, friars' greed, and distinctly pagan philosophy in XXII.273–79a. For Holy Spirit discloses that the graces he gives can be licitly treated as commodities in relations of exchange where "sullyng and buggynge here bileue to wynne" are themselves among his gifts (XXI.227–35).[123] Equally remarkable is the Holy Spirit's gift of dominion and violence to the Church (XXI.245–47).[124] Striking as it is, this perspective confirms that of Holy Church herself in Passus I (I.90–101).

But it does go against the views of Patience. The latter sees poverty as the virtue necessary to free people from the grave risks of dominion and authority, about which he has nothing affirmative to say. Poverty alone, according to Patience, enables people to fulfill Christ's commandment to abstain from judgment (XVI.120–27a; see too XV.277–86, XVI.94–104). But the third person of the Trinity pours out gifts in a manner that seems to sideline the account of the virtues developed by Patience (XV–XVI). The Holy Spirit certainly does call "somme" to a life of contemplation, "longyng to be hennes, / In pouerte and in pacience to preye for alle cristene" (XXI.248–49). These are the people praised in the poem's Prologue, "As Ankeres and Eremites þat holdeth hem in here selles" (Pr.27–32), and praised too by Liberum Arbitrium (XVII.6–16, 25–34). But Holy Spirit offers no support for the Franciscan claims pursued by Rechelesnesse and

Patience about the special perfection of voluntary poverty. Living the life of contemplation in poverty is presented here as just one among many graces given with boundless generosity by God to his Church, a Church for thoroughly embodied and social creatures inhabiting a fallen world. There is no specification, let alone elaboration, of the suggestion that one "craft" is "clenner" than another. Holy Spirit prefers Christians to acknowledge that "all craft and connynge come of my ʒefte" (XXI.250–55). Furthermore, there is an absence that the poem has made extremely conspicuous. Holy Spirit does not apparently give *mendicancy* to anyone, whether "prechours and prestes" or contemplatives living in "pouerte." Such a silence on the topic of religious mendicancy, from such a source, in the context of the Church's foundation, at this stage of the poem, is extremely eloquent.[125] Nor is this silence broken in the poem's extensive account of the further gifts of the Holy Spirit to Piers, or in the details of "þat hous vnite, holy chirche an englisch" which he constructs, or in the successful defense of this Church (XXI.262–390).

Once Christians reject the covenant to which the sacrament of the altar belongs, reject the obligations to do all they can to mend bonds of community unjustly broken, *redde quod debes,* the Church and its members are in dire trouble (XXI.383–48; see chapter 2 of this book). In this situation the superseded sign of poverty returns (XXII.1–64). It seems fraught with many of the disputed problems explored in the poem, and its figuration as Need has generated sharply divergent critical readings.

Need has been read as a demonic, apocalyptic figure composed from a position congruent with the antifraternal work of William of St. Amour and Richard Fitzralph. He has also been read as a Franciscan friar instructing Wille in "a strictly Franciscan" justification for "the mendicant life," one to which the author, "probably a Franciscan," was committed. Given such extraordinarily opposed interpretations, it is not surprising that Need has also been read as "an ethical and representational enigma," one of the poem's "ultimately irresolvable enigmas" who makes poverty "a wholly ambivalent sign."[126] It seems to me that Need's speech at the opening of the final passus is an attempt to reconstitute a Franciscan version of the sign of poverty but in a context and within a dialectical process which gives readers good cause to criticize and reject the attempt. The poet's rhetorical strategy here is extremely complex.

Need confronts a hungry, mobile, and unhappy dreamer (XXI.1–3; cf. XV.1–3, V.48–52). The first part of his speech is a thoroughly traditional, orthodox denial that property is held absolutely (XXII.6–19). In the face of

life-threatening need, a person may take what is needed "his lyf for to saue."
Need is very careful to insist that such taking must be strictly controlled by
extreme need and the cardinal virtue of temperance, the second of the four
grains given to Piers by Grace (XXII.5–19; see XXI.274–75, 281–88).[127]
This is conventional Christian teaching. It leaves unaddressed the questions
put by Reason and Conscience to the mendicant dreamer in Passus V (discussed above). And it leaves unaddressed Liberum Arbitrium's insistence
that he has "neuere" seen Charity "biddyng als a beggare" (XVI.352, also
discussed above). But that does not undermine the orthodoxy and force of
Need's statement about the rights of survival over the rights of private possession and dominion. The first part of Need's speech belongs to Christian
tradition which had nothing to do with Franciscan ideology in particular.

The second part of the speech begins with a claim that the needy individual may take "[w]ithouten consail of Conscience or cardinale vertues."
But Need has just announced that *spiritus temperancie* is central to any licit
act of taking in need, and he reasserts this strongly (XXII.22; see 5–9). So
the second claim does not cohere with the first. Its development makes
matters worse. For Need sets up a hierarchy within the virtues in which
Temperance is supreme: "For is no vertue by fer to *spiritus temperancie*"
(XXII.23). He defends this claim by asserting that other cardinal virtues
easily become vices (XXII.24–33; cf. XXI.451–79a). Doubtless any moral
virtue is fragile, but Need ignores familiar questions about the interlocking,
interdependent nature of the virtues, and he simply contradicts Conscience's
statement that the "cheef seed þat Peres sewe" is *spiritus Iusticie* (XXI.405–6,
297–308).[128] Yet the problems with Need's claims here are not particularly
related to a Franciscan understanding of poverty.

It is not until the third part of his declamation that Need explicitly
moves into Franciscan ideology (XXII.35–50). He identifies the quality
he personifies, Need, with God's Incarnation. God "toek mankynde and
bicam nedy" (XXII.40–41). Need then appropriates Christ's statement that
whereas foxes have holes and birds have nests he has nowhere to lay his head
(XXII.42–47; Matthew 8.20). He relocates the gospel text, having Christ
speak it from the cross. And he rewrites it to insert himself into Christ's language: "'Ther nede hath ynome me þat y moet nede abyde'" (XXII.46).
Wendy Scase recalls that the gospel text Need uses "was a friars' authority
for complete renunciation." Lawrence Clopper too observes that Matthew
8.20 (Luke 9.58) "plays a key role in all Franciscan discussions of poverty
and is always used to support the assertion that Christ and the apostles had
no *dominium* individually or in common."[129] By dislocating the text's place in

the narratives of Matthew and Luke to relocate Christ's saying "in his sorwe on þe sulue rode" (XXII.43), and by representing Christ's journey to the cross in the passive mode ("nede hath ynome me þat y moet nede abyde"), Need composes Jesus in the dominant late medieval manner outlined earlier in this chapter. This mode was central to Franciscan devotion and its representations of Christ, but, as I have shown, it was one that the poet systematically set aside. In its place he composed an active, prophetic figure of immense power, "conqueror" in his ministry, jousting "conqueror" on the cross, "conqueror" in harrowing hell, "conqueror" in the resurrection: very much the Christ of John's Gospel.[130] Need misrepresents these disclosures of Christ in Passus XVIII–XXI. It follows that, in this poem, whatever the case elsewhere, Need's Franciscanizing model of the imitation of Christ is without good warrant. In the Christocentric narratives of *Piers Plowman*, Need is mistaken when he simply claims divine authority for those who decide to "byde and to be nedy" (XXII.48–50).[131] We are thus shown the return of Patience's ideology in a context which confirms the supersession of its Franciscan tendencies which has been unfolding since the departure of Patience from *Piers Plowman* (XVI.164).[132]

The poet now envisages his Church under the assault of Antichrist (XXII.51–386). Only those the culture perceives as "foles" resist this tyrant (XII.58–68, 74–79). Their folly involves deliberate and courageous resistance to "alle falsenesse" and to all who pursue it, however socially powerful and whatever their status (XXII.65–68). These "foles" are thus certainly not "lunatyk lollares," who, we recall, were witless (IX.105–38). Nor is there any indication that their identity as "foles" is bound up with poverty, whether voluntary or involuntary. We do indeed meet people devoted to the sign of poverty, religious mendicants. But these are not among the "foles" who resist Antichrist. On the contrary, they "folewed þat fende for he ʒaf hem copes" (XXII.58).

But why would friars follow Antichrist for copes? These are not as obvious markers of collective and individual transgressions of claims to collective poverty as the building or dining programs associated with mendicants earlier in *Piers Plowman* (III.38–58, XV.38–109). The answer to the question just posed is that the very commitment to living and wearing the fraternal sign of poverty makes people vulnerable to the gifts of Antichrist and the desire these symbolize. A further implication is that those who think they can freely will the state of absolute poverty, mobile and mendicant, chosen as the most perfect form of life, betray the kind of Pelagian delusions about the condition of the fallen will which emerged in the orations of Rechelesnesse and Patience, delusions analyzed earlier in this chapter. We should also recall that neither Christ nor Holy Spirit have given any indication that voluntary and mobile mendicant poverty is a state created and sustained by divine grace in the Church. Here and later in the final passus Langland discloses that those devoted to constructing, exalting, and wearing the sign of poverty have turned out to be no better Christian guides than the sign-bearing pilgrim of Passus VII (VII.155–81; see chapter 2 of this book).

Meditating on the forces attacking his Church, the poet confirms Liberum Arbitrium's view that the priesthood is decisive in determining the form of Christian community and the *habitus* it fosters (for example, XXII.218–31; cf. XVI.242–85, XVII.233–51). Conscience cries out that "inparfit prestes and prelates" overwhelm Christian conscience (XXII.228–29). Those committed to pursuing the allegedly perfect state of life under the sign of poverty present themselves as the solution to the Church's difficulties. Initially Conscience rejects their claim, recognizing that "they couthe nat wel here crafte" (XXII.231). As we observed, in the generous multitude of graced crafts poured into the Church by Holy Spirit, no link was made between the divine gifts forming "prechours and prestes" and those of mendicant poverty. In fact, we recall, there was no mention of religious mendicancy as a calling or state in the Church founded by Holy Spirit (XXI.213–61). Once Conscience has rejected religious mendicants claiming "to helpe" the Church (XXII.230–31), Need reappears. Just as Wille's neediness at the beginning of the final passus had generated the personification Need, so now the friars' neediness briefly conjures up Need once again (XXII.232–41). But whereas Need instructed Wille, a married mendicant with a family (V.1–2, 48–52; XV.1–3; XX.468–72; XXII.193–98), in the rights of the needy and their affinities with a Franciscan model of Christ, his attitude towards religious mendicants is different. He tells Conscience that their offer to help with the "cure of soules" is motivated by covetousness and provides an explanation for their alleged vices. These failings are actually generated by the very sign of poverty to which they are committed. Because they are "pore" and have chosen a lack of "patrimonye," they ingratiate themselves with the rich. They thus abandon the critical, prophetic force of Christian discipleship which we saw in the "foles" who resisted the tyrant Antichrist (XXII.57–64). Abandoning this force, wearing the sign of poverty, they subject themselves to the tyrant. In response to this, Need advises Conscience to make friars live the rigors of the sign they carry, absolute poverty (XXII.236–37). But he acknowledges the ethical dangers of a mendicant life and concludes with two alternatives. Either let them live this morally dangerous life "as beggares" or let them "lyue by angeles fode" (XXII.238–41).[133] At this stage of *Piers Plowman,* Need's alternatives do not constitute a defense of Franciscan ideology and practice. The option of mendicant poverty has not been proposed by Christ or Holy Spirit, and nothing has been done to overturn Liberum Arbitrium's statement that he has "neuere" seen Charity "biddyng als a beggare" (XVI.352; see too XVII.8, 27).[134] Need himself recognizes that working "for lyflode" and giving to beggars in need is a much safer form of life than voluntary mendicancy (XXII.238–39). The other option, living off "angeles fode" by divine miracle, is of course not institutionizable. Need is in fact now mocking the Franciscan project of absolute mendicant poverty in a manner that makes Conscience himself laugh (XXII.242). The critical irony Need thus directs against both options shows that he has been persuaded by the wider process in which he reemerges to repudiate his earlier alignment with Franciscan ideology and practice around the sign of poverty.[135] This undoing accords perfectly with the direction the poem has taken and continues to take.

Conscience laughs at Need's irony but still invites "all freres" into the house called unity, exhorting them to live according to their rule (XXII.242–47, XXI.328). He makes no distinction between different fraternal orders, and what he now proposes is a fundamental challenge to Franciscan ideology. He promises to ensure that the friars have "breed and clothes / And oþere necessaries ynowe; ȝow shal no thing lakke" (XXII.242–49). To be guaranteed all material necessities, to be guaranteed to lack nothing material, is certainly not the Franciscan marriage to holy poverty invoked by Patience (XVI.111–13), certainly not the identification with the destitute envisaged by St. Francis and his most devoted followers. In fact, Conscience's proposal could spell the end of any distinctively Franciscan project. But at this point its implications are not elaborated. Instead Conscience and the narrator focus on the friars' struggles for status and power in the Church (XXII.250–96). One result of this struggle is the subversion of the sacrament of penance with its integration of restitution (*redde quod debes*) and divine pardon (XXII.279–93; see XXI.182–90, 256–61). But the subversion of this sacrament, according to *Piers Plowman,* cuts people off from God's pardon and the sacrament of the altar (XXI.383–408). And Christ himself, we remember, proclaims that without the latter, *semyuief* who has been rescued in baptism will "neuere" gain strength (XIX.89–90; see chapter 2 of this book).

Trying to defend the Church from the powerful attacks of Antichrist, Conscience calls for "a leche þat couthe wel shryue / To salue the þat syke were and thorw synne ywounded."[136] The obedient priest responsive to Conscience's call concentrates on the relations between sacramental healing and restitution, *redde quod debes* (XXII.306–8). But just as Christians had resisted Conscience's insistence that the sacraments of penance and the altar belong to a new covenant calling for transformed practices in the community (XXI.182–90, 383–408), so now some Christians demand a diminution of penitential practices. Their solution is to call for mendicant confessors represented by "frere flaterrere" (XXII.309–15). Conscience denies that there is any need for confessors who do not belong to the secular clergy. But he then gives way to what the friars desire and sends for them, duly licensed (XXII.316–37). Despite encountering an archetypal antifraternal porter (significantly named Peace), the friars are allowed into the besieged Church and welcomed by Conscience (XXII.329–61). The poet represents this decision as catastrophic for individual Christians and the Church (XXII.362–79). The sanctifying sacramental sign of penance is turned into a drug that enchants Christians and makes them utterly indifferent to sin (XXII.378–79). We have been shown why Christian people welcome such intoxicating confessors. But what motivates the friars?

We recall that in his second appearance Need described the friars' motives as covetousness "to haue cure of soules." This covetousness is caused by the fact that "thei aren pore," and this poverty in turn means that they will "flatere to fare wel folk þat ben riche" (XXII.232–35). The final narrative supports Need's analysis. Not only is the representative friar named "frere flaterrere," but he also acknowledges that he wishes to act "for profit and for helthe." In case we miss the multiple meanings of "profit," the poet shows us how the friar "gropeth contricion," offering prayer and Masses by "freres of oure fraternite for a litel suluer" (XXI.363–67).[137] An institutional commitment to the sign of poverty generates the will to accumulate material resources and privileged status in the Church. Many strands in the poem's explorations of the sign have been leading inexorably to this final moment. In colluding with the friars, despite his strong reservations, Conscience has erred.

But whatever his error, he remains the gift of the Holy Spirit in the Church, "constable" of "vnite, holy chirche an englisch" (XXII.213–14, XXI.328).[138] And the Church too remains the gift of Christ and the Holy Spirit (XXI.182–380). So despite the seemingly overwhelming presence of Antichrist's forces in the Church, Kynde himself orders Wille not to leave the "hous" (XXII.204–6, XXI.328). Wille obeys, completely (XXII.199–213).[139] And Conscience responds to his own mistake. He decides to seek for Piers Plowman, the "procuratour" given to the Church by Holy Spirit (XXI.256–61). With this search he proposes an *ecclesiastical* solution to the disastrous effects of the mendicants' commitment to their sign of poverty. He accepts Need's view that the friars' vices are motivated by their poverty, "for nede" (XXII.232–35, 383). Their very quest for perfection in absolute poverty leads them to oppose Conscience. If the Constantinian endowment of the Church could become "venym" (XVII.220–24), we now know that the commitment to absolute voluntary poverty has become a source of the drug that poisons the Church. Conscience's solution takes up earlier suggestions made by Reason in his presence (V.173–77) and more recent ones he himself offered in the final passus (XXII.248–50). Reason associated ecclesiastical reformation with a *fyndynge* for friars from the Church's endowments, a *fyndynge* that would terminate their mendicancy and terminate all possibility of claiming to pursue absolute communal poverty. Conscience, as we saw, suggested that friars should "haue breed and clothes / And oþere necessaries ynowe" (XXII.248–49). He now proclaims that the Church must provide "a fyndynge" for friars (XXII.383). The Church's *fyndynge* will deliver *all* friars, including radical Franciscans, from their identification with the sign of poverty which the poem has so carefully composed, explored, and superseded.[140] The final supersession of "þe signe of pouerte" is thus part of a proposal by the "constable" of the Church for a radical transformation of its current institutionalization. In a complex dialectical process *Piers Plowman* has disclosed how such institutionalization has encouraged a reification of this sign and its mistaken pursuit as the most perfect life in the Church. Tenaciously and inventively working through these contemporary difficulties, the poet created a powerful model for thinking about signs and sanctification in the Church within which and for which he wrote.

chapter 6

HOME, HOMELESSNESS, AND SANCTITY

Conflicting Models

In *Community, Gender and Individual Identity: English Writing 1360–1430,*
I addressed two very different versions of household, home, and sanctification: Margery Kempe's and the aristocratic forms assumed in *Sir Gawain
and the Green Knight.*[1] For Margery Kempe, family life in a merchant home
was a painful impediment to her pursuit of sanctity. Her commitment to
breaking out of her home in Lynn and embracing a mobile, holy life was
seen by the mayor of Leicester as a threat to patriarchal governance: "I
trowe thow art comyn hedyr to han awey owr wyvys fro us and ledyn hem
wyth the."[2] For Margery Kempe, the only family congruent with her own
experience of sanctification was the holy family she imagined so vividly.[3]
But *Sir Gawain and the Green Knight,* like so many surviving visual and verbal productions of the period, assimilates Christianity to aristocratic and
knightly forms of life. The liturgy and its officiating priests permeate
Arthur's court and Hautdesert. Far from casting critical perspectives on the
Church and secular elites, this integration contributes to a sanctification
of the culture's virtues. Characteristically, Sir Gawain's battle shield has
painted on the inside an image of the Virgin Mary, who blesses and protects
the warrior. The poem provides Christianity for courtly subjects and their
households. Whatever the moral complexities emerging in this form of life,
the pursuit of sanctification calls neither for the abandonment of chivalric
practices nor for their transformation.[4] This social world has been richly illustrated by Kate Mertes and C. M. Woolgar.[5] Mertes shows how aristocratic households (c. 1350–1550) came to include "at least one chapel, with
all the liturgical paraphenalia for mass" (124), "at least one resident chaplain,

and numerous *clerici*" (125), and the full performance of the liturgy together with "generational events" (134; baptism, marriage, funerals). These households fostered "the exercise of traditional forms of pious practice open to the layperson," worship, "observance of the liturgical year," reading books of hours, and frequent almsgiving (130; see 123, 129–36). She exemplifies ways in which aristocratic households created forms of sanctification incorporating the households "into the hierarchical structure of society encouraged by medieval Christianity" (129). The materials which Mertes explores are taken mostly from the period after Arundel's Constitutions (1409), but her study does not suggest that the ecclesiastic hierarchy had any anxiety about the forms of Christianity in such homes. Although *Dives and Pauper* disapproved of secular elites withdrawing from parish churches into their households, this does not seem to have been a widespread concern.[6]

I will now turn from these two contrasting forms of sanctification, forms in aristocratic households and in Margery Kempe's abandonment of home, to other lineaments of sanctity in late medieval homes. *Dives and Pauper* takes up the issue under the first commandment of the second table. The mendicant author's initial approach represents the home as a place in which sanctification seems quite unimaginable. Home actually seems a hellish site of disciplinary conflicts. The author looks back longingly to the good old days of Leviticus (20.9): "God bad hymself in þe elde lawe þat hoso cursyd or bannyd his fadir or modir he schulde ben slayn" (1:306). He seems enthralled by this resolution to conflict in the home, for he returns to it when Dives talks about contemporary children longing for the death of their parents so that they can get control of their "heritage" (1:306). The friar recalls Deuteronomy (21.18–21). An "vnbuxum child" who resists household discipline must be led "to þe rewlours of þe cite." Guilty of disobedience which inevitably flows into "ryot, glotonye and lecherye," the child is stoned to death: "God bad þat al þe peple of þe cite or of þat town schuldyn slen þat vnbuxum child with stonys in example of al oþre" (1:308). At once the Christian moralist moves into the present tense, linking contemporary experience with the texts he has chosen from the Old Testament, as though the former provided an intelligible explanation for the latter's violence against the "vnbuxum child": "For whan ȝong folc waxyn rebel to fadir & moodir & ȝeuyn hem to swyche ryot & welfare & to ydylchep, but þey ben chastysyd & withstondyn in þe begynnynge, þei schul schendyn þe comounte of þe peple be roberye & morde & manslaute, be colligaciouns & wyckyd companyys" (1:308). Imagining the present, the friar moves swiftly from acts of disobedience in the home to murder and organized crime.

Home is the place in which subjects must be taught obedience, the basis of all social discipline. The survival of the "comounte" depends on this discipline. Without it, children will become anarchic subjects who "makyn rebellion & rysynge aȝens her souereyns & so be cause of distruccion of þe lond, of þe cite & of þe comounte" (1:308). Here the author of *Dives and Pauper* is not interested in distinguishing size, status, or class of household. Whatever this may be, the home is, for him, traditionally enough, a decisive institution in the polity.

Having invoked the most violent images of household discipline (on three occasions he invokes the Old Testament commands to stone disobedient children; 1:306, 307–8, 322), the author offers another perspective on the contemporary Christian home. He has Dives ask whether it is "folye" for aging parents to give "gouernance of þe houshold" to their children (1:310). Pauper answers that this is better than giving "gouernance" to "strangeris," at least if the children have been "good & kende" so far (1:310). However, even in this case the teacher sees no reason to trust the ethical and affective bonds of the Christian home: "But for ony trost in hyr childryn, Y wolde nout conseylyn hem fully dismettyn hem of her good but alwey reseruyn þe lordchep to hemself & so kepyn her childryn in her daunger" (1:310–11). This anxious counsel of distrust is built on thoroughly materialist beliefs about family relations and motivations in late medieval England. We can also see that these relations belong to a family that is assumed to be a nuclear one, defined by parents and children, rather than a complex, extended one.[7] But does the text's imagination have any identifiable connections with its society? It certainly does. Joel Rosenthal's recent study of old age in medieval England emphasized "the ambiguity of the aged."[8] Given that most English people were agriculturists, how did they face the years in which they could not manage their own lands and tenants? They made maintenance agreements. That is, they made contractual arrangements in which they traded their lands and resources for carefully stipulated benefits. These contracts were enforceable in manorial courts. They were also made "in towns and cities; in the mansions of the great; in abbots' lodgings, priests' houses and bishops' palaces."[9] Such contracts assumed the distrust expressed in *Dives and Pauper*. But how can a Christian moralist justify *contributing* to such dispositions rather than seeking to transform them? By invoking the wisdom literature of the Old Testament. The author quotes Ecclesiasticus 33.19–20 and after translating it observes that one should not give one's possessions to others, "for happely it may repentyn þe & þan schalt þu preyyn to han help of þin owyn good & þu schalt non haue"

(1:311). He emphasizes this carefully self-regarding advice in relations between parents and children, quoting Ecclesiasticus again (33.22), followed by
two *exempla*, one that happened recently, he says, in Colchester (1:311–12).
Vanished from his memory are all traces of Christ's teaching he had quoted
at the beginning of his work: "But a man forsake al þat he hatȝ he may not
ben myn disciple" (Luke 14.33 [mis-cited as 14.23], 55). There is no attempt
to explain, let alone explore, the relations between "Salomon" and Christ,
between the former's self-protective pragmatism and the latter's gospel of
the Kingdom of God. The different implications for familial relations, discipleship, and sanctification are simply ignored, without comment. This is a
remarkable silence in a work of such prolixity.

It is Dives who turns the dialogue to the New Testament here, although
not to recall Christ's teaching on renunciation of possessions (cf. 54–58). He
challenges the friar's attention to parental power and security in the home by
quoting two hard sayings (1:313): "He þat hatiþ nout his fadir & his moodyr,
he may nout ben myn discipule" (Luke 14.26) and "I cam, seyde he, for de-
partyn man & woman aȝens his fadir & moodir" (Matthew 10.35–38)[10] Pauper seeks to deflect the unsettling force of these texts (1:313–14). First, he argues that Christ said these words when most people were "heþene" and all
parents were "in dedly synne," urging "us" to convert our erring parents.
How such conversion missions would work in the power structures of the
homes he has been seeking to shore up, he does not ask. Second, he argues
that in God's cause children should forsake a father and mother who oppose this path of sanctity. Christ's words are restricted, he asserts, to those
parents in "fals belue [*sic*]" (1:313). The teacher's responses to the two texts
Dives has invoked are surprisingly evasive. Banal and bland, they evade difficult issues of authority, discipleship, and conflict raised by the New Testament texts—and by his own book.[11]

However, *Dives and Pauper* does return to the home. It does so in a fascinating context. Dives remarks that nowadays "men seyyn þat þer schulde
no lewyd folc entrymettyn hem of Godis lawe ne of þe gospel ne of holy
writ, neyþer to connyn it ne to techyn it" (1:327). These "men" are, of
course, the rulers of the English Church, currently engaged in their attempt
to destroy Wycliffism and Wycliffites' determination to vernacularize "holy
writ" among the "lewyd folc."[12] The teaching friar responds passionately:
"þat is a foul errour & wol perlyous to mannys soule" (1:327). Here, as in his
sermons, the orthodox writer is hostile to the hierarchy's ideology enshrined
in Arundel's Constitutions.[13] He wants lay men *and* women to know "Godis
lawe" in the ways now being forbidden, as Dives said. But, perhaps as befits

an orthodox cleric, his answer sows an ambiguity carefully excluded from the statement written for Dives. The latter had unequivocally bound the learning of "Godis lawe" to learning the Gospels and "holy writ," just as Wycliffites were doing. Pauper certainly does not question this charged link, let alone challenge it. But after invoking "Godis lawe" he leaves out "þe gospel" and he leaves out "holy writ" (1:327). He also adds a reference to social status: everyone is obliged to learn God's law "aftir his degre" (327). Had the author been interrogated by the hierarchy he could show that while he had not opposed the links made by Dives between "Godis lawe" and the study of Scripture by lay men and women, he had not explicitly validated them.[14] He could also point to his careful maintenance of social status and hierarchy: God's law is to be studied according to the "degre" of the subject.

This still leaves a question for him. If the archbishop and the English Church are currently instituting "foul errour," one "wol perylous to mannys soule," by forbidding "lewyd folc" from concerning themselves with God's law in "holy writ," how does the author of *Dives and Pauper* think lay people should be doing their "besynesse to knowyn Godis lawe"? And how does he answer this question without becoming a disobedient subject to his archbishop, an "vnbuxum child?" One might expect an orthodox answer, especially after *De Heretico Comburendo,* to run along lines such as these: lay people should learn God's law by going to Mass every week to behold the body of their God, by fulfilling the requirement of annual confession and communion, and by attending local sermons when a preacher, like the friar, visits them. But the author says none of this. He places the obligation to teach God's law on "fadris & moodris, godfadris & godmoodris" (1:327). He turns not to ecclesiastic law but to Scripture (Deuteronomy 6.6–9). God commands that the divine precepts and ceremonies are to be taught and meditated upon "sittynge in þin hous amongis þin mene," and everywhere else too (1:327). This is addressed to Dives, the rich man with a "grete mene" (1:58); but the friar wants home, great or small, to be a place of Christian instruction. Despite his earlier emphasis on the hellish conflicts in the home, or perhaps because of this, he now seems to envisage it as a place for training disciples, for sanctification:

> [I]che man in his owyn houshold schulde don þe offys of þe buschop in techinge & correctynge of comoun þingis. And þerfor seiþ þe lawe þat þe offys of teching & chastysyng longyth nout only to þe buschop but to euery gouernor aftir his name & his degre, to þe pore man gouernynge his pore houshold, to þe riche man gouernynge his

mene, to þe housebond gouernynge his wif, to þe fadir & þe moodir gouernynge her childryn, to þe iustice gouernynge his contre, to þe kyng gouernynge his peple. (1:328)

Home is where one is to learn God's law: *and not only when one is a child.* But in the contexts of orthodoxy's battle against Wycliffism this model invites some tricky questions. If the lay person, poor or rich, is to teach as a bishop, what exactly does he or she teach? Can she or he read and discuss God's law as it unfolds in the Gospels and other holy writ? The answer might seem to be that she can. For Pauper did not oppose his interlocutor's inclusion of "holy writ" in God's law, while he argued that restraint on lay engagement with this law to be a dangerous and foul error. Furthermore, nothing in the passage under discussion excludes instruction in vernacularized "holy writ" and theology from the laity's homes. Indeed, such instruction seems fitting for the "offys of þe buschop." However, nothing in the passage directs readers to include it. The writer does not disclose his views on the appropriate resources and authority of the episcopalizing laity. In fact he makes their determination impossible. So we do not know exactly how lay people should be doing their "besynesse to knowyn Godis lawe." Instead of pursuing this any further the friar moves to the safer ground of conventional understanding of governance according to "degre."

It should be noted that this conventional move exemplifies how a culture's reigning "common sense" can block out widely known actuality. I have in mind the large numbers of English homes headed by women, both urban and agricultural, especially among poorer people.[15] Here "common sense" allows the writer to ignore implications of his model that would have added to its difficulties for orthodoxy. For if women head homes, then they will assume "þe offys of þe buschop." Once this is acknowledged, another question might emerge: What should be done if in a household headed by a man the woman is more learned in "holy writ"? What if she is a veritable Saint Cecilia and he someone with the understanding of "Godis lawe" displayed by John the carpenter in Chaucer's "Miller's Tale"? Had the author of *Dives and Pauper* been a wholehearted adherent of the kind of regulations Archbishop Arundel codified in his Constitutions, he would not have generated a model of sanctification and the home which encouraged such speculations, however elusively handled.[16]

This brings me to the point where the potentials of his model of lay sanctity and domestic episcopacy could converge with practices that were classified and persecuted as heretical. These practices are especially well exemplified amongst the Wycliffite victims of the bishop of Norwich, 1428–31.[17] Anne Hudson describes them with great clarity:

> The centre of these East Anglian groups is not the church with its sympathetic or proselytizing clerk, but the domestic room, the *chesehous chambr* or similar, with the secular leader, male or female. As Margery Baxter perceptively observed: "sancta ecclesia est tantum in locis habitacionum omnium existencium de secta sua." In these house churches the implications of the Wycliffite belief in the priesthood of all believers had, whether by choice or by necessity, been absorbed.[18]

The creedal Church [sancta ecclesia] is now located in these Christians' homes, while the modern Roman Church is viewed as the persecuting arm of Antichrist. For example, reflecting on the way that the Church burnt to death her beloved teacher William White in Norwich (1428), Margery Baxter sees the presiding bishop of Norwich as Caiaphas and his ministers as the devil's members.[19] In Margery Baxter's home, one of the "house churches" Hudson mentions, Wycliffite Christians worshipped Christ (44, 46–47, 49, 50) and heard Scripture, the law of Christ (47–48). Margery considered her husband, a wright, an excellent doctor of Christianity (48). Similarly, John Godesell, a parchment maker living in Ditchingham, frequently received well-known heretics in his home, supported them, and allowed them to hold schools and read books there (60).[20] The statement of Hawisia Mone offers a detailed account of home as a place of sanctification in the emerging traditions of Wycliffite Christianity. Hawisia Mone acknowledges:

> Y have be right hoomly and prive with many heretikes, knowyng thaym for heretikes, and thaym Y have recyved and herberwed in our hous, and thaym Y have conceled, conforted, supported, maytened and favored with al my poar—which heretikes names be these, Sir William Whyte, Sir William Caleys, Sir Huwe Pye, Sir Thomas Pert, prestes, John Waddon, John Fowlyn, John Gray, William Everden, William Bate of Sethyng, Bartholomeu Cornmonger, Thomas Borell and Baty, his wyf, William Wardon, John Pert, Edmond Archer of Lodne, Richard Belward, Bertholomeu Monk, William Wright and many others—whiche have ofte tymes kept, holde and continued scoles of heresie yn prive chambres and prive places of oures, yn the whyche scoles Y have herd, conceyved,

lerned and reported the errours and heresies whiche be writen and
contened in these indentures. (140)

In the testimony of John Burell, who had worked for Thomas Mone, we
find "le botery" and "le chesehous chambr" of the Mone's home being used
in Wycliffite rejection of the dietary prescriptions of the Roman Church
(75,76). Hawisia Mone's statement conveys the way such "house churches"
were centered on a nuclear family (Hawisia's daughter is involved in John
Burell's abjuration [75]) but could include many people, "many others" besides the list of names quoted above. Some of these come from far beyond
southeast Norfolk and Loddon. It also evokes the intimacy in which Wycliffite sanctity was fostered: "Y have be right hoomly and prive with many
heretikes," meeting "yn prive chambres and prive places of oures." This is
certainly not Eamon Duffy's medieval England, but it is only excluded from
our account of late medieval Christianity by an ideological fiat.[21] Hawisia
Mone, like her husband (180), and her fellows, was compelled to return to
what the hierarchy understood as "the oonhed of the Churche," recanting
all that might be against the "determinacion of the Church of Rome"
(142–43). Compulsion was accompanied by public punishment.[22] In returning to "the oonhed of the Churche," she, like others, had to renounce all
"felaship" with those classified as heretics; she promised not to be "hoomly
with tham, ne gyve thaym consell, sokour, favour ne confort" (143).[23] She
was to let the Bishop know if she heard of any "prive conventicles or as-
sembles" (143). Her statements show the unorthodox potentials in the
model of the home as place of sanctification where the laity should study
holy writ. But this is also the very model sketched at one point in *Dives and
Pauper*. Such homes provided space and time for cultivating affective and
intellectual bonds (shared texts, shared explorations), theological and ecclesiological reflections. In these the Church, the Roman Church, could
become a topic of wide-ranging critical analysis among Christians gaining
access to Scripture in their own language.[24] Such ruminations and practices
did not in themselves entail schism (like Wyclif himself, these East An-
glians attended parish churches, with whatever reservations). That decision
would depend on the "determinacion of the Churche of Rome." But in the
light of the late-fourteenth-century clergy's petitions for the death penalty
to be given to "heretics," in the light of *De Heretico Comburendo*, of Arundel's Constitutions, and of the rather ambitious determination of the Church
hierarchy to exterminate Wycliffism, it was clear that "the oonhed of the
Churche" had been defined in such a way as to preclude relatively (only

relatively) autonomous artisan homes becoming "house churches" like the Mones' in Loddon.[25]

I will now consider the Church's most widely read English response to Wycliffism in so far as it relates to the topic of this chapter, home, sanctity, and homelessness. It is a work discussed in chapter 1 of this book, a work which Archbishop Arundel himself blessed, ordering it to be disseminated "for the edification of the faithful, and the confutation of heretics or lollards": Nicholas Love's *The Mirror of the Blessed Life of Jesus Christ,* a vernacular version of the Franciscan *Meditaciones Vite Christi.*[26] The "proheme" makes it clear that Love himself represents the very position reported by Dives: "men seyyn þat þer schulde no lewyd folc entrymettyn hem of Godis lawe ne of þe gospel ne of holy writ, neyþer to connyn it ne to techyn it."[27] The mendicant author of *Dives and Pauper,* as we have seen, condemned this current orthodoxy. For Nicholas Love, however, the Gospels and holy writ are simply not appropriate for the laity; instead of Scripture they are to receive the *Mirror.* He claims that Christians who cannot read Latin are better served by "devoute meditacions of cristes lyfe," produced "in holi chirche," than by the vernacularized Scriptures (9–10).[28] These are allegedly "more pleyne in certynge partyes þan is expressed in the gospel of þe foure euaungelistes" (10). As we have observed, the Gospels are aligned with "sadde mete of grete clargye & of hye contemplacion," while the *Mirror,* like its source, is suitable for "symple creatures," the laity who "as childryn hauen nede to be fedde with mylke of lyȝte doctryne" (10). Such milky texts are "steryng specialy to þe loue of Jesu" (10). Love observes that he has adapted the *Meditaciones Vite Christi* to be "moste spedefull & edifyng to hem þat bene of symple vndirstondyng" (10). There are ironies in such claims that need not detain us here: ironies exemplified when one compares Love's neoscholastic defense of the doctrine of transubstantiation in his version of the Last Supper with the Gospels' accounts (150–56); ironies when one compares his version of the "symple vndirstondyng" of lay Christians with the explorations of Hawisia Mone or Sir John Oldcastle.[29] Such ironies highlight the nature of Love's project: to produce a particular version of Jesus Christ, of "þe monhede of cryste," and a particular version of devotion for lay Christians (10). He notes that this calls for "diuerse ymaginacions" that are absent from "holi writte" but that do not go against "þe byleue or gude maneres" (10–11). This task is systematically directed against the version of Christ's humanity emerging from Wyclif's engagement with the Gospels and received by his followers. Wycliffites tend to see Christ as the poorest of men but as a mobile, nonviolent, prophetic preacher of the Kingdom of God, one whose ministry continually involved conflict with the presiding authorities. Such a Christ provided a model for challenging the contemporary Church, with its massive temporal dominion so deeply woven into the structures of contemporary violence.[30] This was the Christ responsible for claims such as those emerging from the "house churches" of East Anglia: "[I]t is not leful to slee a man for ony cause, ne be processe of lawe to dampne ony traytour or ony man for ony treson or felonie to deth, ne to putte ony man to deth for ony cause, but every man shuld remitte all vengeance oonly to the sentence of God" (Hawisia Mone, 142) and "[I]t is not leful ony man to fighte or do bataile for a reawme or a cuntre, or to plete in lawe for ony right or wrong" (John Skylly, 58). Such views come from serious reflections on texts such as the following, and their place in Christ's nonviolent ministry: "Love your enemies. Do good to them that hate you. Bless them that curse you and pray for them that ca- lumniate you. And to him that striketh thee on the one cheek, offer also the other. And him that taketh away from thee thy cloak, forbid not to take thy coat also. . . . [O]f him that taketh away thy goods, ask them not again" (Luke 6.27–30) and "Master, speak to my brother that he divide the inheri- tance with me. But he said to him: Man, who hath appointed me judge or di- vider over you?" (Luke 12.13–14).[31]

Love's strategy is to focus especially on the passion. While this is con- ventional enough in late medieval devotion, Love actually diminishes the role of Christ's ministry from the source he selected.[32] The aim is to dis- solve the dangerous memory of Jesus's ministry given in the Gospels. In fulfilling this task, Love offers a model of Christ and sanctity in the home which is a distinctive alternative to Wycliffite models. It also decisively sets aside the potentially unorthodox model in *Dives and Pauper* discussed above. I shall now exemplify Love's procedures in different stages of "þe blessed life of Jesu crist" (11).

The *Mirror* sets Jesus in a closely bound nuclear family where home is also the workshop: "Joseph wrouht as he miȝt in his craft of Carpentary, oure lady also with þe distafe & nedle, & þerwiþ making hir mete, & oþer office doyng þat longen to housholde." Jesus "meekly" helps them both, "& also in leying þe borde, makyng þe beddes and sech oþere choores" (63). Love emphasizes their common meal "at one litel borde." The food is "symple and sobre," accompanied by "wordes of edificacione ful of wis- dome & of þe holi goste," a feeding of body and soul (63–64). After this "recreacione in comune" the poor family (that they live "in pouerte" is em- phasized, 63) separates for private prayer. It is striking that Love decides to present this artisan family, "in pouerte," as holding a house in which each member of the family has a separate room: "þei wenten to praiere by hem self in hir closetes." Although "þei hade no grete house bot a litel" it contained "þre smale chaumbres, þere specialy to pray & to slepe" (64).[33] Perhaps Love was thinking of his own Mount Grace, but this seems rather like the Mones' home in Loddon: the artisan household as a place of sanctification filled with "wordes of edificacione." There are, however, striking differences. The East Anglian homes disclosed in the Bishop of Norwich's records include readings from Scripture, doctrinal and ethical explorations, critical reflection on the institutions of religion and those who govern them. They are veritable "scoles" of Christian learning (for example, 140) encompassing *both* the nuclear family's home *and* an extremely active network of like-minded seekers in, and beyond, the region. Love's vision of a most holy home excludes such activity, excludes the images of mobility and critical explorations aided by written texts.

Here it is worth noting related elements in Love's treatment of the episode in which Jesus's parents accidentally left him in Jerusalem, losing him for three days (Luke 2.42–50). After the *Mirror* has described the kissing and embracing between reunited mother and son (59), Love alters his source, the *Meditaciones Vite Christi*. There the reader is directed to consider Jesus among the doctors in the temple.[34] Love deletes this. Could this have become too dangerous a memory, the young prophet from an artisan family questioning religious leaders? Be that as it may, Love substitutes speculation about how Jesus spent the days apart from his family:

> In þis forseid processe of Jesu what hope we þat he dide or where & in what manere lyued he þo þre dayes? We mowe suppose þat he went to some hospitale of pore men, & þere he shamfastly praiede & asked herborgh, & þer ete & lay with pore men as a pore child. And sume doctours seyn þat he begget in þo þre dayes. Bot þerof litel forse, so þat we folwe him in perfite mekenes & oþer vertues. For beggyng wiþoutforþe bot þere be a meke herte withinneforþe is litel worþ als to perfeccion. (60)

This is a striking addition to the Franciscan *Meditaciones Vite Christi*, and to Luke's Gospel. It belongs to some of the conversations in which *Piers Plowman* participated (see chapter 5 of this book). Love is troubled by the specter of Christ as *homeless*, Christ as a *vagrant*. Christ, that is, as one of the powerful scapegoats to emerge in the rhetoric of the dominant classes during their struggles with peasant communities and laborers in the years following the Black Death.[35] If Christ was homeless and mobile, what would following him entail? Did not he himself declare, as Franciscans customarily recalled, "The foxes have holes and the birds of the air nests: but the son of man hath not where to lay his head" (Matthew 8.20)? But Love decides that during these three days in Jerusalem Christ must take himself "to some hospitale of pore men" where he can be enclosed. That he turns up not in "hospitale" but questioning the doctors in the temple does not, as Sargent observed, become a topic of meditation in the *Mirror*.[36]

Love's alterations to his sources also relate to another contemporary conversation. This concerns mendicancy, a practice that had preoccupied Langland and so many others.[37] Love acknowledges that "sume doctors" say that Christ begged in those three days, but he dismisses this speculation. As a Carthusian monk, Love is himself of course committed to a life of poverty and common ownership. But this is an enclosed poverty, very different to the mobility of mendicancy, even Franciscan mendicancy.[38] As Sargent observes, "Love's alteration, with its suggestion of the moral ambivalence of mendicancy, is hardly in keeping with the Franciscan spirituality of the underlying Latin text."[39] But then Love's attention was on contemporary England, on contemporary conflicts around forms of Christian discipleship, vagrancy, mendicancy, and ecclesiology.

What then does Love do with the adult Jesus? Was he not homeless, with nowhere to lay his head (Luke 9.58, Matthew 8.20), a vagrant? As noted earlier, one of Love's responses was to diminish Jesus's ministry. But the general tendency of his responses can be seen in his treatment of Christ's temptation in the wilderness. This is read as a call to "go in to solitary place" insofar as this does not conflict with the conventional demands of one's social position: "in als miche as þou maist, sauyng þin astate" (72). After glossing the sequence with Bernard on solitary spirituality (72–73), Love moves to its conclusion, when angels ministered to Jesus (Matthew 4.11).[40] We are shown Jesus "etyng alone, & þe angeles aboute him" (74). The angels ask Jesus what he would like them to prepare for his meal (75). He tells them he wants his family home brought into the wilderness in the form of his mother's cooking: "Goþe to my dere modere, & what maner of mete she haþe redy bringeþ to me, for þer is none bodily mete so lykyng to me as þat is of hir diȝhtyng" (75). Flying to his mother, they are given "of þat symple mete þat she hade ordeynet to hir self and Joseph" (75–76). The angels also pick up a loaf of bread, "a towel, & oþer necessaryes," together with a few

small fishes Mary had prepared (76). Returning to Jesus, they make a picnic
in the desert, with the food prepared at home, by his mother, placed on a
tablecloth: "þe angeles comyng spraddene þe tuwaile vpon þe gronde &
leiden brede þeron" (76). Having neither "bankere nor cushyne," Jesus sits
on the ground but eats "curteysly."[41] Angels wait on him, "one of brede,
anoþer wyne, a noþer diht fishes, summe songen in þe stede of mynstrelsye
þat swete songe of heuen" (76). After his meal Jesus has the angels return
what is left to his mother and promise his return home (76). And that is where
the *Mirror* wants to be as it offers another scene of Jesus's integration in
his family home and its bonds (77). This scene works to defer the ministry,
which, in Love's remarkable and symptomatic judgment, his audience would
find a "longe werke & peraventure tediose" (77–78). It also continues the
sacralization of the home in a form analyzed above, a form conspicuously
different from Wycliffite versions of the home as a site of sanctification. And
it does so without imaging the holy family as a critical alternative to the bonds
and demands of contemporary families, as Margery Kempe did.[42]

Jesus has to leave home, but Love continues to domesticate the prophet
and mobile layman as much as he can. Let me exemplify this tendency.
Luke treats the beginning of Christ's ministry as a prophet's challenge to
the people of Nazareth, one in which he applies Isaiah 61 to himself (Luke
4.16–21). Love, however, has Jesus take up "þe office of a redere as it were
a symple clerke," expounding the text "mekely of him self " (79). But Luke's
account shows that Jesus's preaching was eschatological: liberation to cap-
tives, the gospel to the poor, sight to the blind, *now, in the preacher.* There is
nothing "mekely" said or done. Love observes that all in the synagogue wondered at the words of grace he spoke (Luke 4.22), for he was "souereynly
faire & also most eloquente" (79), but he, like the *Meditaciones Vite Christi*,
leaves the episode here.[43] Luke, however, does not. He recounts that the
people seek to deflect Jesus's eschatological ministry by reinserting him in
his home, domesticating him rather as Love has been doing and, as we shall
see, continues to do: "Is not this the son of Joseph?" (4.22). Jesus comments
on this and continues to elaborate a message in which God's election is
mysterious and uncontrollable, one that brings judgment to Israel (Luke
4.24–27). At this, all are "filled with anger," "thrust him out of the city," and
seek to kill him (Luke 4.28–29). But his time has not come, and he eludes
their murderous will (4.30). For Love the excised completion of this episode
was doubtless one of the passages "þat semen litel edificacion inne" for the
"symple folk" he addressed (78). But the "symple folk" we have encountered

in Loddon, Flixton, or Martham, in Ditchingham or Earsham, would find this a powerful passage, full of "edificacion." For it shows Christ as a prophetic layman whose teaching led to conflict with contemporary authorities and customs; to follow this teacher was to encounter persecutory violence.[44] Love's approach to the Gospels, his domestication of Christ in the household described above, rejects such "edificacion." It had come to have dangerous affinities with Wycliffizing.[45] While the *Mirror*'s treatment of the passion of Christ follows the *Meditaciones Vite Christi* and thus the dominant late medieval representation of Christ's humanity,[46] its mode seems to occlude the political and ecclesiastic implications of the scriptural narratives. Attention is on the bound, scourged, bleeding body of "þat fairest 3onge manne," whether bound naked to a pillar, or "sekyng after hese cloþes," or "alle blody nakede wiþ a maner of schamefastnes gederyng hese cloþes," or being crucified (170–77). The text does mention aldermen, princes, priests, and pharisees (144–45, 168, 172), but we are not led to see these figures of authority as our aldermen, not led to see the passion and crucifixion being produced by *our* systems of justice, *our* lust for dominion, *our* heresy trials, and *our* executions.[47]

The domestication I have traced continues in the treatment of the resurrection. Given the centrality of Christ's mother in late medieval soteriology, it is not surprising that devotional writers felt obliged to correct a strange oversight in the Gospels: the absence of any account of a resurrection appearance to the Virgin Mary. So Love, like his source (*Meditaciones*, ch. 82, 300–301), begins the resurrection sequence with Mary's prayer that God will send Jesus to her on this, the third day (196). Immediately Jesus appears, uttering a greeting in Latin, translated by Love. Mother and son kiss, embrace, and sit down together. Mary looks at Jesus's wounds and asks whether the pain they caused has gone. Reassured that it has, she thanks God the father that he has given Jesus to her: "And so þei boþe louely & likyngly talkyng to gedire, maden a gret ioyful feste & oure lorde Jesus told hir þoo worþi þinges þat he dide in þo þre daies after his passion, & how he delyuerede his chosen peple fro helle" (197). The scene dissolves the strangeness of the resurrection appearances so emphasized in the Gospels.[48] Instead of this, we are given Christ's quite unmysterious return to a familiar domestic intimacy. The conversation concludes when Jesus tells his mother that he will "go shewe him bodily" to Mary Magdalen to comfort her. His mother approves this intention, adding, "Bot I pray 3owe þenkeþ to come a3eyn to confort me, & so she louely clippyng him & kissinge, lete him go" (199; see *Meditaciones,* ch. 83, 304). Such homeliness and domestic continuity are as characteristic of the *Mirror* and late medieval orthodoxy as they are alien to the Gospels. The encounter with Mary Magdalen moves into the same mode, despite Mary's initial inability to recognize Jesus and despite his command, "Touche me not" (200; see John 20.17). Love is confident that Jesus set aside this command and "suffrede hir to touch him, & to kysse boþe handes & feete" (200–201).[49]

As the risen Christ continues to disclose himself, the key word is "homely" (201, 202, 204, 205, 206). This is exemplified in the *Mirror*'s reworking of Luke 24.34–49 (205–8).[50] Jesus forgives the disciples who had forsaken him, instructs them, "spekynge homely," and then "eteþ homely" with them (205–6). Like the *Meditaciones Vite Christi* (ch. 91, 313–14), Love omits a moment in this scene that characterizes the resurrection appearances in the Gospels: "while they yet believed not and wondered for joy" (Luke 24.41). Such complex responses do not fit Love's version. Instead of reflecting on Christ's identity and the disciples' responses, Love elaborates the act of eating into another familiar scene. The disciples serve Jesus and stand around him "myrily" while his mother is "sittyng by him homely & seruynge him fulle gladly." Mary Magdalen contributes to this reconstitution of the past as she sits at Jesus's feet, "after hir olde maner" (206). Love exclaims, "A lorde Jesu, how worþi is þat litel hous, & how likyng & gracious is it to wonne þerinne?" (206). So the resurrection reconstitutes the family household, now including the disciples. They replace Joseph, who has silently disappeared. Love provides a model of the home as site of devotion, of sanctification, and he has consistently formed Christ to fit this. The Carthusian certainly is representing a central component of Christian traditions, early, medieval, and modern: Jesus's sharing of meals, his common table, was a central symbol of the eschatological kingdom. The meals were a symbol which anticipated and instituted the community which was to be the Church, the body and bread of Christ (see Mark 2.15–20, Luke 15.1; 1 Corinthians 10.16–17, Ephesians 5.25–32). And he wishes to emphasize the Gospels' own insistence that the resurrection did restore a communion broken by betrayal and crucifixion, and restore it in sharing food (Luke 24.41–43, John 21.12–14).[51] But his model also systematically opposes Wycliffite forms of making the home a place of sanctification and Christian discipleship, just as it opposes their representations of Christ.

This reading of an aspect of Love's *Mirror* concludes with a memory of the Wycliffite versions of Christ, of sanctification and the home, because, as we saw in this book's opening chapter, Wycliffites were very much on Love's mind as he composed his book, just as they were on the mind of the archbishop of Canterbury, who wanted the work to be communicated to the faithful for their edification and for the confutation of heretics or Lollards (7). I have concentrated on what I term the domestication of Jesus, but this entails no sense that Love's representation of Jesus is formed in some kind of contemplative oasis transcending the battles between Wycliffites and those who spoke for what came to be orthodoxy. On the contrary, taking Love seriously (why read him, or anyone else for that matter, if we don't?) means grasping the full scope of the careful choices he made in his version of Jesus, sanctity, and home. His domestication of Jesus, within the traditional theology of Incarnation and Trinity he shared with his opponents, becomes a thorough domestication of God, as I have just illustrated from the resurrection sequence. It seems to me worth asking whether such domestication of God played an ideological, psychological, and affective role in the struggles in which Love and Archbishop Arundel were involved. The process within which the *Mirror* was composed included the burning of Sawtry, the Constitutions of Arundel, and the burning of Badby: that is, it participated in a process that was novel for the Church in England. The novelty lay in constituting a group of fellow Christians as incorrigible enemies of Christ against whom true Christians must seek the penalty of death by burning. In such circumstances, could the domestication of God become a guarantee that God is indeed homely with us, knowable by us, belonging to our family in a way that will not surprise us with disturbing challenges to our understanding of God? Could such domestication assure us that the agenda of the group to which we belong must be God's agenda? Could the domestication I have traced make it impossible to imagine that God could have solidarity with those who are *not* of our household, those whose ways are *not* our ways and those whose versions of Christ and Church are *not* ours? Of course, these questions do not imply that Wycliffites lacked strategies to foster equal confidence; they only suggest that Wycliffite strategies were different.[52] And because the representational violence in the latter is often obvious, it may discourage us from exploring the collusions with violence in the apparently benevolent and charming domestication cultivated by the Carthusian. Not that recognizing such collusion in Love's devotional modes compels us to assume that in all contexts they would necessarily have a similar political and ecclesiological tendency. Margery Kempe, for instance, was certainly formed within the tradition Love vernacularizes.

But her version of its domesticated Jesus sponsors a Christian subject whose domestic intimacy with Jesus (and the Blessed Virgin Mary) gives her the resources to challenge secular and ecclesiastic powers even as she simultaneously seeks the latter's support and their legitimizing classification of her as "orthodox" rather than "lollard."[53]

I will conclude this chapter with some reflections on the final version of *Piers Plowman*.[54] Tessa Tavormina has written an informative book on Langland's commitment to marriage and the family, to the home. The commitment is displayed both in Wit's sustained celebration of "this wedded men þat this world susteyneth" (X.203–300) and in the use of marital, procreative, generative language in the poem's treatment of the fruits of charity (XVIII.50–116) and relations between the persons of the Trinity (XVIII.184–243).[55] This book gives unprecedented and admirable attention to an important dimension of the poem. Here, however, I will suggest that powerful counterforces in the poem are underestimated in its concentrated approach to marriage in *Piers Plowman*.

Wit's oration in Passus X certainly does include a celebration of marriage, procreation, and affectionate, pleasurable marital sexuality, just as Tavormina maintains.[56] But it is also offered as an antidote to areas of anxiety that have been very prominent in the poem: first, to anxiety about ways in which market relations undermine the traditional hierarchical order, with its particular virtues, and fill the Church with simony; and second, to acute contemporary anxiety about mobile, masterless lower-class people, the so-called "wasters" who challenge Piers's governance in Passus VIII and the beggars with bags whose church is the pub (IX.98–104, 139–75).[57] Against these anxieties Wit offers the marital home as a fortress (see X.203–11, 245–300). Marriage protected from the pressures of the market (X.256–85) will be the sole domain of procreation, thus preventing the emergence of vagrants and wasters (X.294–300). A model of social stability and traditionally imagined social hierarchy will be shored up by marriage. Wit has great expectations of marriages originating in mutual affection and the use of "thy wepene kene" (X.286), an image dealt with rather more critically by Chaucer.[58] He believes that in such a marriage the participants do not engage in those forms of marital cooperation ascribed to the capital sin Couetyse (VI.221–33). The latter contributes to the market practices and their consequences, ones the poet identifies as decisive underminers of the forms of community and the virtues which his poem most values. But how would Wit's vision of marriage preclude what is symbolized in the marriage of "Rose þe regrater" (VI.221–33)? Rose and her practices are perfectly compatible with marital affection and the sexual activity Wit commends. In fact Wit has staked far more than Christian traditions have done in the salvific potentials of mutual affection and sexual pleasures in marriage, as Tavormina appreciates. It seems that the poet has given Wit an attractively simple, "natural" solution to a complex set of social and psychological issues that vex the poem. But he has given this, and its simplicity, as part, but only part, of the long, critical exploration that is *Piers Plowman*. In this light, it can be seen as decidedly inadequate, a utopianism which grossly exaggerates the potentials of marriages originating in affection and sexual pleasure to achieve the ethical and political ends the poet desires. As for specifically Christian virtues, Wit's oration has conspicuously little to say about these.[59] Despite its opening statement about the Creator and its demand that the Church be a missionary Church, it does not begin to engage with the questions about the relations between Christian instruction, home and Church, ones addressed, in their very different ways, by *Dives and Pauper*, Wycliffites, and Nicholas Love. It seems to me that the poem unfolds the deficiencies in Wit's statements and corrects his representation of marriage. It does so through Liberum Arbitrium, "cristes creature . . . and of his kynne a party" (XVI.167–68). Liberum Arbitrium affirms the Church's traditional teaching that marriage is a good, but one that is "beneth" (XVIII.84–85) other Christian forms of life. It must be set within a Christocentric and eschatological vision of salvation history if it is to be properly understood (XVIII.53–116, in the wider, fully relevant context of XVIII.1–XX.478).[60] It is one of the forms of life that "sonnere wollen rotye," encouraging an intenser attachment to the goods of the world than "Wydewhode" and "virginite" (XVIII.55–109). While this seriously qualifies Wit's position on Christian discipleship and marriage, it does so in a deeply traditional way. Although marriage is the lowest form of Christian life, although it leads to "a foule noyse" in our separation from this world, although the other states of life are "more lykynde to oure lorde then lyue as kynde asketh / And folewe þat þe flesche wole and fruyt forth brynge," it is a good that "multiplieth þe peple."[61] At this distance, at this level of generalization, it might be possible to assimilate these evaluations to a comfortable coexistence of different "degres." Perhaps the married readers can feel comfortable in taking a slightly less ironizing version of the Wife of Bath's line as she reflects on Paul's upgrading of virginity over marriage:

Virginitee is greet perfeccion,
And continence eek with devocion,
But Crist, that of perfeccion is welle,
Bad nat every wight he sholde go selle
Al that he hadde, and gyve it to the poore,
And in swich wise folwe hym and his foore.
He spak to hem that wolde lyve parfitly;
And lordynges, by your leve, that am nat I.
(*CT* III.105–12)

But the writer of *Piers Plowman* and the often agonized Wille are less breezy than the Wife of Bath about setting aside models of life given by Christ and Paul. One only has to recall the treatment of *Activa Vita* here (XV.189–XVI.374a) and in the B version (XIII.220–XIV.335).[62] Much in *Piers Plowman* resists Wit's oration, so comforting for the married, so uncomplicatedly confident in the "kynde" of "wedded men," encouraged in these terms: "whil þou art ȝong and ȝep and thy wepene kene / Awrek the þerwith on wyfyng, for godes werk y holde hit" (X.284–85). Amen, say Januarie and the Wife of Bath. But while there are no grounds for taking Wit's oration as providing a model for Christian discipleship and sanctification in the home, and while Liberum Arbitrium invokes traditional teaching on states of life which cast further question on Wit's claims, there are even stronger counterforces to Wit's vision. To these I will now turn, making a long and complex story as short as possible.

This is the story of Christian discipleship and its complex relations to the representations of Christ in *Piers Plowman*. As we have seen, the latter focus on a mobile, powerful prophetic figure, the embodiment of divine luminosity envisaged in John's Gospel.[63] In *Piers Plowman* Christ does not offer the models of domestic piety and space we have traced in Love's *Mirror*. This lack raised the possibility that the way to discipleship, to sanctification, might involve a freely chosen homelessness of the kind cultivated by St. Francis. But such homelessness entailed the cult of absolute poverty, and this, as we saw in chapter 5, became a central topic for exploration in the dialectical processes of *Piers Plowman:* sympathetic but profoundly critical exploration that interweaves theological, ecclesiological, and political dimensions in the poem. Here I wish to follow Wille's journey in relation to the subject of home, homelessness, and sanctity.

Wille begins as a wandering seeker whose mobility is continually challenged and whose status as a married man with a home is emphasized. His refusal to remain in his home is not an obvious mark of sanctification; on the contrary, he has many of the appearances of the vagrant, waster, able-bodied mendicant, the target of the Vagrancy Petition (1376), Statute of Labourers (1351), and Cambridge Parliament (1388).[64] One can see just how Wit would judge this vagrant, home-abandoning seeker. But in the poet's vision, Wille's mobility, his abandonment of home, is made part of the story of salvation history (XVIII–XX). By God's grace his very mobility is led to a direct encounter with the even more mobile, homeless Christ (XIX.48–336; see too XX and XXI.1–14). Home is simply not a site of sanctification. After his visions of Christ, it is to Mass on Easter Sunday that Wille calls "kitte my wyf and Calote my douhter" (XX.467–75). The household that actually obsesses Langland is the one we see being built in Passus XXI. The Holy Spirit enables Piers to build "an hous" founded on the work of Christ and roofed with "all holy writ." It is called "vnite, holy chirche an englisch" (XXI.317–34). Like Paul, the poet envisages this as the place in which the family of faith is formed (Galatians 6.10). Once more we find that the marital home in which Wit invested such confidence does not offer the necessary resources in time of trouble. Wille observes that the disintegration of his bodily energies, so important in Wit's account of marriage, leaves his pitying spouse wishing he were in heaven:

> For þe lyme þat she loued me fore and leef was to fele
> Anyhtes nameliche, when we naked were,
> Y ne myhte in none manere maken at here wille
> (XXII.195–97; see 186–98)

The actual teleology of Wit's vision of marriage "and thy wepene kene" is thus revealed in this passage. It surely also recalls the exemplary warning in Wille's vision of the tree called "trewe loue" (XVIII.9). There we observed how when Elde shakes the tree it is "matrimonye" that "made a foule noyse" (XVIII.109). But Wille is not abandoned here. He is now called, by Kynde, into the Church, "into vnite" (XXII.204–13). True enough, this Church is permeated by the forces of Antichrist and, to our sight at least, seems to have been abandoned by Christ, Holy Spirit, and Piers (XXII). That is why Conscience leaves it, "[t]o seke Peres the plouhman" and Grace outside the divided Church (XXII.380–86). Derek Pearsall rightly observes that this is an "extraordinary ending to a long Christian poem."[65] Its representation of the visible Church might even seem to have converged with that of Wycliffites.[66] But, once again, we must also note that whatever the search Conscience may be called to undertake, and whatever its consequences, Wille himself, every person's rational appetite and the figure of the poet, stays in the Church, obedient to Kynde's commandment, waiting. In the poet's view, *this* is the unlikely household in which Christians are, however late in the day, to learn to love and to learn freedom from anxious attachments (XXII.208–11). If that seems an unlikely story in the light of the poem's massive critique of the Church and its final representation of apparent capitulation to Antichrist, it is the one we are left with, a vision neither Wycliffite nor at all like Nicholas Love's. It seems an appropriate one, however, for a poem in which the divine source of sanctification lived homelessly but left the Holy Spirit to found a house in which all people could find his saving covenant, pardon, and sacraments (XXI.182–390). Grace builds this house from the works of Christ and "calde þat hous vnite, holy chirche an englisch" (XXI.328). This is where Wille went after his first conversion (V.105–8). But it has taken a much longer process for him and the reader to understand what going "to þe kyrke" (V.106) actually means, to grasp what a *corpus mixtum* this community is, how troubled and troubling its "vnite," indeed, how unlikely a place it might seem in which to learn to love. But, as I have observed, Wille now obeys Kynde: "y . . . comsed to Rome / Thorw contriccion and confessioun til y cam to vnite" (XXII.212–13). Whether or not there is a pun in this description of the poet beginning "to Rome" (roam/Rome), as I think there is, we know that his obedience to Kynde is taking him to a struggling "hous" in which, however graced it is with sacraments and "holy writ" (XXI.327), Wille could never feel comfortably at home. But that may be part of its constituent purpose and part of Kynde's meaning in insisting that Wille remain there, whatever quest Conscience may be obliged to pursue (XXII.380–86), and however intractable the resistances to making just communities which would practice kindness (XIX.170–334) and "pay / To Peres pardoun þe plouhman *Redde quod debes* (XXI.186–87).

Augustine can gloss this remark. In the *City of God* he writes that "a household of human beings [domus hominum] whose life is not based on faith is in pursuit of an earthly peace based on things belonging to this temporal life, and on its advantages [commodisque]." But a household of people "whose life is based on faith looks forward to the blessings which are promised as eternal in the future, making use of earthly and temporal things like a pilgrim in a foreign land [terrenisque rebus ac temporalibus tamquam peregrina utitur], who does not let himself be taken in by them or distracted from his course towards God."[67] For those whose goals seem fulfilled by the bounties of mortal life, the earthly city and whatever peace it can yield will indeed be home. But if people are to see the heavenly city they must not expect this mortal life to provide a home. For they will see themselves as "on pilgrimage in this condition of mortality," leading "a life of captivity in this earthly city as in a foreign land." The "hous vnite" is potentially as "wyde as the world" (XXI.332–34), the pilgrimaging city which "calls out citizens from all nations and so collects a society of aliens speaking all languages."[68] Not surprisingly, this collective may seem as like Babylon as it is like Jerusalem. That, after all, is a similarity on which *Piers Plowman* has remorselessly insisted but without being drawn to offer a Donatist or Wycliffite resolution of such painful confusion.[69] As the divinely given place where Wille must learn to love, this strange "hous" cannot be mistaken for home. Designedly so, it must persuade Wille that he and the "foles" he joins "are pilgrims and strangers" (XXII.52–64, 74–75, 206–16; Hebrews 11.13).

NOTES

List of Acronyms

The following are acronyms for series names that are used in the notes and bibliography:

CCCM: Corpus Christianorum Continuatio Medievalis
CCPM: Clavis Patristica Pseudepigraphorum Medii Aevi
CCSL: Corpus Christianorum, Series Latina
EETS: Early English Text Series
PLat: Patrologiae Cursus Completus, Series Latina, 221 vols., ed. J.-P. Migne (Paris, 1879–90)

Preface

1. T. S. Eliot, *The Complete Poems and Plays* (New York: Harcourt, Brace, n.d.).

2. Rowan Williams, *Arius: Heresy and Tradition* (London: Darton, Longman and Todd, 1987), 23. For an exceptionally illuminating meditation on late medieval and sixteenth-century "makings," together with their modern historiography, see Howard Kaminsky, "The Problematics of 'Heresy' and 'The Reformation,'" in *Häresie und vorzeitige Reformation im Spätmittelalter,* ed. Frantisek Smahel and Elisabeth Müller-Luckner (Munich: Oldenbourg, 1998), 1–22.

3. I would like to thank Steven Justice for prompting me to consider this in his comments on the first draft of the present book.

4. See Serge Lancel, *Saint Augustin* (Paris: Fayard, 1999), chs. 26 and 28 (especially pp. 472–74). For reflections on diachronic conversations within Christian

traditions, see Robert W. Jenson, *Systematic Theology* (New York: Oxford University Press, 1999), vol. 2, 278–84.

5. For a range of illuminating studies of this material, from different perspectives, see the following: Eamon Duffy, *The Stripping of the Altars: Traditional Religion in England 1400–1580* (New Haven: Yale University Press, 1992), 160–63, 186–90, 348–76; Patrick J. Geary, *Living with the Dead in the Middle Ages* (Ithaca: Cornell University Press, 1994); Bernhard Jussen, "Challenging the Culture of *Memoria:* Dead Men, Oblivion and the 'Faithless Widow' in the Middle Ages," ch. 10 in *Medieval Concepts of the Past,* ed. Gerd Althoff, Johannes Fried, and Patrick J. Geary (Cambridge: Cambridge University Press, 2002); Stephen Greenblatt, *Hamlet in Purgatory* (Princeton: Princeton University Press, 2001), ch. 3; Chris Chism, *Alliterative Revivals* (Philadelphia: University of Pennsylvania Press, 2002), 14–65, 237–64.

6. This is the place to acknowledge the influence of Alasdair MacIntyre on my thinking over many years. See in particular *After Virtue* (1981; 2d, rev. ed., London: Duckworth, 1985); *Whose Justice? Which Rationality?* (London: Duckworth, 1988); *Three Rival Versions of Moral Enquiry* (London: Duckworth, 1990); *First Principles, Final Ends and Contemporary Philosophical Issues* (Milwaukee: Marquette University Press, 1990); *Dependent Rational Animals: Why Human Beings Need the Virtues* (Chicago: Open Court, 1999).

7. Paul Ricoeur, *Criticism and Imagination* (Cambridge: Polity Press, 1998), 145.

8. Julian of Norwich, *The Shewings of Julian of Norwich,* ed. Georgia R. Crampton (Kalamazoo: Western Michigan University, Medieval Institute Publications, 1994), ch. 86, 154.

9. John Donne, *Devotions upon Emergent Occasions* (Ann Arbor: University of Michigan Press, 1959), V, 30–31.

10. Nancy Griffiths, *Flyer,* Elektra CD, 1994. Thanks to her for this work, as for earlier work and for more recent work.

1. The Sacrament of the Altar in the Making of
Orthodox Christianity or "Traditional Religion"

1. I have found the following especially helpful in seeking to understand the theological history of Eucharistic teaching in the later Middle Ages: Marilyn McCord Adams, "Aristotle and the Sacrament of the Altar: A Crisis in Medieval Aristotelianism," in *Aristotle and His Medieval Interpreters,* ed. Richard Bosley and Martin Tweedale (Calgary: University of Calgary Press, 1991), 195–249; Gabriel N. Buescher, *The Eucharist Teaching of William Ockham* (Washington: Catholic Uni-

versity of America Press, 1950); David Burr, "Scotus and Transubstantiation," *Medieval Studies* 34 (1972), 336–60, and *Eucharistic Presence in Late-Thirteenth Century Franciscan Thought* (Philadelphia: American Philosophical Society, 1984); John Bossy, "The Mass as a Social Institution, 1200–1700," *Past and Present* 100 (1983), 29–61; Henri de Lubac, *Corpus mysticum: L'Eucharistie et l'église au moyen âge* (Paris: Aubier, 1949); Gary Macy, "The 'Dogma of Transubstantiation' in the Middle Ages," *Journal of Ecclesiastical History* 45 (1994), 11–41, and *The Banquet's Wisdom: A Short History of the Theologies of the Lord's Supper* (New York: Paulist Press, 1992); James F. McCue, "The Doctrine of Transubstantiation from Berengar through Trent," *Harvard Theological Review* 61 (1968), 385–430; Miri Rubin, *Corpus Christi: The Eucharist in Late Medieval Culture* (Cambridge: Cambridge University Press, 1991).

    2. For this version of Christ's humanity, dominant in the late Middle Ages, see David Aers and Lynn Staley, *The Powers of the Holy: Religion, Politics and Gender in Late Medieval English Culture* (University Park: Pennsylvania State University Press, 1996), ch. 1. For standard teaching that only duly ordained priests can consecrate, see Thomas Aquinas, "De Articulis Fidei et Ecclesiae Sacramentis," in *Opuscula Theologica*, vol. 1, ed. R. A. Verardo (Rome: Marietti, 1954), 149, para. 620, and Siegfried Wenzel, ed., *Fasciculus Morum: A Fourteenth-Century Preacher's Handbook* (University Park: Pennsylvania State University Press, 1989), 406.

    3. For Corpus Christi processions and their politics, see Rubin, *Corpus Christi*, 243–71, and Mervyn James, "Ritual, Drama, and Social Body in the Late Medieval English Town," *Past and Present* 98 (1983), 3–29. Also relevant here are Eamon Duffy, *The Stripping of the Altars: Traditional Religion in England, 1400–1580* (New Haven: Yale University Press, 1992), 23–27, 44, 92–93; Gordon Kipling, *Enter the King: Theatre, Liturgy, and Ritual in the Medieval Civic Triumph* (Oxford: Clarendon Press, 1998), 11–26, 35–49, 201–9; and Ernst H. Kantorowicz, *The King's Two Bodies* (Princeton: Princeton University Press, 1957), ch. 5.

    4. Thomas Aquinas, *Summa Theologiae [ST]* III.76.1, resp and ad 2. All responses are to the Blackfriars edition (London: Blackfriars, 1964–81); subsequent citations are given parenthetically in the text. For the Office of Corpus Christi, see Thomas Aquinas, *Opuscula Theologica*, vol. 2, ed. R. M. Spiazzi (Rome: Marietti, 1954), 275–81. For William of Ockham's summary of orthodox doctrine in the early fourteenth century, see ch. 2 of his *De Corpore Christi*, where we find Christ's Galilean body under the accidents of a substanceless bread (91), in *Guillelmi de Ockham: Tractatus de Quantitate et Tractatus de Corpore Christi*, ed. Carlo A Grassi, vol. 10 of William of Ockham, *Opera Philosophica et Theologica* (St. Bonaventure, N.Y.: St. Bonaventure University, Franciscan Institute, 1986), 89–234.

    5. Thomas Netter (c. 1370–1430), *Thomae Waldensis Doctrinale Antiquitatum Fidei Catholicae Ecclesiae*, 3 vols., ed. B. Blanciotti (Venice, 1757; facsimile,

Farnborough: Gregg, 1967). Here I refer to Netter's *Doctrinale Fidei Catholicae:* "De Sacramentis" is in vol. 2, and for the Eucharist, see, in that volume, Book V, chs. 17–95 (121–560). Here see especially, from Book V, 21.4 (146), 26.5 (182), 24.1 (158), 24.3 (161), 25.3 (165), and 25.5 (171).

6. Netter, *Doctrinale,* vol. 2, Book V, 20.5 (143–44), 21.4 (146–47), and 23.2 (154). For an attempt to show convergences between Netter's and Wyclif's hermeneutics, see Kantik Ghosh, "'Authority' and 'Interpretation' in Wycliffite, Anti-Wycliffite, and Related Texts c. 1375–c. 1430" (Ph.D. diss., Cambridge University, 1996), ch. 6, and the revision of this dissertation as his book *The Wycliffite Heresy: Authority and the Interpretation of Texts* (Cambridge: Cambridge University Press, 2002), ch. 6.

7. Netter, *Doctrinale,* vol. 2, Book V, 30, especially 30.2 (196–97): "Ecce substantialiter corpus Christi in sacramento, non qualitatium, non figurative, nec quomodocumque imaginarie" (197).

8. Netter, *Doctrinale,* vol. 2, Book V, 56.1 (341) and 58.6 (357): "non sic autem tantummodo Christus per voluntatis consensum, sed etiam corporaliter, carnalis manducatur: ergo item carnaliter, & non tantum spiritualiter manducatur" (357).

9. Netter was, for example, involved in condemning William White to death. See Norman P. Tanner, ed., *Heresy Trials in the Diocese of Norwich, 1428–31,* Camden 4th ser., vol. 20 (London: Royal Historical Society, 1977), 9. For a summary of his and other Carmelite activities relevant to the present context, see Ann E. Nichols, *Seeable Signs: The Iconography of the Seven Sacraments, 1350–1544* (Woodbridge: Boydell Press, 1994), 114–28.

10. Netter, *Doctrinale,* vol. 2, Book V, 2 (151–52).

11. Wenzel, *Fasciculus Morum,* 411.

12. Wenzel, *Fasciculus Morum,* 417 nn. 106–11; see too Duffy, *Stripping of the Altars,* 100.

13. John Lydgate, "The Interpretation and Virtues of the Mass," lines 622–40, in *The Minor Poems of John Lydgate,* ed. H. N. MacCracken, EETS 107 (London: K. Paul, Trench, Trübner, 1911), vol. 1, 87–115. Contrast the benefits of worthy reception in John Wyclif's *De Eucharistia,* ed. John Loserth (London: Trübner, 1892), 178–79.

14. Wenzel, *Fasciculus Morum,* 411; see 410–13 passim. See too Lydgate, "The Interpretation," 114 (lines 641–48).

15. I think particularly of J. Chiffoleau, *La comptabilité de l'au delà: Les hommes, la mort et la religion dans la région d'Avignon à la fin du moyen âge* (Rome: L'Ecole Française de Rome, 1980); Miri Rubin, *Charity and Community in Medieval Cambridge* (Cambridge: Cambridge University Press, 1987), 250–59; Duffy, *Stripping of the Altars,* ch. 10.

16. Studies I have in mind here include Bossy, "The Mass"; James, "Ritual, Drama and Social Body"; R. Faith, "'The Great Rumour' of 1377 and Peasant Ideology," in *The English Rising of 1381*, ed. R. Hilton and T. Aston (Cambridge: Cambridge University Press, 1984), 43–73; Steven Justice, *Writing and Rebellion: England in 1381* (Berkeley: University of California Press, 1994), ch. 4; Rubin, *Corpus Christi;* Sarah Beckwith, "Ritual, Church, and Theatre: Medieval Dramas of the Sacramental Body," in *Culture and History, 1350–1600*, ed. David Aers (Hemel Hempstead: Harvester Wheatsheaf, 1992), 65–89, and *Christ's Body: Identity, Culture, and Society in Late Medieval Writings* (New York: Routledge, 1993); Paul Strohm, *England's Empty Throne: Usurpation and the Language of Legitimation, 1399–1422* (New Haven: Yale University Press, 1998), ch. 2; Margaret Aston, "Corpus Christi and Corpus Regni: Heresy and the Peasants' Revolt," *Past and Present* 143 (1994), 3–47.

17. "Traditional religion" refers to the subtitle of Duffy's *Stripping of the Altars*, "Traditional Religion in England, 1400–1580."

18. I use the edition of Brinton's sermons edited by Mary A. Devlin, *The Sermons of Thomas Brinton, Bishop of Rochester (1373–1389)*, Camden 3d ser., 85–86 (London: Royal Historical Society, 1954), giving page citations parenthetically in the text; see too, on Brinton, W. A. Pantin, *The English Church in the Fourteenth Century* (Cambridge: Cambridge University Press, 1955), 182–85. With Devlin's edition one should note the revisionary observations in H. G. Richardson's review in *Speculum* 30 (1955), 267–71.

19. Brinton's image of the broken mirror is a commonplace: see, for example, John Bromyard, *Summa Praedicantium* (Antwerp, 1614), part 1, 249, and William of Shoreham, *De Sacramento Altaris*, lines 722–28, in *The Poems of William of Shoreham*, ed. Matthias Konrath, EETS, e.s., 86 (London: Kegan Paul, 1902).

20. "Quod credimus est veritas corporis et sanguinis Christi, idem corpus quod natum est de virgine, passum est in cruce, resurrexit et ascendit." See similarly "idem corpus" in Sermon 97 (447). For examples of Brinton's direct concern with Wycliffism, see Sermon 107 (495) and Sermon 101 (446).

21. For "per modum substantiae," see *ST* III.76.1, III.76.3–7, and III.76.7, resp. For a fine critical appraisal of this concept and its development in Aquinas, see P. J. Fitzpatrick, *In Breaking of Bread: The Eucharist and Ritual* (Cambridge: Cambridge University Press, 1993), 15–16, 114–16. The work of this Catholic priest and philosopher has been a constant companion in writing the present book, a perpetual stimulus to the questions that engage me.

22. See once more *ST* III.76.1, ad 2. One question raised here I will address at some length later in the chapter: *deception* in the sacrament. On the issue of

cannibalism within the language and theology of the tradition, see Fitzpatrick, *In Breaking of Bread,* 171–73, 192.

23. For Guillaume de Deguileville's *Pèlerinage de vie humaine,* see *Le pèlerinage de vie humaine,* ed. J. J. Stürzinger (London: Roxburghe Club, 1893); here I use both this edition and the translation by Eugene Clasby, *The Pilgrimage of Human Life (Le pèlerinage de vie humaine)* (New York: Garland, 1992). For Lydgate's translation, see *The Pilgrimage of the Life of Man,* 3 vols., EETS 77, 83, and 92 (London: K. Paul, Trench, Trübner, 1899, 1901, and 1904), and for the prose one roughly contemporary, see Avril Henry, ed. and trans., *The Pilgrimage of the Lyfe of the Manhode,* 2 vols., EETS 288 and 292 (London: Oxford University Press, 1985 and 1988).

24. Clasby, *The Pilgrimage of Human Life,* 21–45 passim, 47, 66, 121, 174, 184. Note the apparently untroubled image of *deception* here (see note 22 above); see Deguileville, *Le pèlerinage de vie humaine,* lines 1465–98, 1503–2004.

25. John Mirk, *Festial: A Collection of Homilies,* ed. Theodor Erbe, EETS, e.s., 96 (London: K. Paul, Trench, Trübner, 1905), page citations are given parenthetically in the text. Fletcher dates the *Festial* c. 1382–90; see A. J. Fletcher, "John Mirk and the Lollards," *Medium Ævum* 55 (1987), 217–24. See too Rubin, *Corpus Christi,* 222–24.

26. Note the attack on "Lollardes" in this same Corpus Christi text (171); see Fletcher, "John Mirk and the Lollards."

27. William of Shoreham, *Poems.* For the section on the poem addressing the Eucharist, see pp. 18–30. Subsequent citations of this work are to line numbers and are given parenthetically in the text.

28. See Thomas F. Simmons, ed., *The Lay Folk's Mass Book,* EETS 71 (London: Trübner, 1879), 20–22.

29. Roger Dymmok, *Liber contra Duodecim Errores et Hereses Lollardorum,* ed. H. S. Cronin (London: K. Paul, Trench, Trübner, 1922); on Dymmok, see Fiona Somerset, *Clerical Discourse and Lay Audience in Late Medieval England* (Cambridge: Cambridge University Press, 1998), ch. 4, and Strohm, *England's Empty Throne,* 61–62, 139–40. Page citations to *Liber* are to Cronin's edition and are given parenthetically in the text. On Dymmok and Richard II, see John Bowers, *The Politics of Pearl* (Cambridge: Brewer, 2001), 27–28, 80, 186.

30. See too Dymmok, *Liber,* 97, 98–99, 100–102, 106. Besides the treatment of these uses by Aquinas in the *Summa Theologiae* discussed above, see his *Summa contra Gentiles,* IV.63.13. Thomas Aquinas, *Summa contra Gentiles,* Book 4, *Salvation,* trans. Charles J. O'Neil (Notre Dame: University of Notre Dame Press, 1975).

31. "Cum Christus ex hoc mundo transiturus esset ad Patrem, ne sponsam suam sanctam scilicet ecclesiam, solacio sue corporalis presencie destituerit, in cena hoc sacramentum instituit" (100).

32. Dymmok, *Liber*, 98; see *ST* III.76.1, ad 2.

33. Dymmok's emphasis on current hierarchy and its sacralization through the Eucharist represents the political theology illustrated in Corpus Christi processions. See Rubin, *Corpus Christi*, 243–71.

34. See Margaret Aston, "Lollardy and Sedition, 1381–1431," *Past and Present* 17 (1960), 1–44, and *Lollards and Reformers: Images and Literacy in Late Medieval Religion* (London: Hambledon, 1984), ch. 4; Peter McNiven, *Heresy and Politics in the Reign of Henry IV: The Burning of John Badby* (Woodbridge: Boydell, 1987), and Strohm, *England's Empty Throne*, ch. 2. H. G. Richardson, "Heresy and the Lay Power under Richard II," *English Historical Review* 51 (1936), 1–28, is still extremely helpful.

35. On the Wycliffite project in this context, see David Aers, *Faith, Ethics and Church: Writing in England, 1360–1409* (Cambridge: Brewer, 2000), ch. 6, and "From Medieval Christianities to the Reformations," *Journal of Medieval and Early Modern Studies* 27, no. 2 (1997), 139–43.

36. On Richard II's victory over London and its sacralization, see Kipling, *Enter the King*, 11–21. Dymmok is a consistent and committed defender of courtly Christianity; see Dymmok, *Liber*, part 6, especially 147–49 and 153–54; part 10 (defense of Christians killing in war and maintaining social regulations); part 12, especially 303–4.

37. See Strohm, *England's Empty Throne*, 61–62, 139–40. Strohm refers, not to the passage on the sacrament I am discussing, but to Dymmok, *Liber*, 130.

38. A few years after Dymmok's *Liber*, one encounters a similar conjunction in Hoccleve's *Regiment of Princes;* see the treatment of Badby's death by burning (288–329) and his desire to witness the burning of "many mo" Wycliffites. Thomas Hoccleve, *The Regiment of Princes*, ed. Charles R. Blyth (Kalamazoo: Western Michigan University, Medieval Institute Publications, 1999). See also Strohm, *England's Empty Throne*, 180–86; Paul Strohm, "Hoccleve, Lydgate and the Lancastrian Court," ch. 24 in *The Cambridge History of Medieval English Literature*, ed. David Wallace (Cambridge: Cambridge University Press, 1999); and Derek Pearsall, "Hoccleve's *Regement of Princes:* The Poetics of Royal Self-Representation," *Speculum* 69 (1994), 386–410.

39. For examples of such miracle stories, see Rubin, *Corpus Christi*, 108–29; Miri Rubin, *Gentile Tales: The Narrative Assault on Late Medieval Jews* (New Haven: Yale University Press, 1999), shows their consequences. See also Beckwith, "Ritual, Church, and Theatre"; P. Browe, *Die eucharistichen Wunder des Mittelalters* (Breslau: Muller & Seiffert, 1938).

40. Mirk, *Festial*, 170–71.

41. Once again Fitzpatrick, *In Breaking of Bread*, is relevant: 15–16, 114–16. It would be wrong to assume that all held Aquinas's views on the mode by which the

accidents were sustained or the mode of Christ's presence, one that became an invitation to write on optics; see, for example, William of Ockham, *Quodlibetal Questions*, 2 vols. (New Haven: Yale University Press, 1991), IV.13, vol. 1, 298–303; in general, see Katherine H. Tachau, *Vision and Certitude in the Age of Ockham: Optics, Epistemology, and the Foundations of Semantics, 1250–1345* (Leiden: Brill, 1988).

42. See especially G. J. C. Snoek, *Medieval Piety from Relics to the Eucharist* (Leiden: Brill, 1995).

43. John Bromyard, *Summa Praedicantium* (Antwerp, 1614), part 1, 247–59; page citations are given parenthetically in the text.

44. Rubin, *Gentile Tales*.

45. See the fine analysis in Beckwith, "Ritual, Church, and Theatre"; with this, David Lawton, "Sacrilege and Theatricality: The Croxton Play of the Sacrament," *Journal of Medieval and Early Modern Studies* 33 (2003), 281–309.

46. Nicholas Love, *Mirror of the Blessed Life of Jesus Christ: A Critical Edition*, ed. Michael G. Sargent (New York: Garland, 1992); citations given parenthetically in the text are to pages in this edition. On Love, see Elizabeth Salter, *Nicholas Love's "Myrrour of the Blessed Lyf of Jesu Christ"* (Salzburg: Analecta Cartusiana, 1974); Anne Hudson, *The Premature Reformation: Wycliffite Texts and Lollard History* (Oxford: Clarendon Press, 1988), 437–40; Beckwith, *Christ's Body*, 63–70; Ghosh, "'Authority' and 'Interpretation,'" ch. 5, and *The Wycliffite Heresy*, ch. 5; S. Oguro, R. Beadle, and M. Sargent, eds., *Nicholas Love at Waseda* (Woodbridge: Brewer, 1997); Katherine C. Little, "Reading for Christ: Interpretation and Instruction in Late Medieval England" (Ph.D. diss., Duke University, 1998), ch. 3. Sargent's introduction to Love, *Mirror*, is invaluable. For Love's thirteenth-century source, the *Meditaciones Vite Christi*, see Iohannis de Caulibus, *Meditaciones Vite Christi*, ed. M. Stallings-Taney, CCCM, vol. 153 (Turnholt: Brepols, 1987).

47. The most impressive of these historians is Duffy; his *Stripping of the Altars* is a work of immense, haunting power. For discussion of its grammar and ideology, see David Aers, "Altars of Power: Reflections on Eamon Duffy's *The Stripping of the Altars*," *Literature and History* 3 (1994), 90–105.

48. On the Latin text and its author see Sargent, introduction to Love, *Mirror*, ix–xx, and M. Stallings-Taney, introduction to Iohannis De Caulibus, *Meditaciones Vite Christi*, ix–xi; see Sargent, introduction to Love, *Mirror*, on Love's treatment of this source (xxx–xliv) and on Love's explicit displaying of his project as against Wycliffism (xliv–lviii).

49. Sargent, introduction to Love, *Mirror*, xliv–lviii. Subsequent page citations are given parenthetically in the text.

50. On Wyclif's ideas about Scripture and hermeneutics, see especially Paul de Vooght, *Les sources de la doctrine chrétienne d'après les théologiens du XIVe siècle et du début du XVe* (Bruges: Desclée, De Brouwer, 1954); M. Hurley, "'Scriptura

Sola': Wyclif and His Critics," *Traditio* 16 (1960), 275–352; Gordon Leff, *Heresy in the Later Middle Ages*, 2 vols. (New York: Barnes and Noble, 1967), vol. 2, 511–16; Ghosh, "'Authority' and 'Interpretation,'" ch. 1, revised in K. Ghosh, "Eliding the Interpreter: John Wyclif and Scriptural Truth," in *New Medieval Literatures*, ed. Rita Copeland, David Lawton, and Wendy Scase (Oxford: Clarendon Press, 1998), 205–24; see too Ghosh, *The Wycliffite Heresy*, ch. 1.

51. Duffy, *Stripping of the Altars*, 3.

52. On the problems of Love's task, see Beckwith, *Christ's Body*, 63–70, especially 70, together with Ghosh, *The Wycliffite Heresy*, ch. 5.

53. On this aspect, see Little, "Reading for Christ."

54. Once again, see Beckwith, *Christ's Body*, 63–70, and Ghosh, *The Wycliffite Heresy*, ch. 5.

55. See the extraordinary, meditative work by Rowan Williams, *Resurrection: Interpreting the Easter Gospel* (New York: Pilgrim Press, 1994).

56. Rowan Williams, *On Christian Theology*, (Oxford: Blackwell, 2000), 216.

57. Note too "contra lollardos" in the margin (153); see also Sargent, introduction to Love, *Mirror*, li–liii.

58. Once again it might not be far-fetched to see this will to identify past and present as the unrecognized effect of too much reading of Wycliffite texts; again, see Beckwith, *Christ's Body*, 63–70, and Ghosh, *The Wycliffite Heresy*, ch. 5. For the treatment of the Last Supper and Eucharist in the standard textbook of late medieval theology, and its antecedents, see Marcia L. Colish, *Peter Lombard*, 2 vols. (Leiden: Brill, 1994), 554, 559–60, 575–76.

59. The same project of identification is maintained at length against Wycliffites in Netter, *Doctrinale*, vol. 2, Book V, 25–26, 56.1, 58.5.

60. *N-Town Play*, Play 27; reference to line numbers in Stephen Spector, *The N-Town Play: Cotton MS Vespasian D.8*, EETS, s.s., 11–12 (Oxford: Oxford University Press, 1991); here directions after line 372 and lines 382–83.

61. For the relevant theological history, see note 1.

62. For the burning of Badby, see McNiven, *Heresy and Politics*.

63. Geoffrey Chaucer, *Canterbury Tales*, III.1271–72, in Larry D. Benson, ed., *The Riverside Chaucer* (Boston: Houghton Mifflin, 1987).

64. Once more, on this tension, see Beckwith, *Christ's Body*, 63–70.

65. For Wyclif on the issue of deceit and illusion in orthodox Eucharistic theology, see Anthony Kenny, *Wyclif* (Oxford: Oxford University Press, 1985), 85–87, and J. I. Catto, "John Wyclif and the Cult of the Eucharist," in *The Bible in the Medieval World: Essays in Memory of Beryl Smalley*, ed. Katherine Walsh and Diana Wood (Oxford: Blackwell, 1985), 269–86, 274.

66. Aquinas quotes from Augustine's *Homilies on the Gospel of John*, tr 26.17; see the English translation in Augustine, *Homilies on the Gospel of John; Homilies on*

the First Epistle of John; Soliloquies, ed. Philip Schaff (Grand Rapids, Mich.: Eerdmans, 1986), 26.17, p. 173, and *PLat* 35.1614.

67. For Scotus's objections, and his alternative account, see Richard Cross, *Duns Scotus* (Oxford: Oxford University Press, 1999), 140–44.

68. This is a characteristic Thomistic position; see *ST* I.1.8 for an especially fine statement of it, also I.1.6, ad 2. On issues of faith, reason, Nicholas Love, and modern Chaucer criticism, see Aers, *Faith, Ethics,* ch. 1.

69. Yet once more I record my indebtedness to Fitzpatrick, *In Breaking of Bread;* for arguments about disguise and cannibalism, see 167–73. Aquinas also addressed the issue of deception in *Summa contra Gentiles,* IV.62.10 (with IV.62.2 and IV.62.14).

70. On this text, see Fitzpatrick, *In Breaking of Bread,* 144–45 (his rendering of *ST* III.75.5, ad 2, lacks, without notice, the phrase I have quoted in the preceding sentence).

71. For a profound discussion of Aquinas and these issues, see Fitzpatrick, *In Breaking of Bread,* ch. 4. Catherine Pickstock's peremptory dismissal of Fitzpatrick is unwarranted; Catherine Pickstock, *After Writing: On the Liturgical Consummation of Philosophy* (Oxford: Blackwell, 1998), 174.

72. For Dymmok, see Dymmok, *Liber,* 100.

73. See chapters 3 and 4 of this book.

74. On this treatise and its place in all known manuscripts of the *Mirror,* see Sargent, introduction to Love, *Mirror,* liii, and for the text, 225–41.

75. See on the issues here Aers, *Faith, Ethics,* ch. 1. Similar to Love is Reginald Pecock's *Book of Faith,* I.7, ed. J. L. Morison (Glasgow: Maclehose, 1909). Pecock maintains that even if Lollards were burnt to death for what was "trewe" they would still be wrong because they had disobeyed prelates.

76. This is a salutary observation on the version of late medieval Christianity in Duffy, *Stripping of the Altars.*

77. See Strohm, *England's Empty Throne,* ch. 2.

78. See Paul H. Jones, *Christ's Eucharistic Presence* (New York: Lang, 1994), 18–19, and Denys Turner, "The Darkness of God and the Light of Christ: Negative Theology and Eucharistic Presence," *Modern Theology* 15 (1999), 143–59.

79. Williams, *On Christian Theology,* 187.

80. Williams, *On Christian Theology,* 190.

2. *The Sacrament of the Altar in* Piers Plowman

1. Robert Adams, "Langland's Theology," in *A Companion to Piers Plowman,* ed. John Alford (Berkeley: University of California Press, 1988), 102. Adams

is here actually quoting Gordon Whatley, approvingly: Whatley's comment is "the only safe generalization about Langland's sacramental theology." For Whatley's essay, see Gordon Whatley, "*Piers Plowman* B 12.277–94: Notes on Langland, Text and Theology," *Modern Philology* 82 (1984), 1–12. Even Wendy Scase, *Piers Plowman and the New Anticlericalism* (Cambridge: Cambridge University Press, 1989), and Lawrence Clopper, *"Songes of Rechelesnesse": Langland and the Franciscans* (Ann Arbor: University of Michigan Press, 1997), have nothing to say on the sacrament of the altar.

2. Respectively, N. T. Gray, "A Study of *Piers Plowman* in Relation to Medieval Penitential Traditions" (Ph.D. diss., Cambridge University, 1984); M. Teresa Tavormina, *Kindly Similitude: Marriage and Family in Piers Plowman* (Cambridge: Brewer, 1995); and M. Vaughan, "The Liturgical Perspectives of *Piers Plowman,* B, XVI–XIX," *Studies in Medieval and Renaissance History* n.s., 3 (1980), 87–155. See too Robert Adams, "Langland and the Liturgy Revisited," *Studies in Philology* 73 (1976), 266–84, and R. St.-Jacques, "The Liturgical Associations of Langland's Samaritan," *Traditio* 25 (1969), 217–30. For an extremely innovative approach to *Piers Plowman* and the liturgy, see Bruce Holsinger, "Langland's Musical Reader: Liturgy, Law and the Constraints of Perfection," *Studies in the Age of Chaucer* 21 (1999), 99–141.

3. For helpful guidance across this complex history, see the following: James F. McCue, "The Doctrine of Transubstantiation from Berengar through Trent," *Harvard Theological Review* 61 (1968), 385–430; David Burr, "Scotus and Transubstantiation," *Medieval Studies* 34 (1972), 336–60, and *Eucharistic Presence in Late-Thirteenth Century Franciscan Thought* (Philadelphia: American Philosophical Society, 1984); John Bossy, "The Mass as a Social Institution, 1200–1700," *Past and Present* 100 (1983), 29–61; Gary Macy, *The Theologies of the Eucharist in the Early Scholastic Period* (Oxford: Clarendon Press, 1984), "Reception of the Eucharist According to the Theologians: A Case of Theological Diversity in the Thirteenth and Fourteenth Centuries," in *Theology and the University,* ed. John Apczynski (Lanham, Md.: University Press of America, 1990), *The Banquet's Wisdom: A Short History of the Theologies of the Lord's Supper* (New York: Paulist Press, 1992), and "The 'Dogma of Transubstantiation' in the Middle Ages," *Journal of Ecclesiastical History* 45 (1994), 11–41; Peter McNiven, *Heresy and Politics in the Reign of Henry IV: The Burning of John Badby* (Woodbridge: Boydell, 1987), 23–29; Anne Hudson, *The Premature Reformation: Wycliffite Texts and Lollard History* (Oxford: Clarendon Press, 1988), 281–90; Miri Rubin, *Corpus Christi: The Eucharist in Late Medieval Culture* (Cambridge: Cambridge University Press,1991); Paul Strohm, *England's Empty Throne: Usurpation and the Language of Legitimation, 1399–1422* (New Haven: Yale University Press, 1998), ch. 2; Eamon Duffy, *The Stripping of the Altars: Traditional Religion in England, 1400–1580* (New Haven: Yale University Press, 1992), ch. 3.

4. For the reception of *Piers Plowman,* see Anne Hudson, "The Legacy of *Piers Plowman,*" in Alford, *A Companion to Piers Plowman,* 251–66.

5. The version of *Piers Plowman* used in this chapter is the C version: William Langland, *Piers Plowman: The C Version: Will's Visions of Piers Plowman, Do-Well, Do-Better, and Do-Best,* ed. George Russell and George Kane (London: Athlone, 1997); passus and line numbers are cited parenthetically in the text. I have found Derek Pearsall's edition and notes unfailingly helpful and have consulted them throughout; see William Langland, *Piers Plowman, by William Langland: An Edition of the C-Text,* ed. Derek Pearsall (London: Arnold, 1978), hereafter cited as "Langland, *Piers Plowman* (Pearsall)." For the B version I use *Piers Plowman: The B Version,* ed. George Kane and E. Talbot Donaldson (London: Athlone, 1988). On "webs of interlocution," see Charles Taylor, *Sources of the Self: The Making of the Modern Identity* (Cambridge: Harvard University Press, 1989), 33–36, and David Aers, ed., *Culture and History, 1350–1600* (Hemel Hempstead: Harvester Wheatsheaf, 1992), 1–3.

6. On this shaping, see H. Leith Spencer, *English Preaching in the Late Middle Ages* (Oxford: Clarendon Press, 1993).

7. For a study of exemplary sensitivity and richness in this domain, see Sarah Beckwith, *Signifying God: Social Relation and Symbolic Act in the York Corpus Christi Plays* (Chicago: Chicago University Press, 2001), passim but especially ch. 5. See too Denys Turner, "The Darkness of God and the Light of Christ: Negative Theology and Eucharistic Presence," *Modern Theology* 15, no. 2 (1999), 143–59, and the work which has been the most important help to me in addressing the issues of this chapter, P. J. Fitzpatrick, *In Breaking of Bread: The Eucharist and Ritual* (Cambridge: Cambridge University Press, 1993).

8. Thomas Aquinas, *Summa Theologiae [ST]* III.65.3, contra, resp, ad 2 and ad 3; III. 73.3, resp and ad 3. All citations are to the Blackfriars edition (London: Blackfriars, 1964–81) and are subsequently given parenthetically in the text. For a characteristic fourteenth-century example, see Roger Dymmok, *Liber contra Duodecim Errores et Hereses Lollardorum,* ed. H. S. Cronin (London: Trübner, 1922), 105, 108–10.

9. Thomas Brinton, *The Sermons of Thomas Brinton, Bishop of Rochester (1373–1389),* ed. by Mary A. Devlin, Camden 3d ser., 85–86 (London: Royal Historical Society, 1954), Sermon 69, 320; see too Sermon 48, 215–16. Contrast the benefits of the worthily received Mass in John Wyclif, *De Eucharistia,* ed. John Loserth (London: Trübner, 1892), 178–79.

10. John Lydgate, "The Interpretation and Virtues of the Mass," lines 622–640, in *The Minor Poems of John Lydgate,* ed. H. N. MacCracken, EETS 107 (London: K. Paul, Trench, Trübner, 1911), vol. 1, 87–115. See Duffy, *Stripping of the Altars,* 100–101.

11. See especially Wyclif, *De Eucharistia,* but also John Wyclif, *Sermones,* 4 vols., ed. John Loserth (London: Trübner, 1887–90), vol. 2, 453–63 (for Corpus Christi), *Tractatus de Blasphemia,* ed. Michael H. Dziewicki (London: Trübner, 1893), 20–31, *Trialogus,* ed. Gotthard V. Lechler (Oxford: Oxford University Press, 1869), 244–77, and *Confessio* in *Fasciculi Zizaniorum Magistri Johannis Wyclif cum Tritico,* ed. Walter W. Shirley (London: Longman, Brown, Green, Longmans, and Roberts, 1858), 115–32. There is helpful commentary in Maurice H. Keen, "Wyclif, the Bible, and Transubstantiation," in *Wyclif in His Times,* ed. Anthony Kenny (Oxford: Oxford University Press, 1986), 1–16; J. I. Catto, "John Wyclif and the Cult of the Eucharist," in *The Bible in the Medieval World: Essays in Memory of Beryl Smalley,* ed. Katherine Walsh and Diana Wood (Oxford: Blackwell, 1985), 269–86; J. A. Robson, *Wyclif and the Oxford Schools* (Cambridge: Cambridge University Press, 1961), 190–95; Gordon Leff, *Heresy in the Later Middle Ages,* 2 vols. (New York: Barnes and Noble, 1967), vol. 2, 549–57; Hudson, *The Premature Reformation,* 281–83; Ian C. Levy, "*Christus Qui Mentiri Non Potest:* John Wyclif's Rejection of Transubstantiation," *Recherches de Théologie et Philosophie Médiévales* 66 (1999), 316–34.

12. Wyclif, *De Eucharistia,* 158–71, 177–79; 90, 98.

13. Strohm, *England's Empty Throne,* ch. 2; on the centrality of the symbol, see Rubin, *Corpus Christi;* Sarah Beckwith, *Christ's Body: Identity, Culture, and Society in Late Medieval Writings* (New York: Routledge, 1993); and Caroline Bynum, *Holy Feast and Holy Fast: The Religious Significance of Food to Medieval Women* (Berkeley: University of California Press, 1987).

14. Dymmok, *Liber,* 3–10. For early examples of orthodox response to Wyclif, see Tyssyngton and Wyntirton in 1381, in Shirley, *Fasciculi Zizaniorum,* 133–80, 181–238.

15. Dymmok, *Liber,* 90–91; on Dymmok, see Fiona Somerset, *Clerical Discourse and Lay Audience in Late Medieval England* (Cambridge: Cambridge University Press, 1998), ch. 4, and Strohm, *England's Empty Throne,* 61–62, 139–40.

16. Dymmok, *Liber,* 93–95; see too 98–99, 100–102, 106. On the miracles, see 99–100. On Eucharistic miracles, with copious examples, see Rubin, *Corpus Christi,* 108–29. Cf. Wyclif, *De Eucharistia,* 19–20.

17. Bossy, "The Mass," 33.

18. Beckwith, *Christ's Body,* 36–37; Beckwith, *Signifying God,* ch. 4; Duffy, *Stripping of the Altars,* 95–102. On "*undifferentiated dorsality*" of the priest, see Fitzpatrick, *In Breaking of Bread,* 210–11; also relevant here are William of Ockham, *Quodlibetal Questions,* 2 vols. (New Haven: Yale University Press, 1991), IV.13–15, 29–31, VI.3, VII.19, and *The De Sacramento Altaris of William of Ockham,* ed. and trans. T. Brune Birch, Latin text and English translation (Burlington, Vt.: Lutheran Library Board, 1930). This last is in fact two distinct but related works, *De Quantitate*

and *De Corpore Christi;* see *Guillelmi de Ockham: Tractatus de Quantitate et Tractatus de Corpore Christi,* ed. Carlo A. Grassi, vol. 10 of William of Ockham, *Opera Philosophica et Theologica* (St. Bonaventure, N.Y.: St. Bonaventure University, Franciscan Institute, 1986). On the textual history, see pp. 5*–19*, 20*–21*. See too Katherine H. Tachau, *Vision and Certitude in the Age of Ockham: Optics, Epistemology, and the Foundations of Semantics, 1250–1345* (Leiden: Brill, 1988), ch. 5.

19. Bossy, "The Mass," 53. Once more I note how illuminating I have found Fitzpatrick, *In Breaking of Bread.*

20. On the date of the C version, see Lucy Lewis, "Langland's Tree of Charity and Usk's Wexing Tree," *Notes and Queries* 240 (1995), 429–33; Anne Middleton, "Acts of Vagrancy: The C Version 'Autobiography' and the Statute of 1388," in *Written Work: Langland, Labor, and Authorship,* ed. Steven Justice and Kathryn Kerby-Fulton (Philadelphia: University of Pennsylvania Press, 1997), 208–317; and Ralph Hanna, "A New Edition of the C Version," *Yearbook of Langland Studies* 12 (1998), 175–88, 186. In the light of this recent work I see no reason for dating Langland's final work on this poem before the late 1380s or early 1390s: a return to W. W. Skeat's suggestion in his great parallel-text edition, *The Vision of William Concerning Piers the Plowman Together with Richard the Redeless,* 2 vols. (1886; reprint, Oxford: Oxford University Press, 1968).

21. On Mede, see David Aers, "Class, Gender, and Medieval Criticism and *Piers Plowman,*" in *Class and Gender in Early English Literature,* ed. B. J. Harwood and G. R. Overing (Bloomington: Indiana University Press, 1994), 59–75; Clare A. Lees, "Gender and Exchange in *Piers Plowman,*" in Harwood and Overing, *Class and Gender,* 112–30; and Stephanie Trigg, "The Traffic in Medieval Women: Alice Perrers, Feminist Criticism and *Piers Plowman,*" *Yearbook of Langland Studies* 12 (1998), 5–29.

22. On the C version, Passus V, see especially Middleton, "Acts of Vagrancy."

23. See Langland, *Piers Plowman* (Pearsall), 115 nn.144, 146.

24. Bossy, "The Mass," 54–56, with Rubin, *Corpus Christi,* ch. 4, and Mervyn James, "Ritual, Drama, and Social Body in the Late Medieval Town," *Past and Present* 98 (1983), 3–29.

25. 1 Corinthians 10:17; see *ST* III.65.1; III.73.4, resp; III.80.1; III.80.4, resp.

26. We should note how Langland's approach to the sacrament precludes many traditional puzzles and their often theologically gross resolutions, as in those caused by the ubiquitous mouse who eats the consecrated host; Fitzpatrick, *In Breaking of Bread,* 164, drawing on Aquinas's commentary on the *Sentences,* IV dist 9, art 2, quaestiuncula 3 (see Fitzpatrick, *In Breaking of Bread,* 163–74). On this see too A. M. Landgraf, "Die in der Frühscholastik klassische Frage *Quid sumit mus,*" in *Dogmengeschichte der Frühscholastik,* vol. 3, part 2 (Regensburg: Friedrich Pustet, 1955), 207–22. For clear examples of the orthodox abstraction of the sacrament

from people's reception, and for the view that the sacrament is *complete* in consecration with reception as a supplement, see *ST* III.73.1, ad 3, and III.74.7, resp.

27. For a rich commentary on the liturgical and scriptural allusions of the passus, see William Langland, *Piers Plowman: B Text (Preface and Passus I–VIII)*, ed. J. A. W. Bennet (Oxford: Oxford University Press, 1972), 182–86, here especially 185. Subsequent citations to this edition are to "Langland, *Piers Plowman* (Bennett)."

28. As we saw in chapter 1, Jesus was said to have enacted the orthodox account of transubstantiation at the Last Supper. *ST* III.81.1 and 3; Nicholas Love, *Mirror of the Blessed Life of Jesus Christ: A Critical Edition*, ed. Michael G. Sargent (New York: Garland, 1992), 146–56. So the question arose: What would have happened to the reserved sacrament in the pyx, or the host consecrated by an apostle during the *triduum*, when Christ's body was separated from his soul and dead? See *ST* III.81.4. Langland resisted such "sacramental" concerns not because he was uninterested in the sacrament but because they were alien to his own sacramental theology. See too note 25.

29. Langland, *Piers Plowman* (Bennett), 182, 186–87.

30. Conventional accounts are amply illustrated in Rubin, *Corpus Christi*, and Duffy, *Stripping of the Altars*, ch. 3; Love, *Mirror*, 225–41, offers a good vernacular example.

31. On Wycliffite attitudes to pilgrimage and signs, see Dymmok, *Liber*, part 8; part 5 is also relevant. See too Hudson, *The Premature Reformation*, 301–9, and Anne Hudson and Pamela Gradon, eds., *English Wycliffite Sermons*, 5 vols. (Oxford: Oxford University Press, 1983–96), vol. 4, 66–68. For the date of the C version of *Piers Plowman*, see note 20 of this chapter.

32. Aunpolles are "small phials containing holy water or oil from shrines." Langland, *Piers Plowman* (Pearsall), 137 n. 165.

33. In this chapter, when quoting the Bible, I use *Biblia Sacra iuxta Vulgatem Clementinam*, 4th ed., ed. Alberto Colunga and Laurentio Turrado (Matriti: Biblioteca de Autores Cristianos, 1965), for the vulgate and *The Holy Bible, Translated from the Latin Vulgate*, rev. Richard Challoner (Rockford, Ill.: Tan Books, 1989), for the English translation.

34. On the plowman here, see Elizabeth Kirk, "Langland's Plowman and the Recreation of Fourteenth-Century Religious Metaphor," *Yearbook of Langland Studies* 2 (1988), 1–21; Hudson, *The Premature Reformation*, 398–408; Pamela Gradon, "Langland and the Ideology of Dissent," *Publications of the British Academy* 66 (1980), 179–205, 197–99.

35. Paraphrasing Augustine, *Confessions*, ed. James J. O'Donnell (Oxford: Clarendon Press, 1992), III.6.11; hereafter cited as "Augustine, *Confessions* (O'Donnell)." For this tradition in relation to *Piers Plowman*, see Elizabeth [Salter] Zeeman, "*Piers Plowman* and the Pilgrimage to Truth," *Essays and Studies* 11 (1958),

1–16; see too J. Wittig, "*Piers Plowman B,* Passus IX–XII: Elements in the Design of the Inward Journey," *Traditio* 28 (1972), 211–80.

36. On the figurative modes here, see Salter, "*Piers Plowman,*" 13–16; see too John Burrow, "The Action of Langland's Second Vision," *Essays in Criticism* 15 (1965), 373–84.

37. See David Aers, *Piers Plowman and Christian Allegory* (London: Arnold, 1975), 80–111, and *Community, Gender, and Individual Identity: English Writing, 1360–1430* (London: Routledge, 1988), ch. 1. For an example of readers who do not see any dialectical processes in the poem, see Traugott Lawler, "The Pardon Formula in Piers Plowman," *Yearbook of Langland Studies* 14 (2000), 117–52.

38. On the political coordinates here, see Aers, *Community, Gender,* 35–55.

39. Bernard McGinn, *The Flowering of Mysticism: Origins to Fifth Century* (New York: Crossroads, 1995), 239. For a convergence of Piers's spiritualizing of the Church to an inner domain with Wycliffism, see examples in Norman P. Tanner, ed., *Heresy Trials in the Diocese of Norwich, 1428–31,* Camden 4th ser., vol. 20 (London: Royal Historical Society, 1977), 77, 73. For Julian of Norwich's version, see Julian of Norwich, *The Shewings of Julian of Norwich,* ed. Georgia R. Crampton (Kalamazoo: Western Michigan University, Medieval Institute Publications, 1994), ch. 62, 127.

40. On eating and drinking in *Piers Plowman,* see A. C. Spearing, "The Development of a Theme in *Piers Plowman,*" *Review of English Studies* 11 (1960), 241–53; Jill Mann, "Eating and Drinking in *Piers Plowman,*" *Essays and Studies* 32 (1979), 26–43; Traugott Lawler, "Conscience's Dinner," in *The Endless Knot: Essays in Honor of Marie Borroff,* ed. M. T. Tavormina and R. F. Yeager (Cambridge: Brewer, 1995), 87–103; Tavormina, *Kindly Similitude,* 119 n. 17.

41. Langland, *Piers Plowman* (Pearsall), 212 nn. 45–47.

42. David Aers and Lynn Staley, *The Powers of the Holy: Religion, Politics, and Gender in Late Medieval English Culture* (University Park: Pennsylvania State Press, 1996), 65, 65 n. 66; Langland, *Piers Plowman* (Pearsall), 213 n. 54.

43. Gray, "A Study of *Piers Plowman.*"

44. There is a substantial literature on Trajan; see especially G. Whatley, "The Uses of Hagiography: The Legend of Pope Gregory and the Emperor Trajan in the Middle Ages," *Viator* 15 (1984), 25–63; Nicholas Watson, "Visions of Inclusion: Universal Salvation and Vernacular Theology in Pre-Reformation England," *Journal of Medieval and Early Modern Studies* 27, no. 2 (1997), 145–87; 153–60; F. Grady, "*Piers Plowman, St. Erkenwald,* and the Rule of Exceptional Salvations," *Yearbook of Langland Studies* 6 (1992), 61–88; A. J. Minnis, "Looking for a Sign: The Quest for Nominalism in Chaucer and Langland," ch. 7 in *Essays in Ricardian Literature,* ed. A. J. Minnis, Charlotte Morse and Thorlac Turville-Petre (Oxford: Clarendon Press, 1997), 143, 165–70.

45. For a brilliant theological and historical study of *corpus mysticum* and *corpus Christi*, see Henri de Lubac, *Corpus mysticum: L'Eucharistie et l'église au moyen âge* (Paris: Aubier, 1949).

46. In the C version the speaker seems to be Rechelessness, but in this passage and in the whole poem there is nothing to subvert its authority, drawing as it does on 1 Corinthians 10.17 and 12.12, 1 Peter 2.2, and the liturgy; see Langland, *Piers Plowman* (Pearsall), 216 n. 109.

47. Love, *Mirror*, 151, 153. Hereafter, page citations to this work are given parenthetically in the text.

48. For a very different reading of the passage in B XII, see D. M. Murtaugh, *Piers Plowman and the Image of God* (Gainesville: University Presses of Florida, 1978), 94–96.

49. Augustine, *Homilies on the Gospel of John*, in *Homilies on the Gospel of John; Homilies on the First Epistle of John; Soliloquies*, ed. Philip Schaff (Grand Rapids, Mich.: Eerdmans, 1986), on John 8.3–18, tr 33.4–8.

50. See Langland, *Piers Plowman* (Pearsall), 288 n. 220; see also Hudson, *The Premature Reformation*, 337–42, 405–6, and Hudson and Gradon, *English Wycliffite Sermons*, 162–72.

51. Langland, *Piers Plowman* (Pearsall), 283 n. 121.

52. John Bromyard, *Summa Praedicantium* (Antwerp, 1614), part 1, 251–52. For Brinton, see Thomas Brinton, *The Sermons of Thomas Brinton, Bishop of Rochester (1373–1389)*, ed. Mary A. Devlin, Camden 3d ser., 85–86 (London: Royal Historical Society, 1954), 251, 306, 447; Dymmok, *Liber*, 99–100; John Mirk, *Festial: A Collection of Homilies*, ed. Theodor Erbe, EETS, e.s., 96 (London: K. Paul, Trench, Trübner, 1905), 170–75; Love, *Mirror*, 154, 225–41.

53. See Aers, *Piers Plowman and Christian Allegory*, 77–109; E. Talbot Donaldson, *Piers Plowman: The C Text and Its Poet*, Yale Studies in English 113 (New Haven: Yale University Press, 1949), 180–96; Tavormina, *Kindly Similitude*, 110–40. On the symbolism of the will to eat the fruit (not just to gaze at it), see David Aers, "Visionary Eschatology: *Piers Plowman*," *Modern Theology* 16 (2000), 6–7 (relating Langland's iconography to Bernard on the Song of Songs).

54. Langland, *Piers Plowman* (Pearsall), 304 n. 262.

55. Here Russell and Kane, in their edition of the C version (Langland, *Piers Plowman*), introduce "Y" at XVIII.288; (contrast the C manuscript in their apparatus, p. 582).

56. There is a fine account of these dialectical relations in Turner, "The Darkness of God," and Beckwith, *Signifying God*.

57. On this, see Ben H. Smith, *Traditional Imagery of Charity in Piers Plowman* (The Hague: Mouton, 1966), 74–93; for the liturgy here, see Vaughan,

"Liturgical Perspectives"; St. Jacques, "Liturgical Associations"; Adams, "Langland and the Liturgy Revisited."

58. Aquinas's argument: *ST* III.65.1, resp, and III.66.2, resp.

59. On "prolongation," his excellent term, see Fitzpatrick, *In Breaking of Bread*, 138, 171–74.

60. Rubin, *Corpus Christi*, 263, see also 243–71; Beckwith, *Christ's Body*, 33–37; James, "Ritual, Drama, and Social Body." Duffy's approach here is idealized and depoliticized; Duffy, *Stripping of the Altars*, 23–28. For the very relevant procession organized after the May 1382 condemnation of Wyclif, in Langland's London, culminating in an orthodox miracle in defense of transubstantiation, see Henry Knighton, *Knighton's Chronicle, 1377–1396*, ed. and trans. G. H. Martin (Oxford: Oxford University Press, 1995), 66; McNiven, *Heresy and Politics*, 38; and Strohm, *England's Empty Throne*, 50–51.

61. For another firefighting Eucharistic miracle, in Bury St. Edmund's in 1464, see Gail M. Gibson, *The Theater of Devotion: East Anglian Drama and Society in the Late Middle Ages* (Chicago: Chicago University Press, 1989), 36, 186 nn. 78–79.

62. For example, see Walter Brut, "Proceedings in the Trial of Walter Brut for Heresy," in *Registrum Johannis Trefnant*, ed. W. W. Capes (London: Canterbury and York Society, 1916), 336–41, especially here 338–39; William Thorpe, *The Testimony of William Thorpe*, in *Two Wycliffite Texts*, ed. Anne Hudson, EETS 301 (Oxford: Oxford University Press, 1993), 24–93, 53. For Wyclif's treatment of reception, see, for example, Wyclif, *De Eucharistia*, 158–71, 177–78. See chapters 3 and 4 of this book.

63. See Smith, *Traditional Imagery*, 90–93. I have been greatly helped by Sarah Beckwith in clarifying the argument in this paragraph. For the use of the Eucharist as a test, described later in this paragraph, see Strohm, *England's Empty Throne*, ch. 2.

64. Augustine, *Confessions*, trans. Henry Chadwick (Oxford: Oxford University Press, 1991), and *Confessions* (O'Donnell), VII.10.16; see the commentary in Augustine, *Confessions* (O'Donnell), vol. 3, 443–45. Aquinas uses this text in *ST* III.73.3, ad 2; after quoting it, he notes, "A man can be changed into Christ and be incorporated into him by his mind's earnest devotion [voto mentis], even though he does not actually receive the sacrament."

65. On this passage, see Aers and Staley, *Powers of the Holy*, 72 and reference in 72 n. 81.

66. See XXI.182–90; on restitution, *"redde quod debes,"* see comments and references in Langland, *Piers Plowman* (Pearsall), 349 n. 187; add to these Britton Harwood, *Piers Plowman and the Problem of Belief* (Toronto: University of Toronto Press, 1992), 43–44, 114–16, 130–32, 151; also Gray, "A Study of *Piers Plowman*," ch. 2, sec. 5; ch. 5; and 416 ff. On this topic in the *Memoriale Presbiterorum*, see

Michael Haren, *Sin and Society in Fourteenth-Century England* (Oxford: Clarendon Press, 2000), 75–76, 82–83.

67. Duffy, *Stripping of the Altars*, 93; for an example of suspicion about frequent communion (in 1378 in Bohemia), see Frantisek Smahel, "Literacy and Heresy in Hussite Bohemia," in *Heresy and Literacy, 1000–1530*, ed. Peter Biller and Anne Hudson (Cambridge: Cambridge University Press, 1994), 252.

68. On the increasingly elaborate separation of clergy and laity in the later Middle Ages, see Bossy, "The Mass," 33; Beckwith, *Christ's Body*, 36–37; Bynum, *Holy Feast*, 57.

69. On these relations, see Augustine, *Homilies on the Gospel of John*, 26.13; see too XXVI.17 and 19, XXVII.1 and 6; also Augustine, *Concerning the City of God*, trans. Henry Bettenson (London: Penguin Books, 1984), X.6 and XXI.25.

70. On the poem's ending, apocalypse, and eschatology, see Aers, "Visionary Eschatology"; R. K. Emmerson, *Antichrist in the Middle Ages: A Study of Medieval Apocalypticism, Art, and Literature* (Seattle: University of Washington Press, 1981), 193–203, and "'Yernen to Rede Redeles?' *Piers Plowman* and Prophecy," *Yearbook in Langland Studies* 7 (1994), 28–76, especially 32–38, 41–49; and Willi Erzgräber, *Mündlichkeit und Schriftlichkeit im englischen Mittelalter* (Tübingen: G. Narr, 1988).

3. *John Wyclif:* De Eucharistia (Tractatus Maior)

1. Reliable and lucid outlines of Wyclif's Eucharistic theology are given by the following: Anthony Kenny, *Wyclif* (Oxford: Oxford University Press, 1985), ch. 7; Maurice H. Keen, "Wyclif, the Bible, and Transubstantiation," in, *Wyclif in His Times*, ed. Anthony Kenny (Oxford: Oxford University Press, 1986), 1–16; Anne Hudson, *The Premature Reformation: Wycliffite Texts and Lollard History* (Oxford: Clarendon Press, 1988), 281–90; Ian C. Levy, "*Christus Qui Mentiri Non Potest:* John Wyclif's Rejection of Transubstantiation," *Recherches de Théologie et Philosophie Médiévales* 66 (1999), 316–34. Gordon Leff is still very useful, despite some exaggeration of the role of realist metaphysics in Wyclif's sacramental thinking; Gordon Leff, *Heresy in the Later Middle Ages*, 2 vols. (New York: Barnes and Noble, 1967), vol. 2, 549–57. Williel Thomson, *The Latin Writings of John Wyclyf: An Annotated Catalog* (Toronto: Pontifical Institute of Medieval Studies, 1983), is an invaluable help in the study of Wyclif. J. A. Robson, *Wyclif and the Oxford Schools* (Cambridge: Cambridge University Press, 1961), includes an account of William Woodford's description of Wyclif's views on the Eucharist, 190–97. See too J. I. Catto, "John Wyclif and the Cult of the Eucharist," in *The Bible in the Medieval World: Essays in Memory of Beryl Smalley*, ed. Katherine Walsh and Diana Wood (Oxford: Blackwell, 1985), 269–86, and Paul de Vooght, *Les sources de la doctrine*

chrétienne d'après les théologiens du XIVe siècle et du début du XVe (Bruges: Desclée, De Brouwer, 1954). For the Church's responses, see especially the following: H. G. Richardson, "Heresy and the Lay Power under Richard II," *English Historical Review* 51 (1936), 1–28; Margaret Aston, "Lollardy and Sedition, 1381–1431," *Past and Present* 17 (1960), 1–44, reprinted in *Lollards and Reformers: Images and Literacy in Late Medieval Religion* (London: Hambledon, 1984), ch. 1; Peter McNiven, *Heresy and Politics in the Reign of Henry IV: The Burning of John Badby* (Woodbridge: Boydell, 1987); Paul Strohm, *England's Empty Throne: Usurpation and the Language of Legitimation, 1399–1422* (New Haven: Yale University Press, 1998); Kantik Ghosh, *The Wycliffite Heresy: Authority and the Interpretation of Texts* (Cambridge: Cambridge University Press, 2002), 197–201, 204–5. Richard Rex's claims that Wyclif is "less forthcoming" about his views on the Eucharist than on what he objects to and that his views are "far from clear" seem to me unwarranted; Richard Rex, *The Lollards* (Basingstoke: Palgrave Press, 2002), 44–45.

2. Anne Hudson, *The Premature Reformation*, 281.

3. Kenny, *Wyclif*, 80, 88–89; Keen, "Wyclif, the Bible, and Transubstantiation," 14; Hudson, *The Premature Reformation*, 282; Catto, "John Wyclif," 273; Levy, "Christus Qui Mentiri Non Potest."

4. Kenny, *Wyclif*, 88; Keen, "Wyclif, the Bible, and Transubstantiation," 14.

5. Roger Dymmok, *Liber contra Duodecim Errores et Hereses Lollardorum*, ed. H. S. Cronin (London: Trübner, 1922), 90–91, from conclusion 1, on the Eucharist; see too 130 (on conclusion 5). The latter is quoted in Strohm, *England's Empty Throne*, 61; see too 139.

6. Strohm, *England's Empty Throne*, ch. 2; Aston, "Lollardy and Sedition"; McNiven, *Heresy and Politics*.

7. For *De Eucharistia (Tractatus Maior)*, see John Wyclif, *De Eucharistia*, ed. John Loserth (London: Trübner, 1892); here see 11, 305. See also John Wyclif, *Trialogus*, ed. Gotthard V. Lechler (Oxford: Oxford University Press, 1869), 248, and Anne Hudson, *Selections from English Wycliffite Writings* (Cambridge: Cambridge University Press, 1978), 17–18, 141–44.

8. For good introductions to such approaches to transubstantiation, see Marilyn McCord Adams, "Aristotle and the Sacrament of the Altar," in *Aristotle and His Medieval Interpreters*, ed. Richard Bosley and Martin Tweedale (Calgary: University of Calgary Press, 1991), 195–249; David Burr, "Scotus and Transubstantiation," *Medieval Studies* 34 (1972), 336–60, and *Eucharistic Presence in Late-Thirteenth Century Franciscan Thought* (Philadelphia: American Philosophical Society, 1984); Richard Cross, *Duns Scotus* (Oxford: Oxford University Press, 1999), 140–44; James McCue, "The Doctrine of Transubstantiation from Berengar through Trent," *Harvard Theological Review* 61 (1968), 385–430; Gary Macy, "Reception of the Eucharist According to the Theologians: A Case of Theological Di-

versity in the Thirteenth and Fourteenth Centuries," in *Theology and the University*, ed. John Apczynski (Lanham, Md.: University Press of America, 1990), *The Banquet's Wisdom: A Short History of the Theologies of the Lord's Supper* (New York: Paulist Press, 1992), and "The 'Dogma of Transubstantiation' in the Middle Ages," *Journal of Ecclesiastical History* 45 (1994), 11–41.

9. Wyclif, *De Eucharistia;* page citations are given parenthetically in the text, as here. We should recall Love's attempt, discussed in chapter 1, to project responsibility for this "school matter" onto Wycliffites.

10. Dating of Wyclif's work, here and below, comes from Thomson, *The Latin Writings*, item 38 (*De Eucharistia*), item 36 (*Tractatus de Apostasia*), and item 47 (*Trialogus*).

11. On Woodford and Wyclif, see Robson, *Wyclif and the Oxford Schools*, 190–95; Catto, "John Wyclif," 271; Ghosh, *The Wycliffite Heresy*, ch. 2. See too, on this issue, Hudson, *The Premature Reformation*, 281 n. 17. For the date of the *Tractatus de Apostasia*, see Thomson, *The Latin Writings*, item 36.

12. Wyclif doesn't cite Augustine here, but he is moving close to one of Augustine's homilies on John 6, one of which he will soon cite (17–18). See Augustine, *Homilies on the Gospel of John; Homilies on the First Epistle of John; Soliloquies*, ed. Philip Schaff (Grand Rapids, Mich.: Eerdmans, 1986), tr 26:12, 18; tr 27: 1, 3, 11. Aquinas, as I observed in chapter 1, insisted that because Christ's presence in the sacrament is in the mode of substance, humans cannot see him. *ST* III.76.7, resp; see too III.75.6, ad 3, III.75.5, ad 2, and III.76.1, ad 3.

13. In this chapter I quote the vulgate from the Douay-Rheims translation, *The Holy Bible translated from the Latin Vulgate*, rev. Richard Challoner (Rockford, Ill.: Tan Books, 1989).

14. See Augustine, *Homilies*, tr 26:18, p. 173: translation adapted to match Wyclif's text.

15. For other characteristic responses to these mice, see Wyclif, *Trialogus*, 247, 257, 258, 260, 271, 273. I return to the mouse later in this chapter, but see Gary Macy, "Of Mice and Manna: *Quid Mus Sumit* as a Pastoral Question," *Recherches de Théologie Ancienne et Médiévale* 58 (1991), 157–66, and Anne Hudson, "The Mouse in the Pyx: Popular Heresy and the Eucharist," *Trivium* 26 (1991), 40–53, especially 40–41, 43.

16. For another example of Wyclif's insistence that it is Augustine he follows, see *Trialogus*, 259–60, and *Sermones*, 4 vols., ed. John Loserth (London: Trübner, 1887–90), vol. 2, 453–54, 455.

17. The complaint about the collapse of this dialectic of the sign into a false *identity* pervades Wyclif's thinking about the Eucharist. Besides comments on this topic in the next paragraph, see Wyclif, *De Eucharistia*, 35–36, 38–39, 47, 53, 126, 216–17, 303–4, 308; Wyclif, *Trialogus*, book 4, chs. 3 and 8; and Wyclif's *Confessio*

in *Fasciculi Zizaniorum Magistri Johannis Wyclif cum Tritico,* ed. Walter W. Shirley (London: Longman, Brown, Green, Longmans, and Roberts, 1858), 115–32. See also Wyclif's two Corpus Christi sermons in *Sermones,* 4 vols., ed. John Loserth (London: Trübner, 1887–90), vol. 2, 453–63, and vol. 3, 277–86 (Thomson, *Latin Writings,* items 175 and 209, dated 1382).

18. See chapters 1 and 2 of this book; also Miri Rubin, *Corpus Christi: The Eucharist in Late Medieval Culture* (Cambridge: Cambridge University Press, 1991); Sarah Beckwith, "Ritual, Church and Theatre: Medieval Dramas of the Sacramental Body," in *Culture and History: 1350–1600,* ed. David Aers (Hemel Hempstead: Harvester Wheatsheaf, 1992), ch. 2; Miri Rubin, *Gentile Tales: The Narrative Assault on Late Medieval Jews* (New Haven: Yale University Press, 1999).

19. For example, 35–53, 83–98, 153, 192–201, 216–17, 218–19, 303–4; consult Hudson, *The Premature Reformation,* 282, and Keen, "Wyclif, the Bible, and Transubstantiation," 12–14.

20. Langland uses this locution in a context that raises related issues; see B XV.212 in William Langland, *Piers Plowman: The B Version,* ed. George Kane and E. Talbot Donaldson (London: Athlone, 1988).

21. See also Wyclif, *De Eucharistia,* 35–38 and 120–23.

22. On the burdensome metaphysical and human inventions laid on modern Christians, see too 48, 61–62, 118, 281. For Wycliffite development of the domestic location of the sacramental sign in Acts 2 and 1 Corinthians 11, see the final chapter of this book, "Home, Homelessness and Sanctity."

23. Characteristic early responses to Wyclif can be found in Shirley, *Fasciculi Zizaniorum*—for example, 133–80.

24. See 83–84, 86, 87, 98, 100, 121, 183, 199, 217.

25. On this passage, see Kenny, *Wyclif,* 89; his concise discussion of Wyclif's theology of the sacrament is very fine.

26. Rowan Williams, *On Christian Theology* (Oxford: Blackwell, 2000), 207; all of ch. 13 is relevant.

27. See Thomas Aquinas, *Summa Theologiae* (London: Blackfriars, 1964–81); citations to this edition are given in my text.

28. Aquinas himself stated that this ceasing to exist was not annihilation; *ST* III.75.3, especially ad 1. But those directly opposing Wyclif and Wycliffites seem to have been more concerned to oppose any doctrines of remanence than in the distinctions Aquinas sought to argue here. A clear summary of fourteenth-century orthodoxy here is in William of Ockham, *De Corpore Christi,* ch. 2, in *Guillelmi de Ockham: Tractatus de Quantitate et Tractatus de Corpore Christi,* ed. Carlo A. Grassi, vol. 10 of William of Ockham's *Opera Philosophica et Theologica* (St. Bonaventure, N.Y.: St. Bonaventure University, Franciscan Institute, 1986).

29. There is a lucid discussion of Wyclif's denial of current accounts of the destruction of the substances of bread and wine in Kenny, *Wyclif*, 83–87; see too Leff, *Heresy*, vol. 2, 551–55.

30. See too 53–54, 129–30, 134–35, 293, 313–14; also Wyclif, *Trialogus*, IV.4, especially 256. Leff, *Heresy*, vol. 2, 551–52, provides copious references.

31. Kenny, *Wyclif*, 85–87; see too Catto, "John Wyclif," 273–74.

32. The major resource here remains Henri de Lubac, *Exégèse médiévale*, 2 parts in 4 vols. (Paris: Aubier, 1959–63). For Wyclif's theory in 1377–78, see John Wyclif, *De Veritate Sacrae Scripturae*, ed. Rudolf Buddensieg, 3 vols. (London: Trübner, 1905–7), I.4, I.6–7, III.30–31; also the works on Wyclif cited in note 34 of this chapter.

33. This is a Thomistic commonplace (see *ST* III.60.4 and III.61.1), but Wyclif begins his own treatment of the sacraments in *Trialogus* by mentioning how necessary signs are to our lives. Wyclif, *Trialogus*, 244.

34. See de Lubac, *Exégèse médiévale*, part 1, vol. 1, 43–118; part 1, vol. 2, 425–88; for Aquinas and scholastic exegesis, part 2, vol. 2, 263–301. On Wyclif's hermeneutics, see the divergent views of de Vooght, *Les sources*, 168–200, and M. Hurley, "'Scriptura Sola': Wyclif and His Critics," *Traditio* 16 (1960), 275–352; more recently, although limited to *De Veritate Sacrae Scripturae* (1377–78), Ghosh, *The Wycliffite Heresy*, ch. 1. For extremely astute critical analysis of Wyclif's hermeneutics, see the Carmelite Thomas Netter, *Thomae Waldensis Doctrinale Antiquitatum Fidei Catholicae Ecclesiae*, 3 vols., ed. B. Blanciotti (Venice, 1757; facsimile, Farnborough: Gregg, 1967), II.19.3–6, II.20.3, II.21.1–2, II.22.10–11, II.23.1–2, II.25.

35. Kenny, *Wyclif in His Times*, 89, makes this very clear. Of course, Wyclif's opponents could invoke the same exegetical tradition against him: they could object that Wyclif dissolves the literal/historical dimension in his treatment of Christ's sacramental presence and the Galilean body. Netter's critique of Wyclif's hermeneutics (Netter, *Thomae Waldensis*) includes sharp observations on its consequences for traditional doctrine accepted by Wyclif. Netter, *Doctrinale*, II.23.2–3. Ghosh, *The Wycliffite Heresy*, ch. 1, seeks to expose allegedly novel tension and contradiction in Wyclif's hermeneutics. In my view, Ghosh seriously underestimates the force of Netter's theological critique of Wyclif in his chapter titled "Thomas Netter and John Wyclif: Hermeneutic *Confrères?* " (ch. 6).

36. Strohm, *England's Empty Throne*, ch. 2.

37. The judgment of the contemporary Church was not formally defined as an article of the faith till Trent. Kenny, *Wyclif*, 87.

38. I am grateful for conversations with Anne Hudson on this. For the practice, see Strohm, *England's Empty Throne*, ch. 2.

39. Catto, "John Wyclif," see especially 277–82; p. 281 discusses *De Eucharistia*, 158–70.

40. I put "Church" in quotation marks here to indicate that Wyclif's ecclesiology massively undermined the status of the visible Church. He observes that nobody knows whether those governing the Church and formulating its articles of faith are actually members of that Church which comprises the mystical body of Christ, the predestinate (272–73). On the problems his position encounters, together with references to relevant literature on Wyclif's ecclesiology, see David Aers, *Faith, Ethics and Church: Writing in England, 1360–1409* (Cambridge: Brewer, 2000), ch. 6. For an attempt to show that Wyclif's understanding of reason introduces "ambiguity" into the paradigms he inherited, see Ghosh, *The Wycliffite Heresy*, 53–54, and, on Wycliffites and reason, 140–42.

41. See, for example, *ST* I.32.4, II–II.5.3, II–II.10.12, and especially II–II.11. For Wyclif on heresy, see *De Veritate Sacrae Scripturae*, III.32, and for his recommendations to the lay powers, see John Wyclif, *Tractatus de Officio Regis*, ed. A. W. Pollard and C. Sayle (London: Trübner, 1887), 228–30.

42. On Wycliffite Christians imitating Christ in their opposition to the Church and for the view that were Christ to return to the modern Church and teach what he'd taught on earth he would be charged as a heretic and, if he did not recant, would be burnt to death, see David Aers and Lynn Staley, *The Powers of the Holy: Religion, Politics, and Gender in Late Medieval English Culture* (University Park: Pennsylvania State University Press, 1996), 46, 46 n. 13. Of course, Wyclif's opponents did not accept Wyclif's understanding of how Christians were to discern "the truth of Scripture"; see Ghosh, *The Wycliffite Heresy*, ch. 2.

43. Catto, "John Wyclif," 282, drawing on John Bossy, "The Mass as a Social Institution, 1200–1700," *Past and Present* 100 (1983), 29–61, 59. For a corrective from the early modern side, one should read Patrick Collinson, *The Religion of Protestants* (Oxford: Clarendon Press, 1982).

44. See Catto, "John Wyclif," 286, 272–80; on the history and ideology of the larger narrative here, see Aers, *Culture and History*, ch. 6.

45. On the Wycliffite theology of penance, see Hudson, *The Premature Reformation*, 294–301; Anne Hudson and Pamela Gradon, eds., *English Wycliffite Sermons*, 5 vols. (Oxford: Oxford University Press, 1983–96), vol. 4, 40–49. On the way that Wyclif's Eucharistic theology diminished the status of priesthood, see Leff, *Heresy*, vol. 2, 525–26, 530–31, 533–34, 538, 557. With the following quotation from *Summa Theologiae* in my text, see similarly Aquinas's earlier statement in his *Contra Impugnantes Dei Cultum et Religionem*, ch. 3, para. 163, in Thomas Aquinas, *Opuscula Theologica*, vol. 2, ed. R. M. Spiazzi (Rome: Marietti, 1954), 36.

46. On translating Scripture, see Hudson, *The Premature Reformation*, ch. 5, and Margaret Aston, "Wyclif and the Vernacular," in *From Ockham to Wyclif*, ed.

Anne Hudson and Michael Wilks, Studies in Church History (Oxford: Basil Blackwell, 1987), 281–330.

47. See the first paragraph of this chapter with references in note 5. On the Caesarean dimensions of Wyclif's vision, see Aers, *Faith, Ethics,* ch. 6. On Richard II here, see Nigel Saul, *Richard II* (New Haven: Yale University Press, 1997), chs. 14 and 15.

48. See, for example, Wyclif, *De Eucharistia,* 318–22, 322–24, 157, 111–12, 126.

49. Wyclif, *De Eucharistia,* 322. For references to *De Simonia,* see John Wyclif, *De Simonia,* ed. Michael H. Dziewicki and Dr. Herzberg-Frankel (London: Trübner, 1899), and *On Simony,* trans. Terrence A. McVeigh (New York: Fordham University Press, 1992). These concerns pervade his work and those of his followers; see Hudson, *The Premature Reformation,* 334–46. For the date of *De Simonia,* see Thomson, *The Latin Writings,* item 35.

50. For an example of Wyclif's use of Acts 4.32–34, see Wyclif, *Trialogus,* 190–91.

51. See Michael Wilks, "Wyclif and the Great Persecution," in *Prophecy and Eschatology,* ed. Michael Wilks (Oxford: Blackwell, 1994), 39–64.

4. Early Wycliffite Theology of the Sacrament of the Altar: Walter Brut and William Thorpe

1. See Walter Brut, "Proceedings in the Trial of Walter Brut for Heresy," in *Registrum Johannes Trefnant,* ed. W. W. Capes (London: Canterbury and York Society, 1916), 278–394, for trial documents with judges' responses. Brut's text is at 285–356. Subsequent citations to pages of this work are given parenthetically in my text. The main commentary on Brut is by Anne Hudson, " '*Laicus Litteratus*': The Paradox of Lollardy," ch. 13 in *Heresy and Literacy, 1000–1536,* ed. Peter Biller and Anne Hudson (Cambridge: Cambridge University Press, 1994), and by Curtis Bostick, *The Antichrist of the Lollards* (Leiden: Brill, 1998), 147–54. The passage of Brut's testimony most noted concerns women and their ability to consecrate the host; see Alcuin Blamires, ed., *Woman Defamed and Woman Defended* (Oxford: Clarendon Press, 1992), 250–60; Margaret Aston, "Lollard Women Priests?" in *Lollards and Reformers: Images and Literacy in Late Medieval Religion* (London: Hambledon, 1984), 52–59. Also relevant here are Alcuin Blamires and C. W. Marx, "Women Not to Preach: A Disputation in British Library MS Harley 31," *Journal of Medieval Latin* 3 (1993), 34–63, and A. J. Minnis, "*De Impedimento Sexus:* Women's Bodies and Medieval Impediments to Female Ordination," in *Medieval Theology and the Natural Body,* ed. Peter Biller and A. J. Minnis (York: York Medieval Press, 1997), 109–39.

2. Hudson, *"Laicus Litteratus,"* 224.

3. See K. B. McFarlane, *John Wycliffe and the Beginnings of English Non-conformity* (London: English Universities Press, 1952), 135–38. McFarlane's conde-scending dismissal of Brut's use of the apocalypse simply overlooks its importance in the claims it makes for "Britones" as an elect people (Brut, "Proceedings," 293–96), its attempts to distinguish medieval fables of Antichrist from scriptural prophecies, and its application of the latter to Church history, with its carefully in-stitutionalizing reading of Antichrist (296–303); see Bostick, *The Antichrist,* 147–54, and Penn R. Szittya, "Domesday Bokes: The Apocalypse in Medieval English Lit-erary Culture," ch. 16 in *The Apocalypse in the Middle Ages,* ed. R. K. Emmerson and B. McGinn (Ithaca: Cornell University Press, 1992), 396–97 (though it seems odd to call Brut's Latin text "popular rather than learned," 396; cf. Hudson, *"'Laicus Litteratus'"*). For remarks on Brut's apocalyptic nationalism, see Ruth Nissé, "Pro-phetic Nations," *New Medieval Literatures* 4 (2001), 95–115, at 111–15.

4. Hudson, *"'Laicus Litteratus,'"* 224. In Anne Hudson, "The Mouse in the Pyx: Popular Heresy and the Eucharist," *Trivium* 26 (1991), 48, however, her state-ment about Brut's "simplified" version of Wyclif's views on the Eucharist seems to me, as my own analysis will argue, not sensitive to Brut's thought in this domain.

5. On Wycliffite hermeneutics, see these differing accounts: M. Hurley, "'Scriptura Sola': Wyclif and His Critics," *Traditio* 16 (1960), 275–352; Paul de Vooght, *Les sources de la doctrine chrétienne d'après les théologiens du XIVe siècle et du début du XVe* (Bruges: Desclée, De Brouwer, 1954), 168–200; Kantik Ghosh, *The Wycliffite Heresy: Authority and the Interpretation of Texts* (Cambridge: Cam-bridge University Press, 2002), chs. 1 and 4.

6. Nicholas Love, *Mirror of the Blessed Life of Jesus Christ,* ed. Michael G. Sar-gent (New York: Garland, 1992). Subsequent page citations for Love in the text are to this edition. On Love, see Sarah Beckwith, *Christ's Body: Identity, Culture, and So-ciety in Late Medieval Writings* (London: Routledge, 1993), 63–70; Katherine C. Little, "Reading for Christ: Interpretation and Instruction in Late Medieval England" (Ph.D. diss., Duke University, 1998), ch. 3; Ghosh, *The Wycliffite Heresy,* ch. 5.

7. The most recent example I have encountered is by Marcia Colish, *Me-dieval Foundations of the Western Intellectual Tradition, 400–1400* (New Haven: Yale University Press, 1997), 255–56.

8. For the vulgate, I am using *Biblia Sacra iuxta Vulgatem Clementinam,* 4th ed., ed. Alberto Colunga and Laurentio Turrado (Matriti: Biblioteca de Autores Cristianos, 1965). For English translation of the vulgate in this chapter, I am using *The Holy Bible Translated from the Latin Vulgate,* rev. Richard Challoner (Rock-ford, Ill.: Tan Books, 1989).

9. For critical but apparently orthodox reflections on the transformation of the sacrament of penance into a punitive, persecutory institution, see the York

Corpus Christi Play as analyzed by Sarah Beckwith in "Coming to Judgment: Church, State, and Heresy in the Trial Plays," ch. 6 in *Signifying God: Social Relation and Symbolic Act in the York Corpus Christi Plays* (Chicago: Chicago University Press, 2001), 103–111.

10. The literature here is immense, and some of it has been cited in chapter 1, note 1. Here the following are especially relevant: Henri de Lubac, *Corpus mysticum: L'Eucharistie et l'église au moyen âge* (Paris: Aubier, 1949); Gary Macy, "The 'Dogma of Transubstantiation' in the Middle Ages," *Journal of Ecclesiastical History* 45 (1994), 11–41; James F. McCue, "The Doctrine of Transubstantiation from Berengar through Trent," *Harvard Theological Review* 61 (1968), 385–430.

11. Thomas F. Simmons, ed., *The Lay Folk's Mass Book*, EETS, o.s., 71 (London: Trübner, 1879), 38–41, 280–88. For my description of the medieval Mass, see John Bossy, "The Mass as a Social Institution, 1200–1700," *Past and Present* 100 (1983), 29–61, especially 33; Beckwith, *Christ's Body*, 33–37, 140; Eamon Duffy, *The Stripping of the Altars: Traditional Religion in England, 1400–1580* (New Haven: Yale University Press, 1992), ch. 3, especially 91; V. L. Kennedy, "The Moment of Consecration and the Elevation of the Host," *Medieval Studies* 6 (1994), 121–50; P. Browe, "Die Elevation in der Messe," *Jahrbuch für Liturgiewissenschaft* 9 (1929), 20–66. On the "undifferentiated dorsality" of the Mass before Vatican II, see P. J. Fitzpatrick, *In Breaking of Bread: The Eucharist and Ritual* (Cambridge: Cambridge University Press, 1993), 209–17. Also relevant here is Edouard Dumoutet, *Le désir de voir l'Hostie et les origines de la dévotion au Saint-Sacrament* (Paris: Beauchesie, 1926).

12. Angela of Foligno, *Complete Works*, trans. Paul Lachance (New York: Paulist Press, 1993), 27; for an example of the host as spectacle, see Angela's account at 146–47. See too Suzanne Lewis, *Reading Images: Narrative Discourse and Reception in the Thirteenth Century Illuminated Apocalypse* (Cambridge: Cambridge University Press, 1995), 260, 263–65.

13. Thomas Brinton, *The Sermons of Thomas Brinton, Bishop of Rochester (1373–1389)*, 2 vols., ed. Mary A. Devlin (London: Royal Historical Society, 1954); see Sermon 69 (320) and similarly Sermon 48 (215–16). For other examples and references, see David Aers and Lynn Staley, *The Powers of the Holy: Religion, Politics, and Gender in Late Medieval English Culture* (University Park: Pennsylvania State University Press, 1996), 26–27. In chapter 1 I exemplified this standard teaching from the Franciscan *Fasciculus Morum*.

14. Respectively, Angela of Foligno, *Complete Works*, 34, and Duffy, *Stripping of the Altars*, 93.

15. Thorpe's text is published in Anne Hudson, ed., *Two Wycliffite Texts*, EETS, o.s., 301 (Oxford: Oxford University Press, 1993), 24–93: here 52. Subsequent citations to Thorpe's work are given parenthetically in the main text.

16. See Paul Strohm, *England's Empty Throne: Usurpation and the Language of Legitimation, 1399–1422* (New Haven: Yale University Press, 1998), ch. 2.

17. Brut's emphasis on the relations between faith and reception is thoroughly Augustinian, as is his whole approach to John 6; see Augustine, *Homilies on the Gospel of John*, tr 26, 27, in Augustine, *Homilies on the Gospel of John; Homilies on the First Epistle of John; Soliloquies*, ed. Philip Schaff (Grand Rapids, Mich.: Eerdmans, 1986). For useful introductions to Augustine on the sacraments, see H. M. Féret, "*Sacramentum, Res* dans la langue théologique de S. Augustin," *Revue des Sciences Philosophiques et Théologiques* 29 (1940), 218–43, and Gerald Bonner, "The Church and the Eucharist in the Theology of Augustine," *Sobornost*, ser. 7, no. 6 (1978), 448–61. Thomas Aquinas's teaching that faithful desire for the sacrament *constitutes reception* involves a similar emphasis on faith, but it separates faith from reception in a way not implied by Brut. See *Summa Theologiae [ST]*, III.79.1, ad 1. This and subsequent citations refer to the 60-volume Blackfriars parallel-text edition (London: Blackfriars, 1964–81). For Brut's teacher on the Eucharist, see John Wyclif, *De Eucharistia*, ed. John Loserth (London: Trübner, 1892), and chapter 3 of this book. See too Anne Hudson, *The Premature Reformation* (Oxford: Clarendon Press, 1988), 281–90; J. I. Catto, "John Wyclif and the Cult of the Eucharist," in *The Bible in the Medieval World: Essays in Memory of Beryl Smalley*, ed. Katherine Walsh and Diana Wood (Oxford: Blackwell, 1985), 43–55; Maurice H. Keen, "Wyclif, the Bible and Transubstantiation," in *Wyclif in His Times*, ed. Anthony Kenny (Oxford: Oxford University Press, 1986), 1–16, especially 6–16.

18. For examples of this mixture, see Ockham's approaches to the Eucharist in *Quodlibetal Questions*, 2 vols., trans. Alfred J. Freddoso and Francis E. Kelley (New Haven: Yale University Press, 1991), 298–310, 369–75, 497–99, and *The De Sacramento Altaris of William of Ockham*, ed. and trans. T. Brune Birch (Burlington, Vt.: Lutheran Literary Board, 1930). For the critical edition of the relevant text, see *De Corpore Christi*, in William of Ockham, *Guillelmi de Ockham: Tractatus de Quantitate et Tractatus de Corpore Christi*, ed. Carlo A. Grassi, vol. 10 of William of Ockham, *Opera Philosophica et Theologica* (St. Bonaventure, N.Y.: St. Bonaventure University, Franciscan Institute, 1986).

19. Love's treatment of the Last Supper in *Mirror*, 146–56, offers an illuminating contrast to Brut's approach, as do the responses of Brut's judges in Brut, "Proceedings," 380–81. On Love and the Last Supper, see chapter 1 of this book.

20. Seriatim, *ST* III.73.1, ad 3; III.74.7, resp; III.78.1, ad 2.

21. See Miri Rubin, *Corpus Christi: The Eucharist in Late Medieval Culture* (Cambridge: Cambridge University Press, 1991), 243–71; and Mervyn James, "Ritual, Drama and Social Body in the Late Medieval Town," *Past and Present* 98 (1983), 3–29. For an extraordinarily rich social, political, and theological account of one urban space, York, see Beckwith, *Signifying God*.

22. See Margery Kempe, *The Book of Margery Kempe*, ed. Lynn Staley (Kalamazoo: Western Michigan University, Medieval Institute Publications, 1996), ch. 67, 157–58.

23. *ST* III.67.2, resp; see also Thomas Aquinas, *Contra Impugnantes Dei Cultum et Religionem*, ch. 3, para. 163, in *Opuscula Theologica*, vol. 2, ed. R. M. Spiazzi (Rome: Marietti, 1954), vol. 2, p. 36.

24. On Wyclif's realist metaphysics, see John Wyclif, *On Universals* (*Tractatus de Universalibus*), trans. Anthony Kenny (Oxford: Clarendon Press, 1988), and Gordon Leff, *Heresy in the Later Middle Ages*, 2 vols. (New York: Barnes and Noble, 1967), vol. 2, 500–510, 512, 515. However, Leff seriously exaggerates the role of realist metaphysics in Wyclif's Eucharistic theology; see chapter 3 of this book, which makes clear how central are the narratives of the New Testament in Wyclif's approach to contemporary theology and ritual around the sacrament of the altar. On this issue see Anthony Kenny, *Wyclif* (New York: Oxford University Press, 1985), 87; Keen, "Wyclif, the Bible and Transubstantiation," 11–12; Ian C. Levy, "*Christus Qui Mentiri Non Potest:* John Wyclif's Rejection of Transubstantiation," *Recherches de Théologie et Philosophie Médiévales* 66 (1999), 316–34.

25. This form of conversion was as unacceptable to the late medieval Church as to the Counter-Reformation Church. For Aquinas's arguments against consubstantiation, see *ST* III.75.2; note the impressive *defense* of the position at III.75.2 obj 1–3 and the uncharacteristic flimsiness of the answer here (uncharacteristic in the lack of support from reasoned argument and Scripture). Note that *ST* III.75.3 argues against the position of the late medieval English Church to which Wycliffites were called to assent, namely, that the substances of bread and wine are annihilated at the consecration. The Wycliffite poem *Pierce the Plowman's Crede* invokes Wyclif and Brut; it also affirms the presence of Christ's body, flesh and blood, in the sacrament because Christ's words convey this. But it resists any attempt to analyze how, since the more the issue is disputed, the more confused it becomes. W. W. Skeat, ed., *Pierce the Plowman's Crede*, EETS, o.s., 30 (London: Trübner, 1867), lines 822–30.

26. Duffy, *Stripping of the Altars*, 91; see ch. 3.

27. In chapter 1, I considered examples of late-fourteenth- and early-fifteenth-century propagation of Eucharistic miracle stories in England from Love's *Mirror*, together with works such as John Bromyard, *Summa Praedicantium* (Antwerp, 1614), 251–52, 254–55; Brinton, *Sermons*, Sermon 40 (179), Sermon 55 (251), Sermon 67 (306), Sermon 83 (446) (see Sermon 40 [179]). Roger Dymmok, *Liber contra Duodecim Errores et Hereses Lollardorum*, ed. H. S. Cronin (London: Trübner, 1922), 99–100; John Mirk, *Festial: A Collection of Homilies*, ed. Theodor Erbe, EETS, e.s., 96 (London: K. Paul, Trench, Trübner, 1905), 170–75 (on this Corpus Christi sermon, see Rubin, *Corpus Christi*, 222–24).

28. For these terms, thoroughly Augustinian in their import, see Denys Turner, "The Darkness of God and the Light of Christ: Negative Theology and Eucharistic Presence," *Modern Theology* 15 (1999), 143–59; this would be fruitfully accompanied by the author's earlier study, *The Darkness of God* (Cambridge: Cambridge University Press, 1995). On *Piers Plowman* in these contexts, see chapter 2 of this book.

29. On the long process in which the English Church's leadership sought to impose the death penalty on those judged to be "heretics," see H. G. Richardson, "Heresy and the Lay Power under Richard II," *English Historical Review* 51 (1936), 1–28, and Strohm, *England's Empty Throne*, ch. 2.

30. Discussed in chapters 1 and 3; see Dymmok, *Liber,* 90–92; see too Strohm, *England's Empty Throne*, 61–62, 139–40, and Paul Strohm, *Theory and the Premodern Text* (Minneapolis: University of Minnesota Press, 2000), ch. 2. On the need for the presence of the Galilean body of Christ, see Dymmok, *Liber,* 100; on the need for its absence, however, see 100–101. Dymmok fails to develop the statements about presence and absence into a dialectical exploration of what is a major theological issue; cf. *ST* III.75.1. Relevant aspects of Dymmok's work were considered in the first chapter of this book.

31. On the Mass as involving the sacrifice of Christ on the altar, see J. Wickham Legg, ed., *The Sarum Missal* (Oxford: Clarendon Press, 1969), 227 ("immolamus tibi patri filium . . ."), with 223 and 221; see too *ST* III.73.4, resp and ad 3, III.79.5, resp. For Trent's views on this, see Session 22 (17 Sep 1562), chs. 1–2 and canons 1, 3, 4; parallel texts in Norman P. Tanner, ed., *Decrees of the Ecumenical Councils*, 2 vols. (London: Sheed and Ward, 1990), vol. 1, 732–34, 735. See too a classic statement of Christ's daily immolation in the sacrament in Emil Friedberg, ed., *Corpus Iuris Canonici* (Leipzig, 1879), vol. 1, part 3, *De Consecr,* d. 2, ch. 52, col. 1333: "cotidie immolatur in sacramento." For Ockham, see William of Ockham, *The De Sacramento Altaris,* 158, stating that Christ is sacrificed [immolatur] daily in the sacrament. For Scotus's views, see Richard Cross, *Duns Scotus* (Oxford: Oxford University Press, 1999), 144–45.

32. See Aers and Staley, *Powers of the Holy,* 24 (with references in nn. 25–27), together with note 30 above. Also relevant here is Thomas H. Bestul, *Texts of the Passion* (Philadelphia: University of Pennsylvania Press, 1996), chs. 2 and 5.

33. Brut's preoccupation with persecution and its place in sanctification represents both a response to his own situation and an important component of Wyclif's own theology, well analyzed by Michael Wilks, "Wyclif and the Great Persecution," in *Prophecy and Eschatology,* ed. Michael Wilks (Oxford: Blackwell, 1994), 39–64.

34. See John Wyclif, *Tractatus de Blasphemia*, ed. Michael H. Dziewicki (London: Trübner, 1893), 62 (see too 72), and *Dialogus sive Speculum Ecclesie Militantis,*

ed. A. W. Pollard (London: Trübner, 1876), 22. See Wilks, "Wyclif and the Great Persecution."

35. For fascinating reflections on the issue raised by Brut, see René Girard, *Things Hidden since the Foundation of the World* (London: Athlone, 1977), and *The Scapegoat* (Baltimore: Johns Hopkins University Press 1986). See also note 9 above.

36. Brut explains inconsistencies in the Church's use of the Old Testament to justify its participation in violence as well as arguing that Christ's "New Commandment" (John 13.34) supersedes any previous justifications for war. Brut, "Proceedings," 313–18, especially 318–19. For Wyclif's arguments on the irrelevance of Old Testament wars for Christians, see John Wyclif, *Tractatus de Officio Regis*, ed. A. W. Pollard and C. Sayle (London: Trübner, 1887), 270; see too 277–79.

37. See the profound account of Pinochet's regime of torture in Chile and the relevant history of the Catholic Church by W. T. Cavanaugh, *Torture and Eucharist* (Oxford: Blackwell, 1998).

38. See Blamires, *Woman Defamed*, 250–60, and Aston, "Lollard Women Priests?"

39. On the symbolic centrality of the Eucharist in medieval culture, see Miri Rubin, "The Eucharist and the Construction of Medieval Identities," and Sarah Beckwith, "Ritual, Church and Theatre: Medieval Dramas of the Sacramental Body," chs. 2 and 3, respectively, in *Culture and History: 1350–1600*, ed. David Aers (Hemel Hempstead: Harvester Wheatsheaf, 1992); Rubin, *Corpus Christi;* Strohm, *England's Empty Throne*, ch. 2.

40. The literature on this is vast, but see Judith M. Bennett, "Medieval Women: Across the Great Divide," ch. 5 in Aers, *Culture and History,* and the very different approach of R. H. Bloch, *Medieval Misogyny and the Invention of Western Romantic Love* (Chicago: Chicago University Press, 1991).

41. Compare Chaucer's "Second Nun's Tale" and the discussion in David Aers, *Faith, Ethics and Church: Writing in England, 1360–1409* (Cambridge: Brewer, 2000), ch. 2.

42. Norman P. Tanner, ed., *Heresy Trials in the Diocese of Norwich, 1428–31* (London: Royal Historical Society, 1977), 142. This position was widespread among these East Anglian Wycliffites; see Margery Baxter, 49; John Skylly, 52, 57; John Godesell, 61; Sibil Godspell [sic], 67; John Skylaw, 147; Edmund Archer, 166; Thomas Mone, 179. William White, who worked with many East Anglian Wycliffites and was killed by his Church, maintained that all women and men who are devout Christians equally have the Church's keys; see Walter W. Shirley, ed., *Fasciculi Zizaniorum: Magistri Johannis Wyclif cum Tritico* (London: Longman, Brown, Green, Longmans, and Roberts, 1858), 422–23. Compare Wyclif's cautious treatment of Acts 2 in *Trialogus* IV.10; John Wyclif, *Trialogus*, ed. Gotthard V. Lechler (Oxford: Oxford University Press, 1869).

43. On John Wyclif, his followers, and the priesthood, see Hudson, *The Premature Reformation,* 325–27, 351–58; Anne Hudson and Pamela Gradon, eds., *English Wycliffite Sermons,* 5 vols. (Oxford: Oxford University Press, 1983–96), vol. 4, 111–20; Leff, *Heresy,* vol. 2, 520–27, 549–57, 579–80.

44. See Aers, *Faith, Ethics,* ch. 6.

45. For Thorpe's *Testimony* I use Anne Hudson's edition (Hudson, *Two Wycliffite Texts*). Page citations are given parenthetically in the text. For what can be construed of Thorpe's life, see xlv–liii.

46. For Love and Arundel, see Love, *Mirror,* 7 and xliv–xlvi.

47. Hudson, *Two Wycliffite Texts,* 107, claims that Thorpe's formulation I have just quoted is "neither clearly heterodox nor unequivocally orthodox."

48. See the richly illustrated discussion in Henri de Lubac, *The Christian Faith* (San Francisco: Ignatius Press, 1986), ch. 5.

49. On Wycliffite ecclesiology see Hudson, *The Premature Reformation,* ch. 7. She comments on this passage in her edition, 107 nn. 276–99. She appears to say that here "Thorpe is not concerned with the institution of the church." This is a puzzling statement since "the institution of the church" is what does concern Thorpe, with people "lyuyng now here in þis liif."

50. On this see McNiven, *Heresy and Politics,* 81–92, and Strohm, *England's Empty Throne,* 40–57. Richardson, "Heresy and the Lay Power," and Margaret Aston, "Lollardy and Sedition, 1381–1431," *Past and Present* 17 (1960), 1–44, remain invaluable.

51. On the rituals of degradation and capital punishment of Sawtry, see Strohm, *England's Empty Throne,* 54–57.

52. On the political and ecclesiastic legislation which made it normal for the involvement of such lay officials in detecting and pursuing heretics, see McNiven, *Heresy and Politics;* Richardson, "Heresy and the Lay Power"; Aston, "Lollardy and Sedition." See too Catto, "John Wyclif," 269–86.

53. See Girard, *Things Hidden* and *The Scapegoat.*

54. See the commentary on Nicholas Love in chapters 1 and 6 of this book.

55. Love, *Mirror,* 79, discussed in chapter 6 of this book. Wyclif had noted that all the saints had habitually fermented sedition; John Wyclif, *De Veritate Sacrae Scripturae,* 3 vols., ed. Rudolf Buddensieg (London: Trübner, 1905–7), I.14 (367–68). See too his account of how Christ himself would be persecuted as a seditious heretic; Aers and Staley, *Powers of the Holy,* 46, 46 n. 13.

56. See note 23 above. The problems for orthodox reforming theologians in this area are sharply shown in the case of Jean Gerson. Mark S. Burrows traces his shifting attitude to preaching after his encounter with Huss and Hussitism at Constance in *Jean Gerson and De Consolatione Theologiae* (Tubingen: Mohr (Siebeck), 1991), 236 n. 57, 257, 261.

57. On Wycliffite understanding of the priesthood, see Hudson, *The Premature Reformation*, 325–27, and Hudson and Gradon, *English Wycliffite Sermons*, vol. 4, 111–20; see too Aers, *Faith, Ethics*, ch. 6.

58. See Augustine, *Homilies on the Gospel of John*, tr 20; see too the works on Augustine and the sacraments cited in note 17 above.

59. See Hudson, *Two Wycliffite Texts*, 119. For Rita Copeland's reading of this exchange and its ideological contexts, see "William Thorpe and His Lollard Community: Intellectual Labor and the Representation of Dissent," ch. 10 in *Bodies and Disciplines*, ed. Barbara A. Hanawalt and David Wallace (Minneapolis: Minnesota University Press, 1996). For a revised version of this essay, see Rita Copeland, *Pedagogy, Intellectuals, and Dissent in the Later Middle Ages: Lollardy and Ideas of Learning* (Cambridge: Cambridge University Press, 2001), ch. 4. This is not the place to elaborate on such reflections, but it seems to me that Rita Copeland's decision to classify medieval theologians and priests as "intellectuals" belonging to an "intellectual community" doing "intellectual work," a classification building on Gramsci's famous typology in his *Prison Notebooks*, is a decision that does strenuous ideological work that is not apparently recognized as such. The categories are committedly secularizing, in Copeland as in Gramsci, and the consequences here include a premature de-Christianization of the contexts, dispositions, motivations, and ideas of the medieval subjects under consideration. For a detailed study of Thorpe's uses of academic discourse, see Fiona Somerset, *Clerical Discourse and Lay Audience in Late Medieval England* (Cambridge: Cambridge University Press, 1998), ch. 6.

60. This process of tradition formation is obscured in Eamon Duffy's history of "traditional religion" in England in *Stripping of the Altars*. See David Aers, "Altars of Power: Reflections on Eamon Duffy's *The Stripping of the Altars*," *Literature and History* 3 (1994), 90–105, and "From Medieval Christianities to the Reformations," *Journal of Medieval and Early Modern Studies* 27 (1997), 139–43.

61. See Hudson, *Two Wycliffite Texts*, 119 nn. 1042–52.

62. Compare William Sawtry, whom Arundel sees as Thorpe's "felow" (36); Shirley, *Fasciculi Zizaniorum*, 408–11. Note that Sawtry cites Augustine from canon law, as Thorpe does (410). On the killing of Sawtry, see McNiven, *Heresy and Politics*, 81–92, and Strohm, *England's Empty Throne*, 40–57. For a later statement of the Wycliffite tradition that Thorpe represents, see William White, burnt to death in Norwich in 1428; he unequivocally affirmed the real presence of Christ's body even as he affirmed the continuity of substantial bread and wine. Shirley, *Fasciculi Zizaniorum*, 418–19.

63. "Ego vero Evangelio non crederem, nisi me catholicae Ecclesiae commoveret auctoritas." In Augustine, *Contra Epistolam Manichaei*, I.5.6, *PLat*, 42:176.

64. For Wyclif's view that the Church consists only of the predestinate, see Leff, *Heresy*, vol. 2, 516–20, and Hudson, *The Premature Reformation*, 314–15.

65. Augustine, *De Doctrina Christiana*, ed. and trans. R. P. H. Green (Oxford: Clarendon Press, 1995), Preface 5.11.

66. Augustine, *De Doctrina Christiana*, Preface 6.12. This vision pervades much of Augustine's preaching and writing against the Donatists. See Serge Lancel, *Saint Augustin* (Paris: Fayard, 1999), 401–2. Augustine's Sermon 47 illustrates the vision I refer to here. Augustine, *Sermons*, trans. Edmund Hill, part 3 of *The Works of Saint Augustine: A Translation for the 21st Century*, ed. John E. Rotelle (Brooklyn: New City Press, 1994).

67. Augustine, *De Doctrina Christiana*, Preface 8.16.

68. William Langland, *Piers Plowman: The B Version*, ed. George Kane and E. Talbot Donaldson (London: Athlone, 1988), X.447, hereafter cited as "Langland, *Piers Plowman* (Kane/Donaldson)." The scriptural text invoked here is Luke 18.19.

69. Augustine, *The Gift of Perseverance*, 2.4, in Augustine, *Four Anti-Pelagian Writings*, trans. John A. Mourant and William J. Collinge (Washington: Catholic University of America Press, 1992); see too Augustine, *Concerning the City of God* XXII.22–23, trans. Henry Bettenson (London: Penguin Books, 1984).

70. See Langland, *Piers Plowman* (Kane/Donaldson), B XV.195–212. The C revision, now given to Liberum Arbitrium, shortens this passage; William Langland, *Piers Plowman: The C Version: Will's Visions of Piers Plowman, Do-Well, Do-Better, and Do-Best*, ed. George Russell and George Kane (London: Athlone, 1997), XVI.337–40a.

71. Quotations from Langland, *Piers Plowman* (Kane/Donaldson), are, seriatim, from lines 198, 200, 210, and 200a. The word "will" is indeed spelt in two different ways in this passage. The Latin text here invokes Luke 11.17 and Matthew 9.4; see D. W. Robertson and B. F. Huppé, *Piers Plowman and Scriptural Tradition* (Princeton: Princeton University, 1951), 183.

72. Here I hope my thinking has been greatly influenced by Rowan Williams, *On Christian Theology* (Oxford: Blackwell, 2000), part 4.

73. Williams, *On Christian Theology*, 216.

74. Williams, *On Christian Theology*, 216.

75. For the role of Scripture in Wycliffite Christianity, see Anne Hudson, *The Premature Reformation*, ch. 5: also see two essays by Beryl Smalley: "John Wyclif's Postilla super Totam Bibliam," *Bodleian Library Record* 4 (1953), 186–205, and "The Bible and Eternity: John Wyclif's Dilemma," *Journal of the Warburg and Courtauld Institute* 27 (1964), 73–89; and Leff, *Heresy*, vol. 2, 511–16.

76. Williams, *On Christian Theology*, 217; see 217–21.

77. Augustine, *Concerning the City of God*, XXII.6. On the lust of dominion, see, for example, III.14, IV.3, XIV.28, XV.7, XIX.15.

78. Augustine, *Concerning the City of God*, XXII.6.

79. Augustine, *Concerning the City of God,* X.6. The Latin text I am using here is Augustine, *De Civitate Dei,* 2 vols., ed. B. Dombart and A. Kalb (Stuttgart: Teubner, 1993).

80. In such aspirations Archbishop Arundel had the unqualified sanction of Aquinas; *ST* II–II.4, resp and ad 1.

5. *The Sign of Poverty:* Piers Plowman *(The C Version)*

1. This is my third contribution to the subject, though it is my first centered on the C version; David Aers, "*Piers Plowman* and Problems in the Perception of Poverty: A Culture in Transition," *Leeds Studies in English* 14 (1983), 5–25, was considerably elaborated in *Community, Gender and Individual Identity: English Writing 1360–1430* (London: Routledge, 1988), which concentrated on relations between the B version of *Piers Plowman* and contemporary social and political conflicts, Franciscan traditions, and opposition to these (especially John XXII and Richard Fitzralph), suggesting that such opposition, together with parliamentary legislation and petitions to fix the price of labor and to control vagrant laborers, were signs of important cultural and ideological transformations. Since this study Anne Middleton has published an exceptionally rich essay on these and other issues, setting out from Wille's "autobiographical" addition to the C version, "Acts of Vagrancy: The C Version 'Autobiography' and the Statute of 1388," in *Written Work: Langland, Labor, and Authorship,* ed. Steven Justice and Kathryn Kerby-Fulton (Philadelphia: University of Pennsylvania, 1997), 208–317. In the same year, Lawrence Clopper published "*Songes of Rechlesnesse*": Langland and the Franciscans (Ann Arbor: University of Michigan, 1997). This erudite work identifies *Piers Plowman* with radical Franciscan ideology and conjures up "a coterie of reformist Franciscans" to compose Langland's primary readership (330): "Langland was probably a Franciscan" (327). Besides the studies of Middleton and Clopper, I have found the following works on *Piers Plowman* especially relevant: Robert Adams, "The Nature of Need in *Piers Plowman* XX," *Traditio* 34 (1978), 273–302; Robert Adams, "Piers's Pardon and Langland's Semi-Pelagianism," *Traditio* 39 (1983), 367–418; M. W. Bloomfield, *Piers Plowman as a Fourteenth-Century Apocalypse* (New Brunswick: Rutgers University Press, 1961); Guy Bourquin, *Piers Plowman,* 2 vols. (Paris: Champion, 1978), especially his summary in part 4, ch. 1 (on pp. 797–98, he also suggests links with Deguileville's *Pèlerinage de la vie humaine*); T. P. Dolan, "Langland and Fitzralph," *Yearbook of Langland Studies* 2 (1988), 35–45; E. Talbot. Donaldson, *Piers Plowman: The C-Text and Its Poet* (New Haven: Yale University Press, 1949); Louise Fradenburg, "Needful Things," in *Medieval Crime and Social*

Control, ed. Barbara A. Hanawalt and David Wallace (Minneapolis: University of Minnesota Press, 1997), 49–69; R.W. Frank, *Piers Plowman and the Scheme of Salvation* (New Haven: Yale University Press, 1957); M. Godden, "Plowmen and Hermits in Langland's *Piers Plowman*," *Review of English Studies* 35 (1984), 129–63; Ralph Hanna, "Will's Work," ch. 1 in Justice and Kerby-Fulton, *Written Work;* Steven Justice, *Writing and Rebellion* (Berkeley: University of California Press, 1994); Derek Pearsall, "Poverty and Poor People in *Piers Plowman*," in *Medieval English Studies,* ed. E. D. Kennedy, R. Waldron, and J. S. Wittig (Cambridge: Brewer, 1988), 167–85; Derek Pearsall, "Lunatyk Lollares in *Piers Plowman*," in *Religion in the Poetry and Drama of the Late Middle Ages,* ed. Piero Boitani and Anna Torti (Cambridge: Brewer, 1990), 163–78; Wendy Scase, *Piers Plowman and the New Anticlericalism* (Cambridge: Cambridge University Press, 1989), chs. 3–4; Geoffrey Shepherd, "Poverty in *Piers Plowman*," in *Social Relations and Ideas,* ed. T. H. Aston, P. R. Coss, and C. Dyer (Cambridge: Cambridge University Press, 1983), 169–89; Penn R. Szittya, *The Antifraternal Tradition in Medieval Literature* (Princeton: Princeton University Press, 1986); Paul Strohm, "Fictions of Time and Origin: Friar Huberd and the Lepers," in *Theory and the Premodern Text* (Minneapolis: Minnesota University Press, 2000), 65–79; Nicolette Zeeman, "The Condition of Kynde," in *Medieval Literature and Historical Inquiry,* ed. David Aers (Cambridge: Brewer 2000), ch. 1. For the important contexts and traditions of the relevant canon law, see Brian Tierney, *Medieval Poor Law* (Berkeley: University of California Press, 1959). On the ecclesiological implications of the poverty controversies, see the extraordinarily informative essay by Yves M.-J. Congar, "Aspects ecclésiologiques de la querelle entre mendiants et séculiers dans la seconde moitié du XIIIe siècle et le début du XIVe," *Archive d'Histoire Doctrinale et Littéraire du Moyen Âge* 28 (1962), 35–151.

2. I refer to the Prologue. All references are to passus and lines; here, Pr.56–65. See with this the vision of Mede, III.38–67. William Langland, *Piers Plowman: The C Version,* ed. George Russell and George Kane (London: Athlone, 1997). All citations are to this edition of the C version unless otherwise stated. I have made full use of Derek Pearsall's fine annotated edition of the C version, *Piers Plowman, by William Langland: An Edition of the C-Text* (London: Arnold, 1978), hereafter cited as "Langland, *Piers Plowman* (Pearsall)." For the B version I refer to *Piers Plowman: The B Version,* rev. ed., ed. George Kane and E. Talbot Donaldson (London: Athlone, 1988); hereafter cited as "Langland, *Piers Plowman* (Kane/Donaldson)." For the A version, I have used *Piers Plowman: The A Version,* ed. George Kane (London: Athlone, 1960).

3. For a fine introduction to the place of the creedal Church in Catholic tradition, see Henri de Lubac, *The Christian Faith* (San Francisco: Ignatius, 1986), chs. 5–6.

4. I.14–40. On measure and the cardinal virtues, see Bloomfield, *Piers Plowman,* ch. 5.

5. See David Aers, *Community, Gender,* 22–35, with the literature in accompanying references.

6. See annotations to this sequence in William Langland, *Piers Plowman* (Pearsall), pp. 46–53.

7. See Langland, *Piers Plowman* (Pearsall), I.86 n. (p. 46).

8. Here I paraphrase standard Franciscan positions from Bonaventure's *Apologia Pauperum,* XIII.30–35; see the English translation by José de Vinck, *The Defense of Mendicants,* in Bonaventure, *The Works of Bonaventure,* vol. 4 (Paterson, N.J.: St. Anthony Guild Press, 1966). A useful compendium of such positions is made by Bonagratia of Bergamo in his *Tractatus de Paupertate Christi et Apostolorum,* ed. L. Oliger, *Archivum Franciscanum Historicum* 22 (1929), 292–335, 487–511. Still indispensable on all these matters is Malcolm D. Lambert, *Franciscan Poverty* (London: Society for Promoting Christian Knowledge, 1961). One of the most illuminating Franciscan contributions to the controversy between John XXII and the Franciscans is William of Ockham's great *Opus Nonaginta Dierum,* translated by John Kilcullen and John Scott as *Work of Ninety Days,* 2 vols. (Lewiston, N.Y.: Mellen Press, 2001).

9. Bonaventure, *Apologia Pauperum,* I.6 and I.10; also VII.37. Ockham claimed that Jesus did not have ownership of the purse or of its contents but only its use; William of Ockham, *Work of Ninety Days,* vol. 2, ch. 94, 633–36.

10. For exegetical traditions deployed by Langland here, see Ben H. Smith, *Traditional Imagery of Charity in Piers Plowman* (The Hague: Mouton, 1966), ch. 1.

11. See David Aers and Lynn Staley, *The Powers of the Holy: Religion, Politics, and Gender in Late Medieval English Culture* (University Park: Pennsylvania State University Press, 1996), ch. 2.

12. See Justice and Kerby-Fulton, *Written Work.* See too Andrew Cole, "Rewriting Langland and Chaucer: Heresy and Literary Authority in Late Medieval England" (Ph.D. diss., Duke University 2000), ch. 2.

13. For "lollar" in the 1380s, see Scase, *Piers Plowman,* 149–60; Middleton, "Acts of Vagrancy," 255, 266, 276–88; Cole, "Rewriting Langland and Chaucer," ch. 2. Cole's work is now revised in "William Langland and the Invention of Lollardy," in *Lollard's and Their Influence,* ed. Fiona Somerset, Jill Havens, and Derrick Pikard (Woodbridge: Boydell, 2003), 37–58.

14. Langland, *Piers Plowman* (Pearsall), V.6 n. See too John Alford, "The Idea of Reason in *Piers Plowman,*" in Kennedy, Waldron, and Wittig, *Medieval English Studies,* 199–215.

15. Or, according to Russell's and Kane's revision of Hm 143, the manuscript they edit (as does Pearsall), he asks what "craft" Wille has "to fynden" for those in need; here I follow Pearsall, as does A. V. C. Schmidt in his edition, *Piers Plowman: A Parallel Text Edition of the A, B, C and Z Versions* (London: Longmans,

1995), V.21. See the critical apparatus to this line in Russell and Kane. My observations on *fynden* and *fyndynge* are unaffected by the differences between Pearsall and Russell/Kane.

16. On *redde quod debes* and justice in *Piers Plowman* there is a substantial literature, referred to in David Aers, *Faith, Ethics and Church: Writing in England, 1360–1409* (Cambridge: Brewer, 2000), ch. 3, especially in 57 nn. 8 and 7.

17. For what is now known and reasonably conjectured about the poet's life, see Ralph Hanna, "Emendations," *Yearbook of Langland Studies* 14 (2000), 185–98, here 185–87.

18. In Langland, *Piers Plowman* (Pearsall), in annotations to V.88, Derek Pearsall notes the repetitions of V.88 by Patience at XV.250 (XV.249 in the Russell/Kane edition). See too W. W. Skeat's annotations in *The Vision of William Concerning Piers the Plowman in Three Parallel Texts Together with Richard the Redeless*, 2 vols., ed. W. W. Skeat (1886; reprint, Oxford University Press, 1968), vol. 2, p. 63, linking B VII.121–29 (VII.126–35 in the Kane/Donaldson edition) and B XIV.48 (XIV.49–50 in the Kane/Donaldson edition). Skeat cites Matthew 4.4 and 6.10.

19. Russell and Kane revise "wordes" in Hm 143 at V.98 to "wyrdes"; I do not see the force of the decision and stay with their base manuscript and Pearsall's text. I read Wille's "hope" as participating in the theological virtue discussed by Aquinas in the *Summa Theologiae*, II–II.16–22; Thomas Aquinas, *Summa Theologiae* [*ST*], 60 vols. (London: Blackfriars, 1964–81). My understanding of the theology of hope invoked in Wille's conversion in Passus V differs from Anne Middleton's neo-Pascalian account of "an absurd wager of faith" ("Acts of Vagrancy," 262, 234). For some of the cultural and theological issues in this difference, see Aers, *Faith, Ethics*, chs. 1 and 2.

20. In quoting the Bible, I use for the vulgate *Biblia Sacra iuxta Vulgatum Clementinam*, 4th ed., ed. Alberto Colunga and Laurentio Turrado (Matriti: Biblioteca de Autores Cristianos, 1965); for English translation, see *The Holy Bible, Translated from the Latin Vulgate*, rev. Richard Challoner (Rockford, Ill.: Tan Books, 1989).

21. Clopper, *Songes*, 301.

22. Perhaps a word about relations between my reading of Passus V and Anne Middleton's in "Acts of Vagrancy" is in order, one that should be taken in the context of my admiration for this essay expressed in David Aers, review of *Written Work, Yearbook of Langland Studies* 12 (1998), 207–17, and in the context of my own writing on the B version's relations to the Statute of Laborers (1351) and the Vagrancy Petition (1376); Aers, *Community, Gender*, ch. 1. I cannot see the challenge of Reason and Conscience to Wille as an "incipient prosecution" by Justices of the Peace of a suspect under the Cambridge Parliament's legislation (Middleton, "Acts of Vagrancy," 254, 260). My own work on prosecutions under the labor

legislation showed justices pursuing artisans and agragrian workers but not Latinate clerics like the figure of the poet; see Aers, *Community, Gender,* 27–31. Clerical conflict in this domain was addressed by *Effrenata* (1350, 1362); see Aers,
Community, Gender, 29, and the text in *The Black Death,* ed. Rosemary Horrox
(Manchester: Manchester University Press, 1994), 306–9. Reason and Conscience
seem to me at this point acting as agents of "kynde knowynge," part of God's
hitherto unrecognized or underactivated gifts to Wille (I.159–60; see I.79–160).
They act here to draw Wille on his journey to Christ and into the Church rather
than as officers enforcing the current labor legislation. There is no good reason to
assume that the poet of the C version identified the journey to Christ with en-
forcement of the labor legislation of 1351 and 1388. As I argued in *Community, Gender,* the temptation to do so had already been addressed and worked through in the
B version (VI–VII) in a sequence that would be kept and revised in C VIII–IX.
For a recent reading that accepts Middleton's identification of the scene as a "prosecution" under the Statute of 1388 and goes on to produce an economistic reading
that is finally different from hers, and even more different from mine, see D. Vance
Smith, *Arts of Possession: The Middle English Household Imaginary* (Minneapolis:
University of Minnesota Press, 2003), 108–10, 115–16 ,137–38, 146–47, 152–53.

23. Here VIII.329–38.

24. For a fine survey of the relevant history of the tradition from which Piers
speaks, see Michel Mollat, *The Poor in the Middle Ages* (New Haven: Yale University
Press, 1986), ch. 3, 6–8; see too the wealth of relevant work collected in M. Mollat,
ed., *Études sur l'histoire de la pauvreté jusqu'au XVIe siècle,* 2 vols. (Paris: Sorbonne,
1974). For a classically functional attitude to the poor (alms sown in the field of the
poor may yield the donor hundredfold returns), see Richard Morris, ed., *Cursor
Mundi,* vol. 3, lines 28,828–28,837, EETS, o.s., 68 (London: K. Paul, Trench,
Trübner, 1892), pp. 1565–66. This is certainly not Piers's relationship to those in
poverty.

25. I follow Pearsall's punctuation rather than Russell's and Kane's here;
Piers is asking a question.

26. David Aers, *Piers Plowman and Christian Allegory* (London: Arnold,
1975), 121–23, *Chaucer, Langland and the Creative Imagination* (London: Routledge,
1980), 20–23, and *Community, Gender,* 49–50; on these occasions the B version was
the focus. I am aware of one other reader who was preoccupied by the disparity between the two lines of the pardon and the long discourse preceding them: Przemyslaw Mroczkowski. He argued that "all the rest of Piers's address was improvised,
with whatever good intentions," although his analysis of this disparity differs
from mine. See Przemyslaw Mroczkowski, "Piers and His Pardon: A Dynamic
Analysis," in *Studies in Language and Literature,* ed. M. Brahmer, S. Helsztynski,
and J. Krzyzanowski (Warsaw: PWN–Polish Scientific Publishers, 1966), 273–92,

quoting here from 288–89; on the pardon, 281–91. From the substantial literature on the pardon I have found the following most interesting: Donaldson, *Piers Plowman*, 161–68; R. W. Frank, "The Pardon Scene in *Piers Plowman*," *Speculum* 26 (1951), 317–31; Adams, "Piers's Pardon"; Denise Baker, "The Pardons of *Piers Plowman*," *Neuphilologische Mitteilungen* 85 (1984), 462–72; Britton J. Harwood, *Piers Plowman and The Problem of Belief* (Toronto: University of Toronto, 1992), ch. 6. D. Vance Smith has twice addressed the pardon, in different ways: see *The Book of the Incipit: Beginnings in the Fourteenth Century* (Minneapolis: University of Minneapolis Press, 2001), 187–94, and *Arts of Possession*, 125–26, 136, 138–46 (here part of his argument about Langland's "approving use of exchange," 126). For a recent and lengthy essay on the pardon, see Traugott Lawler, "The Pardon Formula in *Piers Plowman*," *Yearbook of Langland Studies* 14 (2000), 117–52. This long essay makes "one of its assumptions" the claim that "the poem is recursive rather than developmental" (118). Lawlor's "rather than" seems both odd and mistaken, for there is no either/or here: *Piers Plowman*, in this like books of the *Faerie Queene*, is both "recursive" and "developmental," as the two chapters in this book show and as I showed about its allegorical modes in *Piers Plowman*, ch. 5. For much earlier accounts of the poem's "recursive" nature which I have found far more accurate than Lawler's, see Elizabeth Salter, *Piers Plowman: An Introduction* (Oxford: Blackwell, 1963), 47–57, 104–5; A. C. Spearing, *Criticism and Medieval Poetry* (London: Arnold, 1964), ch. 4; Anne Middleton, "Narration and Invention of Experience: Episodic Form in *Piers Plowman*," in *The Wisdom of Poetry*, ed. Larry D. Benson and Siegfried Wenzel (Kalamazoo: Western Michigan University, Medieval Institute Publications, 1982), 91–122; Baker, "The Pardons of *Piers Plowman*," 462–72, especially 471–72; Greta Hort, *Piers Plowman and Contemporary Religious Thought* (London: Church Historical Society, n.d. [after 1936]), 60.

27. See Pearsall's annotations to IX.283–91 in Langland, *Piers Plowman* (Pearsall), pp. 173–74.

28. It is also followed by Schmidt's parallel-text edition.

29. See W. W. Skeat's punctuation recalled by Derek Pearsall in Langland, *Piers Plowman* (Pearsall), IX.159 n.

30. See the commentaries on this by Shepherd, "Poverty in *Piers Plowman*," and Pearsall, "Poverty and Poor People," especially 178–80. These fine essays share one claim that puzzles me: they both describe the poor here as "the new urban poor" (Shepherd, "Poverty in *Piers Plowman*," 172; Pearsall, "Poverty and Poor People," 179, and "Lunatyk Lollares," 166). I see no reason to classify the landless laborers here as distinctly urban rather than agricultural: they are either and both.

31. Pearsall, "Lunatyk Lollares," 166.

32. Shepherd, "Poverty in *Piers Plowman*," 172. This remark is also quoted by Pearsall, "Poverty and Poor People," 180.

33. See Pr.2–3, 41–46; V.1–104; VIII.73–4, 128–40, 210–30, 263–64, 325–29.

34. On Langland and the term "lollare," see Pearsall, "Lunatyk Lollares"; Scase, *Piers Plowman*, ch. 5; Middleton, "Acts of Vagrancy," 255, 266, 276–88; Cole, "Rewriting Langland and Chaucer," ch. 2.

35. On the political ideology shaping the version of faith and Church, see Aers, *Community, Gender,* ch. 1; for the argument that the C version has the 1388 Cambridge Statutes as its "pre-text," see Middleton, "Acts of Vagrancy"; for objections to Middleton's argument, see George Kane, "Langland: Labour and 'Authorship,'" *Notes and Queries* 243 (1998), 423–25.

36. Shepherd, "Poverty in *Piers Plowman*," 172–73.

37. See Aers, *Community, Gender;* Middleton, "Acts of Vagrancy"; and Kane, "Langland," together with the Franciscan reading proposed by Clopper, *Songes,* ch. 5.

38. Cf. the role of wit and inwit in the following passus, especially X.171–87.

39. Besides the work by Mollat, *The Poor* and *Études,* see the invaluable studies by Tierney, *Medieval Poor Law,* and Margaret Aston, "'Caim's Castles': Poverty, Politics and Disendowment," ch. 4 in *Faith and Fire* (London: Hambledon Press, 1993).

40. Shepherd, "Poverty in *Piers Plowman*," 174; see too Mollat, *The Poor,* chs. 3–4, 6–8, and Morris, *Cursor Mundi.*

41. See Donaldson, *Piers Plowman,* ch. 5, especially 135, 144–47; Langland, *Piers Plowman* (Pearsall), IX.136 n. (p. 167); Pearsall, "Lunatyk Lollares," 171–72; Clopper, *Songes,* 200–217.

42. Clopper, *Songes,* seriatim 203, 207, 215, 21, 3. Clopper's attempt to appropriate Derek Pearsall's work here is rather odd. He claims that Pearsall says these people "are not madmen." But Pearsall actually states that these "lunatyk" people are "*real* [italics in original] fools and madmen" ("Lunatyk Lollares," 172), that these are "literally lunatics" (168; see too 173).

43. Clopper, *Songes,* 207, 215. One should also note Langland's emphasis that these "lunatyk lollares" are "men and women bothe" (IX.106). They are thus *not* Clopper's "brothers": St. Francis and his "brothers" never allowed the sisters to share the brothers' mobility and freedom of preaching but forced them to take the enclosed, monastic model.

44. Clopper, *Songes,* 204.

45. Clopper, *Songes,* 189.

46. On antifraternal literary traditions see Szittya, *The Antifraternal Tradition.* His reading of *Piers Plowman* follows the lines established by Adams, "The Nature of Need" (see *The Antifraternal Tradition,* ch. 7). For an introduction to the Reformation literature on the poor, see Christopher Hill, *Society and Puritanism*

(London: Panther, 1969), ch. 7 and Hill, *Puritanism and Revolution* (London: Panther, 1965), ch. 7. For an important revisiting of Max Weber's *The Protestant Ethic and the Spirit of Capitalism* (London: Unwin, 1971), see Gordon Marshall, *Presbyteries and Profits: Calvinism and the Development of Calvinism* (Oxford: Oxford University Press, 1980).

47. See Aers, *Community, Gender,* 22–26, 34–35, 50–55, 57–60.

48. Whoever is responsible for this gloss does not bother about Piers's anxious reflection that even counterfeits "are my blody bretherne for god bouhte vs alle" (see VIII.215–18).

49. Aers, *Community, Gender,* 53–64.

50. See IX.294 n. in Langland, *Piers Plowman* (Pearsall).

51. Critical responses to the friars and their teaching has been divided. For a recent and unqualifiedly enthusiastic response, see Clopper, *Songes,* 85–87. Contrast Elizabeth Kirk, *The Dream Thought of Piers Plowman* (New Haven: Yale University Press, 1972), 104.

52. See especially *Confessions,* VIII.5.10–6.12, VIII.8.19–9.21, in Augustine, *Confessions,* trans. Henry Chadwick (Oxford: Oxford University Press, 1991). See too the later elaborations in the anti-Pelagian texts such as *On Nature and Grace,* 19.21–34.39, in Augustine, *Four Anti-Pelagian Writings,* trans. John A. Mourant and William J. Collinge (Washington: Catholic University of America Press, 1992). Also, in the same volume, consult *On the Gift of Perseverance.* I am aware of the influential scholarly tradition, now dominant, that reads *Piers Plowman* as a systematically un-Augustinian, even anti-Augustinian work, a "semi-Pelagian" poem. On this see especially Adams, "Piers's Pardon"; Janet Coleman, *Piers Plowman and the Moderni* (Rome: Edizioni di Storia e Litteratura, 1981); James Simpson, *Piers Plowman: An Introduction to the B-Text* (London: Longman, 1990), 93, 124–26, 180 ("his repeated affirmation of the 'semi-Pelagian' idea that men can be saved through full repentance"). This view is rehearsed by Lawler, "The Pardon Formula," for example, 120–21, 126, 138 (Gospels as semi-Pelagian), 142, 147, 151. It emerges in the more sophisticated study by Smith, *Book of the Incipit,* ch. 7. For well-informed reservations towards this tradition of criticism, see A. J. Minnis, "Looking for a Sign: The Quest for Nominalism in Chaucer and Langland," ch. 7 in *Essays in Ricardian Literature,* ed. A. J. Minnis, Charlotte Morse, and Thorlac Turville-Petre (Oxford: Clarendon Press, 1997), 142–78. For examples of Augustinian readings, see Denise Baker, "From Plowing to Penitence: Piers Plowman and the Fourteenth-Century Theology," *Speculum* 55 (1980), 715–25, and "The Pardons of *Piers Plowman,*" in which Baker argues that the pardon allegedly given to Piers is a "false pardon" (469, 470); Britton Harwood, *Piers Plowman,* ch. 6. I have found it very surprising that the advocates of Langland's "semi-Pelagianism" habitually fail to mention, let alone analyze, the representation of "semyuief" and Christ's responses

to this figure (XIX.53–95). I will address this scene later in the chapter. We should recall that Aquinas's *Summa Theologiae* is, in this area, Augustinian; see Joseph P. Wawrykow, *God's Grace and Human Action: 'Merit' in the Theology of Thomas Aquinas* (Notre Dame: Notre Dame University Press, 1995), 143–46 with chs. 3–4.

53. This frivolity is embedded in the exemplum itself, especially in its shorter C version, X.10–55; cf. B VII.26–56.

54. On the exegetical traditions deployed in Langland's rewriting of Jesus's parable of the good Samaritan, see Smith, *Traditional Imagery,* ch. 4.

55. See the dispute between William of Ockham and John XXII in which this subject is addressed; William of Ockham, *Work of Ninety Days,* ch. 94, a classic example of the exegetical details in this controversy. See also, for example, Bonaventure, *Apologia Pauperum,* in *The Works of Bonaventure,* VII.3–9, 11–13, 16, 22, 31–32; XI on Franciscans; and XII on mendicancy (note the claim that Christ accepted the state of mendicancy, XII.30–37). See too Bonagratia of Bergamo, *Tractatus,* especially 325, 327, 328–31, 491–500; against John XXII, see especially 500–502.

56. The A version also has the unambiguous usage; A X.49–51, 105–6. On "rechelesnesse" and its ambiguities, see Donaldson, *Piers Plowman,* 169–75.

57. See Clopper, *Songes,* 83 nn. 33 and 34.

58. For an introduction to some relevant medieval and modern materials on this distinction, see Aers, *Faith, Ethics,* 97–101 with 35–36.

59. Cf. the treatment of grace and "ryȝte" in E. V. Gordon, ed., *Pearl* (Oxford: Clarendon Press, 1963), 481–720.

60. The works cited in note 1 are relevant to this sequence in both B and C versions. On Rechelesnesse see annotations to Langland, *Piers Plowman* (Pearsall), XI.196 and XII.98. On the "myrrour þat hihte myddelerd," see Steven Kruger, "Mirrors and the Trajectory of Vision in *Piers Plowman,*" *Speculum* 66 (1991), 74–95.

61. Clopper, *Songes,* seriatim 88, 220, 92, 223; Langland himself "probably a Franciscan," 327.

62. On the B version and the Franciscan implications of this passage, B XI.270–82, see Clopper, *Songes,* 89–91. He does not explore reasons for the deletion of B XI.273 from the C version.

63. See Aers, *Faith Ethics;* also relevant to the issues here is David Aers, "Chaucer's Tale of *Melibee:* Whose Virtues?" in *Medieval Literature and Historical Inquiry,* ed. David Aers (Cambridge: Brewer, 2000), ch. 4.

64. On the Christocentric nature of the poem and its allegorical modes, see Aers, *Piers Plowman,* ch. 5.

65. See IX.70–87 (discussed above) and XI.40–42, also XV.293–97; Shepherd, "Poverty in *Piers Plowman*"; and Pearsall, "Poverty and Poor People."

66. Thomas Aquinas, *Summa contra Gentiles* [*ScG*], 4 vols., trans. Vernon J. Bourke (Notre Dame: University of Notre Dame Press, 1975), III.133, seriatim 1, 3, 4; see also III.131–35. See, relatedly, Augustine, Sermon 346 A, in Augustine, *Sermons*, trans. Edmund Hill, part 3 of *The Works of Saint Augustine*, ed. John. E. Rotelle (Brooklyn: New City Press, 1994), vol. 10; here see especially section 6, pp. 74–75.

67. Clopper's terms, in Clopper, *Songes*, 88.

68. Pearsall comments: "Imaginatif is interested here in dissociating Christ from beggars (or mendicants: suggested by the mention of the friars, and specified in B XII 46) and rascally poor." Langland, *Piers Plowman* (Pearsall), XIV.90–91, p. 238.

69. On Patience and Franciscan ideology, see Guy Bourquin, *Piers Plowman*, 2 vols. (Paris: Champion, 1978), 404–41 (B XIII–XV) and 649–90 (on the exaltation of poverty in the C version), together with his overall account of the poem's Franciscanism, part 4, ch. 1, 693–736; Pearsall, "Poverty and Poor People," 182–85; Aers, *Community, Gender*, 60–62; Clopper, *Songes*, 238–44. Contrast Adams, "The Nature of Need," and Szittya, *The Antifraternal Tradition*. For a sympathetic account of the political potentials of Patience in the poet's Europe, and our world, see Anna Baldwin, "Patient Politics in *Piers Plowman*," *Yearbook of Langland Studies* 15 (2001), 99–108. In "The Debt Narrative in *Piers Plowman*," Anna Baldwin assumes that Patience has full and final authorial support at B XIV.108–10, 120 (see C XV.285–86, 301), in *Art and Context in Late Medieval English Narrative*, ed. Robert R. Edwards (Cambridge: Brewer, 1994), 37–50. Reasons against this view are offered in the ensuing discussion.

70. In an earlier scene Conscience suggested that if mendicancy were compatible with a state of Christian perfection it would be so within the Church's regular orders (V.90–91).

71. XV.91 puns on the name of a contemporary Dominican friar, William Jordan; see Mildred E. Marcett, *Uhtred de Boldon, Friar William Jordan and Piers Plowman* (New York: privately printed, 1938), 62–64. Clopper acknowledges this allusion, but, wishing to stress "the overall Franciscan character of the scene," suggests that the carnal master is a Franciscan, Brother Elias, the deposed minister general (*Songes*, 239 n. 26).

72. XV.32 and 35. Contrast St. Francis's famous "horror of money"; Mollat, *The Poor*, 122. On this issue note how Ubertino da Casale represented the "spiritual" Franciscan position at the Council of Vienne in 1310; see David Burr, *The Spiritual Franciscans* (University Park: Pennsylvania State University Press, 2001), 125–26. Clopper discusses the debates on crying out for alms in *Songes*, 47–49, 59–61, 63–65. Given this, it is odd that Clopper does not discuss XV.32–34 in this context; cf. *Songes*, 238–45. Kelly Johnson has also noted that Patience is a beggar, though she insists he "is not a literal beggar." See Kelly S. Johnson, "Beggars and Stewards: The Contest of Humility in Christian Ethics" (Ph. D. diss., Duke Uni-

versity, 2001), 84, 94. While it is true that Patience is a personification of a virtue in a poem replete with allegorical writing in different modes, the poet has, at this point, chosen to give Patience a significantly "literal" form of begging and demand for food *or*, most significantly, *money*.

73. See annotations to Langland, *Piers Plowman* (Pearsall), XV.141 (p. 252); see also XVI.137–49.

74. B XIV.29–33a is even more provocatively phrased; this relates to Piers's conversion, deleted in the C version (B VII.122–35).

75. Piers quotes from this in the B version's account of his conversion, B VII.131–35, as does Patience in his B manifestation; B XIV.31–33a, deleted in the C version (XV.232 ff.). Clopper discusses the B version aligning Patience with Bonaventura and other Franciscans (*Songes*, 241–42); Patience, he shows, represents "the Franciscan ideal" (238). On *ne solliciti sitis*, see Konrad Burdach, *Der Dichter des Ackermann aus Böhmen und seine Zeit* (Berlin: Weidmann, 1932), 268–71, 275, 308–11, 351–52; Frank, *Piers Plowman*, 29–33. For a classic example of the debate around solicitude and poverty, see William of Ockham, *Work of Ninety Days*, vol. 2, ch. 76, 481–507.

76. *ScG* III.135.24: see too *ST* II–II.187.7 resp and ad 1–5. With this, consult the Dominican Master General, Hervaeus Natalis, *The Poverty of Christ and the Apostles*, trans. John P. Jones (Toronto: Pontifical Institute of Medieval Studies, 1999), 70–74; the Latin text, *Liber de Paupertate Christi et Apostolorum*, was edited by J. G. Sikes in *Archives d'Histoire Doctrinale et Littéraire du Moyen Age* 11 (1937–38), 209–97. Jones's translation includes an extremely helpful introduction to Hervaeus and his relations both to Aquinas's work and to Franciscan opponents. Once again, Ockham's *Work of Ninety Days* provides a fascinating example of the issues being disputed and the modes of disputation. For examples of conflicts between Dominican and Franciscan theology of poverty, see David Burr, *Olivi and Franciscan Poverty* (Philadelphia: University of Philadelphia Press, 1989), 148–55, and Burr, *The Spiritual Franciscans*, 263–64, 266.

77. Hervaeus Natalis, *Poverty of Christ*, 62–73. Hervaeus Natalis represents in extremely rich and cogent form the resources provided by Dominican tradition for exploring the strengths and limitations of Franciscan theology of poverty and perfection, resources which Langland integrates in his own critical vision.

78. On this theological virtue, see the rich account in *ST* II–II.23–46.

79. It is illuminating to consider Aquinas on this text in *ST* II–II.186.3, ad 4, and in *De Perfectione Vitae Spiritualis*, ch. 7, para. 575, in *Opuscula Theologica*, vol. 2, ed. R. M. Spiazzi (Rome: Marietti, 1954).

80. Langland, *Piers Plowman* (Pearsall) XV.281 n. (p. 259). Augustine reads the text in question without any trace of Patience's irony; see Sermon 311.8–12 in Augustine, *Sermons*, III 9.

81. Russell and Kane revise their base MS (Hm 143) by substituting "þe" for "puyre" and by adding "hit" before "claymeth." I cannot see the force of this decision and so follow Pearsall here. It is interesting that XV. 285–86 reproduces the faulty argument ascribed to Scripture in B X. 347–48 but deleted in C XI (discussed above).

82. Once again consult the powerful elaboration of this tradition in Augustine's *Confessions*, VII.21.27, VIII.5.10–12, VIII.12–25. See note 52 above for studies arguing that *Piers Plowman* is a "semi-Pelagian" work. As will be emerging, in my view the poem generates and explores Pelagianizing voices as *moments* in its dialectical process, moments that are explored, placed, and superseded.

83. *ScG* III.24.

84. Russell and Kane leave MS Hm 143 and select "sute" to replace its "secte." Pearsall (unlike Schmidt in his parallel-text edition) retains "secte." Cf. XVI.98–99, quoted in my text below.

85. Cf. the more parallel statement in B XI.185–89, as Pearsall notes in Langland, *Piers Plowman* (Pearsall), XII.99 n.

86. To some (perhaps "semi-Pelagian") ears this may sound peculiarly Augustinian, but it is actually a commonplace of medieval theology. Consult the treatment of faith in *ST* II–II.1–16 and the fourteenth-century Franciscan handbook *Fasciculus Morum*, ed. and trans. Siegfried Wenzel (University Park: Pennsylvania State University Press, 1989), III.23 (especially pp. 302–6) and, on faith in relation to sloth, V.28–29.

87. On sloth, see Siegfried Wenzel, *The Sin of Sloth* (Chapel Hill: University of North Carolina Press, 1967). For an argument about the centrality of sloth in *Piers Plowman* and its author's anxieties, see John M. Bowers, *The Crisis of Will in Piers Plowman* (Washington: Catholic University of America Press, 1986), chs. 4 and 6.

88. See Romans 7.23; also Augustine, *Confessions*, VIII.5.10–12 and VIII.11.25.

89. See Richard Fitzralph, *Defonsorium Curatorium*, in *Fasciculi Rerum Expetendarum & Fugiendarum*, ed. Edward Brown (London: Chiswell, 1690), vol. 2, 466–86, here 466 and 481. On Fitzralph amd Langland, see James Dawson, "Richard Fitzralph and the Fourteenth-Century Poverty Controversies," *Journal of Ecclesiastical History* 34 (1983), 315–44; Aers, *Community, Gender*, 25–26, 34–35; Szittya, *The Antifraternal Tradition*, 280–83, and, on Fitzralph's ecclesiology, ch. 3; Clopper, *Songes*, 58–65.

90. *Fasciculus Morum*, IV.12 (pp. 387/386).

91. See Bourquin, *Piers Plowman*, 719–20.

92. For Aquinas, see *ST* II–II.188.7 and *ScG* III.135; for Hervaeus Natalis, see *The Poverty of Christ*, Questions 1 and 2a, especially 53–59, 62–76.

93. On Liberum Arbitrium see *ST* I. 83, together with I–II.109.5, ad 1 and ad 4; I–II.109.7, ad 1; I–II.112.2, resp; I–II.112.3, resp; I–II.113.3, resp and ad 2. See

the introduction by J. B. Korolec, "Free Will and Free Choice," ch. 32 in *The Cambridge History of Later Medieval Philosophy*, ed. Norman Kretzmann, Anthony Kenny, and Jan Pinborg (Cambridge: Cambridge University Press, 1982). However, the comments on Aquinas on p. 36 are seriously misleading and also flatten out his intellectual history; cf. ch. 33 in the same volume, Alan Donagan, "Thomas Aquinas on Human Action" and especially the careful study by Wawrykow, *God's Grace and Human Action*. For Clopper's attempt to assimilate Liberum Arbitrium in *Piers Plowman* to his own version of the poem's committedly radical Franciscan ideology, see Clopper, *Songes*, 262–72; cf. Harwood, *Piers Plowman*, 103–12, and Paul Sheneman, "Grace Abounding: Justification in Passus 16 of *Piers Plowman*," *Papers on Language and Literature* 34 (1998), 162–78. Thomas Bradwardine offers a definition of *Liberum Arbitrium* in *De Causa Dei*, ed. Henry Savil (London, 1618; reprint, Frankfurt: Minerva GMBH, 1964), II.1 (443–44).

94. The translation is Pearsall's. Langland, *Piers Plowman* (Pearsall), XVI.271a n., modified by me.

95. On Langland's distinctions and vituperations, see the memorable remarks of Shepherd, "Poverty in *Piers Plowman*," 173; see too Scase, *Piers Plowman*, 64–75.

96. For Hervaeus Natalis, see *The Poverty of Christ* and observations on this above. I am not, of course, claiming "influence." For Langland and hermits, see Godden, "Plowmen and Hermits" and Hanna, "Will's Work."

97. See references in Langland, *Piers Plowman* (Pearsall), XVII.17 n. and 19 n.; to Pearsall's gloss to XVII.19 one should add John 21.1–3, an episode after Christ's resurrection. The significance of such details in the battles around poverty can be seen in William of Ockham's *Work of Ninety Days*, ch. 75: here the Franciscan polemicist insists that the apostles renounced ownership of their nets, keeping only their use. Even less would he countenance their selling their own catch (p. 480). Clopper, *Songes*, 270, overlooks this un-Franciscan emphasis on apostolic trade and commodities. Scase, *Piers Plowman*, 93, notes that the details here are "used untraditionally," but her thesis about the poem's "new anticlericalism" leads her to claim that the "details" are plainly "in accordance with the anticlerical cause." In Langland's context, however, they are nothing of the sort. As I have just observed, Liberum Arbitrium has found Charity among clerics, including the wealthiest ecclesiastics. The point here is to block Wille's path to a mendicant life, a path that was *not* licit for the secular or monastic clergy. Jean de Meun addresses some of the issues here in *Le roman de la rose*, ed. Daniel Poirion (Paris: Garnier-Flammarion, 1974), lines 11293–316, but he ascribes this account of the apostolic rejection of mendicancy to Faux Semblant.

98. I should again mention Clopper's assimilation of Liberum Arbitrium (Anima in the B version) to his Franciscan reading of the poem: Liberum Arbitrium

offers "the same Franciscan orientation that we have seen in Rechelesnesse's and Patience's statements" (267).

99. Scase's fourth chapter of her *Piers Plowman* is on Charity, but unfortunately she assimilates the poem's treatment of charity to her thesis that the poem is systematically "anticlerical" and composed for "anticlericals" and for promoting "anticlerical acts," arguing that "anticlericalism was grounded in charity" here and throughout the poem (84). As I argue here and below, Charity must be understood in a far broader context, one that includes Passus I and Passus XVIII–XXI, together with the roles of the sacraments administered by priests ordained in the Catholic Church.

100. See Skeat, *Piers the Plowman*, vol. 2, 233 n. 227; Langland, *Piers Plowman* (Pearsall), XVII.220 n. and 227 n.; Aers, *Chaucer, Langland*, 70, 74–75; Anne Hudson, *The Premature Reformation: Wycliffite Texts and Lollard History* (Oxford: Clarendon Press, 1988), 336–42; Scase, *Piers Plowman*, 109–10, 208 n. 107. I am grateful for conversation with Anne Hudson around this issue; she rightly warned me against reading back the form disendowment took under Henry VIII and imposing that onto Wycliffites. Their distribution of ecclesial resources seems to have a wider social goal than Henry's; see "The Lollard Disendowment Bill" in *Selections from English Wycliffite Writings*, ed. Anne Hudson (Cambridge: Cambridge University Press, 1978), 135–37, 203–7.

101. See the important work on this by Katherine C. Little, "Reading for Christ: Interpretation and Instruction in Late Medieval England" (Ph.D. diss., Duke University, 1998), and emerging from this, "Catechesis and Castigation: Sin in the Wycliffite Sermon Cycle," *Traditio* 54 (1999), 213–44; also Hudson, *The Premature Reformation*, 294–301.

102. See Aers, *Faith, Ethics*, ch. 6.

103. For an account of allegorical modes around the tree of Charity and their theology, see Aers, *Piers Plowman*, 71–109. Although the analysis here is of the B version, the theological arguments about the organization of Langland's allegory remain relevant to the C version. For a far more materialist account than mine, see Andrew Cole, "Trifunctionality and the Tree of Charity: Literary and Social Practice in *Piers Plowman*," *English Literary History* 62 (1995), 1–25.

104. I cannot see the force of Russell's and Kane's decision to change the word "to" of MS Hm 143 to "in"; cf. Langland, *Piers Plowman* (Pearsall), XVIII.2.

105. To see the expansiveness of the revisions in the C version here, see B XVI.65–72. Kelly Johnson makes an extremely interesting suggestion about the name of the tree: "In the B-version, Pacience is the name of the tree of charity (B XVI.8), but in C the name is changed to Ymago-Dei. The change may have been made to sharpen the precision of the initial picture-allegory of the tree, rather than any particular concern for the pilgrim Patience." Johnson, "Beggars and Stewards,"

84 n. 51. In my view the change may well have had "particular concern" to the treatment of Patience; the change belongs to the processes of supersession I have been describing and analyzing. It also involves fresh theological reflection about the sources of Charity in the image of God in humankind; see *ST* I.93, especially I.93.4–5 and 7.

106. In XVIII.80, Russell and Kane change Hm 143 to "*lyf Actiua.*" Once more I follow the manuscript and Pearsall.

107. See Giles Constable, *Three Studies in Medieval Religious and Social Thought* (Cambridge: Cambridge University Press, 1995), part 1, "The Interpretation of Mary and Martha"; also Langland, *Piers Plowman* (Pearsall), XII.138a (p. 217).

108. Aers, *Piers Plowman*, 102–9.

109. Aers and Staley, *Powers of the Holy*, chs. 1–2: on *Piers Plowman*, 68–74.

110. See quoting and discussion of Angela of Foligno in Caroline W. Bynum, *Holy Feast and Holy Fast: The Religious Significance of Food to Medieval Women* (Berkeley: University of California Press, 1987), 144–45. See Angela of Foligno, *Complete Works*, trans. Paul Lachance (New York: Paulist Press, 1993), 162–63. It should be said, however, that Angela's theology is also informed by the *via negativa;* see the critical edition by Ludger Thier and Abele Calufetti, *Il Libro della Beata Angela de Foligno* (Rome: Editiones Collegii S. Bonaventurae ad Claras Aquas, 1985).

111. See Aers and Staley, *Powers of the Holy*, 68–74.

112. He cites Romans 4, Galatians 3, and Hebrews 11; Langland, *Piers Plowman* (Pearsall), XVIII.183 n.

113. In this context Aquinas cites the text Patience used against Actyf: "Quis est hic et laudabimus eum" [Who is he and we will praise him] (Ecclesiasticus 31.9), quoted and discussed earlier in this chapter. See too Thomas Aquinas, *De Perfectione Vitae Spiritualis*, paras. 573–75, in Aquinas, *Opuscula Theologica*, vol. 2, p. 119.

114. Aquinas, *De Perfectione Vitae Spiritualis*, para. 573.

115. Here I paraphrase from the following passages in *ST*, II–II, seriatim: 186.3, resp, ad 4, ad 2; 188.7, resp. For helpful accounts of Aquinas's teaching on poverty, see Odd Langholm, *Economics in the Medieval Schools: Wealth, Exchange, Value, Money and Usury According to the Paris Theological Tradition, 1200–1350* (Leiden: Brill, 1992), 209–10; John D. Jones, "The Concept of Poverty in St. Thomas Aquinas's *Contra Impugnantes Dei Religionem et Cultum*," *Thomist* 59 (1995), 109–39, "Poverty and Subsistence: St. Thomas Aquinas and the Definition of Poverty," *Gregorianum* 75 (1994), 135–49, and "St. Thomas Aquinas and the Defense of Mendicant Poverty," *Proceedings of the American Catholic Philosophical Association* 70 (1996), 179–92; Jan G. J. van den Eijnden, *Poverty on the Way to God: Thomas Aquinas on Evangelical Poverty* (Leuven: Peeters, 1994); Ulrich Horst, *Evangelische Armut und Kirche: Thomas von Aquin und die Armutskontroversen des 13. und beginnenden 14. Jahrunderts* (Berlin: Academie, 1992), especially helpful on responses to Aquinas. Clopper takes note of the later Aquinas's critical relations to Franciscan

ideology of poverty but is certain that *Piers Plowman* is identified with the radical Franciscanism Aquinas opposed; Clopper, *Songes,* 236–37. For an example of the difference between Dominican and Franciscan emphasis, cf. with the texts of Aquinas I have been outlining William of Ockham, *Work of Ninety Days,* ch. 18 (p. 267) and ch. 76 (p. 589).

116. I refer to the earlier discussion of the two Franciscan friars, Rechelesnesse and Patience. For debate on the poem's relations to Augustine and "semi-Pelagianism," see note 52.

117. For this sequence see Langland, *Piers Plowman* (Pearsall), XIX.47 n.; especially useful here is Smith, *Traditional Imagery,* ch. 4.

118. For an Elizabethan Calvinist's version of Langland's image, see William Perkins, *A Reformed Catholike,* in *The Workes,* 3 vols. (Cambridge, 1616–18), I.559. Perkins insists that the human being must be envisaged as "starke dead" and in need not of healing but of "a new soule" which God must put into the dead person; see pp. 558–61. This is alien to Langland's vision.

119. It is revealing that in even the most nuanced versions of Langland's "semi-Pelagianism," ones that can acknowledge countertendencies to the latter in *Piers Plowman,* this scene is sidelined; see, for example, Smith, *Book of the Incipit,* 171–87. It is striking that Robert Adams considers the Samaritan but asserts that there is no "bondage of the will" shown here; but his claim depends on simply ignoring the "semyuief" victim of XIX.54–58. Adams, "Piers's Pardon," 394–95. This is an issue I am currently pursuing.

120. Augustine, Sermon 299 E, in Augustine, *Sermons,* vol. 8, 299.E.3–5, pp. 266–69.

121. See *ST* II–II.184–3, ad 1; 185.6, ad 1; 188.7, resp.

122. See Langland, *Piers Plowman* (Pearsall), XXI.228 n.

123. For congruent late medieval traditions here in philosophical idioms, see Joel Kaye, *Economy and Nature in the Fourteenth Century* (Cambridge: Cambridge University Press, 1998).

124. Perhaps here Romans 13.1–6, read in a certain way, is favored over Christ's teaching in Luke 6.29–30, 35. For such conflicts in Wyclif's work, see Aers, *Faith, Ethics,* ch. 6.

125. It is worth noting too that no mention is made of those "opere beggares" discussed earlier in this chapter's exploration of the glosses on the two-line "pardoun" of Passus IX, those "lunatyk lollares" who "wanteth wyt" and who actually beg from "no man" (IX.105–38). It should be recalled that some editors maintain that the poet's revision to the B version never reached the final two passus; see Langland, *Piers Plowman* (Kane/Donaldson), 124, and Langland, *Piers Plowman* (Russell/Kane), 62–88, especially 82–83. However, all that we know about the situation is lucidly stated by Derek Pearsall in Langland, *Piers Plowman* (Pearsall):

"The later two passus are relatively little altered, and the last two not at all, but this may be because Langland was satisfied with them, understandably, rather than because he never reached them in the process of revision" (10).

126. I take these three positions, respectively, from Adams, "The Nature of Need"; Clopper, *Songes*, 93–97, 294–95, 304–5; Middleton, "Acts of Vagrancy," 271–72. Also relevant are Scase, *Piers Plowman*, 66, and Fradenburg, "Needful Things," 54.

127. On the conventionality of Need's argument here, see Langland, *Piers Plowman* (Pearsall), XXII.10 n., 15 n., and 23 n.; also Aers, *Community, Gender*, 63–64, and Anna Baldwin, *The Theme of Government in Piers Plowman* (Cambridge: Brewer, 1981), 9. See too William of Ockham, *Work of Ninety Days*, ch. 3 (vol. 1, 88–90), ch. 32 (vol. 1, 334–39).

128. For a classic account of the cardinal virtues and their relations, see *ST* II–II.47–168. For an illuminating recent introduction to the virtues and their traditions, see Stanley Hauerwas and Charles Pinches, *Christians among the Virtues* (Notre Dame: Notre Dame University Press, 1997).

129. Scase, *Piers Plowman*, 66 (see 66–67); Clopper, *Songes*, 94.

130. Aers and Staley, *Powers of the Holy*, chs. 1–2. This vision is perfectly congruent with Matthew 25 and Christ's hidden presence in the poor; see Rechelesnesse at XII.120–26 (we know it is Rechelesnesse speaking here because of XIII.129). See Mary C. Davlin, "*Piers Plowman* and the Gospel and First Epistle of John," *Yearbook of Langland Studies*, 10 (1996), 89–127.

131. For textual and semantic issues around "byde," see the apparatus to XIII.49 by Russell and Kane, together with Scase, *Piers Plowman*, 68–69, and Clopper, *Songes*, 95–96 n. 56.

132. Langland also draws attention, as I pointed out, to Need's exegetical work. He does so be referring us to "the boek" and then having Need both relocate a saying by Jesus and interpolate himself into the divine voice (XXII.42–47). In this way the poet suggests that much hermeneutic work goes into making a "key" Franciscan text (see Clopper, *Songes*, 94). This is a forceful antidote to the reification of the sign of poverty. It is a far more subtle and sympathetic exemplification of a practice polemicized against in the Prologue's comment about friars who "Glosede þe gospel as hem good likede" (Pr.56–58), but it too associates the constitution of the Franciscan sign of poverty with the poem's analysis of the dire trouble in which the modern Church is immersed.

133. On the "old antimendicant joke" here, Scase, *Piers Plowman*, 101.

134. Cf. Patience at XV.263–76; cf. Liberum Arbitrium, XVII.6–16.

135. Cf. Clopper, *Songes*, 98–99.

136. In XXII.304–5 I follow Pearsall's edition with "To" instead of Russell's and Kane's "Go" in XXII.305. I see no problems with "To" and no good reason for "Go."

137. This recapitulates the scene between the friars and Mede where the sacrament of penance and fraternal Masses become commodities for sale; III.38–67.

138. Scase's assimilation of Conscience to her thesis that *Piers Plowman* systematically embodies "the new anticlericalism" fails to grasp the centrality of the Church in Langland's composition of Conscience in the final two passus. This leads her to a mistakenly individualist account of this power; Scase, *Piers Plowman*, 119, 173. This error was also made nine years earlier by Aers, *Chaucer, Langland*, 37. For Aquinas on Conscience, see *ST* I.79.13.

139. In its context, one of absolute freedom from any idealization or sentimentalism about the contemporary Church, this obedience has the inflections of Augustine's attitudes, nicely illustrated in Sermon 47 (probably preached in 414), especially 47.17–18, pp. 311–13, in Augustine, *Sermons*. Against the Donatists, Augustine reflects on Matthew 13.27–30 and Matthew 25.31–32: the Church is for sheep and goats, wheat and weeds, with no human having the powers of final discernment or the authority to separate from the Church in a wish for purification of the field or flock. Such separation is a disastrous usurpation of divine judgment and eschatology, the pathology of apocalyptic politics. Augustine quotes Ecclesiasticus 2.16, "Woe to them that have lost patience." For reflections on Langland's treatment of apocalypticism, see Aers, "Visionary Eschatology: *Piers Plowman*," *Modern Theology* 16:1 (2000), 3–17.

140. The critical literature on *fyndynge* is as diverse as readers' views on the poem's relations to Franciscanism. See especially Frank, *Piers Plowman*, 116–17; Bloomfield, *Piers Plowman*, 147–48; Langland, *Piers Plowman* (Pearsall), XXII.383 n.; Szittya, *The Antifraternal Tradition*, 286–87; Scase, *Piers Plowman*, 101–2; Clopper, *Songes*, 293–96.

6. Home, Homelessness, and Sanctity: Conflicting Models

1. David Aers, *Community, Gender and Individual Identity: English Writing, 1360–1430.* (London: Routledge, 1988), chs. 2 and 4. For a recent essay and bibliography relevant to many of the issues here, see Chris Chism, *Alliterative Revivals* (Philadelphia: University of Pennsylvania Press, 2002), ch. 3. I am grateful to the Center for Medieval and Renaissance Studies at Ohio State University for inviting me to give an earlier version of this chapter.

2. *The Book of Margery Kempe*, ed. Lynn Staley (Kalamazoo: Western Michigan University, Medieval Institute Publications, 1996), ch. 48, 117 (subsequent citations to chapter and page are given parenthetically in the text). Lynn Staley has also translated and edited *The Book of Margery Kempe* (New York: Norton, 2001), while Barry Windeatt has also edited and annotated *The Book of Margery Kempe*

(Harlow: Longman/Pearson, 2000) (hereafter cited as Kempe, *Book of Margery Kempe* (Windeatt).

3. See the following: Sarah Beckwith, "A Very Material Mysticism: The Medieval Mysticism of Margery Kempe," in *Medieval Literature: Criticism, Ideology and History*, ed. David Aers (New York: St. Martin's Press, 1986), 34–57; Sarah Beckwith, *Christ's Body: Identity, Culture, and Society in Late Medieval Writings* (London: Routledge, 1993), 83–88; Aers, *Community, Gender*, 103–8; Lynn Staley, *Margery Kempe's Dissenting Fictions* (University Park: Pennsylvania State University Press, 1994), chs. 2 and 3.

4. Aers, *Community, Gender*, ch. 4, together with Aers, *Faith, Ethics and Church: Writing in England, 1360–1409* (Cambridge: Brewer, 2000), ch. 4, "Christianity for Courtly Subjects."

5. Kate Mertes, "The Household as a Religious Community," in *People, Politics and Community in the Late Middle Ages*, ed. Joel Rosenthal and Colin Richmond (New York: St. Martin's Press, 1987), 123–39; citations to pages are given parenthetically in the text. The essay is reprinted in her invaluable work *The English Noble Household 1250–1600* (Oxford: Blackwell, 1988). Also useful are C. M. Woolgar, *The Great Household in Late Medieval England* (New Haven: Yale University Press, 1999), chs. 5 and 8; C. M. Woolgar, ed., *Household Accounts from Medieval England*, 2 vols., Record of Social and Economic History, n.s., vols. 17 and 18 (Oxford: British Academy, 1992–93); David Starkey, "The Age of the Household," ch. 5 in *The Later Middle Ages*, ed. Stephen Medcalf (New York: Holmes and Meier, 1981); Paul Strohm, *Hochon's Arrow* (Princeton: Princeton University Press, 1992), ch. 6; Margaret Aston and Colin Richmond, eds., *Lollardy and the Gentry in the Later Middle Ages* (Stroud: Sutton, 1997), especially chs. 5, 10, and 12.

6. Priscilla H. Barnum, ed., *Dives and Pauper*, 2 vols., EETS 275 and 280 (London: Oxford University Press, 1976 and 1980); citations to volume and page are given parenthetically in the text. For the objection to the wealthy gentry withdrawing from the parish church and its worship to their "pryue" household chapels, see 1:195–97.

7. On the standard "small and nuclear" size family in late medieval York, see P. J. P. Goldberg, *Women, Work and Life Cycle in a Medieval Economy: Women in York and Yorkshire c1300–1520* (Oxford: Clarendon Press, 1992), 325. (This contradicts a statement on 279 but matches his evidence in chs. 5, 7, and 8; see especially 340–41, 351.) For agricultural England, see Judith Bennett, *Women in the Medieval English Countryside* (New York: Oxford University Press, 1987), ch. 3 (for examples, 48–49, 59, 62, 63), and L. R. Poos, *A Rural Society after the Black Death: Essex 1350–1525* (Cambridge: Cambridge University Press, 1991), ch. 7. Still worth reading, for all its lack of nuance and adequate empirical range, is Alan Macfarlane, *The Origins of English Individualism* (Oxford: Blackwell, 1978), 134–44.

8. Joel T. Rosenthal, *Old Age in Medieval England* (Philadelphia: University of Pennsylvania Press, 1996), see 3, 193 n. 7, with 99–100, 115, 171, 173.

9. Rosenthal, *Old Age,* 100, 111–12. See the following on this issue: Elaine Clark, "Some Aspects of Social Security in Medieval England," *Journal of Family History* 7 (1982), 307–20; Richard M. Smith, "The Manorial Court and the Elderly Tenant in Late Medieval England," in *Life, Death and the Elderly,* ed. Margaret Pelling and Richard M. Smith (London: Routledge, 1991), 39–61, here 52–54, 57; N. Orme, "Suffering of the Clergy," in Pelling and Smith, *Life, Death and the Elderly,* 62–73; Macfarlane, *Origins,* 136–38, 141–43; Bennett, *Women,* 61–62, 151–52, 158–59. *Cursor Mundi* includes children being abandoned and children abandoning their needy parents in its book of penance, lines 28,268–28,275; these acts are evaluated as a capital sin. See Richard Morris, *Cursor Mundi,* vol. 3, EETS, o.s., 68 (London: K. Paul, Trench, Trübner, 1892).

10. On this text in medieval ascetic traditions, see Barbara Newman, *From Virile Woman to Woman Christ* (Philadelphia: University of Pennsylvania Press, 1995), 81–84.

11. Contrast the contemporary letter of Jean Gerson to his brother Nicholas (1401); see Jean Gerson, *Jean Gerson: Early Works,* trans. Brian P. McGuire (New York: Paulist Press, 1998), 198, 424 n. 160; see similarly the previous year, 167, with McGuire's observations, 9–16, 24–32.

12. For the contexts see Anne Hudson, *The Premature Reformation: Wycliffite Texts and Lollard History* (Oxford: Clarendon Press, 1988).

13. For these see David Wilkins, ed., *Concilia Magnae Britanniae et Hiberniae,* 4 vols. (London, 1737; reprint, Brussels, 1964), vol. 3, 314–19.

14. We know that the bishop of Norwich, unlike the abbot of St. Albans, found *Dives and Pauper* a suspect work containing errors and heresies: see Norman P. Tanner, ed., *Heresy Trials in the Diocese of Norwich, 1428–31,* Camden 4th ser., vol. 20 (London: Royal Historical Society, 1977), 99. For related commentary on Wycliffite communities, see Shannon McSheffrey, *Gender and Heresy: Women and Men in Lollard Communities, 1420–1530* (Philadelphia: University of Pennsylvania Press, 1995), and Rita Copeland, *Pedagogy, Intellectuals and Dissent in the Later Middle Ages: Lollardy and Ideas of Learning* (Cambridge: Cambridge University Press, 2001), especially ch. 1.

15. Bennett, *Women,* 149–68; Goldberg, *Women, Work and Life Cycle,* 309–18, 341–48; Macfarlane, *Origins,* 81–82, 91–92, 131–34; Sylvia L. Thrupp, *The Merchant Class in Medieval London* (Ann Arbor: Michigan University Press, 1989), 170. Ralph A. Houlbrooke, *The English Family 1450–1700* (London: Longman, 1984), 208–9, includes an example from Ormbesley (Worscestershire) in 1419: here about 14 percent of the manorial tenants were widows, a figure much increased by the sixteenth century. Suggestive here is Maryanne Kowaleski, "Singlewomen in Medieval and

Early Modern Europe," ch. 2 in *Singlewomen in the European Past, 1250–1800*, ed. Judith M. Bennett and Amy M. Froide (Philadelphia: University of Pennsylvania Press, 1999), especially 41–50. For brief but extremely suggestive comments on the single-parent household in Chaucer's "Prioress's Tale," see Bruce Holsinger, *Music, Body, and Desire in Medieval Culture* (Stanford: Stanford University Press, 2001), 265–67.

16. See Wilkins, *Concilia*, III. 314–19, and Hudson, *The Premature Reformation*, 82–83, 101–3, 355–56.

17. See Tanner, *Heresy Trials;* page citations are given parenthetically in the text.

18. Hudson, *The Premature Reformation*, 450–51, quoting Tanner, *Heresy Trials*, 49; see too Hudson, *The Premature Reformation*, 134–44, 456–72, and Rob Lutton, "Connections between Lollards, Townsfolk, and Gentry in Tenderten in the Late Fifteenth and Early Sixteenth Centuries," in Aston and Richmond, *Lollardy and the Gentry*, 199–228. Wyclif's reading of Acts 2, the faithful breaking bread in their homes, is very relevant; see John Wyclif, *De Eucharistia*, ed. John Loserth (London: Trübner, 1892), 119.

19. Tanner, *Heresy Trials*, 45–46; see too 47. Some of these Wycliffites maintained that the Creedal Church was the soul of any good Christian; see Tanner, *Heresy Trials*, 73, 77. On Antichrist and the Roman Church, see Tanner, *Heresy Trials*, 17 and index under "Antichrist," 221.

20. See similarly Tanner, *Heresy Trials*, 75–76, 85–86, 153–54, 165.

21. On Eamon Duffy's *The Stripping of the Altars: Traditional Religion in England, 1400–1580* (New Haven: Yale University Press, 1992) in this connection, see David Aers, "Altars of Power: Reflections on Eamon Duffy's *The Stripping of the Altars,*" *Literature and History* 3 (1994), 90–105. For an extended attempt to explicate the unimportance of Wycliffites (except in the addled minds of literary historians and Protestant ideologues in need of origins), see Richard Rex, *The Lollards* (Basingstoke: Palgrave, 2002).

22. See Tanner's summary in *Heresy Trials*, 22–25, 29–30.

23. See similar formulations for renouncing such "hoomly" familiarity with Christians now classified as "heretics" in Tanner, *Heresy Trials*, 87, 149, 155, 167.

24. On Wyclif, Scripture, and the vernacular, see Hudson, *The Premature Reformation*, ch. 5 and 375–78.

25. On the processes summarized here, see Paul Strohm, *England's Empty Throne* (New Haven: Yale University Press, 1998), ch. 2.

26. Nicholas Love, *Mirror of the Blessed Life of Jesus Christ*, ed. Michael G. Sargent (New York: Garland, 1992); hereafter, pages are cited parenthetically in the text. On the *Mirror*'s focused attention to Lollardy, see Sargent's introduction, xliv–lviii. For *Meditaciones Vite Christi*, see Iohannis de Caulibus, *Meditaciones Vitae Christi*, ed. M. Stallings-Taney, CCCM, vol. 153 (Turnholt: Brepols, 1997).

234 Notes to Pages 165–68

27. Barnum, *Dives and Pauper*, 327.

28. On these matters see Beckwith, *Christ's Body*, 63–70.

29. On Love's treatment of the Last Supper, see chapter 1 of this book. Alongside Hawisia Mone, I mention Oldcastle here to recall the range of lay Wycliffism; see Wilkins, *Concilia*, III. 354–55, and Beckwith, *Christ's Body*, 71–74.

30. See David Aers and Lynn Staley, *The Powers of the Holy: Religion, Politics, and Gender in Late Medieval English Culture* (University Park: Pennsylvania State University Press, 1996), 44–58.

31. In quoting from the Bible, I use *The Holy Bible, Translated from the Latin Vulgate*, rev. Richard Challoner (Rockford, Ill.: Tan Books, 1989).

32. See Sargent's introduction to Love, *Mirror*, xxxiv, lviii.

33. It is worth noting an alteration to the *Meditaciones Vite Christi* here that Sargent's notes to Love, *Mirror*, do not mention (268). In Iohannis de Caulibus, *Meditaciones*, ch. 15, 70–71, the Virgin Mary is working for money, a wage laborer: Love deletes this. Did he think it was against "gude maneres" for the mother of God to labor for the means of subsistence? On his lack of sympathy with Franciscan poverty, see Love, *Mirror*, 267–68 n. See too the English translation of an illustrated Italian version of the Meditaciones: Isa Ragusa and R. Green, eds. and trans., *Meditations on the Life of Christ* (Princeton: Princeton University Press, 1961).

34. See Love, *Mirror*, 267 n. 60.

35. For the Statute of Laborers and the period to 1381, see Aers, *Community, Gender*, introduction and ch. 1; for the 1380s and the Cambridge Parliament of 1388, see Anne Middleton, "Acts of Vagrancy: The C Version 'Autobiography' and the Statute of 1388," in *Written Work: Langland, Labor, and Authorship*, ed. Steven Justice and Kathryn Kerby-Fulton (Philadelphia: University of Pennsylvania Press, 1997), 208–317. Also relevant here is B. Geremek, *The Margins of Society in Late Medieval Paris* (Cambridge: Cambridge University Press, 1991), ch. 6.

36. Love, *Mirror*, 267 n. 60, 7–11. See the treatment by Aelred of Rievaulx, *Tractatus de Iesu Puero Duodenni*, I.6 (*PLat* 184.853); here too Christ is presented as begging. The Franciscan theologian William of Ockham has Jesus begging from door to door like other poor people but out of voluntary poverty; William of Ockham, *Work of Ninety Days*, 2 vols., trans. John Kilcullen and John Scott (Lewiston, N.Y.: Mellen Press, 2001), ch. 93 (608). Ironically, Love's approach is close to that of the Wycliffite William Taylor, who rejects accounts that Christ begged during these three days; see Anne Hudson, ed., *Two Wycliffite Texts*, EETS, o.s., 301 (Oxford: Oxford University Press, 1993), 20 and 21. Love's stance towards begging may also be convergent with Langland's, but as the previous chapter showed, the poet creates a richly dialectical meditation on and through conflicting positions within Christian tradition.

37. See chapter 5 of this book and its references to the literature on, and around, Langland and mendicancy.

38. See Malcolm D. Lambert, *Franciscan Poverty* (London: Society for Promoting Christian Knowledge, 1961), and M. Mollat, *The Poor in the Middle Ages* (New Haven: Yale University Press, 1986), ch. 7.

39. Love, *Mirror*, 267–68.

40. For temptation of Christ, see Iohannis de Caulibus, *Meditaciones*, ch. 17, 87–88, and for the victorious feast, 89–91. See the illustration of the angels' visit to the Virgin Mary and Joseph to fetch food for Jesus, illustrations 102 and 103 in Ragusa and Green, *Meditations*.

41. Cf. the courtly Jesus of *Cleanness*, 1101–8, in Malcolm Andrew and Ronald Waldron, eds., *The Poems of the Pearl MS* (London: Arnold, 1978). For Abraham's picnic with the Trinity, see *Cleanness*, 601–46, exquisitely described by A. C. Spearing, *The Gawain-Poet* (Cambridge: Cambridge University Press, 1970), 59.

42. On Margery Kempe in this context, see works cited in note 3.

43. Love follows *Meditaciones Vitae Christi* here in leaving out Luke 4.22b–30; Iohannis de Caulibus, *Meditaciones*, ch. 18, 94.

44. On Wyclif and Wycliffites addressing persecution, see Michael Wilks, "Wyclif and the Great Persecution," in *Prophecy and Eschatology*, ed. Michael Wilks (Oxford: Blackwell, 1994), 39–64. This was not a fantasy, of course: see Strohm, *England's Empty Throne*, ch. 2.

45. We remember that learning the *Pater, Ave, Credo,* and *Precepta Dei* in English could now be taken as a sign of Wycliffism; see John Burell in Tanner, *Heresy Trials,* 73. Cf. Love, *Mirror,* 88, discussed by Staley, *Margery Kempe's Dissenting Fictions,* 145. These disciples' "duellynges," like the home of Mary, Joseph and Jesus, are far removed from the East Anglian "house churches" and "schools" discussed above.

46. See Aers and Staley, *Powers of the Holy,* ch. 1, and Thomas H. Bestul, *Texts of the Passion* (Philadelphia: University of Pennsylvania Press, 1996), chs. 2 and 5.

47. Compare the York Corpus Christi plays with this in the profound reading, theological, political, and dramatic, offered by Sarah Beckwith, *Signifying God: Social Relation and Symbolic Act in the York Corpus Christi Plays* (Chicago: Chicago University Press, 2001).

48. For an extraordinarily illuminating work that brings out this strangeness, see Rowan Williams, *Resurrection: Interpreting the Easter Gospel* (New York: Pilgrim Press, 1994).

49. He does keep a trace of the Gospels' emphasis on the difference in the risen Christ by having Mary comment that Jesus's "conuersacion wole not be with vs in maner as it haþ here before" (201), but Love, like his source, does not allow

the brief acknowledgment to dislocate the cosy domestication of the resurrection appearances (see Iohannis de Caulibus, *Meditaciones,* ch. 84, 306).

50. Iohannis de Caulibus, *Meditaciones,* ch. 91, 313–15.

51. Love, *Mirror,* 206, follows Iohannis de Caulibus, *Meditaciones,* ch. 91, 314. On Christ's resurrection meal sharing, see Robert W. Jenson, *Systematic Theology,* 2 vols. (New York: Oxford University Press, 1997 and 1999), vol. 2, 185.

52. See Aers, *Faith, Ethics,* ch. 6. On the specific history here, see Paul Strohm, *England's Empty Throne,* ch. 2.

53. On Kempe in this context, see the works cited in note 3. For examples of the way Kempe's book relates to the *Meditaciones Vite Christi* and Love's *Mirror,* see Kempe, *Book of Margery Kempe* (Windeatt), 11–12, 77 nn. 582 and 585, 162 n. 2207, 180 n. 2584, 204 nn. 3132–33.

54. I use William Langland, *Piers Plowman: The C Version,* ed. George Russell and George Kane (London: Athlone Press, 1997). Derek Pearsall's edition remains a fund of information; *Piers Plowman, by William Langland: An Edition of the C-Text* (London: Arnold, 1978), hereafter cited as "Langland, *Piers Plowman* (Pearsall)." For the B version, see William Langland, *Piers Plowman: The B Version,* ed. George Kane and E. Talbot Donaldson (London: Athlone Press, 1988).

55. M. Teresa Tavormina, *Kindly Similitude: Marriage and Family in Piers Plowman* (Cambridge: Brewer, 1995). For a related attempt to show Langland's unequivocal embrace of human generativity and family, see Andrew Galloway, "Intellectual Pregnancy, Metaphysical Femininity, and the Social Doctrine of the Trinity," *Yearbook of Langland Studies* 12 (1998), 117–52.

56. Tavormina, *Kindly Similitude,* ch. 2.

57. See Aers, *Community, Gender,* 26–35, and Middleton, "Acts of Vagrancy."

58. See Larry D. Benson, ed., *The Riverside Chaucer* (Boston: Houghton Mifflin, 1987), *Canterbury Tales* [*CT*] IV.1839 and X.859.

59. On Christian virtues the most illuminating account is in Aquinas's *Summa Theologiae,* II–II; see Thomas Aquinas, *Summa Theologiae* (London: Blackfriars, 1964–81).

60. On traditional versions of marriage in the fourteenth century, see H. A. Kelly, *Love and Marriage in the Age of Chaucer* (Ithaca: Cornell University Press, 1975), and J. T. Noonan, *Contraception,* rev. ed. (Cambridge: Harvard University Press, 1986).

61. Quoting, seriatim, XVIII.109, 78–79, 85; see the whole passage, 55–109.

62. Note the deleted lines, B XIV.1–4, 323–35; see Tavormina, *Kindly Similitude,* ch. 3.

63. See Aers and Staley, *Powers of the Holy,* chs. 1–2. It should be observed that in *Kindly Similitude* Tavormina seems to have ignored Piers's conversion in the B version and its relations to the book's marriage concerns. Although, as we

discussed in chapter 5 of this book, the C version carefully changes this scene, it too never again shows Piers as the married family man he is in B VI/CVIII.

64. Aers, *Community, Gender,* 27–35; Middleton, "Acts of Vagrancy."

65. Langland, *Piers Plowman* (Pearsall), 376 n. 386.

66. On Wycliffite ecclesiology, see Hudson, *The Premature Reformation,* ch. 7; on some of its unresolved problems, see chapter 4 of this book and Aers, *Faith, Ethics,* ch. 6.

67. I use Augustine, *De Civitate Dei,* 2 vols., ed. B. Dombart and A. Kalb (Stuttgart: Teubner, 1993), and Augustine, *Concerning the City of God,* trans. Henry Bettenson (London: Penguin Books, 1984). Here see XIX.17.

68. Augustine, *Concerning the City of God,* XIX.17.

69. Here I am reflecting on another text by Augustine, his sermon on Psalm 64 (65) in *Enarrationes in Psalmos,* CCSL, vols 38–40 (Turnholt: Brepols, 1956 and 1990), Psalmum LXIV.2, p. 824.

BIBLIOGRAPHY

Primary Works

Andrew, Malcolm, and Ronald Waldron, eds. *The Poems of the Pearl MS*. London: Arnold, 1978.

Angela of Foligno. *Il Libro della Beata Angela de Foligno*. Edited by Ludger Thier and Abele Calufetti. Rome: Editiones Collegii S. Bonaventurae ad Claras Aquas, 1985.

———. *Complete Works*. Translated by Paul Lachance. New York: Paulist Press, 1993.

Aquinas, Thomas. *Opuscula Theologica*. Vol. 1. Edited by R. A. Verardo. Rome: Marietti, 1954.

———. *Opuscula Theologica*. Vol. 2. Edited by R. M. Spiazzi. Rome: Marietti, 1954.

———. *Summa contra Gentiles*. 4 vols. Translated by Vernon J. Bourke. Notre Dame: University of Notre Dame Press, 1975.

———. *Summa Theologiae*. London: Blackfriars, 1964–81.

Augustine. *Concerning the City of God*. Translated by Henry Bettenson. London: Penguin Books, 1984.

———. *Homilies on the Gospel of John; Homilies on the First Epistle of John; Soliloquies*. Edited by Philip Schaff. Grand Rapids, Mich.: Eerdmans, 1986.

———. *Enarrationes in Psalmos*. CCSL, vols. 38–40. Turnholt: Brepols, 1956 and 1990.

———. *Confessions*. Translated by Henry Chadwick. Oxford: Oxford University Press, 1991.

———. *Confessions*. 3 vols. Edited by James J. O'Donnell. Oxford: Clarendon Press, 1992.

———. *Four Anti-Pelagian Writings*. Translated by John A. Mourant and William J. Collinge. Washington: Catholic University of America Press, 1992.

————. *De Civitate Dei.* 2 vols. Edited by B. Dombart and A. Kalb. Stuttgart: Teubner, 1993.

————. *Sermons.* Translated by Edmund Hill. Part 3 of *The Works of Saint Augustine: A Translation for the 21st Century,* edited by John E. Rotelle. New York: Brooklyn: New City Press, 1994.

————. *De Doctrina Christiana.* Edited and translated by R. P. H. Green. Oxford: Clarendon Press, 1995.

Barnum, Priscilla H. *Dives and Pauper.* 2 vols. EETS 275 and 280. London: Oxford University Press, 1976 and 1980.

Bennett, J. A. W., ed. *Piers Plowman: Prologue of Passus I–IV of the B Text.* Oxford: Clarendon Press, 1972.

Benson, Larry D., ed. *The Riverside Chaucer.* Boston: Houghton Mifflin, 1987.

Bible. *The Holy Bible, Translated from the Latin Vulgate.* Revised by Richard Challoner. Rockford, Ill.: Tan Books, 1989.

Biblia Sacra iuxta Vulgatem Clementinam. 4th ed. Edited by Alberto Colunga and Laurentio Turrado. Matriti: Biblioteca de Autores Cristianos, 1965.

Bonagratia of Bergamo. *Tractatus de Paupertate Christi et Apostolorum.* Edited by L. Oliger. *Archivum Franciscanum Historicum* 22 (1929), 292–335.

Bonaventure. *The Works of Bonaventure.* Translated by José de Vinck. Paterson, N.J.: St. Anthony Guild Press, 1966.

Bradwardine, Thomas. *De Causa Dei.* Edited by Henry Savil. London, 1618. Reprint, Frankfurt: Minerva GMBH, 1964.

Brinton, Thomas. *The Sermons of Thomas Brinton, Bishop of Rochester (1373–1389).* Edited by Mary A. Devlin. Camden 3d ser., 85–86. London: Royal Historical Society, 1954.

Bromyard, John. *Summa Praedicantium.* Antwerp, 1614.

Brown, Edward, ed. *Fasciculi Rerum Expetendarum & Fugiendarum.* London: Chiswell, 1690.

Brut, Walter. "Proceedings in the Trial of Walter Brut for Heresy." In *Registrum Johannis Trefnant,* edited by W. W. Capes, 278–394. London: Canterbury and York Society, 1916.

Clasby, Eugene, trans. *The Pilgrimage of Human Life (Le pèlerinage de vie humaine),* by Guillaume de Deguileville. New York: Garland, 1992.

Donne, John. *Devotions upon Emergent Occasions.* Ann Arbor: University of Michigan Press, 1959.

Dymmok, Roger. *Liber contra Duodecim Errores et Hereses Lollardorum.* Edited by H. S. Cronin. London: Trübner, 1922.

Eliot, T. S. *The Complete Poems and Plays.* New York: Harcourt, Brace, n.d.

Friedberg, Emil. *Corpus Iuris Canonici.* Leipzig, 1879.

Gerson, Jean. *Jean Gerson: Early Works.* Translated by Brian P. McGuire. New York: Paulist Press, 1998.

Gordon, E. V., ed. *Pearl.* Oxford: Clarendon Press, 1963.

Guillaume de Deguileville. *Le pèlerinage de vie humaine.* Edited by J. J. Stürzinger. London: Roxburghe Club, 1893.

Henry, Avril. *The Pilgrimage of the Lyfe of the Manhode* (Le pèlerinage de vie humaine), by Guillaume de Deguileville. 2 vols. EETS 288 and 292. London: Oxford University Press, 1985 and 1988.

Hoccleve, Thomas. *The Regiment of Princes.* Edited by Charles R. Blyth. Kalamazoo: Western Michigan University, Medieval Institute Publications, 1999.

Hudson, Anne, ed. *Selections from English Wycliffite Writings.* Cambridge: Cambridge University Press, 1978.

———, ed. *Two Wycliffite Texts.* EETS, o.s., 301. Oxford: Oxford University Press, 1993.

Hudson, Anne, and Pamela Gradon, eds. *English Wycliffite Sermons.* 5 vols. Oxford: Oxford University Press, 1983–96.

Iohannis de Caulibus. *Meditaciones Vitae Christi.* Edited by M. Stallings-Taney. CCCM, vol. 153. Turnholt: Brepols, 1987.

Jean de Meun and Guillaume de Lorris. *Le roman de la rose.* Edited by Daniel Poirion. Paris: Garnier-Flammarion, 1974.

Julian of Norwich. *The Shewings of Julian of Norwich.* Edited by Georgia R. Crampton. Kalamazoo: Western Michigan University, Medieval Institute Publications, 1994.

Kempe, Margery. *The Book of Margery Kempe.* Edited by Lynn Staley. Kalamazoo: Western Michigan University, Medieval Institute Publications, 1996.

———. *The Book of Margery Kempe.* Edited by Barry Windeatt. Harlow: Longman/Pearson, 2000.

———. *The Book of Margery Kempe.* Edited and translated by Lynn Staley. New York: Norton, 2001.

Knighton, Henry. *Knighton's Chronicle, 1337–1396.* Edited and translated by G. H. Martin. Oxford: Oxford University Press, 1995.

Langland, William. *Piers Plowman: The A Version.* Edited by George Kane. London: Athlone, 1960.

———. *Piers Plowman: B Text (Preface and Passus I–VIII).* Edited by J. A. W. Bennett. Oxford: Oxford University Press, 1972.

———. *Piers Plowman, by William Langland: An Edition of the C-Text.* Edited by Derek Pearsall. York Medieval Texts, 2d ser. London: Arnold, 1978. Corrected ed., Exeter: University of Exeter Press, 1994.

———. *Piers Plowman: The B Version*. Rev. ed. Edited by George Kane and E. Talbot Donaldson. London: Athlone, 1988.

———. *The Vision of William concerning Piers the Plowman Together with Richard de Redeles*. 2 vols. Edited by W. W. Skeats. Oxford: Oxford University Press, 1886. Reprint 1968.

———. *Piers Plowman: A Parallel Text Edition of the A, B, C and Z Versions*. Edited by A. V. C. Schmidt. London: Longmans, 1995.

———. *Piers Plowman: The C Version. Will's Visions of Piers Plowman, Do-Well, Do-Better, and Do-Best*. Edited by George Russell and George Kane. London: Athlone, 1997.

Legg, J. Wickham. *The Sarum Missal*. Oxford: Clarendon Press, 1969.

Love, Nicholas. *Mirror of the Blessed Life of Jesus Christ: A Critical Edition*. Edited by Michael G. Sargent. New York: Garland, 1992.

Lydgate, John. *The Minor Poems of John Lydgate*. Edited by H. N. MacCracken. EETS 107. London: K. Paul, Trench, Trübner, 1911.

———, trans. *The Pilgrimage of the Life of Man* (Le pèlerinage de vie humaine), by Guillaume de Deguileville. 3 vols. EETS 77, 83, and 92. London: K. Paul, Trench, Trübner, 1899, 1901, and 1904.

Mirk, John. *Festial: A Collection of Homilies*. Edited by Theodor Erbe. EETS, e.s., 96. London: K. Paul, Trench, Trübner, 1905.

Morris, Richard, ed. *Cursor Mundi*. 7 parts. EETS, o.s., 57, 59, 62, 66, 68, 99, 101. London: K. Paul, Trench, Trübner, 1874–93.

Natalis, Hervaeus. "*Liber de Paupertate Christi et Apostolorum*." Edited by J. G. Sikes. *Archives d'Histoire Doctrinale et Littéraire du Moyen Âge* 11 (1937–38), 209–97.

———. *The Poverty of Christ and the Apostles*. Translated by John P. Jones. Toronto: Pontifical Institute of Medieval Studies, 1999.

Netter, Thomas. *Thomae Waldensis Doctrinale Antiquitatum Fidei Catholicae Ecclesiae*. 3 vols. Edited by B. Blanciotti. Venice, 1757; facsimile, Farnborough: Gregg, 1967.

Pecock, Reginald. *Book of Faith*. Edited by J. L. Morison. Glasgow: Maclehose, 1909.

Perkins, William. *The Workes*. 3 vols. Cambridge, 1616–18.

Ragusa, Isa, and R. Green, eds. and trans. *Meditations on the Life of Christ*. Princeton: Princeton University Press, 1961.

Shirley, Walter W., ed. *Fasciculi Zizaniorum Magistri Johannis Wyclif cum Tritico*. London: Longman, Brown, Green, Longmans, and Roberts, 1858.

Simmons, Thomas F., ed. *The Lay Folk's Mass Book*. EETS 71. London: Trübner, 1879.

Skeat, W. W., ed. *Pierce the Plowman's Crede*. EETS, o.s., 30. London: Trübner, 1867.

————, ed. *The Vision of William Concerning Piers the Plowman Together with Richard the Redeless*. 2 vols. 1886. Reprint, Oxford: Oxford University Press, 1968.

Spector, Stephen. *The N-Town Play: Cotton MS Vespasian D.8*. EETS, s.s., 11–12. Oxford: Oxford University Press, 1991.

Tanner, Norman, ed. *Heresy Trials in the Diocese of Norwich, 1428–31*. Camden 4th ser., vol. 20. London: Royal Historical Society, 1977.

————, ed. *Decrees of the Ecunemical Councils*. 2 vols. London: Sheed and Ward, 1990.

Thorpe, William. *The Testimony of William Thorpe*. In *Two Wycliffite Texts*, edited by Anne Hudson. EETS 301. Oxford: Oxford University Press, 1993.

Wenzel, Siegfried, ed. *Fasciculus Morum: A Fourteenth-Century Preacher's Handbook*. University Park: Pennsylvania University Press, 1989.

Wilkins, David, ed. *Concilia Magnae Britanniae et Hiberniae*. 4 vols. London, 1737. Reprint, Brussels, 1964.

William of Ockham. *The De Sacramento Altaris of William of Ockham*. Edited and translated by T. Brune Birch. Latin text and English translation. Burlington, Vt.: Lutheran Library Board, 1930.

————. *De Corpore Christi*. In *Guillelmi de Ockham: Tractatus de Quantitate et Tractatus de Corpore Christi*, edited by Carlo A. Grassi, vol. 10 of William of Ockham, *Opera Philosophica et Theologica*. St. Bonaventure, N.Y.: St. Bonaventure University, Franciscan Institute, 1986, 87–234.

————. *Quodlibetal Questions*. 2 vols. Translated by Alfred J. Freddoso and Francis E. Kelley. New Haven: Yale University Press, 1991.

————. *Work of Ninety Days*. 2 vols. Translated by John Kilcullen and John Scott. Lewiston, N.Y.: Mellen Press, 2001.

William of Shoreham. *The Poems of William of Shoreham*. Edited by Matthias Konrath. EETS, e.s., 86. London: Kegan Paul, 1902.

Woolgar, C. M., ed. *Household Accounts from Medieval England*. 2 vols. Record of Social and Economic History, n.s., vols. 17 and 18. Oxford: British Academy, 1992–93.

Wyclif, John. *Trialogus*. Edited by Gotthard V. Lechler. Oxford: Oxford University Press, 1869.

————. *Dialogus sive Speculum Ecclesie Militantis*. Edited by A. W. Pollard. London: Trübner, 1876.

————. *Tractatus de Officio Regis*. Edited by A. W. Pollard and C. Sayle. London: Trübner, 1887.

————. *Sermones*. 4 vols. Edited by John Loserth. London: Trübner, 1887–90.

————. *Tractatus de Apostasia*. Edited by Michael H. Dziewicki. London: Trübner, 1889.

————. *De Eucharistia.* Edited by John Loserth. London: Trübner, 1892.

————. *Tractatus de Blasphemia.* Edited by Michael H. Dziewicki. London: Trübner, 1893.

————. *De Simonia.* Edited by Michael H. Dziewicki and Dr. Herzberg-Frankel. London: Trübner, 1899.

————. *De Veritate Sacrae Scripturae.* 3 vols. Edited by Rudolf Buddensieg. London: Trübner, 1905–7.

————. *On Universals (Tractatus de Universalibus).* Translated by Anthony Kenny. Oxford: Clarendon Press, 1988.

————. *On Simony.* Translated by Terrence A. McVeigh. New York: Fordham University Press, 1992.

Secondary Works

Adams, Marilyn McCord. "Aristotle and the Sacrament of the Altar: A Crisis in Medieval Aristotelianism." In *Aristotle and His Medieval Interpreters.* Edited by Richard Bosley and Martin Tweedale, 195–249. Calgary: University of Calgary Press, 1991.

Adams, Robert. "Langland and the Liturgy Revisited." *Studies in Philology* 73 (1976), 266–84.

————. "The Nature of Need in *Piers Plowman* XX." *Traditio* 34 (1978), 273–302.

————. "Piers's Pardon and Langland's Semi-Pelagianism." *Traditio* 39 (1983), 367–418.

————. "Langland's Theology." In *A Companion to Piers Plowman,* edited by John Alford and Anne Middleton, 87–114. Berkeley: University of California Press, 1988.

Aers, David. *Piers Plowman and Christian Allegory.* London: Arnold, 1975.

————. *Chaucer, Langland and the Creative Imagination.* London: Routledge, 1980.

————. "*Piers Plowman* and Problems in the Perception of Poverty: A Culture in Transition." *Leeds Studies in English* 14 (1983), 5–25.

————. *Community, Gender, and Individual Identity: English Writing 1360–1430.* London: Routledge, 1988.

————. "Class, Gender, Medieval Criticism and *Piers Plowman.*" In *Class and Gender in Early English Literature,* edited by B. J. Harwood and G. R. Overing, 59–75. Bloomington: Indiana University Press, 1994.

————. "Altars of Power: Reflections on Eamon Duffy's *The Stripping of the Altars.*" *Literature and History* 3 (1994), 90–105.

————. "From Medieval Christianities to the Reformations." *Journal of Medieval and Early Modern Studies,* 27, no. 2 (1997), 139–43.

————. Review of *Written Work. Yearbook of Langland Studies* 12 (1998), 207–17.

————. "Visionary Eschatology: *Piers Plowman.*" *Modern Theology* 16 (2000), 3–17.

————. *Faith, Ethics and Church: Writing in England, 1360–1409.* Cambridge: Brewer, 2000.

————, ed. *Culture and History, 1350–1600.* Hemel Hempstead: Harvester Wheatsheaf, 1992.

————, ed. *Medieval Literature and Historical Inquiry.* Cambridge: Brewer, 2000.

Aers, David, and Lynn Staley. *The Powers of the Holy: Religion, Politics, and Gender in Late Medieval English Culture.* University Park: Pennsylvania State University Press, 1996.

Alford, John. "The Idea of Reason in *Piers Plowman.*" In *Medieval English Studies,* edited by E. D. Kennedy, R. Waldron, and J. S. Wittig, 199–215. Cambridge: Brewer, 1988.

————, ed. *A Companion to Piers Plowman.* Berkeley: University of California Press, 1988.

Aston, Margaret. "Lollardy and Sedition, 1381–1431." *Past and Present* 17 (1960), 1–44.

————. *Lollards and Reformers: Images and Literacy in Late Medieval Religion.* London: Hambledon, 1984.

————. "Wyclif and the Vernacular." In *From Ockham to Wyclif,* edited by Anne Hudson and Michael Wilks. Studies in Church History. Oxford: Basil Blackwell, 1987.

————. "'Caim's Castles': Poverty, Politics and Disendowment." Ch. 4 in *Faith and Fire.* London: Hambledon Press, 1993.

————. "Corpus Christi and Corpus Regni: Heresy and the Peasants' Revolt." *Past and Present* 143 (1994), 3–47.

Aston, Margaret, and Colin Richmond, eds. *Lollardy and Gentry in the Later Middle Ages.* Stroud: Sutton, 1997.

Baker, Denise. "From Plowing to Penitence: *Piers Plowman* and the Fourteenth-Century Theology." *Speculum* 55 (1980), 715–25.

————. "The Pardons of *Piers Plowman.*" *Neuphilologische Mitteilungen* 85 (1984), 462–72.

Baldwin, Anna. *The Theme of Government in Piers Plowman.* Cambridge: Brewer, 1981.

————. "The Debt Narrative in *Piers Plowman.*" In *Art and Context in Late Medieval English Narrative,* edited by Robert R. Edwards, 37–50. Cambridge: Brewer, 1994.

————. "Patient Politics in *Piers Plowman.*" *Yearbook of Langland Studies* 15 (2001), 99–108.

Beckwith, Sarah. "A Very Material Mysticism: The Medieval Mysticism of Margery Kempe." In *Medieval Literature: Criticism, Ideology and History,* edited by David Aers, 34–57. New York: St. Martin's Press, 1986.

———."Ritual, Church, and Theatre: Medieval Dramas of the Sacramental Body." In *Culture and History, 1350–1600,* edited by David Aers, 65–89. Hemel Hempstead: Harvester Wheatsheaf, 1992.

———. *Christ's Body: Identity, Culture, and Society in Late Medieval Writings.* London: Routledge, 1993.

———. *Signifying God: Social Relation and Symbolic Act in the York Corpus Christi Plays.* Chicago: Chicago University Press, 2001.

Bennett, Judith M. *Women in the Medieval English Countryside.* New York: Oxford University Press, 1987.

———. "Medieval Women: Across the Great Divide." In *Culture and History, 1350–1600,* edited by David Aers. Hemel Hempstead: Harvester Wheatsheaf, 1992.

Bestul, Thomas H. *Texts of the Passion.* Philadelphia: University of Pennsylvania Press, 1996.

Biller, Peter, and Anne Hudson, eds. *Heresy and Literacy, 1000–1530.* Cambridge: Cambridge University Press, 1994.

Blamires, Alcuin, ed. *Woman Defamed and Woman Defended.* Oxford: Clarendon Press, 1992.

Blamires, Alcuin, and C. W. Marx. "Women Not to Preach: A Disputation in British Library MS Harley 31." *Journal of Medieval Latin* 3 (1993), 34–63.

Blanch, Robert J., ed. *Style and Symbolism in Piers Plowman.* Knoxville: University of Tennessee Press, 1969.

Bloch, R. H. *Medieval Misogyny and the Invention of Western Romantic Love.* Chicago: Chicago University Press, 1991.

Bloomfield, M. W. *Piers Plowman as a Fourteenth-Century Apocalypse.* New Brunswick: Rutgers University Press, 1961.

Bonner, Gerald. "The Church and the Eucharist in the Theology of Augustine." *Sobornost,* ser. 7, no. 6 (1978), 448–61.

Bossy, John. "The Mass as a Social Institution, 1200–1700." *Past and Present* 100 (1983), 29–61.

Bostick, Curtis. *The Antichrist of the Lollards.* Leiden: Brill, 1998.

Bourquin, Guy. *Piers Plowman.* 2 vols. Paris: Champion, 1978.

Bowers, John. *The Crisis of Will in Piers Plowman.* Washington: Catholic University of America Press, 1986.

———. *The Politics of Pearl.* Cambridge: Brewer, 2001.

Browe, P. "Die Elevation in der Messe." *Jahrbuch für Liturgiewissenschaft* 9 (1929), 20–66.

———. *Die eucharistichen Wunder des Mittelalters.* Breslau: Muller & Seiffert, 1938.

Buescher, Gabriel N. *The Eucharist Teachings of William Ockham.* Washington: Catholic University of America Press, 1950.

Burdach, Konrad. *Der Dichter des Ackermann aus Böhmen und seine Zeit.* Berlin: Weidmann, 1932.

Burr, David. "Scotus and Transubstantiation." *Medieval Studies* 34 (1972), 336–60.

———. *Eucharistic Presence in Late-Thirteenth Century Franciscan Thought.* Philadelphia: American Philosophical Society, 1984.

———. *Olivi and Franciscan Poverty.* Philadelphia: University of Philadelphia Press, 1989.

———. *The Spiritual Franciscans.* University Park: Pennsylvania State University Press, 2001.

Burrow, John. "The Action of Langland's Sacred Vision." *Essays in Criticism* 15 (1965), 373–84.

Burrows, Mark S. *Jean Gerson and De Consolatione Theologiae.* Tubingen: Mohr (Siebeck), 1991.

Bynum, Caroline. *Holy Feast and Holy Fast: The Religious Significance of Food to Medieval Women.* Berkeley: University of California Press, 1987.

Catto, J. I. "John Wyclif and the Cult of the Eucharist." In *The Bible in the Medieval World: Essays in Memory of Beryl Smalley,* edited by Katherine Walsh and Diana Wood, 269–86. Oxford: Blackwell, 1985.

———. "Wyclif and Wycliffism at Oxford, 1356–1430." Ch. 5 in *The History of the University of Oxford: Late Medieval Oxford,* edited by J. I. Catto and T. A. R. Evans. Oxford: Oxford University Press, 1992.

Cavanaugh, W. T. *Torture and the Eucharist.* Oxford: Blackwell, 1998.

Chiffoleau, J. *La comptabilité de l'au delà: Les hommes, la mort et la religion dans la région d'Avignon à la fin du moyen âge.* Rome: L'Ecole Française de Rome, 1980.

Chism, Chris. *Alliterative Revivals.* Philadelphia: University of Pennsylvania Press, 2002.

Clark, Elaine. "Some Aspects of Social Security in Medieval England." *Journal of Family History* 7 (1982), 307–20.

Clopper, Lawrence. *"Songes of Rechelesnesse": Langland and the Franciscans.* Ann Arbor: University of Michigan Press, 1997.

Cole, Andrew. "Trifunctionality and the Tree of Charity: Literary and Social Practice in *Piers Plowman*." *English Literary History* 62 (1995), 1–25.

———. "Rewriting Langland and Chaucer: Heresy and Literary Authority in Late Medieval England." Ph.D. diss., Duke University, 2000.

———. "William Langland and the Invention of Lollardy." In *Lollards and Their Influence,* edited by Fiona Somerset, Jill Havens, and Derrick Pitard, 37–58. Woodbridge: Boydell, 2003.

Coleman, Janet. *Piers Plowman and the Moderni.* Rome: Edizioni di Storia e Litteratura, 1981.

Colish, Marcia L. *Peter Lombard.* 2 vols. Leiden: Brill, 1994.

———. *Medieval Foundations of the Western Intellectual Tradition, 400–1400.* New Haven: Yale University Press, 1997.

Collinson, Patrick. *The Religion of Protestants.* Oxford: Clarendon Press, 1982.

Congar, Yves M.-J. "Aspects ecclésiologiques de la querelle entre mendiants et séculiers dans la seconde moitié du XIIIe siècle et le début du XIVe." *Archive d'Histoire Doctrinale et Littéraire du Moyen Âge* 28 (1962), 35–151.

Constable, Giles. *Three Studies in Medieval Religious and Social Thought.* Cambridge: Cambridge University Press, 1995.

Copeland, Rita. "William Thorpe and His Lollard Community: Intellectual Labor and the Representation of Dissent." In *Bodies and Disciplines: Intersections of Literature and History in Fifteenth-Century England,* edited by Barbara A. Hanawalt and David Wallace, 199–221. Minneapolis: University of Minnesota Press, 1996.

———. *Pedagogy, Intellectuals and Dissent in the Later Middle Ages: Lollardy and Ideas of Learning.* Cambridge: Cambridge University Press, 2001.

Cross, Richard. *Duns Scotus.* Oxford: Oxford University Press, 1999.

Davlin. Mary C. "*Piers Plowman* and the Gospel and First Epistle of John." *Yearbook of Langland Studies* 10 (1996), 89–127.

Dawson, James. "Richard Fitzralph and the Fourteenth-Century Poverty Controversies." *Journal of Ecclesiastical History* 34 (1983), 315–44.

Dimmick, Jeremy, James Simpson, and Nicolette Zeeman, eds. *Images, Idolatry and Iconoclasm in Late Medieval England.* Oxford: Oxford University Press, 2002.

Dolan, T. P. "Langland and Fitzralph." *Yearbook of Langland Studies* 2 (1988), 35–45.

Donagan, Alan. "Thomas Aquinas on Human Action." Ch. 33 in *The Cambridge History of Later Medieval Philosophy,* edited by Norman Kretzmann, Anthony Kenny, and Jan Pinborg. Cambridge: Cambridge University Press, 1982.

Donaldson, E. Talbot. *Piers Plowman: The C Text and Its Poet.* Yale Studies in English 113. New Haven: Yale University Press, 1949.

Duffy, Eamon. *The Stripping of the Altars: Traditional Religion in England, 1400–1580.* New Haven: Yale University Press, 1992.

Dumoutet, Edouard. *Le désir de voir l'Hostie et les origines de la dévotion au Saint-Sacrament.* Paris: Beauchesie, 1926.

Eijnden, Jan G. J. van den. *Poverty on the Way to God: Thomas Aquinas on Evangelical Poverty.* Leuven: Peeters, 1994.

Emery, Kent, and Joseph Wawrykow, eds. *Christ among the Medieval Dominicans.* Notre Dame: University of Notre Dame Press, 1998.

Emmerson, R. K. *Antichrist in the Middle Ages: A Study of Medieval Apocalypticism, Art, and Literature.* Seattle: University of Washington Press, 1981.

————. "'Coveitise to Konne,' 'Goddes Pryvetee,' and Will's Ambiguous Dream Experience in *Piers Plowman.*" In *"Suche Werkis to Werche": Essays on Piers Plowman in Honor of David C. Fowler,* edited by M. Vaughan, 89–121. East Lansing, Mich.: Colleagues, 1993.

————. "'Yernen to Rede Redeles?' Piers Plowman and Prophecy." *Yearbook of Langland Studies* 7 (1994), 28–76.

Erzgräber, Willi. *Mündlichkeit und Schriftlichkeit im englischen Mittelalter.* Tübingen: G. Narr, 1988.

Faith, R. "'The Great Rumour' of 1377 and Peasant Ideology." In *The English Rising of 1381,* edited by R. Hilton and T. Aston. Cambridge: Cambridge University Press, 1984.

Féret, H. M. "*Sacramentum, Res* dans la langue théologique de S. Augustin." *Revue des Sciences Philosophiques et Théologiques* 29 (1940), 218–43.

Fitzpatrick, P. J. *In Breaking of Bread: The Eucharist and Ritual.* Cambridge: Cambridge University Press, 1993.

Fletcher, A. J. "John Mirk and the Lollards." *Medium Ævum* 55 (1987), 217–24.

Fradenburg, Louise. "Needful Things." In *Medieval Crime and Social Control,* edited by Barbara A. Hanawalt and David Wallace, 49–69. Minneapolis: University of Minnesota Press, 1997.

Frank, R. W. "The Pardon Scene in *Piers Plowman.*" *Speculum* 26 (1951), 317–31.

————. *Piers Plowman and the Scheme of Salvation.* New Haven: Yale University Press, 1957.

Galloway, Andrew. "Intellectual Pregnancy, Metaphysical Femininity, and the Social Doctrine of the Trinity." *Yearbook of Langland Studies* 12 (1998), 117–52.

Geary, Patrick J. *Living with the Dead in the Middle Ages.* Ithaca: Cornell University Press, 1994.

Geremek, B. *The Margins of Society in Late Medieval Paris.* Cambridge: Cambridge University Press, 1991.

Ghosh, Kantik. "Eliding the Interpreter: John Wyclif and Scriptural Truth." In *New Medieval Literatures,* edited by Rita Copeland, David Lawton, and Wendy Scase, 205–24. Oxford: Clarendon Press, 1998.

————. *The Wycliffite Heresy: Authority and the Interpretation of Texts.* Cambridge: Cambridge University Press, 2002.

Gibson, Gail M. *The Theater of Devotion: East Anglian Drama and Society in the Late Middle Ages.* Chicago: Chicago University Press, 1989.

Girard, René. *Things Hidden since the Foundation of the World.* London: Athlone, 1977.

————. *The Scapegoat.* Baltimore: Johns Hopkins University Press, 1986.

Godden, M. "Plowmen and Hermits in Langland's *Piers Plowman.*" *Review of English Studies* 35 (1984), 129–63.

Goldberg, P. J. P. *Women, Work and Life Cycle in a Medieval Economy: Women in York and Yorkshire c 1300–1520*. Oxford: Clarendon Press, 1992.

Gradon, Pamela. "Langland and the Ideology of Dissent." *Proceedings of the British Academy* 66 (1980), 179–205.

Grady, F. "*Piers Plowman, St. Erkenwald,* and the Rule of Exceptional Salvations." *Yearbook of Langland Studies* 6 (1992), 61–88.

Gray, N. T. "A Study of Piers Plowman in Relation to Medieval Penitential Traditions." Ph.D. diss., Cambridge University, 1984.

Greenblatt, Stephen. *Hamlet in Purgatory*. Princeton: Princeton University Press, 2001.

Hanna, Ralph. "Will's Work." Ch. 1 in *Written Work: Langland, Labor, and Authorship,* edited by Steven Justice and Kathryn Kerby-Fulton. Philadelphia: University of Pennsylvania Press, 1997.

———. "A New Edition of the C Version." *Yearbook of Langland Studies* 12 (1998), 175–88.

———. "Emendations." *Yearbook of Langland Studies* 14 (2000), 185–98.

Haren, Michael. *Sin and Society in Fourteenth-Century England*. Oxford: Clarendon Press, 2000.

Harwood, Britton. *Piers Plowman and the Problem of Belief*. Toronto: University of Toronto Press, 1992.

Hauerwas, Stanley, and Charles Pinches. *Christians among the Virtues*. Notre Dame: University of Notre Dame Press, 1997.

Hill, Christopher. *Puritanism and Revolution*. London: Panther, 1965.

———. *Society and Puritanism*. London: Panther, 1969.

Holsinger, Bruce. "Langland's Musical Reader: Liturgy, Law and the Constraints of Perfection." *Studies in the Age of Chaucer* 21 (1999), 99–141.

———. *Music, Body, and Desire in Medieval Culture*. Stanford: Stanford University Press, 2001.

Horrox, Rosemary, ed. *The Black Death*. Manchester: Manchester University Press, 1994.

Horst, Ulrich. *Evangelische Armut und Kirche: Thomas von Aquin und die Armutskontroversen des 13. und beginnenden 14. Jahrunderts*. Berlin: Academie, 1992.

Hort, Greta. *Piers Plowman and Contemporary Religious Thought*. London: Church Historical Society, n.d. (after 1936).

Houlbrooke, Ralph A. *The English Family 1450–1700*. London: Longman, 1984.

Hudson, Anne. *The Premature Reformation: Wycliffite Texts and Lollard History*. Oxford: Clarendon Press, 1988.

———. "The Legacy of *Piers Plowman*." In *A Companion to Piers Plowman,* edited by John Alford, 251–66. Berkeley: University of California Press, 1988.

————. "The Mouse in the Pyx: Popular Heresy and the Eucharist." *Trivium* 26 (1991), 40–53.

————. *"Laicus Litteratus:* The Paradox of Lollardy." Ch. 13 in *Heresy and Literacy 1000–1530*, edited by Peter Biller and Anne Hudson, 222–36. Cambridge: Cambridge University Press, 1994.

————. "Poor Preachers, Poor Men: Views of Poverty in Wyclif and His Followers." In *Häresie und vorzeitige Reformation im Spätmittelalter*, edited by Frantisek Smahel and Elisabeth Müller-Luckner, 41–53. Munich: Oldenbourg, 1998.

Hurley, M. "'Scriptura Sola': Wyclif and His Critics." *Traditio* 16 (1960), 275–352.

James, Mervyn. "Ritual, Drama, and Social Body in the Late Medieval English Town." *Past and Present* 98 (1983), 3–29.

Jenson, Robert W. *Systematic Theology.* 2 vols. New York: Oxford University Press, 1997 and 1999.

Johnson, Kelly. "Beggars and Stewards: The Contest of Humility in Christian Ethics." Ph.D. diss., Duke University, 2001.

Jones, John D. "Poverty and Subsistence: St. Thomas Aquinas and the Definition of Poverty." *Gregorianum* 75 (1994), 135–49.

————. "The Concept of Poverty in St. Thomas Aquinas's *Contra Impugnantes Dei Religionem et Cultum." Thomist* 59 (1995), 109–39.

————. "St. Thomas Aquinas and the Defense of Mendicant Poverty." *Proceedings of the American Catholic Philosophical Association* 70 (1996), 179–92.

Jones, Paul H. *Christ's Eucharistic Presence.* New York: Lang, 1994.

Jussen, Bernhard. "Challenging the Culture of *Memoria:* Dead Men, Oblivion and the 'Faithless Widow' in the Middle Ages." Ch. 10 in *Medieval Concepts of the Past*, edited by Gerd Althoff, Johannes Fried, and Patrick J. Geary. Cambridge: Cambridge University Press, 2002.

Justice, Steven. *Writing and Rebellion: England in 1381.* Berkeley: University of California Press, 1994.

Kaminsky, Howard. "The Problematics of 'Heresy' and 'The Reformation.'" In *Häresie und vorzeitige Reformation im Spätmittelalter*, edited by Frantisek Smahel and Elisabeth Müller-Luckner, 1–22. Munich: Oldenbourg, 1998.

Kane, George. "Langland: Labor and 'Authorship.'" *Notes and Queries* 243 (1998), 423–25.

Kantorowicz, Ernst H. *The King's Two Bodies.* Princeton: Princeton University, 1957.

Kaye, Joel. *Economy and Nature in the Fourteenth Century.* Cambridge: Cambridge University Press, 1998.

Keen, Maurice H. "Wyclif, the Bible, and Transubstantiation." In *Wyclif in His Times*, edited by Anthony Kenny, 1–16. Oxford: Oxford University Press, 1986.

Kelly, H. A. *Love and Marriage in the Age of Chaucer*. Ithaca: Cornell University Press, 1975.

Kennedy, V. L. "The Moment of Consecration and the Elevation of the Host." *Medieval Studies* 6 (1994), 121–50.

Kenny, Anthony. *Wyclif*. Oxford: Oxford University Press, 1985.

———, ed. *Wyclif in His Times*. Oxford: Oxford University Press, 1986.

Kipling, Gordon. *Enter the King: Theatre, Liturgy, and Ritual in the Medieval Civic Triumph*. Oxford: Clarendon Press, 1998.

Kirk, Elizabeth. *The Dream Thought of Piers Plowman*. New Haven: Yale University Press, 1972.

———. "Langland's Plowman and the Recreation of Fourteenth-Century Religious Metaphor." *Yearbook of Langland Studies* 2 (1988), 1–21.

Korolec, J. B. "Free Will and Free Choice." Ch. 32 in *The Cambridge History of Later Medieval Philosophy*, edited by Norman Kretzmann, Anthony Kenny, and Jan Pinborg. Cambridge: Cambridge University Press, 1982.

Kowaleski, Maryanne. "Singlewomen in Medieval and Early Modern Europe." Ch. 2 in *Singlewomen in the European Past, 1250–1800*, edited by Judith M. Bennett and Amy M. Froide. Philadelphia: University of Pennsylvania Press, 1999.

Kruger, Steven. "Mirrors and the Trajectory of Vision in *Piers Plowman*." *Speculum* 66 (1991), 74–95.

Lambert, Malcolm D. *Franciscan Poverty*. London: Society for Promoting Christian Knowledge, 1961.

Lancel, Serge. *Saint Augustin*. Paris: Fayard, 1999.

Landgraf, A. M. "Die in der Frühscholastik klassische Frage *Quid sumit mus*." In *Dogmengeschichte der Frühscholastik*, vol. 3, part 2, 207–22. Regensburg: Friedrich Pustet, 1955.

Langholm, Odd. *Economics in the Medieval Schools: Wealth, Exchange, Value, Money and Usury According to the Paris Theological Tradition, 1200–1350*. Leiden: Brill, 1992.

Lawler, Traugott. "Conscience's Dinner." In *The Endless Knot: Essays in Honor of Marie Borroff*, edited by M. T. Tavormina and R. F. Yeager, 87–103. Cambridge: Brewer, 1995.

———. "The Pardon Formula in *Piers Plowman*." *Yearbook of Langland Studies* 14 (2000), 117–52.

Lawton, David. "Sacrilege and Theatricality: The Croxton Play of the Sacrament." *Journal of Medieval and Early Modern Studies* 33, no. 3 (2003), 281–309.

Lees, Clare A. "Gender and Exchange in *Piers Plowman*." In *Class and Gender in Early English Literature*, edited by B. J. Harwood and G. R. Overing, 112–30. Bloomington: Indiana University Press, 1994.

Leff, Gordon. *Heresy in the Later Middle Ages.* 2 vols. New York: Barnes and Noble, 1967.

Levy, Ian C. "*Christus Qui Mentiri Non Potest:* John Wyclif's Rejection of Transubstantiation." *Recherches de Théologie et Philosophie Médiévales* 66 (1999), 316–34.

Lewis, Lucy. "Langland's Tree of Charity and Usk's Wexing Tree." *Notes and Queries* 240 (1995), 429–33.

Lewis, Suzanne. *Reading Images: Narrative Discourse and Reception in the Thirteenth Century Illuminated Apocalypse.* Cambridge: Cambridge University Press, 1995.

Little, Katherine C. "Reading for Christ: Interpretation and Instruction in Late Medieval England." Ph.D. diss., Duke University, 1998.

———. "Catechesis and Castigation: Sin in the Wycliffite Sermon Cycle." *Traditio* 54 (1999), 213–44.

Lubac, Henri de. *Corpus mysticum: L'Eucharistie et l'église au moyen âge.* Étude historique. Paris: Aubier, 1949.

———. *Exégèse médievale.* 4 vols. Paris: Aubier, 1959–63.

———. *The Christian Faith.* San Francisco: Ignatius Press, 1986.

Lutton, Rob. "Connections between Lollards, Townsfolk and Gentry in Tenderten in the Late Fifteenth and Early Sixteenth Centuries." In *Lollardy and the Gentry in the Later Middle Ages,* edited by Margaret Aston and Colin Richmond, 199–228. Stroud: Sutton, 1997.

Macfarlane, Alan. *The Origins of English Individualism.* Oxford: Blackwell, 1978.

MacFarlane, K. B. *John Wycliffe and the Beginnings of English Nonconformity* London: English Universities Press, 1952.

MacIntyre, Alasdair. *After Virtue.* 1981; 2d, rev. ed., London: Duckworth, 1985.

———. *Whose Justice? Which Rationality?* London: Duckworth, 1988.

———. *First Principles, Final Ends and Contemporary Philosophical Issues.* Milwaukee: Marquette University Press, 1990.

———. *Three Rival Versions of Moral Enquiry.* London: Duckworth, 1990.

———. *Dependent Rational Animals: Why Human Beings Need the Virtues.* Chicago: Open Court, 1999.

Macy, Gary. *The Theologies of the Eucharist in the Early Scholastic Period.* Oxford: Clarendon Press, 1984.

———. "Of Mice and Manna: *Quid Mus Sumit* as a Pastoral Question." *Recherches de Théologie Ancienne et Médiévale* 58 (1991), 157–66.

———. "Reception of the Eucharist According to the Theologians: A Case of Theological Diversity in the Thirteenth and Fourteenth Centuries." In *Theology and the University,* edited by John Apczynski. Lanham, Md.: University Press of America, 1992.

————. *The Banquet's Wisdom: A Short History of the Theologies of the Lord's Supper.* New York. Paulist Press, 1992.

————. "The 'Dogma of Transubstantiation' in the Middle Ages." *Journal of Ecclesiastical History* 45 (1994), 11–41.

Mann, Jill. "Eating and Drinking in *Piers Plowman*." *Essays and Studies* 32 (1979), 26–43.

Marcett, Mildred E. *Uhtred de Boldon, Friar William Jordan and Piers Plowman.* New York: privately printed, 1938.

Marion, Jean-Luc. *God without Being: Hors-Texte.* Translated by T. A. Carlson. Chicago: Chicago University Press, 1991.

Marshall, Gordon. *Presbyteries and Profits: Calvinism and the Development of Calvinism.* Oxford: Oxford University Press, 1980.

McCue, James F. "The Doctrine of Transubstantiation from Berengar through Trent." *Harvard Theological Review* 61 (1968), 385–430.

McGinn, Bernard. *The Flowering of Mysticism: Origins to Fifth Century.* New York: Crossroads, 1995.

McNiven, Peter. *Heresy and Politics in the Reign of Henry IV: The Burning of John Badby.* Woodbridge: Boydell, 1987.

McSheffrey, Shannon. *Gender and Heresy: Women and Men in Lollard Communities, 1420–1530.* Philadelphia: University of Pennsylvania Press, 1995.

Mertes, Kate. "The Household as a Religious Community. In *People, Politics and Community in the Late Middle Ages,* edited by Joel Rosenthal and Colin Richmond, 123–39. New York: St. Martin's Press, 1987.

————. *The English Noble Household 1250–1600.* Oxford: Blackwell, 1988.

Middleton, Anne. "Narration and Invention of Experience: Episodic Form in *Piers Plowman*." In *The Wisdom of Poetry,* edited by Larry D. Benson and Siegfried Wenzel, 91–122. Kalamazoo: Western Michigan University, Medieval Institute Publications, 1982.

————. "Acts of Vagrancy: The C Version 'Autobiography' and the Statute of 1388." In *Written Work: Langland, Labor, and Authorship,* edited by Steven Justice and Kathryn Kerby-Fulton, 208–317. Philadelphia: University of Pennsylvania Press, 1997.

Minnis, A. J. "Looking for a Sign: The Quest for Nominalism in Chaucer and Langland." Ch. 7 in *Essays in Ricardian Literature,* edited by A. J. Minnis, Charlotte Morse, and Thorlac Turville-Petre. Oxford: Clarendon Press, 1997.

————. "*De Impedimento Sexus:* Women's Bodies and Medieval Impediments to Female Ordination." In *Medieval Theology and the Natural Body,* edited by Peter Biller and A. J. Minnis. York: York Medieval Press, 1997.

Mollat, Michel. *The Poor in the Middle Ages.* New Haven: Yale University Press, 1986.

————, ed. *Études sur l'histoire de la pauvreté jusqu'au XIVe siècle*. 2 vols. Paris: Sorbonne, 1974.

Murtaugh, D. M. *Piers Plowman and the Image of God*. Gainesville: University Presses of Florida, 1978.

Newman, Barbara. *From Virile Woman to Woman Christ*. Philadelphia: University of Pennsylvania Press, 1995.

Nichols, Ann E. *Seeable Signs: The Iconography of the Seven Sacraments, 1350–1544*. Woodbridge: Boydell Press, 1994.

Nissé, Ruth. "Prophetic Nations." *New Medieval Literatures* 4 (2001), 95–115.

Noonan, J. T. *Contraception*. Rev. ed. Cambridge: Harvard University Press, 1986.

Oguro, S., R. Beadle, and M. Sargent. *Nicholas Love at Waseda*. Woodbridge: Brewer, 1997.

Orme, N. "Suffering of the Clergy." In *Life, Death and the Elderly*, edited by Margaret Pelling and Richard M. Smith, 62–73. London: Routledge, 1991.

Pantin, W. A. *The English Church in the Fourteenth Century*. Cambridge: Cambridge University Press, 1955.

Pearsall, Derek. "Poverty and Poor People in *Piers Plowman*." In *Medieval English Studies*, edited by E. D. Kennedy, R. Waldron, and J. S. Wittig, 167–85. Cambridge: Brewer, 1988.

————. "Lunatyk Lollares in *Piers Plowman*." In *Religion in the Poetry and Drama of the Late Middle Ages*, edited by Piero Boitani and Anna Torti, 163–78. Cambridge: Brewer, 1990.

————. "Hoccleve's *Regement of Princes*: The Poetics of Royal Self-Representation." *Speculum* 69 (1994), 386–410.

Pickstock, Catherine. *After Writing: On the Liturgical Consummation of Philosophy*. Oxford: Blackwell, 1998.

Poos, L. R. *A Rural Society after the Black Death: Essex 1350–1525*. Cambridge: Cambridge University Press, 1991.

Rex, Richard. *The Lollards*. Basingstoke: Palgrave Press, 2002.

Richardson, H. G. "Heresy and the Lay Power under Richard II." *English Historical Review* 51 (1936), 1–28.

Ricoeur, Paul. *Criticism and Imagination*. Cambridge: Polity Press, 1998.

Robertson, D. W., and B. F. Huppé. *Piers Plowman and Scriptural Tradition*. Princeton, Princeton University Press, 1951.

Robson, J. A. *Wyclif and the Oxford Schools*. Cambridge: Cambridge University Press, 1961.

Rosenthal, Joel T. *Old Age in Medieval England*. Philadelphia: University of Pennsylvania Press, 1996.

Rubin, Miri. *Charity and Community in Medieval Cambridge*. Cambridge: Cambridge University Press, 1987.

———. *Corpus Christi: The Eucharist in Late Medieval Culture*. Cambridge: Cambridge University Press, 1991.

———. "The Eucharist and the Construction of Medieval Identities." In *Culture and History: 1350–1600*, edited by David Aers. Hemel Hempstead: Harvester Wheatsheaf, 1992.

———. *Gentile Tales: The Narrative Assault on Late Medieval Jews*. New Haven: Yale University Press, 1999.

Salter, Elizabeth. [Zeeman]. "*Piers Plowman* and the Pilgrimage to Truth." *Essays and Studies* 11 (1958), 1–16. Reprinted as ch. 6 in *Style and Symbolism in Piers Plowman*, edited by Robert J. Blanch. Knoxville: University of Tennessee Press, 1969.

———. *Piers Plowman: An Introduction*. Oxford: Blackwell, 1963.

———. *Nicholas Love's "Myrrour of the Blessed Lyf of Jesu Christ."* Salzburg: Analecta Cartusiana, 1974.

Scase, Wendy. *Piers Plowman and the New Anticlericalism*. Cambridge: Cambridge University Press, 1989.

Sheneman, Paul. "Grace Abounding: Justification in Passus 16 of *Piers Plowman*." *Papers on Language and Literature* 34 (1998), 162–78.

Shepherd, Geoffrey. "Poverty in *Piers Plowman*." In *Social Relations and Ideas*, edited by T. H. Aston, P. R. Coss, and C. Dyer. Cambridge: Cambridge University Press, 1983.

Simpson, James. *Piers Plowman: An Introduction to the B-Text*. London: Longman, 1990.

Smahel, Frantisek. "Literacy and Heresy in Hussite Bohemia." In *Heresy and Literacy, 1000–1530*, edited by Peter Biller and Anne Hudson. Cambridge: Cambridge University Press, 1994, 237–54.

Smalley, Beryl. "John Wyclif's *Postilla super Totam Bibliam*." *Bodleian Library Record* 4 (1953), 186–205.

———. "The Bible and Eternity: John Wyclif's Dilemma." *Journal of the Warburg and Courtauld Institute* 27 (1964), 73–89.

Smith, Ben H. *Traditional Imagery of Charity in Piers Plowman*. The Hague: Mouton, 1966.

Smith, D. Vance. *The Book of the Incipit: Beginnings in the Fourteenth Century*. Minneapolis: Minnesota University Press, 2001.

———. *Arts of Possession: The Middle English Household Imaginary*. Minneapolis: University of Minnesota Press, 2003.

Smith, Richard M. "The Manorial Court and the Elderly Tenant in Late Medieval England." In *Life, Death and the Elderly*, edited by Margaret Pelling and Richard M. Smith, 39–61. London: Routledge, 1991.

Somerset, Fiona. *Clerical Discourse and Lay Audience in Late Medieval England*. Cambridge: Cambridge University Press, 1998.

Somerset, Fiona, Jill C. Havens, and Derrick G. Pitard, eds. *Lollards and Their Influence in Late Medieval England*. Woodbridge: Boydell, 2003.

Snoek, G. J. C. *Medieval Piety from Relics to the Eucharist*. Leiden: Brill, 1995.

Spearing, A. C. "The Development of a Theme in *Piers Plowman*." *Review of English Studies* 11 (1960), 241–53.

———. *Criticism and Medieval Poetry*. London: Arnold, 1964.

———. *The Gawain-Poet*. Cambridge: Cambridge University Press, 1970.

Spencer, H. Leith. *English Preaching in the Late Middle Ages*. Oxford: Clarendon Press, 1993.

St-Jacques, R. "The Liturgical Associations of Langland's Samaritan." *Traditio* 25 (1969), 217–30.

Staley, Lynn. *Margery Kempe's Dissenting Fictions*. University Park: Pennsylvania State University Press, 1994.

Starkey, David. "The Age of the Household." Ch. 5 in *The Later Middle Ages*, edited by Stephen Medcalf. New York: Holmes and Meier, 1981.

Strohm, Paul. *Hochon's Arrow*. Princeton: Princeton University Press, 1992.

———. *England's Empty Throne: Usurpation and the Language of Legitimation, 1399–1422*. New Haven: Yale University Press, 1998.

———. "Hoccleve, Lydgate and the Lancastrian Court." Ch. 24 in *The Cambridge History of Medieval English Literature*, edited by David Wallace. Cambridge: Cambridge University Press, 1999.

———. *Theory and the Premodern Text*. Minneapolis: University of Minnesota Press, 2000.

Szittya, Penn R. *The Antifraternal Tradition in Medieval Literature*. Princeton: Princeton University Press, 1986.

———. "Domesday Bokes: The Apocalypse in Medieval English Literary Culture." In *The Apocalypse in the Middle Ages*, edited by R. K. Emmerson and B. McGinn. Ithaca: Cornell University Press, 1992, 374–97.

Tachau, K. H. *Vision and Certitude in the Age of Ockham: Optics, Epistemology, and the Foundations of Semantics, 1250–1345*. Leiden: Brill, 1988.

Tavormina, M. Teresa. *Kindly Similitude: Marriage and Family in Piers Plowman*. Cambridge: Brewer, 1995.

Tavormina, T., and R. F. Yeager., eds. *The Endless Knot: Essays on Old and Middle English in Honor of Marie Borroff*. Cambridge: Brewer, 1996.

Taylor, Charles. *Sources of the Self: The Making of the Modern Identity*. Cambridge: Harvard University Press, 1989.

Thomson, Williel R. *The Latin Writings of John Wyclyf: An Annotated Catalog*. Toronto: Pontifical Institute of Medieval Studies, 1983.

Thrupp, Sylvia L. *The Merchant Class in Medieval London*. Ann Arbor: Michigan University Press, 1989.

Tierney, Brian. *Medieval Poor Law.* Berkeley: University of California Press, 1959.

Trigg, Stephanie. "The Traffic in Medieval Women: Alice Perrers, Feminist Criticism and *Piers Plowman.*" *Yearbook of Langland Studies* 12 (1998), 5–29.

Turner, Denys. *The Darkness of God.* Cambridge: Cambridge University Press, 1995.

———. "The Darkness of God and the Light of Christ: Negative Theology and Eucharistic Presence." *Modern Theology* 15, no. 2 (1999), 143–59.

Vaughan, M. "The Liturgical Perspectives of *Piers Plowman,* B, XVI–XIX." *Studies in Medieval and Renaissance History,* n.s., 3 (1980), 87–155.

Vooght, Paul de. *Les sources de la doctrine chrétienne d'après les théologiens du XIVe siècle et du début du XVe.* Bruges: Desclée, De Brouwer, 1954.

———. "La présence réelle dans la doctrine eucharistique de Wiclif." In *Hussiana,* 292–99. Louvain : Bibliothèque de l'Université, 1960.

Watson, Nicholas. "Visions of Inclusion: Universal Salvation and Vernacular Theology in Pre-Reformation England." *Journal of Medieval and Early Modern Studies* 27, no. 2 (1997), 145–87.

Wawrykow, Joseph P. *God's Grace and Human Action: 'Merit' in the Theology of Thomas Aquinas.* Notre Dame: University of Notre Dame Press, 1995.

Weber, Max. *The Protestant Ethic and the Spirit of Capitalism.* London: Unwin, 1971.

Wenzel, Siegfried. *The Sin of Sloth.* Chapel Hill: University of North Carolina Press, 1967.

Whatley, Gordon. "The Uses of Hagiography: The Legend of Pope Gregory and the Emperor Trajan in the Middle Ages." *Viator* 15 (1984), 25–63.

———. "*Piers Plowman* B 12.277–94: Notes on Langland, Text and Theology." *Modern Philology* 82 (1984), 1–12.

Wilks, Michael. "Wyclif and the Great Persecution." In *Prophecy and Eschatology,* edited by Michael Wilks, 39–64. Oxford: Blackwell, 1994.

Williams, Rowan. *Arius: Heresy and Tradition.* London: Darton, Longman and Todd, 1987.

———. *Resurrection: Interpreting the Easter Gospel.* New York: Pilgrim Press, 1994.

———. *On Christian Theology.* Oxford: Blackwell, 2000.

Wittig, J. "*Piers Plowman B,* Passus IX–XII: Elements in the Design of the Inward Journey." *Traditio* 28 (1972), 211–80.

Woolgar, C. M. *The Great Household in Late Medieval England.* New Haven: Yale University Press, 1999.

Zeeman, [Salter] Elizabeth. "*Piers Plowman* and the Pilgrimage to Truth." *Essays and Studies* 11 (1958), 1–16. Reprinted as ch. 6 in *Style and Symbolism in Piers Plowman,* edited by Robert J. Blanch. Knoxville: University of Tennessee Press, 1958.

Zeeman, Nicolette. "The Condition of Kynde." In *Medieval Literature and Historical Inquiry,* edited by David Aers, 1–30. Cambridge: Brewer 2000.

INDEX

DAVID AERS

is James B. Duke Professor of English at Duke University.